PARTY MUSIC

PARTY MUSIC

The Inside Story of the Black Panthers' Band and How Black Power Transformed Soul Music

RICKEY VINCENT

Lawrence Hill Books

Chicago

Published by Lawrence Hill Books, an imprint of
Chicago Review Press, Incorporated
814 North Franklin Street
Chicago, Illinois 60610
ISBN 978-1-61374-492-5

Library of Congress Cataloging-in-Publication Data
Vincent, Rickey.
  Party music : the inside story of the Black Panthers' band and how black
power transformed soul music / Rickey Vincent. — First edition.
      pages cm
  Includes bibliographical references and index.
  ISBN 978-1-61374-492-5 (trade paper)
  1. Lumpen (Musical group) 2. Rhythm and blues music—Political
aspects—United States—History—20th century. 3. Soul (Music)—
Political aspects—United States—History—20th century. 4. Black
power—United States—History—20th century. 5. Black Panther Party.
I. Title.
  ML421.L84V56 2013
  781.6440973—dc23
                        2013026033

Cover design: John Yates at Stealworks
Cover photographs: top, Lumpen onstage, Bill Jennings; left, Smith and
Carlos at 1968 Olympic medal ceremony, Time Life Pictures/Getty
Images; right, James Brown, © Pierre Fournier/Sygma/Corbis
Interior design: PerfecType, Nashville, TN

Printed in the United States of America
5 4 3 2 1

For Gary

Contents

Foreword by Boots Riley   ix

Preface   xiii

Introduction: "Revolution in the Air"   1

1   "Party Music": The Story of the Lumpen   19

2   "Power to the People": Bay Area Culture
and the Rise of the Party   49

3   "The Lumpen Theme": James Brown, the Rhythm
Revolution, and Black Power   87

4   "People Get Ready": Civil Rights, Soul Music,
and Black Identity   125

5   "For Freedom": Cultural Nationalism and the
Black Panther Party   167

6   "Bobby Must Be Set Free": Panther Power
and Popular Culture   217

7   "Ol' Pig Nixon": The Protest Music Tradition, Soul,
and Black Power   263

8   "Revolution Is the Only Solution": Protest Music Today
and the Legacy of the Lumpen   309

Acknowledgments   339

Sources   343

Notes   363

Index   383

Foreword

Contrary to popular belief, some of the most heated debates between revolutionaries are about music. People with the supposedly unlikely dream of changing the whole world love talking about music. Perhaps this is because when you're listening to music, the whole world seems to be summed up for you in an earful of melody and rhythm.

During the 1920s, musical artists close to or in the Communist Party USA were debating the most effective music to accompany the militant strikes, shut-downs, and factory occupations that were happening as a result of their organizing efforts. According to the book *Folk Music and The American Left* by Richard Reuss, composers like Charles Seeger (Pete Seeger's father) were arguing the position that folk music—although popular—was largely apolitical and was not a suitable vessel for revolutionary messaging. It was considered apolitical at the time. They argued that the style most suited to revolution was a more symphonic approach, reminiscent of the Romantic Era music that bore the Internationale. After all, this was the music of the European left, where revolutions were happening. The folk music side of the debate was a logical one—folk music was the music that the people were listening to. This is where they needed to be. Composers like Charles Seeger were eventually won over and became an advocate and producer of revolutionary folk music.

This same debate was happening in the 1990s among folks looking for a way to connect hip-hop music with social movements. The argument was that a certain style of hip-hop—the hip-hop that most people listened to, the hip-hop with more of a blues or funk aesthetic—was base and ignorant, and that the more jazz-influenced aesthetic lent itself to a certain consciousness. I never agreed with this argument, as many of the artists who fell into the conscious hip-hop category talked about the same things gangsta rap did, but with a different style and with less substance about the trials and tribulations of life. Furthermore, folks like Ice Cube were making some of the most politically revolutionary music of the early 1990s, but were called "gangsta" simply due to their funk/blues aesthetic. Later, the group Dead Prez would prove the conscious crowd wrong by making the song "(It's Bigger Than) Hip-Hop," which combined Southern-style crunk aesthetic with lyrics about "getting the po-pos off the block." The song was played all over the country—on radio, in clubs, in Delta 88s and coffee shops.

I've heard much talk from radicals about how we must create a new revolutionary culture, as if the problem with the culture that people are consuming is not the culture, but the style. I've been to countless meetings in which people were consumed with how to create drum circles in certain neighborhoods as a service to the community, while overlooking the fact that ten to twenty people gathered every day by the car with the loudest system and danced or rapped with the music. This schism existed in the 1960s and '70s as well, of course, with some believing that music wasn't really revolutionary unless folks were dressed in dashikis and playing congas.

The gist of the argument has to do with what people see as the primary need in the community. Do people need a cultural change—meaning, do they need to change their behavior—or do they need to be part of a movement that makes material changes in their standard of living and relationship to the wealth they create? If you, as I do, see the latter as the answer, then you understand that the culture that exists is the one we need to harness. The aesthetic is fine. It's the content that needs changing. Yes, there are revolutions and rebellions happening around the world, and we can be inspired by that—but we need to identify with ourselves, as we are now, as powerful vessels of change. Cultural change is guided by material change.

The Black Panther Party was also of the mind that material change was what was needed. The Black Panther Party put forward a serious class analysis that didn't waste time with the idea that changing the culture was the key. So, it follows logically, that when they decided to have a band, it would be a funk band. The Lumpen took the music that black folks in the United States were listening to at the time and changed the lyrics to make revolutionary agitprop grooves. The Lumpen's music, like the Panthers themselves, pointed to the idea that there is no need to call on the us we could be, the us that we are just needs the right map and the right tools. Rickey Vincent just put a very important part of the map in your hand.

—Boots Riley, Oakland, July 2013

Preface

This book explores the *soul* of the black power movement. It puts faces to the revolution and seeks to humanize the black revolutionaries of the day. This book is for anyone who recognizes the transformative soul power of James Brown but still can't find his name in their civil rights history book. It is for anyone who was fascinated by the fearless vision of change put forth by the leaders of the black power era and has wondered how those ideas came about.

This idea has been in the works for many years. One event, perhaps, sparked the basis for this study. In 1988 my mother took me to a memorial for a local activist, Alameda County Supervisor John George, a stalwart community organizer and one of the most respected black politicians in the Bay Area. The humble, spectacled man was a tireless advocate for the working class, and he had died suddenly at the age of sixty. At the memorial, his daughter rose and spoke eloquently of George, reminding us that "he was a revolutionary that could dance."

That phrase stuck with me. A revolutionary that could dance? What did that mean? I always figured that revolutionaries were warriors for the people. Was this to mean that, for the most part, they could not groove with the people? Growing up in the Bay Area, revolutionaries were not hard to find. Militants, hippies, artists, communists: "revolution was in the air" in Berkeley in the 1960s. But there was always a mythology around the black revolutionaries, especially the Black Panthers. Unlike Michael Jackson, they were seen as fighters, not lovers.

A dancing revolutionary? This was not simply about cutting up the floor after a political victory. The implication was, of course, that John George, the tireless public servant, had soul. Whether he could really make the moves was not the point. He could empathize, he could relate, he could feel the people's pain and still stand up and fight the power. His visceral connection to the people is what made him a great leader.

My mother, Toni Vincent, was a Panther, and she knew many of the prominent early Party members. One of my earliest memories is of taking a trip to visit Huey P. Newton in the Alameda County courthouse jail and straining to peep through a tiny window to see him. I've always seen my mom as a revolutionary. As a child she overcame polio, and while she could walk, travel the world, and join the revolution, she did not move with the freedom of a dancer. She was a revolutionary who did not dance.

My late father, Ted Vincent, was an accomplished white historian of black radical politics. His first teaching job at Merritt College in 1964 was energized by the presence of a young, talkative student named Huey P. Newton. He was a fierce counterculture radical and would always get down and funky in his own way, but we all knew that Ted operated just a bit outside the box. So the mythos of the steely eyed black militant remained.

Could one be funky and a revolutionary at the same time? I wrestled with this notion as I wrote my first book, *Funk: The Music, the People and the Rhythm of The One*. The great funk bands and musicians of the 1970s were to me expressions of the freedom that the black power movement fought so hard to establish. These were the dancing revolutionaries I thought I was looking for. For me, Don Cornelius's *Soul Train* was one big black power dance party. But the volumes of history I read gave the impression that the movement people and the entertainers inhabited opposite banks of that river to freedom. How were black power and soul music connected?

Certainly the entertainer and the militant do not typically occupy the same space. At some level it is an absurdity to compare the courage of a militant activist who stares down the barrel of a police rifle to the efforts of an entertainer who might pen some verses of indignation in the comfort of a hotel room. Yet somehow these people are connected. Somehow, the fighters and the lovers inspire one another and force us to consider that we all possess elements of both.

The spark for this discussion of black power and soul music came from a small, short-lived rhythm and blues band that operated out of Oakland, California, in 1970. The group performed for less than a year, but in that short window of time they represented all that was revolutionary about black politics and black culture in that era. The band was the Lumpen, and this book tells their story, and the story of the Black Panther Party, and of the revolution that created them.

Party Music: The Coup

I was made aware of the Lumpen in 2002 through conversations with Boots Riley, leader of the rap group the Coup. The title of this book is borrowed from the name of one of Boots Riley's albums. The Coup's fourth album, *Party Music*, released in late 2001, garnered its own controversy before the record was even distributed, as the cover artwork depicting the destruction of the World Trade Center (a few months hence) was seen at the time as all too prophetic. The artwork was withdrawn before the CD hit the stores, and the new art featured a photo of a filled martini glass, as if a party were taking place, with a gasoline can in the background. This image fused the idea of a party with the symbol of rebellion implied in a Molotov cocktail. With songs like "5 Million Ways to Kill a C.E.O," "Pork and Beef," and "Get Up," Riley and DJ Pam "the Funkstress" Warren used humor, irony, verbal acrobatics, and wicked grooves to promote their message of radical social change. Showered in praise by critics, the Coup's *Party Music* effectively used the funk to bring about an urgent call to action, as well as a call to the dance floor.

In one discussion in 2002 about the "party music" theme, Riley told me that he had heard that the Black Panthers had a funk band. For both of us the proposition seemed remote and absurd, almost comical, but Riley suggested I investigate further. I asked my associate at KPFA radio, Walter Turner, a journalist and former Party member, and he confirmed to me that the Party had a band. Turner said the group was called the Lumpen, and that he owned a copy of their music.

He showed me a seven-inch, 45 rpm single with the titles "Free Bobby Now" and "No More" printed on each side. It was credited as a Seize the Time production, and the artist was listed as the Lumpen. The single is one of the most sought after oldies records by music collectors. Through Walter Turner, I was able to digitize the single as well as other cultural productions of the black radical movement, including the two music albums recorded by former Panther Party leader Elaine Brown.

In the fall of 2002, Riley put me in contact with Greg Morozumi, a local organizer at the Oakland-based East Side Arts Alliance. Morozumi informed me that a remnant of the Black Panther Party (BPP), then represented by former BPP chief of staff David Hilliard, had recently released a rap album, and that one of the members of the rap group was the son of an original Lumpen member. I invited the Panther-oriented rap group—the Fugitives—and David Hilliard onto my KPFA radio program. Through Jamil Calhoun of the Fugitives, I was able to contact William Calhoun, founder and former leader of the Lumpen. When William Calhoun gave me a brief telephone interview during a break from his workplace at an at-risk youth facility in Sacramento, everything I had been working on fell into place.

Calhoun put me in touch with Billy "X" Jennings, organizer of the It's About Time Committee, a Sacramento-based organization of former rank-and-file BPP members dedicated to maintaining the legacy of the BPP through a range of community, educational, and cultural activities. Jennings provided a great deal of archival information on the Lumpen as well as access to the remaining Lumpen members. With the help of Jennings, and occasional support from David Hilliard, I was able to contact and interview a cross-section of former Party members and supporters who had affiliations with the Lumpen.

In the fall of 2003, I obtained a tape of a live performance of the Lumpen from the Huey P. Newton Archives housed at Stanford University. The recording was a grainy dub (apparently from a cassette) of a performance at Merritt College in North Oakland (located just a few blocks from the original BPP central headquarters), recorded on a Tuesday night, November 10, 1970. With the assistance of engineer Deverol Ross at KPFA radio, I was able to upgrade the sound quality to create a digital CD recording and carefully analyze each selection in the forty-minute, seven-song set.

Despite the grainy sound, the songs exploded out of the speakers with high-quality singing, skilled musical support from the band, and the presence of an energized, interactive audience. This live performance represented the essence of what was at the core of the activist-artist aesthetic within the black power and Black Arts movements. Artists were increasingly political, and political leaders were eminently soulful. Members of the two movements fed off each other and inspired the actions that we remember today as the black revolution.

As a radio host and DJ, for me a playlist or a musical group's set list can be seen as a work of art in its own right. I was captivated by the song choices made by the group—all classic soul songs parodied and reworked to fit the party line of the Black Panther Party. This live recording of the Lumpen told a story that demanded to be told, a story about a superior soul music performance, a story about a band of performers unlike any other, and a story about a revolutionary time and a revolutionary Party that led to this entity coming into being.

The research on the Lumpen, and the circumstances that created a band such as this, would become my 2008 doctoral dissertation, "The Lumpen: Music on the Front Lines of the Black Revolution." Publication of the work proved problematic, and it was through Noelle Hanrahan of Prison Radio that I sent a copy of the dissertation to Mumia Abu-Jamal. Mumia enjoyed the dissertation, gave it his endorsement, and facilitated my relationship with the Frances Goldin Literary Agency, which led to the placement of *Party Music* with Lawrence Hill Books.

It is important to note that the Lumpen singers, all full-time Panthers, were each adamant that any discussion of their work be placed in context of the movement they were a part of and the organization they were working in. They did not want to be placed in front of the larger movement story, because they were not the movement leadership; they were rank-and-file Panther Party members and are proud of that fact. Their story is a part of a revolutionary moment that inspired musicians and activists to take things to the extreme because this was the tenor of the times. Years later, generations raised on the rhythms of revolution, in music and in spoken word, see the black power era through a different lens. A new breed is yearning to know the story of the black revolution, as told through the music. This is it.

Introduction

"Revolution in the Air"

E very song tells a story. The songs in this book tell the story of a revolution—of multiple revolutions taking place at once. Within the black music tradition, one finds that all things flow along multiple rhythms. The rhythms of change were everywhere in the United States at the end of the 1960s: in global war and conflict, in the arena of social justice, at the personal level of identity, and in popular culture. Everything, it appeared for a moment, was undergoing a radical transformation.

The revolution discussed here is what was called the black revolution. The black revolution involved radical, confrontational ideas of dramatic change, yet the topic was well established in the mainstream of American discourse at the time, and nearly every American had an opinion about it. The black revolution encompassed dreams of overturning the social order, of confronting white racists and destroying the racial caste system in America, of destroying the capitalist dominion over Western economies, of purging the culture and history of Eurocentric distortions and replacing them with ones that would be vibrant and empowering to all, and of transforming black life from one of perpetual crisis into one of black- and African-inspired celebration.

On a structural, economic level, the revolution did not materialize. On a cultural level, the repercussions were long lasting and indelible. On

1

the level of identity formation, on the essential transformation from the flaccid term *Negro* to the prideful *black*, the revolution was triumphant. Yet even the term *black*, as a revolutionary symbol, would eventually lose much of its significance. Perhaps the most lasting example of the radical changes that took place during this period was the revolution in black music. From the transformations of soul music by Curtis Mayfield, Sly Stone, Aretha Franklin, and James Brown to the bold sonic assaults on the status quo by the likes of Nina Simone and Jimi Hendrix, the evidence was clear that a radical moment was upon us.

The radical moment was fueled by the idea of "black power!" Black power was more than a political movement driven by nationalism and enmity toward whites, it was a resistance culture, a means of reclaiming one's identity through the events and actions of one's daily life during this time of radical change. The music and other cultural productions of the times played a significant role in this process. People heard the speeches and went to the rallies, but they also danced to the music and felt the fire of revolution flow through their bodies in motion. The cultural politics of black power were crucial to the times.

Stokely Carmichael (later Kwame Ture) was one of the most prolific black radicals of the 1960s. In his early years leading the Student Nonviolent Coordinating Committee (SNCC), and later as a key proponent of black power, Carmichael was one of the most prominent and effective organizers in the civil rights/black power era. He was a frequent ally and foil to Dr. Martin Luther King Jr. and was an undisputed leader of the movement. While he was seen as a political activist, he was influenced by the music, by the culture of the people, just like everyone else. In his memoir, *Ready for Revolution*, he discusses the impact of black popular music on his movement: "I really dug into the popular music aspect—soul, rhythm and blues, even funk a little—of this uprising of political and cultural consciousness, and not just because it reached millions of our people. We are an African people, so it was natural that from the beginning, from the spirituals right on up, music would be our weapon and our solace."

Carmichael recognized black music as the weapon that it is and expressed an understanding of its evolution as a parallel to the many social movements with which he was well acquainted. For those of his generation, knowledge and pride in the history of black music went hand in hand with knowledge and pride in the history of the black struggle. Carmichael further explains:

Indeed, certain jazz musicians had always incorporated a high social and cultural consciousness into their work. And in the early sixties, artists like Sister Odetta, Oscar Brown Jr., Max Roach and Abbey Lincoln with their *We Insist! Max Roach's Freedom Now Suite*, or Nina Simone's "Mississippi Goddam" and "Young, Gifted and Black" had reflected the Southern struggle.

But now something slightly different. Political consciousness moved into the popular arena. Soul, rhythm and blues, stuff that had been purely commercial, dance music, entertainment. I think Bro Sam Cooke (peace be unto him) might have got in first with "A Change Is Gonna Come." After that we talking about people like Marvin Gaye, "What's Going On," Brother Curtis Mayfield, "We're a Winner," "Keep On Pushing," "People Get Ready," Sister Aretha Franklin's "Respect," and of course, the King of Soul, Brother James Brown's "Say It Loud (I'm Black and I'm Proud.)" This music reached people we couldn't otherwise reach. How effectively I can't say. But from it, one sensed an exuberant mood in the community.[1]

Carmichael was aware of the relationship between the revolution in the social structure he was fighting for every day as an activist and the revolutionary changes taking place in the daily lives of the people he had chosen to serve. Carmichael reveals himself as a soul brother, someone likely as adept on the dance floor as on the rally stage. Indeed it was Carmichael's soulfulness—his personal style and ability to flow and improvise within his community—that made him a great movement leader.

Carmichael also makes the valid point that soul music reached many more people than he did, emphasizing that in many cases the sounds may have been different, but the impulse was the same. As comedian Dick Gregory said at the time, "You'd hear Aretha three or four times an hour. You'd only hear [Dr. Martin Luther] King on the news."[2] The dissemination of the ideals, the ideologies of the movement, were in an important way accomplished through the popular culture of the day: in the language used by radio DJs, in the fashions deployed by entertainers, the slang used by activists that sought to affirm their street credentials as well as validate their analyses of the movement, and in a dozen other ways.

"Black power," like soul, was an elusive slogan to define at the time, yet you knew it when you *felt* it. The live black music show was one site at which people from all walks of life were given a communal space—a radical concept at the time—to behave with abandon. While this might be dismissed as simply a recreational respite from the true grind of the movement, many of the movement's goals and ideals were formed, focused, and quite literally brought to life there. In the early 1960s, audiences of youth were *living* integration on the dance floor, witnessing equality—and quite clearly experiencing freedom—with each beat and freeform physical gyration to the music. Their pleasure was in itself a form of political expression, and the politics of pleasure were on full display, shouting down the politics of partisanship.

As the great soul singers began to dominate black popular music— James Brown, Aretha Franklin, Otis Redding, the Temptations, and others—their concerts became spaces of celebration of far more than dance moves. As James Brown put it, "The word soul meant a lot of things, in music and out. It was about the roots of black music, and it was kind of a pride thing too, being proud of yourself and your people. Soul music and the civil rights movement went hand in hand, sort of grew up together."[3]

By the end of the 1960s a new, more militant strand of black music emerged. From within the black radical movement, the poets, jazz combos, and a few courageous rhythm and blues performers pushed a message of total revolution on their audiences and received a response of exhilaration and righteous indignation that resonated with the power of Malcolm X's speeches. For the militant performer, the production involved a performance of blackness, of hypermasculinity and hyperbole, of smack talk that put the Man in his place and exalted everything gloriously black and proud among the people. The collective soul experience was no longer the ideal; this was about becoming—or re-becoming—black, and if it made whites uncomfortable, well then it was about time they too felt isolation in their own land.

During this heated time in American history, entertainers were often political and political leaders were unmistakably entertaining. Often the tenor of the times blurred the roles of each. The multifaceted pianist and singer Nina Simone was an enigmatic advocate for social causes. As an entertainer, the classically trained prodigy had established herself as a musical tour de force as she played concert halls from her native North Carolina to Paris in the early 1960s. However, as events in the civil rights movement compelled a reorganization of her views, she developed a protest music repertoire and produced piercing commentary on the changes evolving at the time. In her concerts she openly defied and challenged her predominantly white audiences, often claiming from the stage, "This next song is only for the black people that are here." In her memoir *I Put a Spell On You*, Simone positioned herself within the movement:

> I realized that what we were really fighting for was the creation of a new society. When I had started out in the movement all I wanted were my rights under the constitution. But the more I thought about it the more I realized that despite what the President or the supreme court might say, the only way we could get true equality was if America changed completely from top to bottom. And this change had to start with my own people, with *black revolution*.[4]

Simone, as a touring artist, was one of the most prolific artists to emerge as an activist from the stage, with songs like "Mississippi Goddam," a blistering (yet comical) rant against Southern Jim Crow racism in 1963 and "Why? (The King of Love Is Dead)," a ballad for Martin Luther King Jr. cowritten with Weldon Irvine just days after Dr. King's death. Nina Simone, as an entertainer, longed to be a part of the movement as a full-time participant:

> When I went on marches or played benefits I watched all the full-time activists embracing and laughing, grooving together, and I knew that when it was over they'd go home to eat, argue politics, listen to music, make love and sleep. The next day they'd make plans to meet up again on the next march and then go back into their communities to live out the ideas they believed in. They belonged; I didn't.[5]

In her revealing lament, Nina Simone understood just how exciting, how fulfilling, and how soulful movement life was for the many activists she knew. She understood that the movement was not merely a series of political actions and position papers. It involved thousands of young people (and others) in the prime of life taking action on behalf of their people for the purpose of justice—not for profit or for popularity. The politics of pleasure were working in tandem with the politics of revolutionary change.

In his memoir of life as a Black Panther, *We Want Freedom*, Mumia Abu-Jamal recounts the narrative of Naima Major, a young high school student and National Negro Scholar, who was transformed by the movement and by the Black Panther Party. Major recalled the feeling and the energy of her political transformation, and the organic way her experiences cohered with her social growth:

> I went to a Free Huey Rally at the federal building in SF, and met many brave Panthers. Went on a mission with Kathleen Cleaver in Hunter's Point because my beloved was one of her self-appointed guards. Captured body and soul by the rally and the love and energy of black people. My favorite retort to almost anything soon became "And how does that free the people?" I was dogmatic and insufferable, but could dance you down at a house party![6]

Major's movement catechism was part and parcel of the lived experience of soul at the time, as young people were being educated, energized, and transformed by a movement that evolved on their terms.

Many of the most memorable changes in black music—Marvin Gaye's transformation from pop crooner to movement preacher on "What's Going On," Jimi Hendrix's evolution from blues rocker in the Jimi Hendrix Experience to thunder-funk pioneer in the Band of Gypsys, from James Brown's ruggedly intimate ballads to his outburst of righteous, primal funk—occurred as the civil rights movement exploded into the black power movement in a cataclysm of rage and rebellion.

At the dawn of the 1960s, black popular music was established in three fairly self-contained, self-defined, and self-segregating formats: rhythm and blues, jazz, and gospel. Rhythm and blues was the most popular form of dance entertainment, led at the time by Ray Charles and the early pop icons from Motown such as Smokey Robinson. The earliest of the 1960s soul crooners, Sam Cooke and Jackie Wilson, were just beginning to make their mark, and Aretha Franklin was toiling away at Columbia recording comparatively tame pop and jazz standards. Some of the strongest yet most mysterious sounds of discontent were coming from the avant-garde jazz community, with artists such as Charles Mingus Jr., Max Roach, and Archie Shepp and free-thinking experimenters such as Ornette Coleman, Cecil Taylor, and John Coltrane musing upon ideas of what radical change is all about.

When the 1960s began, rock and roll as a pop phenomenon was defined by Elvis Presley gyrating his hips on national television in an imitation of the Memphis soul brothers he had learned from. When the sixties ended, rock was defined by Jimi Hendrix abusing the "Star-Spangled Banner" at the Woodstock concert in August 1969. When the sixties began, jazz was defined by John Coltrane's soaring spirituality and Quincy Jones's pop sophistication. When the decade ended, jazz was defined by Miles Davis's electronic swamp dirge at the *Bitches Brew* sessions. Black dance music began the sixties with the joyous, rowdy rocking of Ray Charles and ended with James Brown and Aretha Franklin righteously ripping into the souls of their audiences.

The one constant through the musical machinations was the role of gospel music. Eventually gospel music would be changed by the movement as well, but it is important to note that as an autonomous institution of black self-definition and success, the recorded spirituals, first developed as a recorded idiom in 1932 by Rev. Thomas Dorsey, had become a standard bearer for the survival of blacks in the Jim Crow South and throughout the country.

During the early years of the civil rights movement, the black church was the central organizing structure and spiritual home base for a generation seeking to work up the courage to challenge white racist violence. One fundamental element of the black church experience was and is the music, the timeless sounds of salvation that have passed from generations of slaves to the present day. These sorrow songs would eventually morph into freedom songs, and the church became the source of inspiration for the movement. Martin Luther King Jr. utilized the power of spirituals to keep him going through the desperate times, and specifically requested that Mahalia Jackson perform before his "I Have a Dream" speech at the March on Washington in 1963. Jackson was on the stage during Dr. King's famous speech and urged King to leave his scripted text, shouting, "Tell them about your dream, Martin! Tell them about the dream!" Mahalia Jackson's presence may have been the spark that made a legend out of the man on that unforgettable day.[7]

As a representation of the bittersweet past and as a symbol of the promise of the future, the music of the black church was and remains a core element in the coherence of the black experience. Waldo E. Martin Jr. explains the nature of gospel music as a social movement force:

> It might appear that gospel is the least political and worldly of African American musics. In fact the opposite is true. Gospel

music—like the spirituals—is highly political in a broad sense of
the term, if for no other reason than that it functions as a means to
constitute a unified community to forge a collective consciousness.
It likewise functions as a locus of unrestrained celebration as well as
a soothing balm. It offers hope and possibility.[8]

To offer hope and possibility in the face of the unspeakable terrors facing civil rights activists in the South bears witness to the unique powers
of the gospel music experience. The physical reality of the dangers, the
uncertainty, and the fear involved in the struggle would sway in the
moment of the music, in the netherworld of sensation, as a collective
emotional state takes over as one gives themselves away to the song.
Through the innate healing power of the music—of the sounds, of the
rhythms, of the collectively shared physical motion, the exhilaration
of the unified harmonies—a sense of unbounded power emerges, and
the terrestrial fears and trials are suspended for the moment. Gospel
music forges a sustainable moment of courage out of one of despair and
retreat.

The civil rights movement was a time when improvisation was the
standard for both movement activities and the music the activists produced. Many traditional gospel songs were reformulated for the needs
of the moment. The urgent and triumphant traditional song "Keep Your
Hand on the Plow" was reimagined by civil rights activist Alice Wine
and transformed into "Keep Your Eyes on the Prize," while the simplest
of gospel standards, the melodic "Amen"—sung with the word extended
"aaa-men!"—was transformed by young activists at the early sit-ins to
become "free-dom!" The use of the song, and so many others, was pig-
gybacking on the moral-spiritual backing of the church, and was brought
into a new secular realm of social justice.

Gospel songs, and the sounds of gospel music, would continue to be
used as fodder for civil rights workers through the decade. But as black
power began to emerge as a theme, a new sound of resistance emerged,
and the range of songs used by the movement expanded to popular
rhythm and blues tunes. Chants and riffs from the radio became a part
of the movement lexicon. Titles like "Tell It Like It Is," "Get Ready," and
"Take Me as I Am" were imbided with meanings beyond their intended
lyrics. One marcher in 1966 on the long March Against Fear in Mississippi (also known as the Black Power March) came up with a revision to

the lyrics of Wilson Pickett's hit song "Land of 1000 Dances," which was known at the time to bounce along with an effervescent beat with lyrics such as: "Put your hand on your hips, yeah / Let your backbone slip / Do the Watusi / Like my little Lucy." The improvised black power lyrics and crowd response went as follows:

> I said freedom got a shotgun / oh yeah!
> I said freedom got a shotgun / oh yeah!
> You know freedom gonna shoot it / oh yeah!
> At those segregated bigots! / oh yeah!
> I said freedom got a shotgun! / oh yeah!
> Naaa na-na-na naaa

The singer and the crowd then joined in with the familiar vocal hook of the song "naa na-na-na naaa," wrapping the audience of marchers in a collective interpretation of popular song, reinterpreted for the movement.[9] Soul music—black popular music—would become the template for new movement songs. Conversely, the movement in the streets would inspire a rhythm-driven awakening of music in jazz, in funk, and in soul that captured a people's aspirations just as the people were awakening.

Framing the Black Revolution

The rhetoric of revolution was a common thread throughout the discourse of the civil rights / black power movements. The revolution carried a set of meanings among black Americans that evolved dramatically during those years. From the outset of the civil rights movement in the mid-1950s, the struggle for black equality developed with a spirit more hopeful than at any time since the American Civil War a century prior. When NAACP lawyer Thurgood Marshall successfully argued to the Supreme Court in the famous 1954 *Brown v. Board of Education* case that segregation was unconstitutional, a number of new social constructs were unleashed. The idea that Negroes possessed some form of self-determination, and that their own actions could bring about changes in the racial caste system, was a revelation. For so long, generations of impoverished and terrorized Negroes had been at the mercy of their white neighbors. By the time of the Rosa Parks incident in Montgomery, Alabama, in 1955, which challenged and eventually brought an end to segregated busing in the South, the idea began to take hold that Negroes themselves could be the initiators of social change.

In addition, the prospect that equality could be imagined with an increasing sense of realism meant that black culture, black life, black values, black morality, and black thought were worthy on their own terms. Even within the context of Dr. Martin Luther King Jr.'s vision of nonviolent civil disobedience, for a young and hopeful generation a "revolution within" was taking place.

As organizational activity spread and the agitation for equal rights increased, a proportional increase in cultural pride emerged, as black people found within their culture—their writing, their drama and visual arts, their scholarship, their folkways, and especially their music—the evidence that equality was their birthright. The example of self-reliance displayed by the Nation of Islam and its fiery spokesman, Malcolm X, affirmed that Negroes had not only the same inalienable rights as whites, but also possessed their own moral, spiritual, and physical resources to create a new society on their own terms.

One universally acknowledged cornerstone of the movement was the work of Dr. Martin Luther King Jr. His charismatic leadership and advocacy of nonviolent civil disobedience in the face of raw southern violence earned him the indisputable mantle as leader of the movement. And it was Dr. King's iconic August 1963 speech at the March on Washington that served as a celebration and a summary of the movement to that point. It is important to note that during the early portion of Dr. King's speech, he did not temper the tone of the social revolution that was taking place on the streets of America:

> It would be fatal for the nation to overlook the urgency of the moment. This sweltering summer of the Negro's legitimate discontent will not pass until there is an invigorating autumn of freedom and equality. . . .
>
> There will be neither rest nor tranquility in America until the Negro is granted his citizenship rights. The whirlwinds of revolt will continue to shake the foundations of our nation until the bright day of justice emerges.[10]

This was not the idealistic imagery that Dr. King is so well known for. On this most revered of occasions, Dr. King threatened the nation with death, claiming it would be fatal to overlook the crisis at hand. The revolution had clearly arrived at Dr. King's doorstep. Dr. King was keenly aware of the simmering rage that was dwelling within his people, and he sought to harness it in a useful way. The "whirlwinds of revolt" would continue to spiral out of control as the decade progressed, despite Dr. King's best efforts.

A confluence of events in 1965 sparked a new branch of the movement, one in which the aspects of nonviolent civil disobedience began to lose their relevance. The assassination of Malcolm X on February 21 initiated a widespread reappraisal of his writings and speeches by a new generation of young rebels. Fractures within the movement began to emerge, which brought contradictory value systems among blacks into view. The passage of the Voting Rights Act in August 1965, only weeks after the brutal beatings of civil rights marchers in Selma, Alabama, was considered a fallacy by many dispossessed people (though liberal lawmakers considered it a hard-fought victory against staunchly racist opposition). The frustration reached a breaking point when South Central Los Angeles exploded in the Watts uprising on August 11, 1965.

The growth of ideas contrary to integration—which included the rise of black nationalism, the emergence of independent African nations and the spread of Marxist revolutionary thought, the reappraisal and affection for Africa, and the daily outrages of black life in the cities—all became fuel for an ideological explosion of antiassimilationist ideas in black America. Stokely Carmichael's chant of "black power," introduced midway through the Mississippi March Against Fear in the summer of 1966, became the new rallying cry of the dispossessed and coalesced a growing, yet still unfocused, feeling among a new generation of black youth.

As the leaders of the civil rights movement met resistance and deeper-entrenched problems in the northern cities in the latter half of the 1960s, a less hopeful mood set in. A new perspective emerged among many in the black community disillusioned with the system, yet still determined to agitate for change. In many urban areas a sense of inevitable confrontation with the power structure began to emerge. The black revolution began to take on increasingly literal physical interpretations.

The construct of *revolution* was galvanized by the words of Malcolm X. The Nation of Islam's minister of mosque number seven in Harlem was well known on the New York streets as the champion orator of black causes in the early 1960s. Malcolm X consistently derided the established civil rights leaders at the time, whom he claimed were only seeking superficial change and access to a society that Malcolm and others saw as corrupt. Malcolm X did not validate the idea that a revolution was taking place merely because people were marching for voting rights or for access to public facilities or businesses. He did not entertain the idea of access to white institutions as a goal. He used the model of the anti-colonial struggles for freedom in Africa, Asia, and Latin America as his frame of reference. These struggles frequently involved violent battles over land utilizing guerilla warfare. As a veteran of the violence of urban black survival, Malcolm was able to bring this comparison down to the street level for his audiences. He made this point clear in Detroit in 1963 in his "Message to the Grass Roots":

> You don't know what a revolution is. If you did, you wouldn't use that word. A revolution is bloody. Revolution is hostile. Revolution knows no compromise. Revolution overturns and destroys everything that gets in its way. Who ever heard of a revolution where they lock arms . . . singing "we shall overcome"? You don't do that in a revolution. You don't do any singing, you're too busy swinging.[11]

Within a few years, many of Malcolm's predictions would come to pass. At the end of the 1960s the spirit of the revolution was everywhere: in the marches, in the chants, in the rebellions, and in the arts.

This defiant energy gave rise to many black radical ideas, pronouncements, and organizations. Young people wanted to get in on the revolution by any means necessary. They began study groups and newsletters, organized picket lines and rallies, confronted people in power, and in the process shed their fears of the police, of the justice system, and of the omnipresent aura of white privilege. They wrote about their actions in journals and in fiction; they designed, painted, and sketched posters and banners and flyers with vibrant black revolutionary symbols; they danced and sang songs with African rhythms; they wrote plays that imagined a racial apocalypse; and they screamed poems and played music with the pulse of their newfound black fire. The black power movement and the Black Arts movement emerged and thrived simultaneously.

As the writings, rallies, organizations, and number of participants in black radical groups increased, a more fully formed sense of "blackness" began to take hold. Not created or maintained by whites, it was a new, decidedly autonomous identity. This was a lasting legacy of the revolution. Lerone Bennett Jr. explains the nature of the cultural revolution that took place during the 1960s:

> The important point emerging from this is that the Movement was a double revolution, a revolution in the streets and a revolution in symbols, images and ideas—a revolution, in a word, of the word. The two revolutions unfolded at the same time and were complimentary facets of the same reality: the historical explosion of a people in the sudden labor of self-discovery, self-determination, and self-legitimization.[12]

The revolution would become a popular catchphrase, a catchall term for use by anyone ready and willing to rally around people's outrage at the power structure. Rock star and former Beatle John Lennon publicly proclaimed the need for a revolution as he agitated for his anti–Vietnam War protests in 1971. When the Last Poets released "Niggers Are Scared of Revolution" in June 1970 and Gil Scott-Heron re-recorded his sarcastic "The Revolution Will Not Be Televised" in April 1971, the songs captured just how omnipresent and yet versatile the idea of revolution was at that moment. Eventually the term would be manipulated and maligned, and its literal and symbolic meaning would be lost. For a time, however, there was quite clearly revolution in the air.

The Black Panther Party took the idea of revolution seriously. The organization crafted itself as an outgrowth of the vision of Malcolm X and proclaimed itself the vanguard of the revolution. Early on, with their menacing image—wearing black leather, black berets, and carrying weapons—the Panthers stood uncompromisingly on the national scene as defiant black militants willing to take on the US power structure. New recruits joined the Party with the notion that they were going to be in a life-or-death encounter with law enforcement at some point in the near future and committed themselves to that inevitability.

As rank-and-file members of the Black Panther Party, the young men who became members of the Lumpen had also made this commitment. None of them joined the Party to play songs. They joined to give their lives to the struggle, to the revolution. Eventually, as a result of a number of dramatic events, the Black Panther Party broadened its scope, and the Lumpen group was created to popularize that black revolution.

The "Great Transformation"

The impact of the black power movement in general and the Black Panther Party in particular on the landscape of American culture and identity formation was nothing short of transformative. It is important to note that the role of identity politics in modern American life emerged from the black power era movements. As Michael Omi and Howard Winant write in *Racial Formation in the United States*: "The black movement redefined the meaning of racial identity, and consequently of race itself, in American society."[13] The popularity of the phrase "black is beautiful" was perhaps the simplest and most elegant example of what transpired during those years. Blacks generated a new cultural value system on their own terms and marked their own reference points of value in a contemporary American context.

These new matrices of meaning were also fundamental to the struggles of other *racialized* groups in America. As Jeffrey Ogbar explains: "It was the Black Power movement that had some of the most visible influences on the radical activist struggles of Latinos, Asians, and Native Americans, giving rise to a visible movement of radical ethnic nationalism and new constructions of ethnic identity. Young activists of all backgrounds had been impressed and inspired by the militancy, political analysis, organization and symbolism of black nationalists and Black Power advocates."[14]

A new vocabulary of hyphenated Americans would emerge, and members of these racialized groups would be both *defining* and *defined by* these new terms. America would become a nation of racialized interest groups, what Omi and Winant would call the "racial state." Omi and Winant termed the creation of the racial state the "Great Transformation," which "irreversibly expanded the terrain of political contest" and set in motion the array of identity-driven politics that form the national body politic today. This Great Transformation was a result of black power, and the focal point of black power politics and culture was the Black Panther Party, which combined political theater, social work, and urban warfare at the flashpoint of racial unrest in twentieth-century America.

Framing the Panthers

The Black Panther Party for Self-Defense, as it was originally called, was a multifaceted black revolutionary organization whose initial membership, while primarily from the urban working class, was composed of a broad cross-section of the San Francisco Bay Area's African American community. Their early public actions (from 1966 to 1968) were designed to confront symbols of the power structure directly and to provide a critique and working alternative to the traditional nonviolent methods of protest. Cofounders Huey P. Newton and Bobby Seale designed Party activities to impress new recruits with their fearlessness and willingness to die for the people. Their courageous stance sparked a rapid increase in membership and the establishment of more than thirty chapters across the country by the end of 1968.

Party membership transcended class or ideological barriers as many rank-and-file participants were introduced to an alternative communalistic lifestyle. During the early years this included weekly lessons in political education, or "P.E." classes. This was the primary means of indoctrination/transformation of new recruits, to help turn "brothers off the block" into Black Panthers. There were codes of personal conduct, and most chapters offered forms of self-defense and firearms training. Party duties included work in the many "Survival Programs" such as the breakfast for children program and "liberation schools," as well as production and distribution of the *Black Panther* paper, regular security detail, and participation in a wide range of community events. The commitment was extremely rigorous, as there were duties twenty-four hours a day, compounded by the constant threat of attack by law enforcement and, in later years, from rival black radical factions.

The Black Panther Party went through three distinct phases of its existence. The early years of 1966 through 1970 were characterized by projections of militarism and black nationalism, as well as an affection for socialism, a rapid growth in numbers, and a compelling presence in the American popular imagination. The second phase, from 1970 to 1973, can be characterized as a transitional period in which Party leader Huey P. Newton consolidated his power in Oakland, redirected the organization toward programs to serve the people, and sought to run Party leaders for elective office. The final stage, 1974 to 1982, involved the growth of a local infrastructure in Oakland, initially under the leadership of Elaine Brown, within the context of a gradual decline of black radical politics nationwide.

Despite being raised in black working-class families with little political education, the young Panther Party leaders re-created themselves as theoreticians and intellectuals of the revolution who daily engaged with the power structure on the streets as revolutionaries. Party members and supporters from all walks of life were able to identify with their leaders and to see themselves as analysts as well as agents in their revolutionary cause.

A number of young Panthers incorporated their artistic talents in the pursuit of their revolutionary dreams. Emory Douglas, who survived incarceration in a youth reform school by learning the printing trade, became involved with playwright and activist Amiri Baraka during Baraka's visiting lectureship at San Francisco State in the spring of 1967. Douglas designed the sets for the traveling plays that Baraka and others would perform in the area. Douglas then worked with Bobby Seale to design the first editions of the *Black Panther* newspaper, and joined Seale and other Panthers on their famous visit to the Sacramento state capitol to protest pending gun restrictions. As minister of culture for the Black Panther Party, Douglas would design the vast majority of issues of the *Black Panther* through the 1980s. Through sharp and vivid imagery he celebrated the revolutionary warrior, and revolutionary ideals, while characterizing police and members of the power structure as filthy pigs. Douglas would become—and remains—a central figure in the propagation of the revolutionary ideology of the Black Panther Party.

Douglas designed the artwork on the first album release of Panther-based music by Elaine Brown, titled *Seize the Time*. In 1968 Elaine Brown, then a young Los Angeles chapter leader, began to write songs—revolutionary ballads—that she sang while playing the piano. In the crisis following the 1969 UCLA shoot-out in which Panthers John Huggins and Alprentice "Bunchy" Carter were killed, Elaine Brown sang some of her songs to a group of grieving Panthers that included David Hilliard. Hilliard anointed one of Brown's songs ("The Meeting") the Black

Panthers' national anthem and proclaimed that Brown should record her music for the revolution. Her album was recorded in Los Angeles under the guidance of iconoclastic jazz arranger Horace Tapscott. The album, *Seize the Time*, was a vivid representation of Panther Party ideals that included Brown's written commentary as well as Douglas's artwork. It was sold at Party functions and was advertised in the *Black Panther* as part of the Party's early efforts to disseminate their message to the community through music. Elaine Brown's music was compelling message music, sung as dramatically arranged ballads. Brown's music, however, did not move with the rhythms of the streets: soul music.

Despite the cultural productions of Emory Douglas and Elaine Brown, the stoic Panther mythos lived on in the nation's imagination. It is only through later revisions of the narrative that the Black Panthers' image began a process of reconstruction that has revealed Party members to be the soul brothers and soul sisters that they were.

Framing Party Music

As a political history, *Party Music* offers an insider's narrative of the Black Panther Party during its crucial transformative phase, 1969–1971. As a soul music history, *Party Music* explores the motives of many of the great artists and great songs performed during that tumultuous period. At a turning point in history, with many dramatic events playing out on the national stage, black power and soul music are explored as one resonant note, a scream actually, from the people themselves.

Some books are organized in a linear, chronological fashion. This book is not one of them. *Party Music* is structured along a set of songs performed by the Lumpen at a concert in Oakland in November 1970. The live Lumpen experience is an important element here. Their approach to soul music, and their skillful infusion of explicitly political lyrics onto established black popular music songs during their performances, presents us with an experience worthy of study in and of itself. Their approach went far beyond the use of gimmicks and chic radical slogans. The Lumpen transfused an entire rhythm and blues concert with the lifeblood of the revolution. Every lyric, every harmonized verse, every chant, every grunt, every shout carries a weight of meaning in their performance. Rather than transcribe an entire concert at once, each song of the evening is examined individually, as a guide to each chapter. All of the chapters begin with an immersion into the live Lumpen show, followed by a brief take on the original hit song the group had chosen to reinterpret and politicize. From there the discussion goes in many directions, from radical politics to music and culture and back again. Each chapter discussion is a deliberation on a theme inspired by a Lumpen song.

At this unique moment in time, a generation of spirited people were challenging the state, challenging the social order, taking up causes on their own, and initiating social change in a variety of ways. As the sage philosopher Bushwick Bill of the Geto Boys has said: "There are three types of people in the world: those who don't know what happened, those who wonder what happened, and people on the streets like us who make things happen!" For those people who make things happen, here is their *Party Music*.

1

"Party Music"

The Story of the Lumpen

As the backing band, the Freedom Messengers, winds down their final song in the Merritt College auditorium, the packed audience of hundreds of students, young radicals, and community members from the North Oakland area feel the anticipation building in the room. The lights go down, a drum roll starts, and a voice from the shadows bellows out:

"Ladies and gentlemen, brothers and sisters. The Black Panther Party very proudly presents, [drum roll]. . .

"The Lumpen!"

The sound of the band crashes in with a high energy rhythm and blues groove. The Lumpen members rush the stage and begin to step, kick, and spin—the show is off and running.

This is how the Lumpen began their concert on November 10, 1970, as well as their many other shows during a ten-month span from midsummer 1970 to the spring of 1971. They were billed as "The Black Panther Party's Revolutionary Band," and like many of the community programs produced by the Black Panther Party at the time, they delivered the goods. The Lumpen represented the goals and ideals of the Party and performed their radicalized renditions of popular black music through some of the most tumultuous moments in the Black Panther Party's existence. This is their story.

The story of the Lumpen began in San Jose, California, in 1968, just as the student uprisings that had been taking place at college campuses nationwide landed at the small South Bay campus of San Jose State University, fifty miles south of San Francisco. The cataclysmic events of that year—the murders of Nobel Peace Prize–winner Dr. Martin Luther King Jr. and presidential candidate Robert F. Kennedy—and the continuing horrors of the Vietnam War and racial conflict at home had fostered the rise of a radicalized student movement on many campuses. Northern California students and activists in particular had been inspired by the leaders of the Third World Liberation Front (TWLF) at San Francisco State University, which had successfully mobilized a student walkout to demand the creation of a Third World College. As a result of the TWLF, students on college campuses throughout Northern California began a series of walkouts in an effort to address inequalities at their schools and to support causes in the larger community. As Dr. Jason Ferreira states: "It was as if the students throughout the region were engaging in one big strike."

For entirely different reasons, San Jose State was becoming world famous in its own right. San Jose State was the home of the world-renowned United States Olympic track team, and its most celebrated members: Lee Evans, Tommie Smith, and John Carlos. While the student athletes trained at "Speed City," they also found themselves on the front lines of social change. A year earlier, the protests of disenfranchised blacks at SJSU—including a young, fiery black sociology instructor named Harry Edwards—had led to the unprecedented cancellation of the 1967 college football season opener due to the threat of an athletic boycott by the black players. The success of the black boycott emboldened the athletes, who along with Smith and Edwards spearheaded the Olympic Project for Human Rights, an effort that advocated a total black American boycott of the Olympic Games to be held in October 1968 in Mexico City.

The drama of the proposed Olympic boycott was one of the most consuming international stories of 1968. Some black athletes, such as Lew Alcindor (later known as Kareem Abdul-Jabbar), then an All-American basketball star at UCLA, honored the boycott and refused to participate in the Olympic games. The climate of protest was pervasive and tense, and as a result, the boycott plan and Edwards himself would fade into the background as the games approached. The remaining athletes were left to choose their own method of protest. On October 16, after their medal-winning performances in the Olympic two-hundred-meter final, San Jose State students Smith and Carlos would shock the world by raising their black power fists on the victory stand in Mexico City.

The impact of that moment at the Olympic games would be felt far and wide and would consume the lives of Smith and Carlos for decades. Yet the Olympic protest events were only part of a larger movement for social change taking place in the black community. Black college students who were facing daily insults, disorienting and often racist curricula, segregated and second-class facilities, and little or no administrative support felt a strong compulsion to participate in protests and challenges to the status quo. However, many black students also felt a different type of pressure, as the act of simply attending college was seen by their families as a personal breakthrough, and one not to be sacrificed on the altar of social protest.

In the streets of the Bay Area, young people were witnessing a visible assault on the black community, and on Black Panther Party members in particular. The imprisonment of Huey Newton in the fall of 1967 and the April 6, 1968, killing of young Bobby Hutton and wounding of Panther leader Eldridge Cleaver by Oakland police were clarion calls for many black youth that in 1968 a war with the power structure was imminent—if it had not already begun.

Into this mix, three black militant students arrived at the center of a storm of social upheaval at San Jose State. These young men had the conviction that they would take the struggle further than the student strike at SF State, further than the Mexico City events. They were prepared to seize the time.

That fall semester of 1968, a recent Berkeley High School graduate and former youth NAACP member named Michael Torrence enrolled at San Jose State. He was one of the first participants in the statewide Equal Opportunity Program (EOP), an emerging program spawned from student activism that sought to increase minority college enrollment. Torrence immediately began to organize black students on the campus, using as his guide the image of the Black Panther Party. "At that time I wanted to be a Panther. That was my goal," he recalls.[1] Torrence and his allies developed a coalition with the Black Student Union at nearby

San Jose City College, where they met William Calhoun, leader of the BSU there. The larger Black Student Alliance they formed then began a regimen of Black Panther Party functions, including the distribution of the *Black Panther* newspaper and political education classes. The young would-be Panthers also volunteered their time (along with many others) for some of the basic work of the Black Panther Party. They worked the weekly shipping detail in San Francisco, binding copies of the *Black Panther* for distribution nationwide.

As the fall 1968 semester progressed, the San Francisco State TWLF student protest had grown in size and intensity, involving almost daily confrontations between police and protesting students. Under Torrence and Calhoun's leadership, the San Jose State BSU attempted to generate a student walkout in solidarity with the San Francisco State actions. However, with the proposed walkout scheduled to take place only days after the Olympic games, the San Jose student body was not as prepared (nor was the community as effectively involved) as San Francisco, and the BSU leaders found that their brand of politics faced stiff resistance. Torrence recalls:

> In November of '68, we did vote to go out on strike. That was my first arrest; I got arrested for inciting a riot. When we got out of jail—there was me and three other brothers—we got out of jail, came back, and found out that the students had voted to call the strike off. They—I guess they got intimidated . . . you know, so there were probably some threats of suppression coming down.[2]

Torrence and the others attempted to recruit the Olympic athletes but found the track stars had little interest in controversy after the noise they had already made. "We supported them, but then when it came down to the strike, they didn't support us. . . . The athletes' position was basically, 'I'm not going to blow my scholarship for this here,'" Torrence recalls. Lumpen founder William Calhoun had a similar recollection of the young men who had nevertheless become heroes within a global movement of resistance with their symbolic gesture on the podium at the Olympic Games:

> [To us] they were not seen as revolutionary types, they were just track runners. Myself, Harry Edwards, people who had made

speeches, people who had been on the stage, people who had been at demonstrations, those were the "movement people." Tommie, Lee, and them, they were supportive, they were part of it. . . . They were at meetings, and they clapped their hands and all of that stuff, but that's all there was.[3]

With the chaos surrounding the Olympic boycott and the backlash forced upon the track runners, their return to San Jose State was fraught with controversy and conflict—hostile administrators, a hostile national media, a virulent backlash from self-described "patriotic Americans" against a gesture deemed offensive by some, and ironically, an impatient black radical community that was often urging them to take further protest action. It was perhaps understandable that under the circumstances the athletes' support did not extend beyond the track field. Calhoun states:

I knew Tommie Smith, Lee Evans, and John Carlos and all those guys. We were trying to talk them out of going to Mexico at all. Just not even showing up. It was Harry's thing to go down there and boycott or whatever. We didn't think they should show up at all. From our position, if you're going to boycott, boycott. But things kind of got diffused. And because it wasn't organized—it was kind of like the Million Man March; everybody wanted to do it but nobody kind of quite knew what we were doing or why we were doing it. So it kind of got diffused in terms of its actual application. So people went, and you had the protest with Tommie and John, but that was strictly spontaneous. They were very serious brothers, and I love them both with all my heart, but that wasn't planned.[4]

The young would-be Panthers continued on with their plans to organize the black students and the community of San Jose. In early 1969 Michael Torrence was elected chair of the San Jose State Black Students Union and set about recruiting other politically adept black students, one of whom was fellow EOP student Clark "Santa Rita" Bailey. Bailey had gone to Oakland's Castlemont High School and had enrolled at San Jose State in the spring of 1969. "Michael and them, they basically bombarded me with information, and they wouldn't leave me alone," Bailey recalls. "With that being said, some of the material that I read was very interesting to me, and it was material from Huey [Newton]."[5] Bailey joined the campus BSU and quickly immersed himself in the campus protest movement.

The paths of student activists Torrence, Calhoun, and Bailey would take another turn. Panther leader Eldridge Cleaver had been in exile since the summer of 1968, and his whereabouts were a complete mystery for a time. He had been recently "discovered" in Cuba, thanks to a cover story in the *Black Panther* in the spring of 1969, which incensed the law enforcement community. As the San Francisco Panther chapter prepared for a May Day rally, the San Francisco police raided the Panther Party headquarters, which was Eldridge Cleaver's former home. Tensions grew, and a call was put out for "reinforcements." Torrence recalls the situation:

> The SWAT team in San Francisco had vamped on the Fillmore office. That was two days before the rally, and they made a lot of arrests to try to disrupt the rally and they [the Panthers] had called us and asked if we could send some cadres up there, any sort of support we could—money and bodies. So about two carloads of us rolled up to San Francisco and camped out in the Panther houses for a couple of days, you know, behind the barricades and stuff.[6]

Torrence remembers the nature of his own particular experience of "firearms training" that first chaotic night at the San Francisco offices:

> So the first night they put myself and another brother, we call him Poison, up in the front window, and gave me what was called a Panther special [a rifle] and basically told us, "You got the front window; if the Tac squad pulls up in a Safeway van, they're gonna have a spotlight in it. If they open up the spotlight, your job will be to shoot out the spotlight and fall back." That was the first night.
>
> The only training at that point was, "Here's the safety; here's the trigger. And don't let it go off because you got twenty people behind you that are sleeping but they all got guns next to 'em." That first night was really intense. The police were at all corners. As time went on you learned more. It wasn't a real trigger-happy operation by no means.[7]

Through this trial by fire the young activists were on their way to earning the responsibilities and respect of being a Panther. As difficult and frenzied as the process of becoming Party members was, Torrence, Bailey, and Calhoun had a shared commitment to revolution that was not going to waver in times of crisis. This inner drive would serve all of them well over the next few years.

> And from that point on, we pretty much kind of became sort of like a cadre of the Party; we were at that time called Panthers in Training or community workers, and that summer we picked up two properties on the east side of San Jose, which was the community, and we opened up the [Panther Party Chapter and Community] Center.[8]

Eventual Lumpen founder and songwriter William Calhoun was just as committed as Torrence and Bailey. "I was tired of jiving," Calhoun recalls. "If we were going to have a revolution, then I wanted to be part of something that was revolutionary. And the only thing I could see was Huey P. Newton's Black Panther Party. And when Michael and Santa Rita [Bailey] and myself all hooked up at San Jose State, I guess we all had that kind of in mind."[9] Calhoun was the most experienced organizer of the trio. The jump to join the BPP was a part of a process of growth, activism, and soul-searching for him:

> The one thing as I made my progression through the movement years, from SNCC—I was one of the West Coast coordinators for the Poor People's Campaign right after the Prophet [Dr. Martin Luther King Jr.] was shot—I kind of progressed very quickly, but I touched a lot of different groups. I was the national cochairman of the House of Umoja for a very little while. But with each of these groups, there was something missing. There was a disconnect between that which we espoused and that which we did. I sensed in the Black Panther Party that disconnect was not there. And the more the brothers came down with the P.E. classes, the chief of staff [David Hilliard] came down one time, and brought some brothers and sisters with him, we got to meet them, we got to see them and see that these were some serious people. They're not just talking junk, they are out here doing it. And when the thing happened with Eldridge [the spark for the police raid], I was gone. It was a phone call, and I was in the car.[10]

After the May Day crisis had abated, the young men returned to San Jose and continued to organize the Panther chapter there, but they were just marking time until they were assigned to the central offices.

Through their daily organizing work, Torrence, Calhoun, and Bailey discovered that they each had a musical background, and the trio would sing as they passed the time. "A lot of evenings after we were through with whatever political work we were doing, we would like to just sit around and sing," Torrence recalls.[11] They sang as they worked the Wednesday night routine of binding the *Black Panther* at the Howard Quinn Printing Company on Alabama Street in San Francisco. They sang along with what was on the radio—soul music—as well as traditional blues standards and gospel music. Shipping night involved many volunteers, and the three singing Panther paper handlers became known to the Party staff and leadership. Calhoun recalls:

> This was a big coming together on Wednesday night. If there was a social event, if you want to consider it social, this was a social event. Food was prepared, and Panthers came from everywhere to do this work to get this paper out. And as it goes with black folks—I'm sure it goes with other cultures, but I know ours better—as it is with black folks, once you get a little beat going, a little rhythm going, pretty soon someone starts humming and off we go.
>
> We were just singing popular songs. Clark Bailey, Michael, and I, as we were racking and stacking, whatever we would do, we would hum songs, sing songs, whatever. We were just singing popular songs, nothing revolutionary. We may throw a little something in like we did with the Isley Brothers' "It's your thing, do what you wanna do, whitey can't tell you what the f— to do," we changed the lyrics a little bit.
>
> Emory Douglas, he heard us, and he asked me to develop something, to try to make it into something, because he said this was something that would help get the message of the Black Panther Party out.[12]

In the fall of 1969 the three San Jose State organizers were assigned full-time to the San Francisco chapter of the Black Panther Party. While Calhoun started working on the idea of a Panther musical group, they were all were kept busy with their rank-and-file Panther duties. The work involved a continuation of their efforts at organizing black students on the local college campuses in addition to their regular duties of selling the *Black Panther*, preparing breakfasts for the children, securing donations for the Survival Programs, pulling security duty guarding Panther offices, preparing and teaching the political education classes, and mobilizing for all types of events and crises that faced the organization.

Each member went through a gradual process of gaining responsibility and rank as a Black Panther based upon the needs of the organization. The work was often tedious but interrupted by dramatic moments of clarity. "There were times in my life in the Party that I didn't expect to make it," Clark Bailey recalls. "We've been woke up in central headquarters with police as far as your eye can see. On every building with guns pointed down to our office. And you just say to yourself at that time, 'This is it.' "[13]

In the spring of 1970, Torrence, Calhoun, and Bailey were assigned duties at a local festival in the Fillmore District, which was then a predominantly black neighborhood. Since Party member Elaine Brown had recorded an album of Panther-oriented music in 1969, the Party members at the Fillmore event were aware of the powerful impact that blending their politics with the culture, with daily life, could have on people. As a means of contributing to the spirit of the festival, the members decided to perform with a piano on the back of the Panther paper distribution truck and sing two songs that William Calhoun had written: "Free Bobby Now" and "No More." Minister of Culture Emory Douglas saw the trio perform and committed at that point to make a "cultural cadre" out of the group. The idea was that the group could be used as a recruitment vehicle to spread the message of the Party through a means familiar to the people. "That's what Emory recognized immediately, especially watching the people's reaction that afternoon in San Francisco. They wouldn't let us stop singing them two little songs. We had to sing them over and over and over again," Calhoun recalls.[14]

They were given the name the Lumpen by Chief of Staff David Hilliard. Most of the local Party members who took regular political education classes on Sundays were aware of the meaning of the name, which, as Calhoun explains, "is based on Karl Marx's social analysis which says that the *lumpenproletariat* are the lowest strata of social society."[15] The lumpenproletariat, according to Marx, were the "social scum" of society, the "refuse of all classes," including "swindlers, confidence trick-sters, brothel-keepers, rag-and-bone merchants, organ-grinders, beggars, and other flotsam of society."[16] This group was of a social status below the proletariat, the masses of the working classes that Marx envisioned would spearhead the uprising that would defeat capitalism. Karl Marx frequently referred to the lumpenproletariat with derision and in *The Communist Manifesto* proclaimed: "The Lumpenproletariat, that pas-sively rotting mass thrown off by the lowest layers of old society, may, here and there, be swept into the movement by a proletarian revolu-tion; its conditions of life, however, prepare it far more for the part of a bribed tool of reactionary intrigue."[17] There appeared to be little use for the lumpenproletariat in a class analysis of revolutionary change. How-ever, Black Panther Party founder and ideological leader Huey Newton found value and political potential in the lumpenproletariat and differed from Marx in that sense. While Marx believed that this subclass was too unstable and vulnerable for co-optation by the bourgeoisie and the rul-ing classes (and to their own habitual vices), Newton believed that the "social scum" at the bottom could be organized and politicized into a new vanguard of revolutionary change.

Newton's model was the revolutionary transformation of Malcolm X and the work of the Nation of Islam to reclaim thousands of lost mem-bers of the black community. The Nation of Islam, through Malcolm X's oratory, went a long way toward eradicating the shame associated with downtrodden, drug-addicted, and imprisoned black Americans because the Nation presented a path to redemption. To Newton and many others, Malcolm was a shining example of the possibilities of reclaiming one of the lumpen, the lowest of the low. In the streets, to be lumpen was to be hood, one of the brothers off the block, and so in Panther parlance, *lumpen* was a term of praise and allegiance for Party members.

The name itself was also a means of indoctrinating potential Pan-thers into a Marxian analysis of social conditions and to familiarize the audience with some of the vocabulary used to foment one's political consciousness in the 1960s. To present the idea of lumpenproletariat to first-time potential recruits of the Black Panther Party in a lecture might have come across as too dogmatic and abstract. But by presenting a liv-ing, breathing, *singing* representative of that vanguard, the spearhead of the revolution, the Lumpen had the potential to stimulate, educate, and encourage skeptical members of the community they were targeting.

The group was not simply a weekend hobby; they were an official part of the cultural apparatus of the Black Panther Party. As David Hilliard explains:

> We had an entertainment agenda because the whole point of coming to a Black Panther Party event was the totality of it all. You get the cultural and the political as a complete medium for connecting with people, so people were entertained but they were also educated, which was most important. And they left there not just with a piece of paper or leaflet, they left there wanting to be signed up in one of the BPP's Survival Programs.[18]

The singing Panther members developed their musical craft through the spring of 1970 as they continued their work as rank-and-file Party members. They worked in and around the central headquarters in Oakland and San Francisco, so their activity was a part of the daily routine of Panther life at the time. Clark Bailey recalls that the leadership knew of them early on:

> They would come and check us out, and we would sing at different functions that the organization would have. A lot of times we would have functions just for Panthers, you know, in more like a family atmosphere where we would barbecue and cook, and just be able to pass information of what was going on at the different community levels, where the community centers were. And of course the leadership was there. They were more hands-on in the central area.[19]

Shortly after the Fillmore park performance, William Calhoun was assigned the task of developing the singing trio into a complete rhythm and blues band. Emory Douglas and David Hilliard had succeeded in getting the Panthers' governing body, the Central Committee, to agree to the experiment in Panther Party community outreach through soul music. Torrence recalls:

> David and Emory, being our advocates, made sure the funds were allocated. David said, "Y'all got to have your own equipment. You got to have some good equipment, 'cause if we gonna put you out there,

we don't want to put out no secondhand thing." So they allocated and we went out and shopped for the PA system, the piano, mics and speakers and stuff, and picked it up; we were responsible for it.[20]

At this point in the Party's history, both cofounders Huey Newton and Bobby Seale were in jail awaiting trials, Minister of Information Eldridge Cleaver was in exile, and Chief of Staff David Hilliard, a childhood friend of Huey Newton, was essentially running the Party. Hilliard had also authorized the recordings of Elaine Brown's first album, *Seize the Time*, in 1969, so he saw the potential for a reconnection with the community in the Lumpen.

As the group became established as an official Panther project, a fourth singer, Sacramento chapter cofounder James Mott, was added to the group. Mott had more experience than the others and, William Calhoun believed, was there to keep the situation running smoothly:

> James Mott was put in to make sure we stayed in line, I think. That we didn't turn out to be a bunch of musicians. 'Cause James came from national headquarters. The three of us came up from San Jose, you know, college students. I think they wanted to make sure we didn't turn out to be dilettante little musicians. So they put a hardcore brother in with us.[21]

James Mott was a veteran of the Sacramento chapter and had dealt with serious police actions from the force there that was said to be trained in riot control by the LAPD. Mott and others had withstood the police raids on the Panther office that sparked the Oak Park riots in Sacramento on Father's Day 1969, and he had earned the respect of the Panther leadership. In addition to his credibility as a trusted Party member, Mott had his own musical skills that he shared with the others, and a natural bond was formed. As Mott recalls: "We'd be sittin' up on security at night front and back, and we would just start singing. Or they would start singing, I would join in. . . . We gave our history of singing groups and all that . . . and we just hit it off."[22]

Once the group was solidified, a band was recruited from the local musical community. Many talented local musicians were enthusiastic about volunteering to perform for the Party, and a varied group of supporters (including politically progressive white musicians) played for the band. Torrence explains their status:

Brother Bill Calhoun had experience in terms of forming bands and directing bands, and so he was able to take these brothers who volunteered. They were not paid, [and] they were not Panthers—they were what we designated as community workers. And then we named them the Freedom Messengers. And they did this for free, strictly out of dedication to the people, which I think came through in the playing, because they were not motivated by anything other than what we were all motivated by, and that was to serve the people.[23]

"I grew up with Santa Rita [Clark Bailey] in the Brookfield Village projects," recalls guitarist Mack Ray Henderson. "We went to church together. He knew I could play. When he asked me to play for the Panthers I jumped at the chance."[24]

The Lumpen began to perform at local Party-sponsored events in the summer of 1970. They started out performing as an unannounced addition to BPP events featuring well-established artists and activists. But their look and sound made people take notice. Onstage, the group had the look of established rhythm and blues groups such as the James Brown Revue and the Temptations. One Panther supporter donated his time and money to make snappy uniforms for the singers, and they hit the stage in style.

The band deliberately chose to perform songs that were familiar to members of their community, and they established a repertoire of popular songs. The Lumpen revised them with lyrics that uncompromisingly asserted the Panther Party ideology. Calhoun developed the premise of working around the remakes of popular songs:

> The whole idea of the covers thing came to me from James Cleveland, the gospel artist. James would take a popular song and make it gospel. And he'd do it in a New York minute, 'cause I remember my mother buying a lot of those records. They were just covers of some popular song, but James Cleveland has now made it into a gospel song.
>
> When it came around to the Black Panther Party and my time in the Black Panther Party, I used his example. Why not take a popular song and make it relevant—because right now it ain't relevant, and we need to be pushing relevance, twenty-four seven.[25]

In performance, the Lumpen singers would mix the harmonizing styles of popular Motown groups with the grooving, scatting, ad-libbing funk of the James Brown sound. The Lumpen's upbeat songs were often variations on a James Brown performance technique. For example, on "The Lumpen Theme" one can hear the group compelling the crowd to move to the music, chanting, "We want freedom / to determine / the destiny / of our community" interspersed with "good God" and "say it louder."[26]

The group was adept at the multipart harmonizing that was a large part of black popular music at the time. Soul music required skilled singers who were capable of both individual and collective vocalizing. It was important to the credibility of the act that they be able to *perform* soul music of high quality, or the entire performance might degenerate to a grotesque comedy and give the appearance of a shallow mockery of soul. This would be an insult to the popular soul singers (recognized as heroes in the black community), an insult to the young black radical audience they sought to entertain, and an insult to the revolutionary cause of the group. The Lumpen did not take their task lightly.

By working with what was familiar to their audience, by using the driving, sensuous rhythms and heartfelt, earnest vocalizing inherent in soul music, all the while bringing the audience along into their revolutionary ideology through the lyrics, the Lumpen fused the politics of pleasure with the politics of revolution. The crowd responses to live Lumpen performances reveal that the experience was clearly an entertaining affair to their followers. They brought out the joy in the struggle. "They would sit in the chairs, they would stand in the aisles and cheer, and sometimes people would come down in the little foyer in the front and groove, and some would come down front and do a little move," recalls band member Mack Ray Henderson. "It was a very, very free, 'do what you wanna do' type thing. But the important thing was the message."[27] A young Elvie McLellan Jr. (now Basheer Muhammad) saw the Lumpen when they played a small bar in Watts in 1970: "They reminded me of the Delfonics, only they made themselves a little bit more political. They did all the steps and moves that every soul group at the time was known to do."[28] The Philadelphia-based Delfonics were among the best of the harmonizing soul-singing groups of the day, and McLellan's impression was just what the Lumpen wanted to present to their audience. Rhythm and blues legend Lenny Williams was a close friend of

Huey Newton and attended many of the Panther functions during their heyday. Williams recalls the range of styles the Lumpen performed:

> They did a variation of things. You know, they did songs that were topical songs, you know, inspirational songs that talked about the movement and the people, and then they did love songs because, you know, love is an essential part of a people. We love ourselves and we have to love our women and the women have to love the men so that we can procreate. So they sang a whole potpourri of material. It ran the gamut from songs that talked about the issues of the day and songs that talked about love and happiness.[29]

"We did some ballads, but they all had a revolutionary message," Michael Torrence recalls. "We did one for Ericka Huggins, a slow song, 'Set Sister Ericka Free.'"

And the Lumpen were more than just revolutionary singers: Torrence, Bailey, and Mott were adept dancers too. As Michael Torrence recalls, the group had a well-choreographed "revolutionary" experience prepared for their audience:

> We got a lot of choreography. Again, we wanted to take the model that was popular and recognizable to the people in the community, particularly the black community, and that is along the model of say a group like the Temptations, but also with a strong rhythm such as a James Brown but with moves. So along with the singing and the harmony we wanted to do choreography, but our choreography was not just about spinning, the choreography was part of the story.
>
> So with our steps you would see us throw grenades, you would see us pump shotguns, you would see us . . . do a whole choreographed dance routine. Actually, it was a pantomime, but it was a whole dance routine, based upon brothers on the block playing craps, a racist cop comes along, brutalizes one brother, the brothers rise up, defend the other brother that's been brutalized, and death of the fascist pig. And we did all that with dance. So we tried to use all of those aspects, the music, the visual, the steps, the choreography, and all these various modes to try to get across these messages to the people in a way that was entertaining too, but at the same time hopefully inspirational and educational.[30]

At the time, the militant public posture was still a significant element of the Black Panther Party ideology and iconography, and the Lumpen did not temper the tone of the message. Ironically, the Lumpen were delivering their militant message just as Huey Newton and his faction of the leadership of the Party were moving the organization away from the tactics of direct confrontation with the power structure. As William Calhoun recalls, Huey Newton saw one of their performances and found that one song was too militant for his own tastes:

> There was a tune I wrote called "Killing" that Huey made us stop singing. The Party was making this transition. We were making the transition from being the guys on the posters with the guns to breakfast programs and political work and that kind of stuff.
>
> And when the minister got out of prison, he was trying to make the transition too. He came to a show at the Sportsman's Club in San Francisco and that's when I introduced this particular song. It was kind of a blues thing, and the hook was, "There's got to be some killin' if you want to be free." And that was a little too strong for the minister and the breakfast for children programs. So "Killing" got cut out of the repertoire.[31]

Calhoun's lyrics revealed the troubled narrative of the Panthers at that time.

Nevertheless, by providing an inspirational shout of revolutionary commitment, the Lumpen succeeded in popularizing the organization through the trope of the mythic black revolutionary ready for battle. Further, they were able to use the soul power inherent in the black music of the streets to galvanize a collective spirit within their audience.

While their shows were seen as entertaining by their followers, the seriousness of the Lumpen message is consistent with their overall approach as rank-and-file Panthers. In fact, all of the Lumpen members maintain that their emphasis at all times was their commitment to their duties as Panthers. As Lumpen member Clark Bailey recalls:

> We worked as much as possible. There were times when the pressures that were put upon us by the police were so great that we couldn't really put the time in, 'cause we were more concerned with the survival of the organization, which was primary, of course.

That's very important to understand. What we were doing in terms of that was a secondary project. Our main project was we were members of the Black Panther Party and considered revolutionary in every sense of the word. So we studied hard, we worked hard. And there really wasn't a whole lot of time to work on this project.[32]

The 45 rpm Single

In August 1970 the Lumpen went to the Tiki Recording Studio in San Jose and recorded two songs that would be released on a 45 rpm single: the original Calhoun compositions "Free Bobby Now" and "No More." As far as bandleader Calhoun was concerned, the recording was just a test pressing to see what the group sounded like. However, as soon as the tape was heard by Party leadership, it was out of his hands. The single was pressed, advertised in the *Black Panther*, and sold at local Panther Party events and at Lumpen performances. Party members also took the single to local Bay Area black radio stations requesting airplay but were told repeatedly that the music was too radical for the airwaves.[33]

The first side of the single, "Free Bobby Now," featured a dance rhythm driven by percussive guitar chops and an aggressive, energetic drumbeat that was contemporary with the James Brown sounds of the time. The vocals, each Lumpen member taking different lines, would bring the first verse:

> He walked the streets and carried a gun
> To save his people . . . and family
> From those who kill us for four hundred years
> Bobby must be set free!
> We're sayin'
> Bobby must be set free!
> We're sayin'
> Good God almighty
> Set our chairman free[34]

The vocal vamping in between the chorus reflected the James Brown influence, as Brown was known for using religious references as part of his repertoire of rhythmic, soulful inflections. This was an essential element of soul music: the fluid fusion of sacred and secular, the gospel and the blues. The aesthetic contradictions were ripe because the Black Panther Party was a revolutionary organization, a self-described Socialist organization that did not emphasize organized religion as a means of organizing people. Yet the conventions of soul music—the spiritual references—were employed with predictable results. The burning track works out in under two and a half minutes.

The flip side of the single, the second Calhoun composition, "(Won't Be) No More," comes in at four minutes and twenty seconds and resonates with the blues-heavy soul sound of Ray Charles. With a looping piano and rolling guitar licks coming and going with each swaying verse, "No More" has the sound of a slow religious song, but the lyrics, and eventually the voices, take the message over the top.

> From Watts to Brownsville, we find misery
> But there won't be no more, won't be no more
> There won't be no more, won't be no more
> Rats, dirt, and kids who are hungry
> There won't be no more, won't be no more
> There won't be no more, won't be no more
> 'Cause we've seen how to be free
> How to be free
> The pigs on our streets and poverty
> To this way of life, we're closing the door
> So there won't be no more
> There were times we stood by—we stood by
> Like we could not see
> But there won't be no more, won't be no more
> Can't be no more, can't be no more
> We'll get guns—we'll get guns
> To defend our community
> There won't be no more, won't be no more
> Can't be no more, can't be no more[35]

"From Watts to Brownsville" in the first line refers to bitter episodes in the black struggle. In the summer of 1970 a series of riots broke out in the Brooklyn neighborhood of Brownsville. Initially in protest of lacking sanitation services, the protest expanded to pickets about public schools and police brutality and consumed the neighborhood. "When the New York Panthers came out here, they told us Brownsville was the worst place out there, worse than Harlem," Billy Jennings recalled.[36] The Watts reference is clearly to the untenable conditions in South Central Los Angeles that gave rise to the 1965 revolt there. The Lumpen were providing a movement newscast within a musical experience.

As the verses continue to roll on, the singing takes on more passion as lead vocalist Calhoun utilizes the patented Ray Charles formula for soaring over the verses with repetitions designed to bring home the message. "No More" is, in this sense, a familiar soul song that builds in intensity throughout its four-minute length. One is informed by the compelling lyrics and absorbed by the passionate performances of the singers and musicians in unison. It is interesting that in the final verse the singers announce a solution to the evils around them, a *militant* solution: "We'll get guns to defend our community." These lyrics represent the effective climax of the song both emotionally and ideologically.

It is no accident that Calhoun's composition appears to become increasingly passionate as it becomes increasingly militant. Borrowing from the gospel music tradition of revelation, of expressing an increasingly emotional intensity as a buildup to the climactic reference to Jesus or to the Lord, great soul music accomplishes a similar feat in the secular realm, and the Lumpen appropriated the same methods for their politicized rendition of soul. The convincing aesthetics, the all-encompassing experience of soul music performance, were not missed by Calhoun or the other singers in the group.

In the fall of 1970, the Lumpen were appearing at Panther Party events around Northern California and the West Coast. The single was available for sale, and a steadily increasing amount of publicity was afforded their performances. Initially the Lumpen were just part of the entertainment within a larger Panther event. Calhoun explains:

> Usually it was a Black Panther Party function so there would be somebody there who would be doing the political analysis. And we would either be used as the warm-up for that if it was a high-ranking Party member such as Kathleen [Cleaver] or Emory or David [Hilliard], because everybody else was in jail at this time. If it was a high-ranking member, we would be the warm-up act.

If not, we were the show, and the political stuff would go in front.
But it was always about recruiting. It was always about spreading
the Party message. And everything I wrote was harmonious with
the ideology of the Party or the Ten Point Platform and program.[37]

As their reputation grew, and as Emory Douglas placed larger and
more prominent advertisements in the *Black Panther*, the Lumpen
became headliners. They performed at the Sieze the Time benefit for
Bobby Seale along with Elaine Brown on October 11, 1970, at the Oak-
land Sportsman's Club near Merritt College. They performed in San
Francisco at the People's Free Benefit at the Sportsman's Inn on November 1, which a full-page ad in the Panther paper promoted as their "First
Major San Francisco Performance." They performed in Los Angeles at
Patrick's Payton Place on December 8 along with legendary R&B singer
Carla Thomas. On December 27 the group headlined a bill with well-
known local singing group the Natural Four at the Blue Gardenia in
West Oakland. The Lumpen played along with the rock band Gold at
the Free Breakfast Program Benefit in East Oakland on January 9, 1971,
and at San Jose City College along with R&B singing group the Persuasions on Thursday, January 14. The group performed at UC Berkeley's
Pauley Ballroom on Saturday, January 23, in a program sponsored by
the Arab Students Association there. On March 5 they performed at
the Revolutionary Intercommunal Day of Solidarity for Bobby Seale,
Ericka Huggins, Angela Davis, and Ruchell Magee at the Oakland Auditorium. The Grateful Dead also performed at the all-day event, though
the groups did not meet.[38]

The Lumpen traveled to the northeastern United States in November 1970 for a Revolutionary Tour. They performed at the University of
Madison–Wisconsin, Amherst College in Massachusetts, Temple University in Philadelphia, and Howard University in Washington, DC, as
well as at local parks, union halls, and nightclubs in Boston, New Haven,
Connecticut, and New York City. They were often the opening act for
speeches by the Party leadership in a series of Party fund-raisers. The
Lumpen made an impression everywhere they went. By many accounts
the "tour" was a successful representation of the Panther Party ideology
as well as the Lumpen as a musical force. Saxophone player David Levinson recalls the energy of their New York City performance:

I remember we did the Roseland Ballroom in New York. I remember that was amazing. Because of not only the R&B that we played but also the political message that the Panthers were putting out—and what they said was so germane and so key and so relevant to what people were living and the high energy of the politics and the political realities of the time. There was so much going on at that time; people just went wild, they loved hearing this stuff, which wasn't talking about the usual sappy love stuff. It was a real eye-opener, and a heart-opener for people to hear the Lumpen talking about real daily life struggles. And that's what sort of set them apart. In the context of some of the concerts we did, the energy was just off the wall.[39]

When the group performed in New Haven, the site of Party chairman Bobby Seale's controversial murder trial, there were more police than supporters. Chairman Seale, Party leader Ericka Huggins, and others were awaiting trial on a murder conspiracy charge, and the Panther activists and their supporters throughout the region were on edge. But the Lumpen group was there for a reason, and they persevered. James Mott explains:

We found out that they [the police] had cleared the area and told everybody they had better not come to the park that day. These cops, the FBI, drove up and they were calling us all kind of names: "You m-f so-and-so, we're gonna kill all of ya." But finally we got the power on, 'cause they tried to stop us from doing that. Then a handful of brave souls came out there that day.

And we sang the songs "Bobby Must be Set Free," "(Won't Be) No More," and maybe one other song. We found out that Bobby and Ericka heard us singing. And we could hear people hollering from the jail over there: "Right on, right on brothers." "Right on, sing the song." "Right on for Bobby, right on for Ericka," "Right on, power to the people." We could hear that.[40]

The performance itself was only one component of the revolutionary nature of the Lumpen. The act of defying the authorities by playing music is one of the storied methods of cultural resistance in social movements. Because of their high profile as a stage act, the Lumpen assumed some of the same risks associated with political leaders and other visible activists. Because they were only secondarily musicians and primarily Panthers, they accepted their responsibilities as part of their duties. Mott recalls the background to their guerilla performance:

> So after we were done, we were breaking down our equipment, and I remember the FBI drove up they started calling us names again and then we would tell them things like, "Gee, you guys are late, you were supposed to be here for the concert." Then they followed us everywhere we went on the freeway . . . everywhere we drove, they were there. They were right behind us; sometimes they would tailgate us. You could see them giving us the finger and doing that, like they're going to shoot you sign, they want to kill you type of thing. It was really interesting.
>
> I never will forget—because it was a stage set I said, "Hey man, you know they may plan on killing us." I remember Calhoun saying, "Well, if that is, so be it, we'll die for the people." And Clark and Michael said, "Right on, we're just gong to do what we got to do." 'Cause we didn't know, we said we could be up here and a sniper shot could ring out and down us all.
>
> Nobody was there except for a brave handful who ended up coming, saying we don't care. The rest of them, they [law enforcement] had intimidated the community, telling them they better not show up. "You'll get arrested, they'll do this to you"; this is what the people were told.[41]

The Lumpen performed outside in the cold at the aborted second Revolutionary People's Constitutional Convention (RPCC) in Washington, DC, on Friday, November 27, 1970. The convention was intended to be a follow-up to the Philadelphia RPCC and an opportunity for thousands of activists to finalize their ideas for a new antiracist, anticapitalist, pro–gender equality, gay-tolerant society. However, problems with the unpaid rent for the venue at Howard University left hundreds of delegates literally out in the cold. The impromptu Lumpen performance was one of the only high points of the gathering. They were met once again by the FBI. William Calhoun recalls, "The FBI guy walked past us and said, 'What took you so long to get here? We lost you in New York and we thought you'd never get here.' 'Cause they followed us down from Boston."[42]

Had the RPCC met in Washington, DC, that Thanksgiving weekend, they might have noticed that the Lumpen represented in many ways the revolutionary community that the RPCC organizers were striving for. The Lumpen, despite their designation as the official Black Panthers' band, frequently had two white members in the group, one of whom was David Levinson. This fact was representative of the Black Panthers' larger "intercommunalist" vision, but it also reflected the problems and conflicts the Party had with other black nationalist organizations.

In San Francisco, the presence of integrated rhythm and blues groups was not uncommon. The Bay Area has a rich tradition of racially mixed rhythm and blues acts, from Johnny Otis to Tower of Power and Sly and the Family Stone. However, when the Lumpen performed in the racially charged spaces in which black nationalism was the primary ideology, they encountered a peculiar type of "reverse racism." Levinson recalls one example of the unity that the band expressed with all of its revolutionary members:

> I remember we were up in the Midwest. We were playing some college campus. It was a huge turnout; it was in a gym. We got to this place and it was late and snowing and difficult to get to. By the time we finished the concert, which was sponsored by the BSU, at the end they offered to put us up because it was snowing, but they wouldn't put the black guys and the white guys up together. And out of principle, the Panther members, the Lumpen itself, refused to accept that offer. We drove back rather than put the white guys up somewhere else. That is something I always remember with great affection and fondness. We were very tight.[43]

Clark Bailey recalls that the racial conflict on the road was a test of the Lumpen and the Panthers' principles, and they did not compromise when it came to Levinson or to the idea that their revolution was not for one group only.

> David Levinson can tell you. One thing he realized from the trip is the ideology of the Party. . . . They [concert organizers] didn't want David to play. They didn't want to help him, so there was a couple of times the Lumpen said, "Fuck you, he's a member of our group, and if you can't recognize that he's a part of our group . . .

then we're not gonna participate." That happened a couple of times on the road. That's living up to the principles you're talking about.[44]

The Lumpen returned to the Bay Area in early December 1970 and began the humbling daily duties of Panthers all over again. They played the role of stars on the stage, but they lived the life of duty in the Black Panther Party. "We went as revolutionaries, not as R&B stars," Clark Bailey recalls. "People gave us shit like, 'So you the rock stars for the revolution now,' but that's not what it was about."[45]

The Lumpen did attract some of their own recruits as a direct result of their success onstage. Fredrika Newton, eventual widow of Party leader Huey Newton, was one of many teenagers fresh out of Berkeley High School when a Lumpen concert came her way: "I remember the Lumpen. I used to go to all of their shows," she recalled in an impromptu telephone conversation with me in 2006. "I was a groupie for the Lumpen. I used to go with [singer] James Mott. My girlfriend Val [Valerie Trahan] went with Clark [Bailey], my other girlfriend Jan [Thompson] went with Mike [singer Michael Torrence]. I joined the Party because of the Lumpen."[46] While groupies may not have been the primary goal for the Lumpen, it appears that the band members were clearly doing their share of entertaining their audience.

Michael Torrence and the others each had experiences in rhythm and blues groups and understood that the notion of groupies could be a misnomer. "They were our cheerleaders. Every opportunity they'd come, and if they could they'd bring some friends with 'em. And a lot of what was happening was about that word of mouth, 'You should've seen the show,' that kind of thing. That was the way we were able to pack out Merritt [the show that was recorded]. We weren't getting any radio coverage or nothing like that." Moreover, in no way were the young followers of the group going to be treated the way groupies for rock and roll bands were. Torrence explains:

The difference was that these sisters here were political. They were trying to be part of the movement; they were trying to support the Party and the worst thing that we could do would be to try to exploit them behind that sexually or whatever. Because we're supposed to be a whole 'nother model. At the same time, these are our supporters, and hopefully recruits. So we see ourselves as being a recruiting tool for the Party. So if you turn around and try to turn that into some sexual opportunist type of thing and exploit them and pimping them out and all this stuff here, just use them and toss them aside, we would get severely disciplined for that anyway.

There was a policy in the party. We had political education classes on male chauvinism. David [Hilliard] and them would take a very hard line about it. 'Cause there had been some problems with that, some revolutionary pimping going on. And we had some sisters in that Party that were as hardworking and more courageous than a lot of brothers up in there. . . .

Part of the black culture is that male chauvinistic thing, but inside the Party, we're all comrades here, and if you try to exploit these sisters here you're going to get disciplined, you're going to get severely disciplined. And even more if you're out there representing the Party publicly, and it gets around and you're in the Lumpen, oh no.[47]

Despite their personal charisma and skill as performers, the trappings of fame were minimal for the Lumpen members. This was not a group that was going to be pampered by local promoters or the media. The Lumpen singers were given few if any special privileges and were rarely given days off to rehearse or rest up for shows. And there were many shows. During their heyday, the group performed almost weekly, headlining Panther Party events through the fall of 1970 and into the spring of 1971. Entire pages of the *Black Panther* were devoted to prominent advertisements for Party events at which the Lumpen played as the main attraction.

Despite their apparent popularity and legitimacy in the Bay Area music scene, the band was not given high priority within the Party's organizational structure. The popularity of the Lumpen as a Panther Party musical group was a small but noticeable distraction to some Party members who did not consider dancing and singing to be revolutionary activities. As minister of culture, Emory Douglas was the primary advocate for the Lumpen, and Douglas participated in the meetings of the Party Central Committee, the organizing entity for all Party activities.[48] As the primary visual artist for the Party, whose artwork was featured in almost every edition of the weekly paper, Douglas had earned a degree of credibility within the organization and put it to use in support of the Lumpen. Douglas wrote articles in support of the band, designed their advertisements in the *Black Panther*, and advocated for the Lumpen at the Central Committee meetings. Douglas explains the dynamics involved:

> Sometimes you have the attitude in the Party of these people who just had this rigid focus; [they] didn't care about the cultural aspect, just straight politics. So I was kind of like a buffer between those and them and that as it related to the leadership. They [the Lumpen] would get a hard time sometimes and not be allowed to practice. They would ask me if I would talk to so and so and see if that could happen, and do what I could to work it out, and most of the time it worked out.[49]

The Lumpen members themselves have consistently supported the notion that the Party goals were always primary and that their musical adventures were only a secondary exercise in their overall commitment to the Party and to their revolutionary service to their community. Lumpen member Michael Torrence explains:

> The music was just another tool or another weapon to further that cause but we were Panthers first, and so in that regard we were required to do all that was required of any Panther—to get up in the morning and feed the children for the breakfast program, to sell the newspapers, to secure the offices to do whatever community work was needed, to pick up donations. Because we were Panthers first.
>
> By no means were we ever entertainers. By no means were we anything separate or different or above any other rank-and-file member. We didn't want that designation, we never tried to get that designation.
>
> We were required even more so to participate in political education classes because the things that we wrote had to reflect the line of the Party and be educational, or at least informative to stimulate some thought.
>
> So again we were a cadre, and in terms of the Black Panther Party, a cadre is a unit. We were considered a cultural educational cadre, under the leadership of the minister of culture.[50]

The consistent justification for the entertainment element of the Lumpen by its members is important when one considers the proclamations of the Black Panther Party and leader Huey P. Newton's anointment of the Black Panther Party as the vanguard of the coming black revolution. The individuals who joined the Party in the late 1960s were drawn to the organization because of the militant, revolutionary vision of the Black Panthers. The idea that the organization would eventually be putting their ideology into a stage performance was not a consideration of the early recruits. It took a great deal of growth for some Party members to embrace the emerging priorities of the organization in 1970. Calhoun explains:

> I came in very much a nationalist, not a socialist. This [was] the last of the Black Nationalism phase of the Party. It was beginning to make its transition to Socialism and it was also making a transition to dealing with more community programs rather than those of us who wanted to go around shooting people. I'm saying that so that the Lumpen makes some sense.
>
> When I first came into the Black Panther Party I don't think anybody would have paid any attention to the Lumpen, because we were too busy organizing around other things. But as the Party was maturing and getting ready to start doing more community stuff without us all walking in with .38s strapped on our sides, the atmosphere [became] conducive to the Lumpen coming into being.[51]

The Lumpen were active during a tumultuous, transitional period in Party history. As a result of major events internally during this time (mid-1970 through mid-1971), cofounder and leader Newton moved to dramatically reorganize. In February 1971 Newton expelled Eldridge Cleaver from the Party after a critical public confrontation he had with Cleaver by phone from Algeria. Cleaver had been considered one of the Party leaders and advocated the more militant, confrontational actions Newton was trying to distance the Party from. This action fractured the Party into factions that supported either Cleaver's militarist stance or Newton's longer-term vision of revolutionary change. Fueled by COINTELPRO infiltration, agent provocateurs, and disinformation fomenting suspicion, the resulting internal friction devastated the rank-and-file membership and led to the deaths of dedicated Panthers Robert Webb and Sam Napier.[52] Calhoun recalls the chaos:

> When the split happened between Eldridge and Huey, Eldridge's people were really based in New York. And in Oakland . . . people

that I had known very well in Oakland sided with Eldridge, and some of the people that I had met in New York when the Lumpen had been back there performing had declared, "Eldridge said the streets aren't safe for Panthers."

I was one of the people designated to become one of David Hilliard's bodyguards when that split happened. So I had the Lumpen thing going, yes. And I was still writing for the Party paper, yes. I did a couple more runs to New York, but after Sam Napier got killed we stopped doing that. And I became one of David's bodyguards.[53]

Newton ordered many chapters to be closed across the country and recalled volunteers to Oakland. By the end of 1971, Newton had developed a plan to run political campaigns for Party leaders: Elaine Brown for Oakland City Council and Bobby Seale for mayor. As a result of these significant changes, tasks and duties for rank-and-file members were redirected and the Lumpen stopped performing. On May 23, 1971, the Lumpen carried out their final performance as a Black Panther Party operation at the Sacramento City Auditorium. Bandleader William Calhoun, with a child on the way, left the Party a few days later, the same day Bobby Seale returned from prison in Connecticut—Bobby indeed had been set free. The remaining singers performed at smaller Panther Party functions but were no longer advertised and didn't carry a band with them.

The remaining three Lumpen singers each remained active Party members, working on the Oakland municipal elections and various other duties. Michael Torrence left in 1973 and continued his singing career; he toured with Marvin Gaye in 1974. When Marvin Gaye performed his classic "Distant Lover" to thousands of screaming fans live in Oakland for that now-legendary recorded performance, Michael Torrence was onstage as a background singer. Torrence worked as a staff writer for Motown as well before settling in Los Angeles. Clark Bailey continued on in the Party through much of the 1970s, working on a variety of duties, including the maintenance of certain "technical equipment" for the Party. James Mott continued with the Party until 1978, working for the Community Learning Center until its leader, Ericka Huggins (Mott's wife at the time), resigned.[54]

The 1973 Oakland city elections were close contests, but the Party candidates lost. Having lost their bid for mainstream political power, and after years of law enforcement infiltration and isolation working to eliminate their revolutionary political thrust, by 1974 the Black Panther Party appeared to be little more than a conventional social-work organization with a controversial name. Nevertheless, their effectiveness at organizing the black vote in Oakland led to the eventual election of Lionel Wilson as the city's first black mayor in 1977 and helped to reconfigure the racial composition of the city's political, cultural, and economic infrastructure.

The Black Panther Party was part and parcel of a tradition of innovative Oakland political and cultural formations. The Lumpen qualify as well. "We put together a product that was successful for its time. It was a unique theory, a unique idea," Clark Bailey recalls.

> Anyone else, trust me, if any other organization would have tried to do that, they would have fought with greed, they would have had different members of the band and the group wanting to get paid, they [would] see money coming in, they [would] want to know where the money's going and, "Hey man you just got all that money at the door, all these people, I didn't get paid?" You would have that happen. The only way that it didn't happen is because we had principles that we lived by.[55]

The Lumpen members continued to live by their principles long after they left the Party. William Calhoun, after a stint as a Bay Area DJ, joined the Baptist ministry and cofounded the Wo'se Community Church in Oakland. Michael Torrence continues his work with at-risk youth in Los Angeles, Clark Bailey recently retired from the Sacramento Regional Transit District where he had worked as a bus driver for twenty-five years, and James Mott, now known as Sataru Ned, is assistant pastor of Agnes Memorial Christian Academy, located in the heart of violence-torn East Oakland.

The members of the Lumpen survived their post–black power years relatively intact. While they each moved on to the struggles of life and family as working-class members of black America, they did not denounce the Party, their revolutionary principles, or other former members. Nor did they seek to profit from their years of service to the people. Only as a result of a younger generation's growing interest in black radical culture and the "Party music" they produced have William Calhoun, Michael

Torrence, Clark Bailey, and James Mott recently begun to indulge in the exercise of telling their story.

The members of the Lumpen traversed the crossroads between revolutionary politics and revolutionary culture. As musicians they represented the high standards of soul music production and presentation and honored the musical traditions they had inherited. As rank-and-file Panthers, they were representative of the commitment and selflessness that embodied the thousands of young people who took that rare opportunity to act upon their beliefs and desires for total revolutionary change in America. And they lived to tell about it.

2

"Power to the People"

Bay Area Culture
and the Rise of the Party

On this Tuesday evening in November 1970 in North Oakland, a rousing rhythm and blues performance is under way. Looking upon the classic architecture of the Merritt College auditorium from Grove Street, one can hear the unmistakable rhythms of black popular music. Inside the hall, the chairs on the auditorium floor are filled by an enthusiastic crowd. Backstage the headliners, decked out in bright shirts and dark vests, prepare to go onstage. After a series of speakers and announcements, an instrumental set from the backing band—known as the Freedom Messengers—gets under way. The multiracial band of casually dressed funky young musicians grooves on instrumental jazz and R&B standards, setting the mood for the stars of the show. The Freedom Messengers are composed of a cross-section of young East Bay musicians, most fresh out of high school and thrilled to be volunteers for the Black Panther Party in any capacity.

The Freedom Messengers' final song is a pop hit known to everyone in the crowd. It's a rousing dance number, driven by sharp horn blasts and a throbbing beat. "Dance to the Music" has been a black radio staple since its release in the spring of 1968, the first of many major worldwide hits from the groundbreaking, beloved San Francisco–based band Sly and the Family Stone.

As the pulsing staccato horn blasts drive across the auditorium, one can expect to hear the familiar chant given by Family Stone member Cynthia Robinson:

"Hey, get up! And dance to the music / Get on up! And dance to the music!" For this performance, Panther supporter "Sister Candace" brings the same energy and cadence, but chants, "Hey, get up! And make revolution! / Get on up! And make revolution!"

As the song progresses in a note-for-note rendition, a different band member sings a refrain leading into a hot riff from the band. "Pick up the gun and get ready / Revolution has come, yeah!" is followed by a drum solo. "Don't you know that it's time / to protect yourself with the gun yeah yeah," is followed by a guitar solo. As the bass player sings in the lower range, "If you want to change this system / You got to fight to get what you want," the verse is followed by the familiar bass guitar solo. Another singer is heard bringing out the chorus, "You might like to hear the horns blow / a little power from the front, yeah, yeah!" as the horns bring the song into the upper ranges.

After smoking the groove, in unison the band shout-sings the chorus, "We got a message to the people / saying off the pigs! Off the pigs!" as the stirring horns punctuate the groove and elevate the energy of the space.

The verses of the entire song are repeated (just as Sly and the Family Stone were known to do in concert), adding to the excitement and embellishment of the new message in the familiar music. The song then crashes down to a splash of applause from the audience. The fiery, celebratory, revolutionary tone for the evening had been set.[1]

There is a certain synchronicity between the groundbreaking musical upheaval brought about by Sly and the Family Stone and the parallel development of the Black Panther Party. Both revolutionary entities emerged at almost exactly the same time, from the same community, and both changed the thinking of a generation.

"Dance to the Music"

If ever there was a party starter during the late 1960s, Sly and the Family Stone's spring 1968 breakthrough hit "Dance to the Music" was the one. The urgent, spirited shouts, the throbbing, upbeat pulse from the drummer, the punching horn riffs that soar above and wiggle below, were just the beginning of this revolutionary romp. The guitar, the bass, the key-boards all take solos as the relentless beat builds to a peak of excitement. By the end of the song you've not only sweated up a storm, you know each member of the band.

The rhythm and blues performance aesthetic was slow to break out of its time-tested formula of glitter and glamour. The matching suits, the conked hair, the coordinated dance steps in support of the lead singer, backed by an anonymous band, were all staples of the black dance music formula until "Dance to the Music" changed everything. These three minutes of power and fury from an unbelievable band of players that introduce themselves in each verse completely transformed the way black popular music was approached. Almost overnight, the formalized uniforms gave way to individualized outfits as "funk bands" sought to celebrate the individuality of their performers while generating unity through their irresistible grooves.

It was one of the great game changers in the history of black popular music; an entire generation of musicians trained to perform in obscurity behind a self-absorbed lead singer now shared the multicolored spotlight. Ambitious, originally styled musicians from all walks of life now had an opening to pursue their funky dreams and aspirations. Sly and the Family Stone was the most influential black band of its time, and generations later the musical and social formulas the band employed continue to be studied by upstart musicians seeking to take their music, and their audience, higher.

For the Lumpen show to open with a note-for-note rendition of a Sly and the Family Stone standard speaks volumes about the Lumpen band's sense of the popular pulse of the people. "Dance to the Music" was a song played by nearly every rhythm and blues act at the time. The Lumpen group was aware of the popular appeal and the potential to engage with and elevate the audience with the song.

In many musical circles, Sly and the Family Stone is considered a revolutionary act in its own right. With a multiracial and multigender lineup of musicians, each bringing forth diverse yet inclusive identities, the Family Stone was in many ways a pioneering collaboration from the outset. San Francisco–based music critic Joel Selvin, in his commentary celebrating what he pronounced the "number one San Francisco band of the twentieth century," expressed a widely felt feeling about the group:

Sly & the Family Stone changed the way music was played—from the way Stevie Wonder sang to the funky rumblings behind Miles Davis. They pointed the future of jazz to Herbie Hancock and made the Temptations grow up. There would be no Prince if there hadn't been a Sly Stone. Michael Jackson is such a fan, he bought the publishing rights.[2]

The "Family Stone" was a stage name created by the leader of the group, Sylvester "Sly Stone" Stewart. The band was in fact composed of the four youngest members of the Stewart family, which had migrated—literally overnight as a result of a racial confrontation—to the San Francisco Bay Area. Originally from Denton, Texas, the family settled in the small north bay town of Vallejo in late 1943 where there was work in and around the war industry.[3] While the Stewart children grew up in the Pentecostal church (Church of God in Christ), rich with spirited music and strong family values, by the time they were teenagers in the early 1960s they began to thrive on a new form of liberated Bay Area pop culture. Sylvester was the eldest brother, the ringleader, court jester, and gadfly. Younger brother Freddie was a dedicated musician and bandleader of his own group, Freddie and the Stone Souls, and younger sisters, Rose and Vaetta (Vet), had developed their own talents as vocalists.

Sylvester went to work in San Francisco as a DJ and music producer, calling himself Sly Stone. Sly worked at local black radio station KSOL and also wrote songs and produced records for the emerging rock scene at Autumn Records, producing hits for the Beau Brummels ("Laugh, Laugh") and Bobby Freeman ("C'mon and Swim") in 1964. Sly Stone cowrote Freeman's pop hit "S-W-I-M" and put his stamp on pop music before he was known to anyone outside of the Bay Area. He sang in one of the only integrated doo-wop vocal acts (the Viscaynes), and through his radio program he merged pop, soul, and rock styles using his energetic on-air presence to create an unbounded, spirited experience for his listeners.

Sly Stone's music was infectiously positive and uplifting, and it only grew when Sly merged his own band with Freddie's to become Sly and the Family Stone in 1966. The original band included their high school classmate Cynthia Robinson on trumpet and shouts, and Jerry Martini on saxophone. The two—a tall black woman and a stocky Italian American man—were an odd but funky pair perfectly suited for the new sound and new energy delivered by the band. The Oakland-bred Larry Graham Jr. played bass, and he is now known for creating the "slap bass" technique of thumping and plucking bass strings in time with the music, which became the signature funk sound of the 1970s. Drummer Gregg Errico, who came from Freddie's band, was a floppy-haired Italian American who had an incredibly propulsive and energizing drumming style that worked perfectly with the entire band, which was completed by brother Freddie on guitar and sister Rose on piano. Sly was out front and outrageous with his sterling grin, flamboyant costumes, kinetic performance, and multitalented instrumentalism, singing and playing guitar, piano, organ, and harmonica.

All of the members dressed wildly and individually, as there were no uniforms, no patterned appearances to reference the days of chitlin' circuit rhythm and blues. Yet the singers—and everyone sang—were clearly drawing upon and identifying with the traditional black gospel spirit within the music. Women were prominent in the group and presented as equals. They were not treated simply as background singers or dancers, but rather as musicians who performed, chanted, stomped, danced, and contributed to the overarching message that "everybody is a star."

The magic of the band's unity was a radical proposition to some, and the equality of the group members was no simple thing to engineer during those times, as Sly Stone explained in a 2010 interview:

> There was people saying, "You gonna pay the girls as much as you pay the guys?" I said, "Why not?" I never caught on to that thing, discrimination. I wanted the band to represent as much variety of soul as possible. And I thought if people could see that, see all these different people having fun on stage, they can go ahead and relax, you know.[4]

The band produced a seamless fusion of musical forms and styles, sparking an unbounded new energy in the music. Jagged bebop horn lines could be heard riding along a thunderous bass while whimsical guitar chords, delicate doo-wop harmonizing, and scorching church choir wails could be heard all in the same verse. The songs ranged from lighthearted romance to racial confrontation, all with an undergirding positive spirit of renewal, peace, and love. Greil Marcus wrote a definitive critique of the group in his 1973 essay, "Sly Stone and the Myth of Staggerlee":

There was an enormous freedom to the band's sound. It was complex because freedom is complex; wild and anarchic, like the wish for freedom; sympathetic, affectionate and coherent, like the reality of freedom. And it was all celebration, all affirmation, a music of endless humor and delight, like a fantasy of freedom.[5]

The Family Stone in many ways personified the new society that the young counterculture generation was striving for. By not simply tolerating, but *celebrating* difference, by making collective diversity work, the Family Stone was actualizing the type of democratic ideals that America's youth had been raised on. Yet the American youth of the time had found those ideals to be corrupted in the real politics and social formations of the day. The Family Stone exploded those contradictions and transcended them with music that spoke of individual expression and affirmation within a revolutionary new and inclusive community.

"Don't Call Me Nigger, Whitey"

After the Family Stone's star turn in early 1968 with "Dance to the Music," the entire country endured a set of serious crises, and by early 1969 a new vision was truly needed. Into this leadership void emerged the Family Stone's masterpiece, the *Stand!* album. A tour de force of resilient energy and unity, the album featured some of the most iconic, uplifting songs of the era: "I Want To Take You Higher," "You Can Make It If You Try," "Stand!," "Sing a Simple Song," and the number one pop hit "Everyday People." One song stood out beyond the others because of its harsh sound and biting social statement. The second song on the album was the stirring "Don't Call Me Nigger, Whitey." A rugged blues-rock rhythm underscores some wailing harmonica and chanting vocals: "Don't call me nigger, whitey!" And their refrain, sung slowly with emphasis: "Don't call me whitey, nigger!" The six-minute song did not feature the group's typical uplifting crescendo or turn into positive-minded whimsy. It was stark and undeniably direct—and strategically placed on the album directly after the title track and before their anthem "I Want to Take You Higher."

The song served a stronger and more significant purpose than the typical protest song. Sly Stone and the band were performing racial anger, across the racial divide—in both directions—as equal parties involved. Neither racial group was seen as above or below the other, and the racial confrontation was in fact a bold, if implicit, statement of equality among the combatants. Despite the harshness of the song's tone, it was as important as any of the band's other songs in affirming that everyone is of equal worth. On the album, once the song is finished, the exaltory "I Want to Take You Higher" explodes, emphasizing just what can come after the racial confrontation is over. Sly had made his point. There is a new world on the other side of the race war, and *everyone* is invited.

The music of Sly and the Family Stone inspired a wave of songs in which artists celebrated a new and authentic self image, one no longer in need of racial or social acceptance. Shortly after *Stand!*, the Isley Brothers recorded "It's Your Thing," Isaac Hayes sang "Do Your Thing," Charles Wright and the Watts 103rd Street Rhythm Band urged people to "Express Yourself," and a flowering of social commentary from the Temptations emerged on songs such as "Message from a Black Man," "Cloud Nine," and "Ball of Confusion." This wide-open, reality-driven, affirming brand of funk and soul was directly related to the breakthroughs, musically and socially, of Sly and the Family Stone.

The Family Stone looked and sounded like no other act when they hit the national pop music scene in the spring of 1968, and the Bay Area rock scene was central to their rise—and to the rise of the 1960s counterculture that was catalyzing a revolution of youthful minds in San Francisco.

The Bay Area and the Counterculture Revolution

The San Francisco Bay Area was home to the youthful rebels, antiwar and civil rights activists, drug and lifestyle experimenters, hardcore militants, beat poets, and general outcasts who comprised the burgeoning youth rebellion that had just celebrated its "Summer of Love" in 1967. Sly and the Family Stone was one of the banner-waving exponents of this unbridled new energy and attitude among the hippie generation.

By the mid-1960s, the baby boomer generation was entering its teen years, and the males were approaching draft eligibility. The generation was also coming of age in terms of its relationship with the black struggle. Some young whites, such as the young graduate student Mario Savio, had participated in the southern civil rights movement and fought for the moral cause of black freedom before transforming the mantra of social justice to their own causes. In the case of Savio, it was the free speech movement at UC–Berkeley in 1964.[6] Others simply found the agitation attractive and rebelled against their own uptight and racist middle-America family environments, fleeing to the cities. These rebel youth experimented with alternative lifestyles, alternative drugs, alternative living spaces, and alternative music. For some, the experimentation was short-lived; for others it was a harbinger of a deeper commitment to personal and social change. As I wrote in my first book, *Funk*:

> As harder drugs, violent street clashes over civil rights and the War, and ultimately the draft made white males experience the vulnerability of oppression, the poets, artists, and rock musicians became their saviors. What began as a primitive teenage youth movement in the 1950s, preoccupied with sex and abandon, evolved into a global belief system with an ethos of peace and love, and a collective vision of redemption that piggybacked on the ideals of the civil rights movement.[7]

Among the musical leaders of this revolution were the iconoclastic folk singer turned social commentator Bob Dylan, the adventurous British rock and roll quartet the Beatles, the Seattle-bred guitarist Jimi Hendrix, the Afro-Latin rock stylist Carlos Santana, the psychedelic troubadours the Grateful Dead, and the meteoric Sly and the Family Stone. With national hits that appealed to both black and white audiences, Sly and the Family Stone was the most universally popular.

Sly Stone and his band in many ways symbolized the potential for community that so many disaffected, idealistic youth were striving for: women musicians were empowered and treated onstage as equals to men; blacks and whites worked together and sang, danced, and played complex, exhilarating music that exploded the standards for black music presentation. The Family Stone was an established leader of a type of social change, a different type of revolution—one attuned to the politics of pleasure that a multiracial generation of youth had immersed itself into. The Lumpen players understood this, tuned in, and followed their lead.

Oakland Stroke

It is no accident that the groundbreaking methodology of Sly and the Family Stone emerged from the San Francisco Bay Area—the East Bay in particular—where a black revolution was also taking place. The black working-class neighborhoods in Oakland, Berkeley, Richmond, Vallejo, and San Francisco were ground zero for many of these emergent new lifestyles and visions. Politics and culture were intertwined in a mix of activity, bringing together black activist roots and rocking blues bars, southern folk wisdom, labor union politics, and the illicit economy of the mean streets.

Filled with a rush of migrants from the South lured by the promise of work in the war effort, the Bay Area's black population increased dramatically during World War II. Between 1940 and 1950, the Bay Area's black population grew from 21,000 to 150,000.[8] Initially, many of the new blacks on the West Coast thrived. They set up commercial districts and cultural spaces in the Fillmore District in San Francisco and along Seventh Street in West Oakland that drew popular black jazz and blues stars from across the country.

Oakland and the East Bay had a tradition of black organizing that went back to the 1930s and the West Coast leadership of the Brotherhood of Sleeping Car Porters. This first major national black union was represented by black men who were revered in the black community, yet the nature of their work was to serve white patrons on cross-country railroad trips before the rise of air travel.

The Brotherhood of Sleeping Car Porters was the strongest black labor union during World War II. When national union leader Asa Philip Randolph organized a March on Washington Movement in 1941 to protest segregation and shame the United States during its war against the racist German regime, Randolph's threat secured the integration of the war industries, which led to the desegregation of the armed forces in 1948—and ultimately opened the legal precedent for *Brown v. Board of Education* and the civil rights movement a decade later.[9]

The cross-country train route ended in Oakland, and the Brotherhood on the West Coast was led by Oakland resident C. L. Dellums, vice president of the union under Randolph. Dellums was a leader in the growth of unions and equal rights issues in the East Bay for thirty years. The elder Dellums's legacy in progressive community service was eclipsed by his nephew, the former US representative and Oakland mayor Ronald V. Dellums. The younger Dellums maintained his uncle's strident position in favor of social justice causes. He was elected to Congress from the Black Panthers' home district (Oakland and Berkeley) in 1971, served for twenty-seven years, and was praised as "the conscience of the Congress."

This West Coast tradition of political radicalism and self-determination developed apart from the southern civil rights struggle. While the proscriptions of Jim Crow—presumptions of black inferiority, enforced segregation, police brutality, and inherent white privilege—were commonplace in the American West in the mid-twentieth century, West Coast blacks did not witness the daily references to slavery, nor were they forced to traverse Civil War memorials at every turn. They were also distant from the multigenerational networks of churches and predominantly black colleges and had to be innovative and progressive in their far-reaching efforts at black self-determination. One might say that this generation of black migrants was able to imagine freedom in a different way from their southern counterparts as they watched the sun set across the infinite California coastline.

Academic resources, from the local community colleges—Oakland City College in downtown Oakland and Merritt College right in the heart of black North Oakland—to the nearby University of California at Berkeley, were frequented by young blacks who organized among themselves on campuses and developed student organizations that interfaced with community groups and their causes. Huey Newton and Bobby Seale met as they were navigating their student group activities at Merritt College. Federal monies for antipoverty programs and job-training projects provided resources for ambitious young student-activists from the community to share their wares, have access to reading materials, and develop their ideological positions as they interacted within the diversity of their East Bay community.

Robert O. Self, in his book *American Babylon: Race and the Struggle for Postwar Oakland*, describes the physical and social geography of the region and how it all lent itself to revolutionary formations.

> The long corridor from West Oakland north through South Berkeley to the University of California campus, between San Pablo and Telegraph avenues, formed one of the most vibrant political

landscapes anywhere in the nation in this period. Intellectual, social and physical geographies intersected here in powerful combination. Home of the East Bay's largest African American community—representing all ages and classes—as well as thousands of white Berkeley college students, in these neighborhoods a quarter century of American labor and civil rights movement politics and the burgeoning student and antiwar movements overlapped with some of the poorest districts in the East Bay. . . . In early October 1966, the same month that Newton and Seale wrote the party's Ten Point Program, "What We Want, What We Believe," ten thousand people organized by the Vietnam Day Committee marched down Telegraph from the Berkeley campus to the Oakland city line to protest the war and the draft.[10]

And as the turmoil of the 1960s escalated, a vibrant counterculture emerged from the East Bay that contributed to a national awakening. Oakland was a hotbed of blues travelers during the same period. Blues and R&B clubs such as Esther's Orbit Room, Slim Jenkins', and the Continental Club, and bars such as the Lamppost and Bosn's Locker where Huey Newton spent his off time, were hangouts of the blues crowd. Yet they were not alone. Counterculture folk artists on college campuses commingled with an equally diverse array of musical/cultural practitioners. The music of the church, the righteous rhythm and blues tour stops by giants such as Little Richard and Ray Charles, the Latin cultural influence in the nearby Mission District in San Francisco, the decades-long Bay Area Asian American cultural influence, the freewheeling psychedelic explorations of the alternative jazz and rock scenes in Berkeley and San Francisco all contributed to an approach and an inclusive culture that created space for musical fusions not imagined or attempted anywhere else. This creative stew led to the formation, and the rise, of Sly and the Family Stone in 1966.[11]

Economically, however, the Bay Area was as racially restrictive as any other metropolitan region in America. The end of World War II sent the black economy spiraling downward. Racism and red-lining operated to keep blacks from purchasing property outside of "their" neighborhoods. In the East Bay, the black underclass was also growing in size and influence as alternative economies of drug trafficking and prostitution became established elements of urban life. San Francisco was a navy port city and tourist attraction, and the gambling and prostitution was well regulated by its famously corrupt police force. Across the bay was a different matter. There was more freedom for individual hustlers to operate. Thus, the ghetto pimp culture, so popularized by contemporary rap stars such as Too $hort and E-40, was established during the 1950s and 1960s in Oakland (and glorified in the 1973 movie *The Mack*).

Power grabs by the right-wing establishment in Oakland from then-mayor John Reading, and the newspaper monopoly held by *Oakland Tribune* publisher William Knowland, led to a series of bitter turf battles that seemed to affect the local black communities in the worst way. During and directly after World War II the Seventh Street corridor of West Oakland was a thriving business and cultural space. Blacks had work in the nearby shipyards and railroad yards, and the transportation hub brought musical travelers and merchants to the thriving coastal community. However, by 1960 the city leaders had implemented a vision of "redevelopment" that destroyed the black neighborhoods while allowing for suburban sprawl. In 1946 Oakland dug up its railroad lines through town, making a wasteland of the city railroad headquarters, and then claimed miles of black homeowners' property through eminent domain to make the Grove-Shafter Freeway that cut through the heart of black West Oakland neighborhoods. Black homeowners were forced to move to East Oakland or outlying cities while suburban whites drove down the new freeway running right over the devastated area to their jobs in San Francisco.

The crushing poverty and simmering tensions were made all the more palpable when the Los Angeles Watts District exploded in August 1965. Considering the situation, many were compelled to pose the question: "Is Oakland next?" With the rise of the Black Panthers, one might say an even larger conflagration erupted than anyone expected. Warren Hinckle, editor of *Ramparts* magazine (which hired Eldridge Cleaver straight out of prison in 1966) wrote a foreboding exposé on Oakland in February 1966, a few months before the Black Panther Party would take shape.

> As all American cities in trouble, Oakland needs more than new Federal programs and new industries. It desperately, essentially requires a revitalization, a redefinition of itself as an heterogeneous community. And this rebirth can only come, as the Phoenix, from the ashes of the ghetto. Only such a revolutionary awakening,

stirring in the slums and accepted in the hills, can save Oakland from the deepening and eventually disastrous war between the two worlds.[12]

The Rise of the Black Panther Party

Out of this confluence of elements arose black youth such as Huey P. Newton and Bobby Seale. Both were raised in the Oakland flatlands, went to public schools there in the late 1950s, studied politics at junior colleges, got work in the local poverty programs, read up on revolution, hung out in intellectual hot spots around Berkeley, explored radical black nationalism in local organizations, and experienced the charisma and compelling voice of Malcolm X. Newton and Seale also witnessed the economic hardships felt by their families, felt the brunt of the billy club, suffered the dehumanization of police brutality, and experienced the claustrophobia of local jail cells long before they created the Black Panther Party.

Bobby Seale was born in Dallas in 1936, and his family traveled throughout Texas before settling in Oakland during World War II. After tumultuous experiences in high school, he dropped out and joined the air force. Seale wound up stationed in South Dakota and spent his off time developing his craft as a jazz musician playing drums. "I wanted to keep my drums because I was engrossed in being a righteous jazz drummer. . . . It was an outlet, because you couldn't go anywhere. . . . In the afternoon I would go with these other cats who were musicians. We had a righteous group."[13] Seale's smart mouth got him in trouble with his military superiors, and problems with his loan for the drum kit left him in bad standing on the South Dakota military base. He was dishonorably discharged, and he returned to Oakland. He found work as a sheet metal mechanic—often only lasting until his discharge was revealed—and wound up at the Kaiser Aerospace and Electronics laboratory in Foster City, California, testing metals on the Gemini missile project. While they knew of his discharge, Seale was able to work there for fifteen months until, according to Seale, he quit "because I felt I was aiding the government's operation."[14] Seale also tried his hand as a stand-up comedian, delivering routines, impressions, and poems whenever gigs presented themselves. One such impromptu recital on top of a café table on Telegraph Avenue would later get Huey and Bobby arrested together.

Seale earned his high school diploma through night school. He began to attend Merritt College in north Oakland in 1962, where he met Newton. There were a number of emergent social organizations on the campus, and the two had joined the Afro-American Association (AAA), led by Donald Warden (now Khalid al-Mansour). Warden hosted intensive study groups that included some of the brightest minds in the black struggle. The AAA also put on events that brought black students together to raise their political consciousness. Warden was media savvy and hosted a radio show (and later a television program) dedicated to black issues. However, Warden's "pro-capitalist brand of black nationalism" grated on Seale and Newton, who were studying socialism and were wary of business schemes by blacks that could be as exploitative as those from whites. They soon left the AAA. Seale briefly joined the West Coast branch of the Revolutionary Action Movement (RAM), founded by Max Stanford of Philadelphia, a close confidante of Malcolm X. RAM advocated black militancy and a Marxist-inspired brand of economic restructuring in the community. The group sought to act as an underground organization influencing others. However, RAM inexplicably refused to allow Newton to join. While Bobby Seale was surprised by this, considering his friend Newton's involvement in black radical ideology, he was even more surprised that when Malcolm X was assassinated, RAM didn't take to the streets. Seale was outraged:

> When Malcolm X was killed in 1965, I ran down the street. I went to my mother's house, and I got six loose red bricks from the garden. Every time I saw a paddy roll by in a car, I picked up one of the half-bricks and threw it at the motherfuckers. I threw about half the bricks, and then I cried like a baby. I was righteously crying. I was pissed off and mad. Every paddy I'd see, *whop!* I'd throw a brick, and it would hit the cars, and *zoom!* They're driving down the street, and I'm throwing bricks for a motherfucker. I thought that was all I could do. I was ready to die that day.[15]

Seale quit RAM and began to search once more for the appropriate vehicle for his outrage. At the time, police brutality was the most pressing issue in the Oakland communities, and both Newton and Seale wanted to be part of an organization that addressed it. As a spinoff group to RAM, Merritt student Kenny Freeman started the Soul Students Advisory Council (SSAC), which had a little more of an activist commitment. Newton and Seale were able to work with SSAC to push for a black history course on the campus and began to address the police brutality that was becoming more acute on the streets.

Huey and Bobby wanted to model SSAC after the Louisiana-based Deacons for Defense and Justice, a group of black veterans that created a disciplined armed patrol group in 1964 to defend against violent white racists.[16] Huey and Bobby saw SSAC as the type of organization that could become a substantial player on the scene. Huey approached the SSAC leadership with the idea of armed patrols. He pointed out that since local police had begun to display their shotguns in the front seat of their cars, young blacks should do the same. The SSAC members denounced the idea, which they said gave the two men little chance to even survive, let alone create an organization capable of what the young men were attempting to do.

Ironically, Bobby and Huey were able to develop their own program courtesy of the state. Bobby obtained steady work at the North Oakland Neighborhood Service Center as a community liaison with the War on Poverty office. He was given funding to staff an assistant, and he hired Huey. The two were able to debate, discuss, and develop their Ten Point Plan for the Black Panther Party for Self-Defense while on the US government payroll.[17]

Huey Newton was born in Monroe, Louisiana, in 1942, the youngest of seven children. Huey's father brought his family west, like so many others, to seek work in the wartime industry; the family moved to Oakland when Huey was three years old. The family struggled and lived in poverty, but Huey's childhood was relatively benign considering what was to come.

> We shared the dreams of other American children. In our experience we planned to be doctors, lawyers, pilots, boxers, and builders. How could we know that we were not going anywhere? Nothing in our experience had shown us yet that the American dream was not for us. We too had great expectations. And then we went to school.[18]

Huey Newton experienced a series of conflicts with the educational institution. He was constantly humiliated by teachers who claimed he was stupid and inferior. "At the time I did not understand the size or seriousness of the school system's assault on Black people. I knew only that I constantly felt uncomfortable and ashamed of being Black. This feeling followed me everywhere without letup. It was a result of the implicit understanding in the system that whites were 'smart' and Blacks were 'stupid.' "[19] Newton insists his real education came from the streets and from his family. His father, Walter, was a strict disciplinarian, and through Walter's guidance Huey learned to fight and learned to stand for justice at all times. Huey learned to stand up for himself and to hold his ground from his oldest brother, Lee Edward, who was the first of the siblings to face jail time. He learned about the street life and being a "player" from "Sonny Man," Walter Jr., who took Huey to the racetrack and other hipster hangouts. And he learned the value of education from his brother Melvin, who was a dedicated student at Oakland City College during Huey's youth.

Huey's mother gave him piano lessons. Childhood friend David Hilliard was impressed with Huey's diverse talents and recalls, "Huey loved classical music. His mother had furnished him with piano lessons, so he introduced me to the music of Tchaikovsky. He loved *The Nutcracker*. One of his favorite songs was Rimsky-Korsakov's 'Flight of the Bumblebee.' "[20]

The dance music of Newton's day was not a significant part of his lifestyle. Huey Newton's social skills left him wanting when it came to parties. He did not see himself as a good dancer and spent much of his time at social gatherings in back rooms conversing about ideas rather than stomping the floor or slow dancing with the ladies as his friends were doing.[21]

Once out of high school, Newton taught himself to read and became a voracious consumer of ideas, from philosophy and economics, to law and revolutionary violence. Once he was able to go to Merritt College and enjoy his intellectual pursuits on his own terms, Newton thrived. He was an enthusiastic student who always asked questions in class and challenged instructors to defend the assigned works and to apply them to real-world ideas.

Newton also indulged in some alternative lifestyles that were emerging in the Bay Area. He knew a fellow student named Richard Thorne, who promoted the beliefs of "free love" and "nonpossessive relationships" and would later become an influential leader of the nationally known Berkeley-based Sexual Freedom League. Huey gravitated toward this idea, as much for the access to women as the philosophical underpinnings:

> My doubts about marriage were reinforced when I met Richard Thorne. His theory of nonpossessiveness in the love relationship was appealing to me. The idea that one person possesses the other, as in bourgeois marriage, where "she's my woman and he's my man" was unacceptable. . . .
>
> Although much of this involved a new philosophy about the family, another part of it was exploitative. I was serious about our attempt to question matters through practice, but I also felt that we were taking advantage of the women for practical reasons. Women paid my rent, cooked my food, and did other things for me, while any money I came by was mine to keep. . . .
>
> While I loved many women, only twice did I feel an impulse to marry. . . . No matter how deeply I felt, I could not share her goals if they led to a compromise with society.[22]

Newton's pronounced aversion to a "compromise with society" was perhaps a typical reflection of his generation. Newton's life choices showed he sought to change society rather than compromise with it.

Newton's ambivalence toward women's equality would be mirrored in the organization he would later found. As a black radical trumpet of aggression on the national scene, the Black Panther Party was a phallocentric outlet of political theater. On the other hand, many Panthers in daily practice were challenged as revolutionaries and taken (dragged perhaps) through an introspective process of acknowledging the equality of women within their ranks. To the women in the Party, the growth appeared to be marginal, but in the context of black radicalism in the 1960s, the Black Panther Party may have been the most inclusive black radical group of them all.

Huey Newton was also familiar with the alternative lifestyles of the residents of the Haight-Ashbury district of San Francisco, who were leading their own social revolution. Newton followed the activities of the Diggers, an infamous group of actors, artists, and rebels who promoted a vision of society free from private property. The Diggers gave away food

at a series of "free stores" and used the energy of the people and donations from the community to maintain them. They performed guerilla
street theater (such as the "End of Money Parade") and also began the
first "free clinic" in the Haight. All of these activities would become
central elements of Black Panther community practices. In 1967 Newton
secured the use of the Diggers' "communication company" to print the
first issues of the Black Panther paper.[23]

Through Donald Warden's Afro-American Association, Huey Newton was exposed to a broad spectrum of black radical ideologies and
personalities. Warden's organization provided a crucial stepping stone to
the rise of black radicalism on the West Coast, and included the members of two other competing groups that called themselves Panthers; the
San Francisco–based Black Panther Party of Northern California (led by
Ken Freeman and Ernie Allen) and the Los Angeles–based Black Panther
Political Party, which briefly included John Floyd and Angela Davis.[24]

In 1963 the AAA put together the Mind of the Ghetto Conference
at McClymonds High School in Oakland. It was there that Huey saw
Malcolm X for the first time. A young boxer named Cassius Clay was
there also, but Malcolm X was clearly Huey's inspiration.

> Malcolm X impressed me with his logic and with his disciplined,
> dedicated mind. Here was a man who combined the world of the
> streets and the world of the scholar, a man so widely read he could
> give better lectures and cite more evidence than many college pro-
> fessors. He was also practical. Dressed in the loose fitting style of
> a strong prison man, he knew what the street brothers were like
> and he knew what had to be done to reach them. Malcolm had a
> program: armed defense when attacked, and reaching the people
> with ideas and programs that speak to their condition. At the same
> time, he identified the causes of their condition instead of blaming
> the people.[25]

With Newton's supportive family background, the wide-open social
formations on the Merritt College campus, and the presence of fearless leaders such as Malcolm X, Newton and other young blacks were
inspired to challenge their dehumanizing social and economic status and
to reach beyond what established civil rights and Black Nationalist leaders had attempted. The AAA didn't work for them; RAM was not the

answer; the SSAC did not go far enough. Out of the action and energy generated by Malcolm X's death, the upheaval in Watts, and the increasingly repressive police presence on the streets of Oakland, the time was ripe for Newton and Seale to form their own unique organization to address their community's needs.

The Ten Point Program

On October 15, 1966, after weeks of discussion and study, Newton and Seale finalized a platform for their new organization, with two components: a basic, readable treatise of "what we want" followed each time by a lengthier explanation of "what we believe." In this way, Newton and Seale could run off the primary points of the program to those who wanted a quick summary, yet they provided more information to support their points.

After writing a draft, Huey took it to his brother Melvin for grammatical editing. Once it was ready, Bobby's wife, Artie, typed up a final draft on mimeograph paper. It was only after that draft was written that Bobby and Huey chose the black panther as the symbol for the group. It had come in the mail as the logo from the Lowndes County Freedom Organization in Mississippi. Huey saw the logo and decided to name his group the Black Panther Party for Self-Defense. It was not the first black panther party, but it would become the best known.

The ten points directly addressed the problems of living in the working-class black areas of Oakland. Point one was, "We want freedom. We want power to determine the destiny of our community." Point two, "We want full employment for our people," was from the outset a challenge to the economics of capitalism and its deleterious effects upon the black community. Point three followed directly: "We want an end to the robbery by the CAPITALISTS of our black community." Point four demanded decent housing, and point five demanded proper education. Point six was far-reaching: "We want all black men to be exempt from military service." This bold move was supported by the claim, "We believe that black people should not be forced to fight in the military service to defend a racist government that does not protect us." Similarly, point eight demanded the release of all black men from jails, as they were not given fair trials by juries of their peers, which was point nine. Point ten was more or less a summary of the points: "We want land, bread, housing, education, clothing, justice, and peace." In addition, point ten demanded a United Nations–administered plebiscite (vote) to allow blacks to determine their own destiny. They supported the final demand with a passage from the July 4, 1776, United States Declaration of Independence:

> We hold these truths to be self evident, that all men are created equal; that they are endowed by their Creator with certain inalienable rights; that among these are life, liberty, and the pursuit of happiness . . .
> But, when a long train of abuses and usurpations, pursuing invariably the same object, evinces a design to reduce them under absolute despotism, it is their right, it is their duty, to throw off such government, and to provide new guards for their future security.[26]

Their first order of business was to implement point number seven: "We want an immediate end to police brutality and murder of black people." Newton explained the direction in his autobiography, *Revolutionary Suicide*, in 1973:

> This is a major issue in every black community. The police have never been our protectors. Instead they act as the military arm of our oppressors and continually brutalize us. . . . We recognized that it was ridiculous to report the police to the police, but we hoped that by raising encounters to a higher level, by patrolling the police with arms, we would see a change in their behavior. Further, the community would notice this and become interested in the Party. Thus our armed patrols were also a means of recruiting.
> At first, the patrols were a total success. Frightened and confused, the police did not know how to respond, because they had never encountered patrols like this before. They were familiar with the community-alert patrols in other cities, but never before had guns been an integral part of any patrol program. With weapons in our hands we were no longer their subjects but their equals.[27]

The patrols got the attention of the community, and of law enforcement. They also served to create a new breed of young black men in the process. Newton and Seale had formed a space in which young black men could act upon their own feelings of outrage and injustice in a way that was relevant to their community. Elbert "Big Man" Howard, one of the first Panthers to join the organization, recalls those times:

> At this period in time the struggle for civil rights was raging out of control. Malcolm X was telling the nation it's the ballot or the bullet. He was telling us to defend ourselves. If any man put his hand on you or yours, you had a right, you had an obligation to fix him so he would never be able to do it again. I believed in these teachings and still do. I was truly angry.
>
> I think that my anger was always tempered with discipline and reasonable thought. I like to think that my patrols in the street never led to unnecessary bloody confrontations. The young brothers that rode with me had to follow the rules of engagement set forth by Chairman Bobby Seale and Minister of Defense Huey P. Newton. I think that the big red pick-up truck with a bunch of Black brothers in it was on the Oakland P.D. blotter to avoid confrontation. As a result, there was no loss in the community or of Panthers or police. That is not to say there were not ambushes, harassment, and false arrests.[28]

In April 1967 Richmond, California, police shot and killed an unarmed black youth named Denzil Dowell. Dowell's family asked the Panthers for help, and after requesting an investigation and being rebuked, Newton, Seale, and the Panthers realized it was time to expand their reach. They planned a large rally in support of Dowell, and they promoted it by printing up a pamphlet discussing the Dowell case. This would become the first issue of the *Black Panther* newspaper. What began as an ad-hoc means of reaching out to the black community and supplementing the word of mouth that was already working effectively became one of the Party's greatest achievements. Eventually the *Black Panther* newspaper would have a weekly worldwide circulation of more than 100,000 copies. The eclectic, multiracial population of the region may have been one of the reasons why. David Hilliard recalls:

> The *Black Panther* newspaper was born during the height of the counterculture revolution and the hippie underground newspaper movement. We used to put together the newspaper to the strains of

Bob Dylan's *Highway 61 Revisited*. Huey's favorite song was "Ballad of a Thin Man." Publishers who were sympathetic to the Black Panthers and their Ten Point Program regularly printed weekly editions of various alternative press, circulating everything from leaflets to full-blown, newsprint periodicals such as the *San Francisco Oracle* and the *Berkeley Barb*. Consequently, one publication offered Huey and the Black Panthers use of their mimeograph machines. If Huey and the Party provided the necessary paper, ink, and staples, they could assemble their own leaflets.[29]

The leaflets eventually became newsprint, with full-page articles, artwork, commentary, and announcements of events. Support for the Party and its causes grew as the *Black Panther* grew in size and circulation. Volunteers began to work for the paper on a weekly basis, combining local issues with global revolutionary news, updates on Party activities nationwide, and striking revolutionary artwork from a young San Francisco artist named Emory Douglas and the first female Panther recruit, Matilaba, a.k.a. Tarika Lewis.

Sacramento

To bring their case to a larger venue, Huey and Bobby planned a "colossal event" that would make the Panthers known worldwide. The event was a staged march into the state capitol building in Sacramento. The Panthers went to protest the Mulford Act, pending legislation that was designed to prohibit the public display of weapons. The bill was written by a Republican, Alameda County State Assemblyman Don Mulford, who was based in the Panthers' home district. On Tuesday, May 2, 1967, Bobby Seale led a delegation of armed Panthers (twenty-four men and six women) to the California state capitol; they walked into the legislature chambers dressed in black leather jackets and black berets (despite the heat that day), brandished firearms, and read from a proclamation that stated in part:

> The Black Panther Party for Self-Defense calls upon the American people in general and the black people in particular to take careful note of the racist California Legislature which is now considering legislation aimed at keeping the black people disarmed and

powerless at the very same time that racist police agencies throughout the country are intensifying the terror, brutality, murder and
repression of black people. . . .

Vicious police dogs, cattle prods, and increased patrols have
become familiar signs in black communities. City Hall turns a deaf
ear to the pleas of Black people for relief from this increasing terror.
The Black Panther Party for Self-Defense believes that the time has
come for black people to arm themselves against this terror before
it is too late.[30]

Photographs of Seale, Lil' Bobby Hutton, and the others were trans-
mitted worldwide. The news spread fast: GUNMEN INVADE WEST COAST
CAPITOL crossed the front page of the *Chicago Tribune*; ARMED NEGROES
ENTER CALIFORNIA ASSEMBLY IN GUN BILL PROTEST was the *New York
Times* tagline; ARMED GANG INVADES STATE CAPITOL was the headline
from London's *Guardian*. The Panthers had shocked the world.[31]

Amiri Baraka was a visiting lecturer (and organizer) at San Francisco
State University that spring semester, and he recalled the energy in the
air that day:

The day Bobby Seale and the Panthers went up to Sacramento with
their guns, the state campus sparkled with anticipation. The word
spread like only good news can. Black students were beaming from
one end of the campus to the other. The real shit was not too far
away, was what was in some of our minds. The real revolution is just
around the corner, we felt. The photos of Bobby [Seale] and Bobby
Hutton on the front page with their heat strapped on or in hand did
something wonderful to us. It pumped us up bigger than life. Black
men demanding democracy and justice and ready to fight about it!
Those were heady times.[32]

Because of the media surrounding that day, the Panthers became a
worldwide sensation. Young blacks nationwide wanted to join the Party
or create their own chapters. One of those young people was James
Mott, a Sacramento native who just happened to be on the site of the
capitol building the day the Panthers arrived. "I was there that day and
saw Ronald Reagan talking to these schoolgirls. He saw those Panthers
and cut and ran like he was trying out for the Olympics!"[33] Within the

year, Mott and some of his associates started up the Sacramento chapter of the Black Panther Party.

Lumpen Members' Road to the Black Panther Party

William Calhoun

The same forces that led Newton and Seale to create the Party led the members of the Lumpen toward involvement in the Party. William Calhoun grew up in San Jose. His family had headed west from Arkansas, when his father, after some "incidents" in the army due to racist treatment, left the area and settled where few would know who he was. William Calhoun would experience the same racist treatment once he was drafted in 1964.

Calhoun was raised in a close-knit, diverse, working-class community, where he learned an appreciation of music and started his own rock and roll bands. He thought he was ready to take on the world with his adolescent brand of music until he was transformed like so many other artists of his generation by Brother Ray:

> I thought I knew what music was about until I heard my first Ray Charles record. What little I know about piano, I learned sitting down imitating Ray Charles records. Michael McDonald has said that "when you first hear Ray Charles, the first time, he touches something down inside you didn't even know was there. And you spend the rest of your career trying to find it again." And that's exactly what happened to me.[34]

Calhoun developed a career as an R&B singer and nightclub host, or emcee. He wound up at the world-famous San Francisco strip joint, Big Al's, singing songs and introducing the dancers. His gig lasted a year. Then things really got interesting.

> When I finished at Big Al's, the next gig was at a place called the Idle Hour Supper Club in Anchorage, Alaska. I was there for about a month and a half and some Eskimos who were in the National Guard came into the club. They had been out on maneuvers for the weekend, and they refused to serve the Eskimos in the club. This reminded me very much of when I was in New Orleans in full dress

uniform—they wouldn't let me in the clubs on Basin Street. So I notified the NAACP, which got involved with the club owner. They found out I called [and] we got fired. I came back to San Francisco. . . . I tried Big Al's again, but I couldn't take it anymore.[35]

Calhoun returned to the Bay Area and began his political career by organizing students at San Jose City College in the fall of 1967, which he did with characteristic zeal. "My job was to organize all the black folks on the campus of San Jose City college, which we did. Janitors, teachers, everybody. By the time we had been there a year, every black person on the campus of San Jose City College was a member of the Black Student Union." During Calhoun's first year in college he was introduced to Kenny Freeman—by then the leader of the Black Nationalist group House of Umoja. Freeman had originally formed the San Francisco–based Black Panther Party of Northern California, but after a run-in with the Oakland-based Black Panther Party, his group changed its name. Freeman was then known as Mamadu Lumumba. Calhoun joined the group and was given the name "Mdamase," which he was told was a South African name given to one of "royal or regal bearing." Calhoun was not impressed with the activities of the group. "I was getting very bugged about the direction of the House of Umoja because we were spending a lot of time in Swahili classes, learning all this cultural crap, and I wanted to be out doing something a little more aggressive in terms of the revolution." Calhoun decided the group needed to be more visible and relevant in the community, so he voluntarily sought out some firearms for the organization:

A friend of mine in the organization and I, we went down to Pacoima [near Los Angeles] and got a couple of carloads of what in the Black Panther Party we called "technical equipment." I brought the technical equipment to my house and had Kenny Freeman come over and, you know, to inspect it because I bought it for the organization, and he just about freaked. When he saw the stuff laid out on the bed, and the clips and all that, he just went nuts. "Hey, what are you doing, you gonna get us all killed!"

So that's when I decided these cats are not serious. And I wanted to find somebody who was. And that's when I heard about Huey P. Newton.[36]

Clark "Santa Rita" Bailey

Clark Bailey had a rough time as a youth, growing up in the Brookfield Village projects in East Oakland. The nickname "Santa Rita" came from his familiarity with the Santa Rita Jail, the county lockup in Dublin, twenty miles outside of Oakland in eastern Alameda County. "I was a pretty wild and crazy kid. I was basically a young hippie-like guy, because that was what was going on during that period of time," he recalls. Bailey toiled in foster care through most of his teens. However, there was one unique aspect of his disrupted family life: he continued with his musical studies despite the chaos in his life.

> So if I moved here or there, one thing consistent for me was my music. I was able to continue to take these lessons that I had been taking. I took lessons all the way through all the bullshit. And it was basically the classical background, it wasn't rhythm and blues or anything. I was playing Beethoven and stuff. I got this scholarship at Stanford playing "Flight of the Bumblebee" on the piano. That was my way of keeping sane through all the madness that was going on in my life as a young man.[37]

Bailey didn't take the scholarship to Stanford, but his grades were steady despite his troubled background, and he made his way to San Jose State. Once there he was repeatedly asked to join the Black Student Union by Michael Torrence, who was the leader of the BSU. Clark Bailey was skeptical about the entire movement thing until he witnessed the distribution night at the San Francisco offices of the Black Panther Party.

> On a Wednesday night, one night every week, people from all walks of life would come in there and help us put this newspaper out. And we're talking about folding the newspaper, stapling it, taking wrapping paper, wrapping each newspaper. We were putting out thousands and thousands of issues all across the country. Licking labels, it took all night. And this was amazing to me. I couldn't believe that people would actually do this for free. 'Cause I was, you know, I come from the streets, everything is about money. So that was the most impressive thing that I had ever seen.[38]

Witnessing the power of the people inspired Bailey to pursue the responsibilities of Black Panther Party membership, which he took on with his typical zeal. He would join the organization and devote his entire life to the work and duties of a Panther:

> The procedure that you had to go through during that period of time was study first. And so I started reading different publications. Mao, Fanon, and really started getting into what revolutionary struggle really meant. We were young. And we felt that we could change the world. And if it was necessary to put our lives on the line for that, then that's what we would do.[39]

Michael Torrence

Berkeley High graduate Michael Torrence, the one responsible for recruiting Bailey at San Jose State, began his political career as a chairman of the Berkeley youth chapter of the NAACP at the age of fourteen. He was also involved in Berkeley High choral groups as well as his church choir. Torrence had come from accomplished stock, as his mother Frankie Bowman was the first black woman in the US Forest Service in California. The pioneering spirit led young Michael far beyond the NAACP.

> I had a cousin, his name was Frank Jones, who opened up one of the first black bookstores in Berkeley—used to be called Brain Power— down on San Pablo [Avenue]. He was working as one of the original editors of the *Black Panther* paper. I used to work in his bookstore after school, and he took me to a few meetings and got me my first "red book," but I hadn't joined full-time. By the time I got to San Jose State my politics had definitely changed to what you would call revolutionary, and I got involved with the student strike my first year there in '68.[40]

It would not take long before Torrence, Calhoun, and Bailey moved beyond the typical struggles for resources of student groups at San Jose State University. The model they drew upon was the exploding Black Panther Party. Torrence recalls:

> That following semester I became the chairman of the Black Student Union there and we organized the BSU along the lines of the Black Panther Party. We began to sell papers on campus and come up to San Francisco to work the distribution. Eventually, in the

summer of '69, we established a community center in East San Jose with the notion of forming a chapter out of the colleges. So we set up a breakfast for schoolchildren program, a liberation school down there, had some police confrontations and some other things that went along with it.

And long story short, that particular chapter dissolved, but myself, Clark Bailey, Bill Calhoun . . . and some other brothers and sisters, we all went up—basically left school and joined. We wanted to be full-time Panthers so we started in the San Francisco chapter in the Fillmore District.[41]

Michael Torrence had a rich musical background as well. Like the others, he disregarded his musical background when he joined the revolution, not knowing that it would return to him and be of use one day.

I grew up around music. My mother is very musical; my mother used to be a drummer. There was just always music in the house. Music from the '40s, you know, Sarah Vaughan, Billy Eckstine, you name it, then all the way up to James Brown, Sam Cooke, Lou Rawls, there was always music around the house.

Then I also had another uncle, Bobby Mclain, who was a singer in the '50s, a doo-wop singer. So I was exposed to that at a very early age. And it just seemed to be something kind of natural.

As far as any formal training, in high school I sang with some chorus groups and things of this nature here, but I really began performing with groups, I think at thirteen was the first group that I performed in, singing groups and bands and stuff, and it was just something that I just really loved to do.[42]

James Mott and the Sacramento Black Panther Party

James Mott grew up in Sacramento, seventy miles northeast of the Bay Area. Yet he shared the same convictions about social change as his colleagues, and as a high school student he mailed a request for the paperwork to start a chapter of the Student Nonviolent Coordinating Committee (SNCC) in 1966, which was the best-known black radical organization at the time:

We ended up getting buttons and membership paperwork out here; we started recruiting. . . . Eventually Stokely Carmichael came out here. And I was able to speak, meet, and greet him. He was very happy what was going on in the area, that we were organizing.

In a small, socially conservative city such as Sacramento, it was considered—even in the black community at the time—a radical act to participate in a civil rights organization. This was particularly so for young people. Mott and his small group of youth activists encountered resistance from their own elders: "I remember when we went to church . . . at that time I don't think they were ready. They actually told us that unless we stopped affiliating ourselves with the organization [SNCC] we would have to leave the church. We left the church."[43]

James Mott crossed paths with the Black Panther Party in the spring of 1967 when they came to Sacramento and put on a show for all the world to see. As a young man, the event at the state capitol sunk in deeply with Mott. "I think what Bobby and Big Man, Lil' Bobby and the rest of the members who came through at that point in time demonstrated to us, was 'enough was enough.' That us having a right to defend ourselves was the American way." It would be another year before Mott saw the Panthers again and was moved to join, shortly after the death of Lil' Bobby Hutton in April 1968.

One day I remember these brothers marching in the community in all black, in their leather, and they were talking about Bobby Hutton, and they were talking about how you can join the Black Panther Party, and how you can join and how Bobby was killed, murdered. And what struck me was the fact that he was seventeen years old. I asked myself what would motivate a seventeen-year-old to take it to that level, to where he would put his life on the line?[44]

Shortly afterward, Mott, Charles Brunson, and a few others organized their own Sacramento chapter of the Black Panther Party. The group included Jack Strivers, Gloria Abernathy, Melvin Whitaker, Mark Teemer, and Shirley Finney (who would become an actress and play the lead in the 1977 film *Wilma*, about the life of track star Wilma Rudolph).

According to James Mott, the Sacramento Party chapter thrived. It featured one of the first breakfast for children programs, and its relationship with the multiracial community was a positive one. The educational program was also very effective under the leadership of the chapter. "We used the Ten Point Program to teach people to read," Mott recalls.

> The membership here in Sacramento was typical. You had some brothers who were out there hustling, doing their thing, who became members. And they were great as far as being able to go and talk to businesspeople once they became politically educated and understood the purpose. They were able to go in and eloquently voice the need for the program and its support. So they put their hustling talents to use.[45]

James Mott's enthusiasm for the Party was marked by his regular routine of distributing the *Black Panther* paper in and around the state capitol building. As part of his weekly distribution rounds, he would hit up the staffers. He earned a reputation in the hallways and helped the Party's image in the eyes of some state lawmakers. Mott recalls how he would approach the secretaries to "give" copies of the *Black Panther* to governor Ronald Reagan:

> I had three copies. I said, "I want to make sure that the governor gets these." She looked at the papers, you know the artwork on the old Panther papers was very prolific, right? "I will make sure that he gets it." I would come back, and I said, "Did he get 'em?" and she said, "Oh yes." I said, "Did he read them?" And she said, "Oh yes, he did, and he wasn't very happy." So I would give her more papers. I'd say, "Here's some more."
>
> At noon, we would make it a point to be downtown because we would take a stack of papers, maybe about five hundred, and what would happen was, the state workers, they would make it a point to get downtown and they would buy those papers, twenty-five cents. State workers in their suits in shirts and ties, women in business dresses would come by. These were white people that would buy these papers. We had a certain clientele down there.
>
> That's how Jesse Unruh, at that time state attorney general, came out with that statement because they had been informed— the information had been given to them every time they opened

up that paper. They would read about another breakfast program. This one is in L.A., this one is in Baltimore, New York, wherever. It was there. So he's the one that came out with that statement: "The Black Panther Party is feeding more children in the nation than the United States government."[46]

In addition to his presence at the state capitol, James Mott was a regular in the Bay Area, participating in Party functions and soaking up the wisdom of the leadership there.

Just about every Saturday, myself and Charles Brunson, we would come down to the Bay. We'd come down and we would go to the meetings and retreats that Bobby and Eldridge and Kathleen, George Murray at that time, [would have]; we would come to all the retreat meetings.

Then after that we would go over to Bobby's and sit with Bobby and John Seale and brainstorm all night long. We would have our little drinks and we would be sitting there talking about organizing and some of the things we could do in the area. We would sound off suggestions.

Charles and I would go down there sometimes, we would be dead tired. We would go down there and we would have this opportunity to sit up after these meetings, all night long with Bobby and just brainstorm. I'm talking about us coming from Sacramento and you have this mass organization of people in the Bay Area, but here we are having this quality time every weekend with Bobby about organizing. I was like a sponge. I was absorbing it all. It helped put me on the course to define what my responsibilities were.[47]

James Mott was well trained musically as well. Active in his church, he was a soloist in the Jubilee Choir there.

I had a good music teacher by the name of Sister Simmons. I learned vocal tonation, pitch. I learned how to pronounce words correctly in terms of singing emphasis, all that. Breathing techniques, and of course that was the beginning. And then later on when I went to college I was in the concert choir. Singing things like the "Hallelujah Chorus" and all that. I learned a lot more vocal techniques. And I loved the music.

Also we had a little group. A three-man group, I think we were called the Satins, we would perform in local talent shows. Back in the day, we would go to the teen centers, and I remember having a piano in there—you go in there and you start singing songs. People would start playing, you know, some of the Motown songs. I even started writing some songs. At that point in time we had a little idea of polishing our group, getting a little demo recording, getting into Motown or some other musical organization where we can go into the music business.[48]

Early on in his musical development, Mott was influenced by the lyrical mastery of the Motown groups and their positive portrayal of life. "When you heard that music in our era, it sent a message . . . so the lyrics, the content, that gave that message was something that stuck in my mind. At that point in time, I said that the music that we write is going to send a message. The music that we do is going to send a message."[49] Mott would prove himself prophetic on this point.

At some of Mott's visits to Bay Area Panther after-hours gatherings, he would dabble in doo-wop singing with other young men. While it was evident that Mott had the political commitment from his work in the Sacramento chapter, once it became known he had the singing talent to support the others, Emory Douglas had him assigned to the newly formed Black Panther singing group. After some conversations with Party chief of staff David Hilliard, who had dubbed the group the Lumpen, Emory Douglas began to secure resources for the act to become a visible part of the Panther cultural thrust in the community.

The Lumpen members from the outset were straddling contradictions. Bandleader Calhoun had experience working in bars and strip clubs. This knowledge allowed him to effectively emcee the proceedings of the Lumpen live shows from behind his electric piano. Calhoun's experience in the seedy underworld of entertainment ironically gave his delivery of funky rhythm and blues a certain credibility. Clark "Santa Rita" Bailey's soulful lead singing was an amalgamation of his Panther politics, his classical musical training, and his extralegal past. James Mott was talkative offstage, but onstage he let his dynamic visuals—his large facial features and towering afro—make the strongest impression. Michael Torrence was politically well read, astute, and analytical, yet his dancing steps were smooth enough to stabilize the stage show. Each of these young men had learned music for the joy of it and had so deeply internalized the politics of their time and place that they were willing and able to transform their fiercely revolutionary spirit into song.

The Lumpen Band

As was typical of rhythm and blues outfits of the time, the backup band changed membership often. The initial session players on the group's first single were local musicians Calhoun knew from the San Jose area. As the group became more established, they drew together a stronger lineup of musicians, many of whom would go on to established careers of their own. Although the musicians were not full-fledged Party members, their sympathies clearly led them to donate their time to the Lumpen while they pursued diverse careers. "People don't realize how many people loved us as a Party," Clark Bailey recalls. "We were in the community all the time. So you meet people. It wasn't really that hard to pull together a band. Guys were wanting to play. When I was a young kid, I would play anywhere. You didn't have to pay me, I didn't care, I just wanted to play."[50]

This was the case for guitarist Mack Ray Henderson, bass player Thomas Wallace, drummer Minor Williams, and the rest of the young players. These three rhythm section players joined when Clark Bailey asked high school classmate Minor Williams to play. The musical opportunity was a great one for the youngsters. However, life in the Lumpen band was unlike the typical R&B gig. The lack of pay was only one inconvenience; the threat of police confrontation was a constant concern, and the volunteer musicians were not as trained or prepared as the Panthers were to deal with it. "I think about that stuff sometimes," Lumpen drummer Williams recalls. "I say, 'Wow, I was really lucky to have survived the Lumpen group.' Man, it was a lot going on in those days."[51]

The band membership changed frequently. One incarnation of the group performed locally in the autumn of 1970 and went on the "revolutionary tour" in November and December. After the tour, however, many of the band members left and were replaced. Some of the new players wound up in the studio doing postproduction recordings for the live album, and the finished product contains elements of both band incarnations.

Some of the Lumpen band members developed successful musical careers. Saxophone player Raheem Roach was Calhoun's musical director and led the players when they performed their opening set as the Freedom Messengers. Bailey recalls that Roach went on to perform with jazz iconoclast Sun Ra shortly after his Lumpen gig. Drummer Minor Williams was starting out as a session drummer and played with the Lumpen just as his cousin Lenny Williams was gaining fame as a local singer who would later join the R&B headliners Tower of Power. Minor Williams continues to perform in various bands in the Bay Area to this day. Bassist Melvin Coleman was also just starting out his career, but later picked up a gig with the soul group the Whispers, which lasted more than thirty years and garnered multiple platinum hit records. Coleman just recently retired from the Whispers and settled in North Carolina. Guitarist Mack Ray Henderson and bass player Thomas Wallace continue to perform locally in the Oakland area.

Trumpet player David Levinson was one of many politically conscious youngsters at the time just happy to participate in the group.[52] Levinson says he came from a radical activist background, and his parents, Saul and Cece Levinson, had helped to create the Intercommunal Committee to Combat Fascism (ICCF) in 1969, which was essentially a white adjunct of the Black Panther Party. While playing in the Lumpen, David Levinson volunteered at one of the health clinics sponsored by the ICCF. Shortly afterward, he left the ICCF to attend medical school. Levinson became a doctor and remains to this day a trauma surgeon in San Pablo, California, patching up bodies every weekend in the emergency ward of Doctor's Medical Center (just outside of Richmond), trying to fend off the human tragedy the Panthers sought to alleviate.[53]

There were other members of the band who came and went. But it should be remembered that there was an essential commonality among the San Francisco Bay Area community of activist-musicians who participated in the social experiment that was the Lumpen: they all shared the hope and vision of a liberated community, they were all highly skilled at their craft at a young age—they could give up the funk—and they were all willing to take up the task for the cause without expectations of profit or commercial or public recognition.

The NCCF

By 1969 the Black Panther Party was taking initiative in coalition-building with white radicals. It sought to create spaces where allied and adjunct Party offices could be created in which nearly identical Party functions took place and all community members could participate. In July 1969 the Panthers sponsored a United Front Against Fascism Conference in Oakland specifically to draw support for Panther goals from a broader community. Shortly after the conference, David Hilliard announced the formation of the National Committee to Combat Fascism (NCCF) as a non–racially exclusive adjunct to the Panthers.

While there had been a dedicated core of white radical supporters in the San Francisco Bay Area and other northern cities, the Party established NCCF chapters throughout the country, especially in southern cities such as Memphis, Dallas, Houston, New Orleans, and Greensboro, North Carolina. Curtis J. Austin, author of *Up Against the Wall: Violence in the Making and Unmaking of the Black Panther Party*, writes: "When the Panthers attempted to look beyond issues of race and began to include whites as a significant part of their base of support, they attempted to fight racism with solidarity while at the same time making up for the lack of black bodies to put upon the front lines of their revolutionary advance."[54] A great deal of organizing took place in these offices, and the FBI and law enforcement officials treated them as Panther chapters. Los Angeles Panther leader and Vietnam veteran Elmer "Geronimo" Pratt was sent to the southern chapters to train recruits and to fortify the chapter offices.[55]

The Black Panther Party was implementing its own form of radical antiracist organizing as early as the summer of 1969. The traditional civil rights organizations such as SNCC and Dr. King's SCLC were not as visible in many black communities by the end of the 1960s. Through the NCCF chapters, the Black Panther Party was challenging police brutality, establishing Survival Programs, and organizing local community members in cities that by this time had little multiracial political activity or infrastructure. Their presence in the South represented a newer wave of antiracist activism in which southern blacks and whites operated on common ground. Unlike SNCC, which had become radicalized and had essentially purged its white membership by 1967, the Panthers were creating a common space in which young radicals of all persuasions could organize and participate. In addition, the Party was tapping into a larger sense of imminent upheaval and change that was taking place among youth worldwide, particularly after 1968.

Sly Stone, Interracialism, and the Panthers

Much of the revolutionary spirit shared by so many at the time transcended the traditional racial conflicts because the social transformations were taking place at all levels of society. The concept of "integration" was fast becoming an anachronism, because a generation had come to feel that the institutions people were fighting for access to were in need of complete transformation. What was the point of integrating into an assortment of corrupt institutions in the first place? This was one of the fundamental issues confronting members of the counterculture generation at the end of the 1960s. Kenneth Rexroth discussed the changes in a 1969 essay:

> Today there is growing up throughout the world an entirely new pattern of life. For several years I have called it the subculture of secession but this it is no more—it is a competing civilization, "a new society within the shell of the old." It has come about not through books or programs but through a change in the methods of production. It is a society of people who have simply walked into a computerized, transistorized, automated world, a post-industrial or post-capitalist economy, in which there is an ever-increasing democratization of at least the possibilities for a creative response to life.
>
> What does democratization of the arts mean in practice in America? What happens when an entire subculture takes to poetry, rock groups, folk songs, junk sculpture, collage pop pictures, total sexual freedom, and costumes invented ad lib? What is the relationship of this literary and artistic activity in which everyone can take part to the official, professionalized culture? What is the relationship of the Establishment and the Secession? Obviously the younger people are both seceding from something and acceding to something. What?[56]

At this moment of social rupture and change, the revolutionary words of youthful idealists carried particular weight and potential and were transmitted through a variety of forms that included musical recordings played live, heard on the radio, and seen on television.

The resonance of Sly and the Family Stone on Bay Area culture should not be underestimated. The pioneering outfit certainly transcended racial categories and was equally popular among whites and blacks. They were not divested from their black audience as Jimi Hendrix was, nor were they bound to it as James Brown was. Sly and the Family Stone, for a brief period, put forth an entirely new concept of integration. It was transcendent, because it celebrated a space in the imagination far beyond the premise of equal participation in the stale institutions that created the racial conflicts in the first place. Sly, in his vision, conceived a new space in which "Love City" was the address, followers were leaders, and leaders had no titles. This new space was accessible to anyone, yet the director of the operation, the subtle and slippery ringmaster, puppeteer, and pied piper of the social revolution was a black man, Sly Stone. This black man had been raised in the working-class streets of the Bay Area black community and had not abandoned his ties to the pool-hall homeboys of his adolescence, even as he wrote pop anthems for rock groups in San Francisco. Like Huey Newton, Sly Stone would rocket to worldwide stardom from humble Bay Area roots with a revolutionary new way to look at the world. Also like Huey Newton, Sly Stone would withdraw to his street life and disappear from the scene in a few short years. Generations later, rebel youth are still studying Huey Newton's revolutionary politics—and Sly Stone's revolutionary music.

Sly Stone had a peculiar relationship with the Black Panther Party. His music rarely took on specific causes, yet he was a lightning rod for issues of race, violence, and community values simply by virtue of the depth of ideas in his work. Members of the Black Panther Party were known throughout that period to approach popular figures and ask for their support, either financially or through some type of endorsement. Some Party members at the time did more than request that grocers donate eggs for the breakfast program. There were constant rumors that the Black Panther Party was putting pressure on a number of popular entertainers to support the Party in some way. In a rare in-depth interview in the 2010 Sly Stone documentary *Coming Back for More*, Sly reveals surprising details of his relationship to the Panthers.

> Kathleen Cleaver, . . . she wanted one hundred thousand dollars. I said OK, but you got to first make me know—give me a reason to why I should do that. They were trying to make me feel like I needed for them to remind me I'm black. That it would be a good thing to do so that I'd be secure and black. I ain't got no problem being black, in the first place. I'm not into that violence you guys do though. So I don't want to contribute to that. You know, it's not good to fight the police, you're gonna lose.[57]

Sly Stone and his band, regardless of any financial contribution to the militants in his hometown, served to further the cause of freedom for an entire generation on his own terms. The Black Panther Party, in many of their pronouncements, demanded, "We want freedom" and typically explained it by saying, "We want freedom to determine the destiny of our community." While Sly and the Panthers may not have been the best of friends, they were definitely allies in a cultural revolution taking place on their doorstep.

For the Lumpen to begin their live concert recording with their own rendition of Sly and the Family Stone's definitive song of inclusion, "Dance to the Music," the Panthers were, in their own way, acknowledging what the legendary Bay Area band was professing to the world. "Listen to the voices!" was the chant from the original hit song. A new world of freedom and inclusion was at the doorstep; one only needed to make the move. In music and in politics, the world was tuning in to a new groove, with dreams of giving "all power to the people."

3

"The Lumpen Theme"

James Brown, the Rhythm Revolution, and Black Power

After their introduction following the Freedom Messengers' rousing opening act, the Lumpen storm the stage with a high-energy singing and stepping performance. The instrumental groove takes center stage as "The Lumpen Theme" works around a variation of James Brown's "There Was a Time." Brown's original 1967 composition was in itself a tour de force of raw rhythm, and for many, it is considered the primordial funk groove. The burning track had been rerecorded and released on Brown's live album *Sex Machine* that summer of 1970, and the Lumpen represented the percolating groove with fury and dedication.

As the band jams for the first two minutes, the Lumpen lead members step, spin, stomp, wave, clap, and sing to the beat of the rhythms, coming together for the background verses: "We want freedom / to determine / the destiny / of our community." The energy is high as drummer Minor Williams keeps a steady pulse with guitarist Mack Ray Henderson chopping the strings with a double-time rhythmic riff and bass player Thomas Wallace improvising a bottom bounce that works against the rigid rhythmic lock to make for an irresistible funk groove. The horns sweep over the rhythms with crisp, sustained notes, providing a towering melody that announces the unmistakable influence of James Brown.

As the singers repeat the chant "freedom," bandleader and piano player William Calhoun introduces the group, to the rhythm of the song:

> *Freedom!* / Hah! / *freedom* / Lookie here / *freedom* / James Mott / *freedom* / Michael Torrence / *freedom* / Clark Bailey / *freedom* / Hah! / *freedom* / good God / *freedom* / My name is Bill Calhoun / *freedom* / We're from the Black Panther Party / *freedom* / Hah! / *freedom* / . . . I want you to / *freedom* / to sing along with me.
> We want Freedom / to determine / the destiny / of our community . . .
> Say it louder.
> *We want Freedom / to determine / the destiny / of our community . . .*
> Say it like you mean it.
> *We want freedom / to determine / the destiny / of our community . . .*

The singers then begin a series of chants calling out incarcerated Panther Party members before the band takes over with a stirring, energetic groove session.

> Free Bobby / *freedom* / free Bobby / *freedom* / free Bobby / *freedom* / free Bobby / *freedom* / Free Ericka / *freedom* / Free Ericka / *freedom* / Free Ericka / *freedom* / Free Ericka

Lead singer William Calhoun chants and shouts "good God!" in between the background voices, providing another percussive layer of vocals, and signifying on the rich vein of rhythmic soul music that the band is representing on this night. As the band plays for another two minutes, the singers vary their choruses and continue the percussive vocalizing "hah," "unh unh unh," "hah" until the song is brought to a crisp, sharp ending, followed by sustained crowd applause.[1]

Throughout their thrilling opening song, the Lumpen utilized the standards and techniques of the James Brown band. Through the use of call-and-response audience interaction, the effective use of physicality on stage, the driving rhythms and counter-rhythms by the band, and the percussive improvised vocalizing, the group signified on the rhythms of the streets while framing the political thrust of the Black Panther Party on the people's terms. James Brown at this time was an immensely popular icon of black pride, and to some he was considered a revolutionary artist. By using the James Brown performance aesthetic, the Lumpen were asserting the revolutionary black power of their music. "Everything about my stage production I got from James Brown," recalls Lumpen bandleader William Calhoun.[2] Lumpen singer Michael Torrence recalls:

> I was fourteen when I saw him at the Oakland auditorium. It was one of those shows he used to do, which was really more of a dance than a concert. It was high, high energy, nonstop. James Brown would be driving on you—he really was the hardest-working man in show business, but so was everybody up there with him. And if you were out there in the audience, same thing. So by the time you came out of it, you were ready to take a deep breath too. Once you left, you walk out the concert and say, "Whooo. How 'bout that." So that was the same thing we wanted to do, to have them coming out of Lumpen performances like that, going "Whooo!"[3]

James Brown left an indelible stamp on the collective social values and standards of expression in black American culture. In this sense, Brown and his body of 1960s-era work can be rehabilitated in terms of his impact on black consciousness, and this chapter will reexamine the achievements of James Brown as an agent of black power during the height of the black revolution.

"There Was a Time"

The burning groove chosen by the Lumpen to enter the stage to at their packed Merritt College concert was a staple of the James Brown show at the time. Recorded in June 1967 during a ten-day stint at the Apollo Theater in Harlem, a four-minute version was released as a B-side to the single "I Can't Stand Myself" in late 1967 and became a flip-side hit early in 1968, reaching number three on the R&B charts. The entire fifteen-minute performance was heard when *Live at the Apollo Volume 2* was released in the summer of '68. The song is not so much a song as a rhythm workout, with just a semblance of melody from punching horn riffs to begin the journey. With a hyperactive rhythmic interplay between guitarists Jimmy Nolen and Alphonso "Country" Kellum, and both Clyde Stubblefield and Jabo Starks doubling up on drums (with the addition of bongos, a revolutionary idea for R&B then, played by Ronald Selico), the band keeps an incessant wiggle to the groove, making it impossible to sit still throughout the song. A heavy emphasis on what Brown calls "the One," providing a punch on the downbeat of the song, creates yet another level of rhythmic twist. The Godfather of Soul ad-libs in time with the groove, vamping on dances, places, and party chants over a wicked riff. This song, recorded during the politically heated summer of 1967, is a prime example of James Brown's ability to capture the moment—rhythmically—in black America.

James Brown can be heard improvising a series of rhyming verses to bring about each dance he performs, perhaps introducing the first freestyle rapping of the hip-hop era: "Lookie here, dig this / Now there was a dance / That I used to do / The name of the dance, ha / They call the boogaloo." It was not a simple coincidence that James Brown referred to popular dances during his extemporaneous riffing on the song. Brown was as much a stage performer as a singer. His body was in motion throughout his performances. Members of his audience at this time developed their own sense of motion and rhythm by watching, imitating, and interpreting the incessant motion of Soul Brother Number One. Larry Neal writes:

> The hit song "There Was a Time" traces the history of a people through their dances, and achieves in the process something of a rhythm and blues epic poem. . . . Quoting these lyrics hardly does justice to Brown's genius. He invokes dances like the Camelwalk and the Boogaloo. Each dance conjuring up a definite feeling and memory. Black poetry is best understood, as the powerful force that it is, when it is recited and danced.[4]

James Brown onstage was providing a cultural history in every verse, in every rhymed couplet, celebrating a time and place in black cultural memory that could be collectively referenced through the dance—the collective experience of a people. In his performances—there is no studio recording of "There Was a Time," only live recordings—James Brown was both present and past, a summation of the black experience and a signpost toward a people's future.

Brown, with a forceful emphasis on the rhythmic groove, was forging a new approach to black poetry that would emerge in rap music only a decade later. The hard-driving, rhythm-based American music (funk and hip-hop) of the following decades can trace its existence to the Godfather of Soul and the work he was doing in the late 1960s. As for "There Was a Time," it is ironic that a song with a title referencing the past could reflect so much of what was ahead in the music of America.

James Brown and the Rhythm Revolution

Not enough has been written about what Brown and his band did to revolutionize the rhythms of American music in the 1970s, and by extension the aesthetics and cultural politics of the world's music. Rarely accounted for in his public biography (until his passing on Christmas Day in 2006) is the fact that James Brown was the most prominent popular entertainer to openly promote and celebrate black pride. The music of James Brown in the late 1960s was the single most unifying facet of popular black culture of the time. With recordings such as "Papa's Got a Brand New Bag" in 1965, "It's a Man's Man's Man's World" in 1966, "Cold Sweat" in 1967, "Say It Loud (I'm Black and I'm Proud)" in 1968, and "Mother Popcorn" in 1969, Brown pushed an assertive, black masculine aesthetic into popular music in ways never before heard in America. A decade of Brown's steady musical output and consistently energetic stage shows earned him a reputation as the acknowledged essential musician of the streets. His accolades and self-proclaimed titles such as "the Hardest Working Man in Show Business," "Mr. Dynamite," "Soul Brother Number One," and "the Godfather of Soul" were never seriously disputed.[5]

Brown's music of this period combined no-nonsense, straight-talking delivery with a unique form of rhythmic contrast and tension that exuded confidence, strength, and pride. Brown was at the forefront of a collective race conscious awakening that was taking place in black America at the time. In a 1968 essay, LeRoi Jones (later known as Amiri Baraka) wrote figuratively of Brown's singular ability to transform public space:

> If you play James Brown (say, "Money Won't Change You / but time will take you out") in a bank, the total environment is changed. Not only the sardonic comment of the lyrics, but the total emotional

placement of the rhythm, instrumentation and sound. An energy is released in the bank, a summoning of images that take the bank, and everybody in it, on a trip. That is they visit another place. A place where Black People live.

But dig, not only is it a place where Black People live, it is a place, in the spiritual precincts of its emotional telling, where Black People move in almost absolute openness and strength.[6]

The James Brown experience, whether heard live or on the radio, was one that made public celebrations of blackness plausible, permissible, and overtly enjoyable.

In the early 1960s a new "Negro mood" of hope and pride had entered the public sphere, and Brown's music was a sharp reminder of those aspirations. As the movement became more militarized and assertive, the rhythms of Brown's music captured the essence of that aggression. In a symbolic fashion, in much the same way that the direct talk of Malcolm X served to bring about a direct dialogue about race and equality in society, Brown's late 1960s music pushed against the traditional modes of music making to become something explicit, articulate, and assertive in ways never before heard in popular music. "Don't give me integration / Give me true communication," Brown sang in his 1969 black power opus "I Don't Want Nobody to Give Me Nothin'." "Don't give me sorrow / I want equal opportunity to live tomorrow."

Brown's funk music did not turn the other cheek. It did not speak in metaphors or double meanings (as was the blues tradition), and it did not speak vaguely of longing for the future (as was the gospel music tradition). Brown's music reflected the harsh, unvarnished truths of black American life. Yet Brown was capable of utilizing elements of the black performance tradition to generate transcendent moments of triumph and celebration above all of the trials.

Generally, soul singers were judged by their sincerity and the passion of their delivery. No other artist performed with more conviction, with more force onstage, than the Godfather of Soul. One could feel that James Brown meant what he said. Brown, in reality, did not have to sing a verse to deliver a message. As Ben Sidran writes:

It should be stressed that James Brown's screams and the two drummers he employed to generate an enormous rhythmic dynamism were more revolutionary than were his somewhat controversial lyrics . . . especially because they were not recognized as being revolutionary. The techniques of the oral culture thus met with little opposition and altered the perception, and so the behavior, of young Americans in the privacy of their own homes.[7]

James Brown was at the center of a process of identity formation for a generation (black and white) that was beginning to understand on an intuitive, visceral, personal level what *freedom* was really about.

James Brown was born into poverty in 1933 in a one-room shack outside of Barnwell, South Carolina, and from the age of six was raised in his aunt Handsome "Honey" Washington's brothel in Augusta, Georgia. Living day-to-day meant that at a young age Brown understood the bitter necessities and desperate ambitions of black life in the Jim Crow South. Sentenced to eight years for a petty crime at the age of sixteen, Brown seemed to be headed down the road of many of his contemporaries.

An epiphany involving the possibilities of stage performance led Brown to write to the parole board requesting early release to perform gospel music. Brown's inspired gambit earned him an early release and, with the help of the family of local singer Bobby Byrd, Brown began his singing career in 1952 in the Gospel Starlighters. The Starlighters soon moved to rhythm and blues and changed their name. Once Brown became established as a backup singer and later lead singer of the Famous Flames, he took hold of his career and set new standards for black entertainers at every turn.

His first recording, "Please Please Please" for the King Records subsidiary Federal in 1956, with its sparse lyrics and repetitive soulful begging, remains a testament to Brown's ability to reach people on their own terms. Subsequent recordings such as "Try Me" (1958) and "I'll Go Crazy" (1960) established Brown among the most authentic and charismatic black singers of the day. On October 24, 1962, Brown recorded a live performance at the Apollo Theater in Harlem (just as the Cuban Missile Crisis had gone public). The performance solidified Brown's reputation as an authentic soul singer. As one critic wrote: "The ten-minute-plus rendition of 'Lost Someone' captures the sound of Brown baring his soul with an almost unbearable intensity, which drives the audience into a manic chorus of shouts and screams."[8] The subsequent chart-topping release of the live performance cemented Brown's reputation as Soul Brother Number One.

Throughout the decade, the James Brown performance was a centerpiece of working-class black popular culture. Even in small cities like Sacramento, hometown of Lumpen member James Mott, the influence of JB was supreme:

> I remember the purple satin shirts, the tight pants, the birdies shoes, those little boots. . . . We looked forward to this. We would go to the fields. We picked tomatoes, we picked peaches, cut grapes, I did it all. We would take our little money. We would go buy our James Brown clothes. We would go to his concert. Under twelve or thirteen it was ninety-nine cents to see James Brown at the Memorial Auditorium. . . . And every time he came to town, we would make sure that we were not on restriction, that we were not grounded; we would plan for it a month in advance.[9]

By 1964, Brown had grown frustrated by his label's refusal to grant him a new contract. The success of *Live at the Apollo* should have garnered him a new deal, Brown figured. So Brown took the bold step of recording at another label (Smash) while still under contract to King Records. The legal complications created an impasse that Brown himself crossed by creating some of the greatest music of his life. With promises from King label owner Syd Nathan, Brown returned home with a vengeance.

The February 1965 recording of "Papa's Got a Brand New Bag" was a peace offering to his record label and a turning point in Brown's career. The jerky, percussive recording reflected a change in more than Brown's contract status. Brown was developing a revolutionary new process for making dance music. With important new musicians in the fold, including rhythm guitarist Jimmy Nolen, drummer Melvin Parker, and Melvin's younger brother Maceo Parker on saxophone, Brown packaged the soaring talent into an efficient, propulsive rhythm machine, and Brown surfed the waves with his own particular vocal acrobatics. Brown explained the breakthrough himself:

> I didn't need melody to make music. That was, to me, old fashioned and out of step. I now realized that I could compose and sing a song

that used one chord or at the most two. Although "Papa's Got a Brand New Bag" has just two chords, and a melody sung over what is really a single note, it is just as musical as anything Pavarotti has ever sung. More important, it stood for everything I was about— pride, leadership, strength, intensity. And it went straight to number one on every pop and R&B chart in the world.[10]

Nothing else sounded like this song anywhere on the radio. The groundbreaking, hugely popular song was recorded in Charlotte, North Carolina, in February 1965, the same month Malcolm X was assassinated in Harlem. It was released on July 17, 1965, three weeks before the so-called Watts riots. Papa had a new bag indeed.

"The One"

In what would later be called the first of the funk beats, on "New Bag" Brown and his band developed an exotic new rhythmic orientation, a means of arranging the music around the downbeat. The downbeat is the first pulse in a four-beat bar in Western music, what Brown would call "the One." Most of American popular music to this time had been written around a melody that emphasized the two and the four. Handclaps are applied on the two and the four, employing foot stomps, pauses, or silence on the downbeat. James Brown explained the breakthrough in a 1993 interview: "I turned all of them around because I went on one and three as opposed to the music being written on two and the four. Then I took gospel and jazz and defied all the laws. If I played eight bars and felt like I should play nine or ten, I would play nine or ten. As long as I felt the people grooving."[11]

The new rhythmic emphasis created a choppy, bouncing energy in the music. Songs seemed to percolate over layers of rhythms that had no perceptible starting or stopping points. Brown utilized the One to bring the musicians together, providing structure for rhythm players to improvise around, with a regular reference point. Meanwhile, the horns, keyboards, and vocals were typically written out in traditional songwriting fashion (hum a melody, write a verse, hum a chorus, write lyrics). A young bass player named William "Bootsy" Collins went through a funky musical apprenticeship under the mentorship of Brown when Collins joined the group in March 1970: "He always told me, 'Son, you've got to play it on the one.' And I was like, on the one? What the heck is he talking about? He said, 'On every one, you've got to play a dominant note.' "[12]

By playing melodies and singing in traditional modes that created an expectation of the spaces around the downbeat, Brown was able to redesign black dance music in a unique fashion, creating what is now called "funk." Funk music plays off the rhythmic expectations implied in Western music, yet is driven percussively from a collaborative groove that could go on indefinitely, and as such was allied with the popular dance rhythms of the Caribbean islands and West Africa.

Brown's new approach to music making was rhythm based. Unlike music derived from the blues, it was not built around a melody, or even an implied melody. This music came from the drums, bass, and guitars. And, for the first time in America, this music spoke directly from Africa. "I was hearing everything, even the guitars, like they were drums," Brown recalled in 1986.[13] The direct impact Brown's music had on his predominantly black audience in the late 1960s was an upswelling of unbridled excitement, affirmation, and allegiance.

James Brown knew he was on to something. He understood that Papa's new groove was a game changer. "I had discovered the power of the percussive upbeat," he said. While he was celebrated as a soul singer extraordinaire, he was pushing the limits of self-expression, and he drove his band into the new musical space of funk. Brown explained the scope of his invention of funk music in his compelling 2005 memoir *I Feel Good*:

> It was like opening the floodgates to a rhythm-based extension of soul, a physically performed, roots-derived configuration of music that comes straight from the heart. In that sense, soul became the perfect marching music for the civil rights era, a way to choreograph the burgeoning pride that could be found everywhere. It was, to me, like the jump beat that we always saw in films from Africa, when the Blacks were organizing against Apartheid. We'd always see them jumping in place, with the sound of the drum beneath them, giving them weight, lending them focus, providing them unity.
>
> What was missing for me and my people was the rhythm of our own revolution—a soundtrack strong enough to bring us to the outside rather than keep us on the inside.[14]

Brown, for many, provided a "rhythm of our own revolution" in the late 1960s. It is interesting that in 2005 Brown spoke of "bringing us to the outside" rather than "keeping us on the inside." The essence of Brown's music provided a counterpoint to the integration efforts of the mainstream civil rights movement associated with Martin Luther King Jr. and to the integration-oriented black popular music associated with Motown Records, the popular black-owned soul music label out of Detroit. Brown's music captured the aspirations of young people who were framing a new anti-integrationist impulse of their own. The Watts upheaval in the summer of 1965 and the release of the *Autobiography of Malcolm X* later that year were sentinels of a new spirit of antiassimilation that was emerging within the movement and within black American society. The emergence of the Black Panther Party on the national scene in May 1967 was part of this nationalistic evolution.

On tour through Oakland in the mid-1960s, Brown encountered Donald Warden (now Khalid al-Mansour), who had organized black radical discussion groups through his Afro-American Association and was established on local radio and television. The nationalist Warden was not a fan of the "singing and dancing of black folks," but he saw an opportunity to spread his message through Brown's popularity and invited Brown to his shows and to events in the community. Similarly, Brown saw an opportunity to develop his race-first politics with someone equally media savvy, and the two had frequent discussions about race politics over the years.[15]

In 1966 Brown began recording and releasing "message" songs with direct statements about black self-pride and achievement. "Money Won't Change You" and "Don't Be a Drop-Out" were the first, but there were others to follow. They were delivered with the characteristic rugged rhythms and direct dialogue for which Brown was known. In 1967 Brown and his band stretched the rhythmic contrast even further with the intense rhythms of "There Was a Time" and the inside-out grooving on "Cold Sweat," which provided a new structure and formula for his many followers to aspire to.

Brown's ballads began to radiate with a black masculine aesthetic. His now classic 1966 recording of "It's a Man's Man's Man's World" became a symbol of Brown's approach to black patriarchy. Steeped in emotion and longing, the song captures the listener with its piercing strings and even more piercing screams. In the chorus, Brown exhorts "It's a man's, man's, *man's* world" with such pain that one almost feels he regrets the point, and the following line seems to close the deal: "but it wouldn't be *nothing* / without a woman or a girl." As a demonstration of the soul music aesthetic, Brown appears to almost break down emotionally on the recording. Yet despite the theater, Brown was also revealing his tortured background with women. Having been abandoned by his mother at the age of four and raised by his aunt in a brothel, Brown's family values emerged from a state of crisis that appeared to manifest in his volatile relationships with his three wives. Domestic disturbance calls to local police appeared to confirm an image of a misogynistic, out-of-control black patriarch. Yet Brown understood that his role as a black public figure was to present a public face of black success that he saw as patriarchal, driven, and in control. When Brown ad-libbed lyrics such as "Man makes everything he can / but a woman makes a better man," they fit and reinforced what was seen by many as traditional male patriarchal roles. Brown's personal values resonated with the prevailing black masculine aesthetic of black power on the streets in an unmistakable fashion.[16]

James Brown and Black Power

The concept of "black power" in the American social justice movement of the 1960s followed an awkward path to prominence. Radical black writers and artists such as Harold Cruse and LeRoi Jones explored the concept in articles and plays, yet it did not take on an air of inevitability until the death of Malcolm X and subsequent efforts to organize in the black community. In the summer of 1966, on James Meredith's Freedom from Fear March through Mississippi, Stokely Charmichael introduced the term *black power* to crowds of marchers, initiating polarizing reactions among established activists across races and political persuasions. The march itself was hastily organized as a result of the assassination attempt on James Meredith, who had vowed to walk the 220 miles from Memphis, Tennessee, along the northern border of Mississippi to the capital of Jackson. Meredith was shot on the second day of his march. The resulting notoriety brought the full weight of the civil rights leadership—including James Brown—to organize and rally the community to complete the march for Meredith. Brown flew into Memphis to visit Meredith and performed at Toogaloo College in Jackson in support of the march, which turned out to be one of the sparks for the black power movement.

In his 1986 autobiography *Godfather of Soul*, Brown recalled that period: "There was a lot of ferment going on, and a lot of tension inside and outside the movement. . . . Martin [Luther King] was trying to keep things going in a nonviolent way, and Stokely [Carmichael] and them were starting to talk about Black Power—and upsetting a whole lot of people with it too. Whitney Young and Roy Wilkins pulled out of the march because of it." Brown, however, was unfazed by the implications of the term, and embraced it:

> Black Power meant different things to different people, see. To some people it meant black pride and black people owning businesses and having a voice in politics. That's what it meant to me. To other people it meant self-defense against attacks like the one on Meredith. But to others it meant a revolutionary bag. . . . I wanted to see people free, but I didn't see any reason for us to kill each other.
>
> Stokely [Carmichael] said I was the one person who was most dangerous to his movement at the time because people would listen to me.[17]

In his memoir, Brown refers to his conversations with James Meredith as being the starting point for Brown's forays into social activism. Within days of visiting Meredith, Brown recorded "Money Won't Change You," and later that summer he recorded "Don't Be a Drop-out," which he used as the centerpiece of his social activism. Brown spoke frequently to Vice President Hubert Humphrey and contributed to Humphrey's Stay in School program, visiting schools and telling his story of the value of education. Throughout 1967 Brown found himself a consultant to the White House on issues of race.

1968

The crushing violence and social upheavals of 1968 proved to be a turning point in the careers of many public figures, and Brown was no exception. In February Brown purchased his first radio station, WGYW in

Knoxville, Tennessee. He changed the call letters to WJBE and upgraded
the format of soul, jazz, and gospel music to include news, public affairs,
and children's programs. Brown was adamant about using his clout as a
black entertainer to provide for his community.

During his live stage shows, Brown would frequently bring the
music down and deliver a speech or share some personal sentiments
with the audience. Often Brown would have a local civic leader, activist,
or entertainer come onstage to receive recognition. He did this throughout a weeklong set at the Apollo Theater in March 1968. At one of
the shows he brought his accountant onstage to present a check to the
civil rights organization the Congress of Racial Equality (CORE), and
a check to the H. Rap Brown Defense Fund. H. Rap Brown was one
of the most prominent black militants at the time and was under government harassment for inciting violence. The Louisiana-born Hubert
Brown (now Jamil Abdullah Al-Amin) earned the name "Rap" in the
early 1960s while developing his quick-witted rhyming style and playing
the dozens with his neighborhood homies. He attended Southern University and quickly emerged as an activist leader. He was elected chair
of the Student Nonviolent Coordinating Committee (SNCC) in 1967,
replacing Stokely Carmichael. Rap Brown followed Carmichael's path
of making proclamations of black power, and he urged direct action to
challenge the racial status quo. At one rally in Cambridge, Massachusetts, in June 1967, Rap Brown directly challenged protestors to take
over some white-owned businesses: "I don't care if you have to burn him
down or run him out, you better take over them stores." Shortly after
Rap Brown left Cambridge, fires broke out in the district Rap Brown
appeared to have threatened. Rap Brown was charged with arson and
inciting a riot and was in and out of jails and courtrooms through the
end of the decade.

Rap Brown was a compelling speaker with a penchant for memorable one-liners. Among his most famous were: "Violence is as American
as cherry pie" and "If America don't come around, we're gonna burn it
down." Rap Brown was well versed in street slang and had a massive
following of young and antiestablishment supporters. James Brown, perhaps ironically, was among them. Brown wrote, "I disagreed with Rap
about a lot of things, but I also didn't like the way the government was
harassing him. And as bad as things were getting, I thought we needed to

stick together. I was against violence, but I was not against self-defense."[18] Brown's open dialogue with black power militants made him a singularly equipped black celebrity to respond when the masses exploded.

In late March, Brown visited Africa for the first time as a guest of the president of the Ivory Coast (now Côte d'Ivoire), Félix Houphouët-Boigny. There he got a taste of his formidable global cultural influence as a successful black American entertainer.

> When I got there and got off the plane, I felt I was on land I should have been on much earlier. The Africans were full of pride and dignity, and they were very warm, too. It was hard to believe that they knew my music. . . . We were there for only two days, but I was overwhelmed by the spirit of the place. I think it made me understand some things about my roots as well.[19]

Brown landed in New York City on Tuesday, April 2, planning to sleep off his lengthy flight and prepare for a big night at the Boston Garden on Friday. Brown's sleep was interrupted on Thursday with the news that Martin Luther King Jr. had been shot in Memphis. Brown had to cope with the news, figure out how to grieve, prepare to move forward with the concert, and help to ameliorate the state of his own people. James Brown was in crisis-management mode throughout that weekend and the days that followed. Local officials wanted to cancel the concert, a plan that would just as likely have sent thousands of outraged blacks into downtown Boston without a place to go.

A deal was struck: the local PBS affiliate would broadcast the James Brown concert from the Boston Garden that night, and James Brown fans would be urged to stay home to watch an entire, uncut performance on television. The event, and the complex negotiations between a desperate big-city mayor and a former shoeshine boy from Augusta revealed just how much leverage the Godfather of Soul had amassed. The show would go on.

After some somber introductions by black city councilman Thomas Atkins—the first black city official elected in Boston in the century—and a stark plea from Mayor Kevin White, James Brown ushered in the band on cue and began his regular show. The James Brown Revue was a finely tuned operation, with Brown running his band with split-second efficiency. Despite the horrors of the past few hours, James Brown produced a top-notch performance, replete with exhilarating dance steps, smiling banter with his band, a delightfully sensual interlude with Marva Whitney, and the awkward comedy routines of Maceo Parker. These things could all be considered out of step with the somber moment, but Brown had to carry on and had to bring the audience up with his own brand of entertainment. James Brown had a lot on his mind that night:

> Throughout the show, between songs, I talked about Dr. King and urged the people to stay calm. I announced a song title and tried to work the title into a little rap about Dr. King and the whole situation. I talked about my own life and where I'd come from. At one point, when I was reminiscing about Martin, I started to cry—just a few tears rolling out, you know, nothing anybody could really see— but it was like it was all starting to really sink in what we lost. But I pulled myself together—I thought that would do the most good— and went on with the show.
>
> "I'm still a soul brother," I said at one point, "and you people have made it possible for me to be a first class man in all respects. I used to shine shoes in front of a radio station. Now I own radio stations. You know what that is? That's Black Power."[20]

As Brown entered into his finale, the crowd became understandably excited, and some began to rush the stage. Initially they were politely restrained by security, but as things progressed, one white security officer shoved a young black audience member into the crowd, almost inciting a riot at the moment. Brown had to stop the music, raise the lights, and admonish the audience—and let the security officials know that he had control of the situation. Brown addressed the crowd, and the viewing audience in Boston, and patiently but authoritatively kept the place from turning to chaos.

By breaking down the show and taking charge of the moment, Brown used his considerable clout not only to maintain order at his venue, but also to address the seething frustrations of a people so deeply wounded that night. As chaotic as the moment was, the interlude was necessary for a grieving audience to witness: soul about to explode kept contained by the Godfather of Soul himself. Brown's cool but assertive command of the crisis was striking, as Martin Luther King himself had trouble containing unruly crowds during his final years. But Brown did not utilize religious or moral grounds to pacify his audience. Brown understood the raw racial tone of the moment, and he addressed his people accordingly: "We're black" he told the seething, grieving crowd, "we're black, we're black, I know I can get some respect from my own people." Brown got the respect of the people—and the respect of the authorities, who understood the unique hold James Brown had on his people.

The next day Brown was in Washington, DC, to speak to another unruly crowd that had just spent the previous night torching black neighborhoods in the city. In all, riots in 110 cities shook the nation in the aftermath of King's murder. Boston was one of the few major cities that was not torched that sad weekend. Brown spent the rest of the spring telling Negroes in ravaged cities across the country, "learn, don't burn." His ongoing relationship with Vice President Humphrey helped solidify James Brown's self-image as a voice of his people in a critical time. Yet the overture was not universally praised. In addition, Brown's release of a fairly patriotic song, "America Is My Home," that summer sparked friction from his progressive supporters who were forging a deep critique of the American experiment at that time.

James Brown then made a fateful decision. He pushed forward with his plan to play for the American troops stationed in Vietnam. Brown had seen this as a no-brainer, an effort to do his patriotic duty as well as showcase his status as a national and international talent. He had repeatedly sought to travel with the regular USO organizations but was denied. In June 1968 he obtained permission from the State Department to take a small group and perform for the troops. The trip could be seen both as triumphant and tragic. The band performed in Japan and Korea, which helped to internationalize his appeal, and Brown took a small entourage to Vietnam, playing to troops directly in the fighting zone, literally dodging bullets to get from show to show. Upon his return, Brown was treated with disdain by the very community he sought to uplift. He was seen by many as a lackey of the Lyndon Johnson administration, which had supported the Vietnam war, while the vast majority of young people and African Americans opposed it.

Determined to perform there for "all of the troops" and not just the black ones, James Brown risked his reputation, and his life, in the poorly secured war zone to perform to thrilled GIs. Brown and his band did not enjoy the support of the US government at any level for his gesture.

"I was packed and ready to go," recalls Alfred "Pee Wee" Ellis, James Brown's saxophonist, regarding the Vietnam trip. "Then at midnight the night before we were to leave, I got a call from the FBI. They said that I had an outstanding drug warrant against me from high school, and I couldn't leave the country." In retrospect, the level of engagement by the federal government into the actions of a rhythm and blues band in 1967 is striking.[21] Brown later claimed, quite accurately it turns out, that he was put under federal surveillance after the Vietnam trip.

"Say It Loud"

As was his custom during the early years of his career, Brown constantly engaged with local leaders, activists, entertainers, and interested locals in the communities in which he performed. After-hours talks in his dressing room, while often entertainment-related, could quickly become a hot spot for debates regarding nationalism, blackness, militancy, violence, Vietnam, and black capitalism. Brown encountered members of the Black Panther Party and other black radical organizations that urged him to deliver a more direct political message. One account by Brown sideman Hank Ballard states that "machine-gun-toting Black Panthers" intimidated Brown into writing direct message songs. Brown denied the claim but in his autobiography writes of finding a grenade at his door in a hotel in Los Angeles in 1968.[22] Progressive leaders questioned Brown's politics, and in an interview, journalist Earl Wilson asked Brown directly what it was like to be called an Uncle Tom. By the summer of 1968 James Brown knew he was under fire to deliver an unmistakable message song.

In early August, James Brown went to Los Angeles to appear on the *Joey Bishop Show*. The next day, August 7, 1968, Brown went to the Vox studio on Melrose Street in Los Angeles, had some staffers gather some children (few, if any, were black) to sing a chorus, and set about the recording of one of his most important records. Trombonist Fred Wesley's first recording experience with Brown was on this song. In his autobiography, *Hit Me, Fred: Recollections of a Sideman*, Wesley recalls the event:

> Just then, Mr. Bobbitt, the road manager and a bunch of people, mostly kids, walked into the studio. We stopped playing, and Mr.

Brown went over and greeted them like he had expected them. I had no idea what they had to do with this recording. . . .

Mr. Brown was in control now. Pee Wee took his place in the reed section, and James counted it off. The groove was already strong, but when James counted it off and began to dance and direct it, it took on a new power. All of a sudden, the fatigue I had been feeling was gone. The kids were doing their chant with a new energy. In fact the energy level in the whole studio was lifted. James went straight through the whole tune and that was it. After about four hours of preparation, "Say It Loud, I'm Black and I'm Proud" went down in one take.[23]

The song hit the airwaves on August 16, less than two weeks after its one-take recording session. Brown incorporated it into his tour across Texas that same week, rousing the crowd to chant "I'm black and I'm proud!" On September 14, "Say It Loud" was in stores, soaring to number one.

The impact of "Say It Loud" could be felt everywhere. It is not an exaggeration to say that the song may have been the most important black popular music recording ever released. " 'I'm Black and I'm Proud,' that was the most beautiful thing that ever happened!" recalls guitarist Mack Ray Henderson. "Because before that, it was 'I'm black and I'm ashamed!' "[24] In October 1968, when Olympic athletes Tommie Smith and John Carlos raised their black-gloved, clenched fists on the victory stand in Mexico City during the playing of the national anthem—the effect itself causing a surge in black pride—"Say It Loud—I'm Black and I'm Proud" had just peaked as the number one R&B song in the country.

The record was also a crossover hit and garnered pop radio airplay as well as a couple of awkward television performances in front of predominantly white audiences. James Brown performed the song on ABC television on Hugh Hefner's *Playboy After Dark* in front of a roomful of scantily dressed women, who chanted the chorus of the song with gusto. Brown's lifelong friend Al Sharpton described the impact of the song: "He made people all over the world, whites in America, Asians, like black music and identify with it. He had them actually singing 'I'm black and I'm proud,' people that weren't even remotely black, didn't know what the chant meant to be black in America."[25] Because of Brown's mainstream popularity, the song was heard everywhere.

However, the song would be James Brown's last pop top-ten hit for the next seventeen years.

"Say It Loud" proved to be a turning point in black popular music and a watershed in black popular culture. Black popular music up until that point had not reflected the bitterness of blacks toward the white man in such explicit fashion. Other, more somber critiques of white supremacy, such as Billie Holiday's 1939 "Strange Fruit" and John Coltrane's "Alabama" in 1963, were powerful in their own way, but they were melancholy and steeped in the blues. Nina Simone's blistering 1964 performance of "Mississippi Goddam" worked as a show-tune parody and certainly reflected the bitterness of the southern civil rights struggle. Brown, on the other hand, was triumphant. The subtle symbolism of the other upbeat civil rights era songs such as "People Get Ready" and "Dancing in the Streets" gave way to Brown's lyrical form of direct action: "Now we demand a chance to do things for ourself / We're tired of beatin' our head against the wall' / And workin' for someone else" was one of the revealing verses. Brown concluded the song with his trademark fire: "We're people, we're just like the birds and the bees / We'd rather die on our feet / Than be livin' on our knees." "Say it LOUD," he demanded, and the chorus of young people *shouted* back, "I'm black and I'm PROUD!" It was one thing to be accepting of one's own worth, but to shout to the world that, as a member of a once-derided race, you were now black and proud was an entirely new and triumphant state. Brown also captured the tenor of the times, using a phrase his father had taught him: "We would rather die on our feet than be livin' on our knees." Brown brought it into the movement of the sixties with vibrant new meaning.[26]

"Say It Loud" popularized the term *black* as the proper and preferred nomenclature for African Americans across the country and across the generations and finally ushered the term *Negro* out of mainstream use. In previous eras, to call someone black was a deeply seated term of derision in the community; to empower and liberate the word helped to liberate an entire population. The term *Negro* was an anachronism when it appeared on the 1970 census as the official designation of choice for African American citizens. Al Sharpton commented after Brown's passing: "There were many in the movement who wanted to raise the consciousness of black America from Negro to black. James Brown did it with one song. He could reach the masses much quicker than a lot of the leaders."[27]

"Say It Loud" captured the possibilities inherent in the soul aesthetic, the idea that black entertainment could generate another level of consciousness in its listeners. Further, the prevalence of Africanized rhythms aligned Brown's music with a musical tradition that had deep roots in moralizing through the music. In a sense, Brown made far more connections with his opus than he originally anticipated.

James Brown's song was not entirely revered by black radicals. While the Black Panthers recognized James Brown to be a consummate entertainer, their official doctrine on his black power sloganeering was that it was a superficial effort. Oakland Panther Linda Harrison wrote a critical essay in a 1969 issue of the *Black Panther*, "On Cultural Nationalism," where she treated James Brown's hit song as a distraction from the real revolution:

> In the United States, cultural nationalism can be summed up in James Brown's words—'I'm Black and I'm Proud.' . . . Those that believe in the 'I'm Black and Proud' theory—believe that there is dignity inherent in wearing naturals; that a buba makes a slave a man. . . . A man who lives under slavery and any of its extensions rarely regains his dignity by rejecting the clothiers of his enslaver; he rarely regains his dignity except by a confrontation on equal grounds with his enslaver.[28]

The Black Panther Party saw itself as going beyond cultural nationalism, beyond identity politics, toward revolutionary action. The Panthers had their reasons at the time for disparaging cultural nationalism (see chapter 5), but Harrison's position and the Panthers' public posture of dismissing the party music of James Brown perpetuated the illusion that the Panthers, as revolutionaries, would not dance. Had the Lumpen managed to release their live album and become nationally known, they might have completely shattered that stoic image of the Panthers and through their performance given recognition to the impact of James Brown on black American life and culture.

For Brown himself, "Say It Loud" turned his career upside down. He stopped receiving offers to play in predominantly white venues. He rarely was invited to perform in the pop festivals, was given no more movie appearances, and with the exception of a few invitations from liberal TV talk show hosts, largely disappeared from the pop apparatus. Brown discussed this in 1986:

> The song cost me a lot of my crossover audience. The racial makeup of my concerts was mostly black after that. I don't regret recording it, though, even if it was misunderstood. It was badly needed at the time. It helped the Afro-Americans in general and the dark-skinned man in particular. I'm proud of that.[29]

While James Brown never showed regret for recording the song that turned his career on its head, he did lament the implication that "Say It Loud" was fodder for a militant uprising. This was not Brown's vision of black pride. "Say It Loud" popularized black radicalism and indirectly served to sanction the activities of publicly known black radicals such as H. Rap Brown, Stokely Carmichael, Eldridge Cleaver, Seale, and Newton. Many of their books, such as Cleaver's *Soul on Ice* (1968) and Hamilton and Charmichael's *Black Power* (1967), were selling well—in addition to the *Autobiography of Malcolm X* (1965)—and now it seemed that James Brown had provided the movement with a black power soundtrack.

Within a year of the release of Brown's song, there were black pride anthems appearing on the airwaves from black-oriented radio stations. The Temptations' "Message from a Black Man," the Impressions' "Choice of Colors," and Sly and the Family Stone's "Don't Call Me Nigger, Whitey," presented an entirely new discourse across the racial divide in 1969. Frank discussions of racial inequality were commonplace in the daily lives of black people, and in part because of Brown they were increasingly common in mainstream black popular music.

Brown's song generated interest in music that could "tell it like it is," and the song energized the careers of radical poets and jazz musicians who had been seeking a larger space for their fiery antiracist, anti-integrationist, and often blatantly antiwhite works to be heard. In 1969 the political novelist and jazz poet Gil Scott-Heron was given a contract by legendary jazz and pop producer Bob Thiele to record a night of his political poetry backed by a jazz ensemble. Thiele was responsible for many of the classic 1960s sides by John Coltrane. The inner fire heard in avant-garde jazz as instrumental music was now exploding with the black fire of a new breed of righteous, straight-talking jazz poets. The recording of *Small Talk at 125th and Lenox* provided an early rendition of Gil Scott-Heron's anthem of outrage and anticommercialism, "The Revolution Will Not Be Televised."

Gil Scott-Heron was born in Chicago in 1949. After his parents divorced, he was raised by his grandmother in rural Tennessee. Scott-Heron witnessed southern racism firsthand as one of the first grade-schoolers to integrate the schools in Jackson, Tennessee. He spent his teenage years in the chaos of early 1960s Harlem and was writing biting poetry and fiction between stints in college. Once he began recording, a new tone of angry black soul emerged in his work. Gil Scott-Heron produced music with an angular, righteous voice of discontent that captured the imagination of a rebellious generation. Through Thiele's Flying Dutchman records, Scott-Heron would release such biting jazz poetry as "Whitey on the Moon," "Home Is Where the Hatred Is," and "Who'll Pay Reparations on My Soul?" Developing a musical collaboration with fellow Lincoln University student Brian Jackson, throughout the 1970s the two recorded many socially conscious—and funky—rhythm and blues songs such as "Johannesburg," "The Bottle," "Angel Dust," and "B-Movie." Gil Scott-Heron would go on to become one of the most important politically oriented black artists of his generation.

A New York–based stable of militant writers known as the Last Poets brought their radical street verse, recorded with minimal accompaniment (typically just a conga player), and became iconic voices of a violent time. They used their words to imagine a violent black uprising on songs such as "When the Revolution Comes," "Black People What Y'all Gonna Do," and "Niggers Are Scared of Revolution," while expressing antiwhite enmity in works such as "Opposites" and "The White Man's Got a God Complex."

"We tried to keep that whole sense of revolutionary thought alive," founding member Abiodun Oyewole recalled in 2009.

Are we ready to be together, are we ready to live, are we ready to die in order to live better? I mean it was like some heavy questions but it was all about black people coming together finally and trying to get rid of the negative aspects.

Now those negative aspects became the nigger. The whole movement of the Last Poets was to "de-niggerify" black people. A nigger is slovenly, a nigger is unreliable. We didn't wage war against white people, we waged war against black people that were not being black, and those people were niggers.[30]

The Last Poets began when three New York street poets—Gylan Kain, Felipe Luciano, and Abiodun Oyewole—came together for a 1968 memorial on Malcolm X's birthday, May 19. They named themselves the Last Poets, referencing a concept from the South African–born Harlem poet Keorapetse "Willie" Kgositsile, who foretold that when the inevitable uprising began, the writers would become the soldiers. The group believed that their efforts signified that they were the last of the poets before the cleansing. "The Last Poets, the last words before the guns start talking," as Alafia Purdim stated.[31]

They began to work out of a Harlem art space they called East Wind. The volatile ensemble quickly grew, splintered, and diverged into two groups. One incarnation of the Last Poets, consisting of Oyewole, Umar Bin Hassan, and Alafia Purdim, recorded a groundbreaking album engineered by rock producer Alan Douglas that sold 400,000 copies on the strength of Ben Hassan's iconic rap "Niggers Are Scared of Revolution." Another faction, calling itself the "Original" Last Poets, composed of Kain, Luciano, and David Nelson, produced an album and film of their works in 1970 that included tracks such as "Die Nigger," "Into the Streets," and a track titled "James Brown," a tribute to the Godfather's singular impact on black identity. The passionate poem refers to "James Brown the witch doctor" who "screams, falls, scoops the moon from the river" and "showers the power of his cold sweat as his sweat becomes the river!" The crescendo of screams at the conclusion expresses the centrality of the pure soul force that James Brown delivered to his audience, an audience that included the Original Last Poets.

Collectively, the Last Poets' first three albums and film of poetry in performance (all released between 1969 and 1971) reveal both the popularity of black radicalism and the increasing militancy found in black popular entertainment. While the membership of the Last Poets would vary through the years, their incendiary poems of black revolutionary consciousness were released to wide acclaim and became known

The Lumpen
publicity photos

(Left to right) James Mott, William Calhoun, Michael Torrence, Clark Bailey.

Photos by Ducho Dennis, courtesy of It's About Time Archive

The Lumpen in action at the Memorial Auditorium at Merritt College
in Oakland (above) and in Brownsville, New York (below).
Photo by Ducho Dennis, courtesy of It's About Time Archive (top); Stephen Shames/POLARIS Images (bottom)

Lumpen at Defermery Park in Oakland, 1970. They are performing the skit involving police brutality and the resistance of brothers off the block.
Stephen Shames/POLARIS Images

THE ARAB STUDENTS-ASSOCIATION PRESENTS

THE LUMPEN & *THE FREEDOM MESSENGERS*
Revolutionary Musicians

FROM THE BLACK PANTHER PARTY

PLUS

THE VANGUARDS
Revolutionary Jazz Ensemble

Donation $2.00

8:30 SATURDAY JANUARY 23
PAULEY BALLROOM U.C. BERKELEY

FREE BOBBY

THE LUMPEN

Flyer for the Lumpen performance at UC Berkeley, sponsored by the Arab Students' Association.
From the H.K. Yuen Social Movement Archive, UC Berkeley. Courtesy Lincoln Cushing/Docs Populi.

The Lumpen perform in San Francisco. (Left to right) Mott, Torrence, and Bailey, with Calhoun at the piano. Note saxophone player Raheem Roach and trumpeter David Levinson.
Photo by Ducho Dennis, courtesy of It's About Time Archive

The Lumpen backstage at Merritt College

Bailey, Mott, Torrence, and Calhoun getting ready (top).
Michael Torrence prepares to take the stage with Bailey looking on (bottom left).
Calhoun, Bailey, and Torrence in a lighter moment (bottom right).

Photos by Ducho Dennis, courtesy of It's About Time Archive

William Calhoun, leader of the Lumpen, at the studio controls at the Tiki Studios, San Jose, 1970, recording the single.

Photo by Ducho Dennis, courtesy of It's About Time Archive

Torrence, Mott, "Sister Candace," Calhoun, and Bailey.

Photo by Ducho Dennis, courtesy of It's About Time Archive

Calhoun with studio musicians at a Lumpen rehearsal.

Photo by Ducho Dennis, courtesy of It's About Time Archive

Drummer Minor Williams.

Photo by Ducho Dennis, courtesy of It's About Time Archive

James Mott (second from left) and Michael Torrence (center) in formation with other Panthers at the United Front Against Fascism Conference in Berkeley in 1969.
Photo by Ducho Dennis, courtesy of Its About Time Archive

Panthers on duty

James Mott and Clark Bailey coordinate a free food giveaway at the Black Community Survival Conference at Bobby Hutton Park in Oakland in 1972.
Courtesy of Department of Stanford Special Collections and University Archives, Stanford University Libraries

Lumpen members Mott, Bailey, and Torrence generating music in support of the 1971 Cal Pak boycott. This famous photo appeared in *Jet* magazine in 2011.
Stephen Shames/POLARIS Images

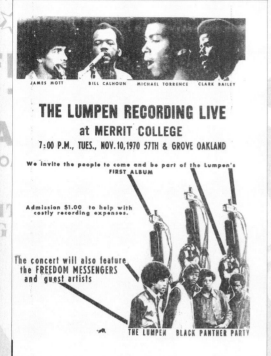

Flyer for the Lumpen concert discussed in the text.
Courtesy of It's About Time Archives

Full-page advertisement for the Lumpen in the *Black Panther* from December 1970. *Courtesy of It's About Time Archives*

Flyer for Ladies Choice, a singing group featured on tour with Marvin Gaye in 1974. Michael Torrence is directly to the left of Marvin Gaye, in the center.
Photo courtesy of It's About Time Archives

The Lumpen in present day: (left to right) Bailey, Torrence, Mott, Calhoun.
Photo courtesy of Ayesha Walker Photography

Mott, Bailey, Calhoun, and Torrence reunite for the first time in forty-two years.
Photo courtesy of Ayesha Walker Photography

as precursors of the politically charged rap music that would emerge from the Bronx a decade later.

With Brown's recording of "Say It Loud" and the explosion of musical militancy that appeared to follow it, one might have concluded that James Brown had entered the movement. As the most popular black entertainer of the decade, James Brown was a celebrity of undisputed credibility with his audience. His message songs, charitable contributions, investments in black businesses such as soul food restaurants and black radio stations, made Brown an indispensable icon of black success and social responsibility. In 1969 *Look* magazine published a cover story on Brown, and along with his picture on the cover was the curious phrase, "Is James Brown the most important Black man in America?"[32]

Brown's music influenced the entirety of the black music spectrum, including the Motown standard bearers. A young Michael Jackson emulated Brown's dances during the Jackson 5's audition for the storied Motown label in 1968. Jazz musicians expanded their repertoire to include rhythm-driven instrumentals inspired by Brown's supremely talented backing band. Brown's performance was one space where blacks of all political and economic persuasions could enter and be validated.

Brown was also the envy of the burgeoning Black Arts movement. The poets and playwrights, visual artists, novelists, social theorists, and jazz critics that composed a palpable wave of new black arts activity in major cities saw Brown as the pinnacle of what the black arts could become if properly directed. Amiri Baraka referred to Brown as "Our No. 1 black poet."[33] Black Arts movement activist Larry Neal explained Brown's influence in a 1987 essay that summarized the "Social Background to the Black Arts Movement" of the 1960s:

> We began to listen to the music of the rhythm and blues people, soul music. . . . The big hero for the poets was James Brown. We all thought that James Brown was a magnificent poet, and we all envied him and wished we could do what he did. If the poets could do that, we would just take over America. Suppose James Brown had consciousness. We used to have big arguments like that. It was like saying, "Suppose James Brown read Fanon."[34]

To imagine Brown reading Frantz Fanon is of particular interest, as the Martinique-born psychologist and theorist of a "Third World Revolution" was required reading in the political education classes in the formative years of the Black Panther Party. Fanon's 1961 opus, *Wretched of the Earth*, written as he was battling cancer as well as working alongside the Algerian resistance against French colonial rule, was for many the bible of the Third World revolution. That book and other of his writings resonated because of Fanon's ability to deconstruct the psychology of colonization, which girded Fanon's prescriptions for violence in the overturning of the colonial state. *Wretched of the Earth* was popular worldwide and was widely read in the United States once it was translated in 1963. For the Black Panthers—who were Fanonists in a very strong sense—to produce a James Brown–styled band like the Lumpen speaks volumes about the potential—the revolutionary potential—of the music, of the culture, of the people. Larry Neal's fanciful notion of James Brown reading Fanon was perhaps best incarnated in the music and performances of the Lumpen.

The revolutionary potential of a funky black entertainer was not missed by the state. Brown was correct when he assumed he was put under surveillance in 1968. In a siege of his finances initiated by the FBI, the IRS, and the FCC, Brown was forced to sell off his radio stations, private property, and the lease to his private jet plane to pay millions of dollars in back taxes he claimed he knew nothing about. Despite his public appearances with Presidents Johnson and Nixon and Vice President Humphrey (or perhaps because of them), nothing could stop the pressure applied to him by the federal government. Brown discussed this in 2005:

> It has since been proved that J. Edgar Hoover, with who knows whose permission, had a mandate to prevent the rise in America of a new Black leader. All of us who were Black and in the public eye were put under intense surveillance, harassed by the IRS, and subjected to all forms of underhanded activities to discredit us in an effort to take away our hard-earned money, and therefore our potential political power. No matter what it took.
>
> Sure enough, I suddenly had new troubles with the IRS. Out of nowhere—or at least it seemed that way to me—they claimed I owed four million dollars in back taxes, which was crazy. There's no

other word for it (except maybe prejudicial, vindictive, politically motivated, etc.) . . . The next thing I knew, the IRS and the FCC had taken away the rest of my few remaining radio stations in order to satisfy that tax lien. In doing so, they also happened to silence one of the strongest and most vital voices that spoke directly to America's Black community.[35]

In 1970 Brown's amassed wealth and public presence as a black media entrepreneur was a highly admired aspect of Brown's cultural leadership. While his many business ventures often appeared haphazard, to many of Brown's fans it appeared inexplicable that a steadfast black capitalist of the stature of Brown, whose properties were well known and admired throughout the black community, could manage to lose control of his empire within a few short years. It was later revealed that Brown was a victim of the Special Services Committee of the IRS, which illegally spied on US citizens in an effort to harass, discredit, and destroy political opponents of President Richard Nixon. In 1974 a congressional investigation of the doomed Nixon administration found that, at the request of the president, the IRS illegally spied on thousands of individuals and organizations that it claimed harbored "extremist views and philosophies." The investigation produced a list with more than eleven thousand names. James Brown's name was on it. While Brown continued to record and perform worldwide, his empire was quietly dismantled, and his ability to build a black-oriented economic infrastructure based upon his vast popularity was sabotaged. It was done quietly, but a case can be made that Brown was seen by the government as a political threat and was made an example by forces beyond his control specifically because he was a black entertainer with a political vision for his people.[36]

James Brown and Third World Revolution

The amount of state repression imposed on black entertainers who had the potential to energize, politicize, and call to action their constituency leaves intriguing evidence as to how much of a threat to the social order these individuals appeared to be. Robert Nesta (Bob) Marley, the Jamaican singer and adherent to Rastafarianism, for example, was known worldwide for music that railed against an unjust social system. Marley delivered reggae, a hypnotic, humanistic brand of rhythm-based music, to the world. Although Marley remained publicly neutral about Jamaican politics, his musical message of redemption for the impoverished was closer to that of the socialist-leaning Jamaican prime minister, Michael Manley. Street gang violence was rampant at the time, but the 1976 shooting attempt on Bob Marley's life, only days before a massive Smile Jamaica concert supported by Manley and only weeks before national elections, was considered by many to have been initiated by Manley's opponent, Edward Seaga. Bob Marley's visibility and perceived influence in Jamaican politics revealed the significance of Marley's power as an entertainer.[37]

While he is recognized worldwide as a creative visionary, much of Bob Marley's musical orientation owes a debt to black American soul music in general, and James Brown in particular. Many of the vocals in Jamaican popular music are finely crafted interpretations of American R&B, sung over the syncopated rhythms of the island. The early 1960s Jamaican singing groups, including Bob Marley and the Wailers, initially had the look and feel of doo-wop singers in the states.

But the music of Jamaica has always had a heartbeat pulse to it. Reggae is an amalgam of Western pop melodies and harmonies performed over traditional African-rooted rhythms. "The basic parts of the music were the drum and the bass. Because you know drums are the first instruments in music. So the drum is the heartbeat, and the bass is the backbone," says Wailers bass player Aston Barrett. "Reggae is a concept of all different types of music," Barrett continues. "You got funk, you got rhythm and blues, you got soul, and it's very jazzy, when it's ready."[38]

In the 1950s the rhythms of Jamaican music were heavily influenced by British pop music and the swinging rhythms of ska music that combined gentle calypso-styled syncopations with a two-step swing borrowed from jazz. Marley biographer Timothy White asserts that it was the music of James Brown that influenced Jamaican musicians to abandon the Euro-pop influenced ska sound in favor of a more roots-oriented, downtempo rhythm of rocksteady (a direct precursor to the edgier riddims of reggae). When American rhythm and blues developed a more assertive rhythmic foundation in the mid-1960s, Jamaican musicians followed suit. Brown's focus on the One was a key to the transformation of American popular music, and evidently Jamaican music as well. In *Catch a Fire*, the definitive biography of Bob Marley, White claims: "Marley was on target when he linked James Brown with the transition, since R&B was to ska what soul was to rock steady."[39]

Bob Marley spent most of 1966 in the United States, living with his mother in Delaware. There, he soaked up the sounds of soul music on the radio and developed a deeper sense of his own style, as well as a keen affection for the smooth croonings of Curtis Mayfield and the raw soul of James Brown. (Ironically, Marley missed the much-heralded April 21, 1966, visit to Jamaica by Ethiopian emperor Haile Selassie, the legendary "King of Kings" to the Rastafarians, whose worldview Marley was beginning to immerse himself in.) When Marley returned to Jamaica in the fall, he is said to have told Bunny Wailer that he "no longer wanted to be a smooth singer, but rather he preferred to be a rough and militant vocalist like James Brown."[40] In 1969 Marley and his group recorded a militant race pride oriented single, "Black Progress," which featured verses from Brown's "Say It Loud—I'm Black and I'm Proud," some Brown-influenced black power chants, and an opening guitar riff from Sam and Dave's "Soul Man."

On the first album attributed to Bob Marley and the Wailers, called *Soul Rebel*, Marley is heard shouting out black American popular dances like the mashed potato, the funky chicken, and the alligator on the song "Soul Almighty." The album also features an interpolation of James Brown's "Try Me." Soul was an undeniably strong influence on Bob Marley (and most Jamaican musicians), and Marley was an avid follower of the Godfather's music, as he stated in a 1975 interview:

> People like I, we love James Brown an' love your funky stuffs, an' we dig inta dat American bag. We didn't want ta stand around playin' dat slower ska beat anymore. De young musician, deh had a different beat—dis was rock steady now! Eager ta go![41]

That "slower ska beat" would develop into a downbeat as a result of American R&B, and the work of James Brown. In America, Brown is the one credited with pushing R&B into what was called *soul*. Brown's adaptation of funky rhythms and his unapologetic and urgent celebrations of pride and pleas for social justice served to push a new worldview onto an international audience that was searching for a method to voice its own aspirations.

"The African James Brown"

Brown's influence traversed the Atlantic as well. The Nigerian bandleader Fela Anikulapo Kuti gained worldwide prominence as a musician playing his own variation of the popular highlife African music style in the 1970s, employing the techniques of music popular among the people combined with explicit messages of resistance to oppression. This world-renowned bandleader and social critic developed a strong stance against what he saw as corruption within the Nigerian government in the 1970s. On extended tracks like "ITT (International Thief Thief)," "Coffin for Head of State," and "Teacher Don't Teach Me Nonsense," Kuti railed against the colonial mentality of the elites in his land and abroad, openly preaching that music is the weapon for social change.

Kuti's career, like that of many West African musicians, was heavily influenced by James Brown. As one of the most popular artists in Africa in the 1960s and 1970s, James Brown's highly percussive rhythms, fiercely aggressive vocals, and improvisations carried over radio in Africa and had a transfixing and transforming effect on the younger generations. As African nations such as Ghana, Nigeria, and Côte d'Ivoire sought out their political independence, the strikingly anti-Western (yet still Western) music of James Brown was exhilarating. From city to city on the west coast of Africa in the mid to late 1960s, American soul music was the dominant musical entertainment form, and James Brown was the undisputed king. James Brown imitators with names like Geraldo Pino, Pepe Dynamite, "Elvis J. Brown," and "James Brown Jr." performed regularly along the African west coast, competing in scream contests and soul contests along the way. Fela Kuti saw it all happening and tried to find his own space.

> Soul music took over. James Brown's music, Otis Redding took over the whole continent, man. It was beautiful music though, I must agree. I said to myself, I must compete with these people. I must find a name for my music, so I gave my music [the name] "afrobeat" to give it an identity.[42]

Seeking to expand his music beyond an imitation of Africanized soul music, Kuti traveled to the United States to study jazz. However, he arrived at the height of the black revolution in 1969. In Los Angeles, Kuti met the young activist Sandra Smith (later Sandra Isadore), who had ties to the Black Panther Party. Her influence on Fela Kuti would change the world's music. Smith exposed Kuti to the works of Malcolm X, Stokely Carmichael, Martin Luther King Jr., and Elijah Muhammad. They were a revelation to Kuti, who would return to Africa on a mission to energize his audience with politically conscious music under the slogan "Music Is the Weapon." Kuti explained the revelation of Malcolm X in 1982:

> This book, I couldn't put it down. The Autobiography of Malcolm X . . . This man was talking about the history of Africa, talking about the white man. . . . I never read a book like that before in my life. . . . I said, "This is a man!" I wanted to be like Malcolm X. . . . I was so unhappy that this man was killed. Everything about Africa started coming back to me.[43]

Sandra Isadore was an adept musician herself and had keen observations about Fela's musical experiments at the time. She imparted upon Fela the necessity of a message in the music. She recalled:

> At that time, James Brown had "Say It Loud, I'm Black and I'm Proud." Fela was singing in Yoruba, you couldn't understand anything he was saying, but the music was getting better and better. He was getting deeper into his African roots. African music is about the chanting. Fela had all these rhythms and all these arrangements, and it was getting so dynamic! But when I asked him what he was saying, he said he was talking about what he likes in his soup! And I was saying, "No. You need to sing some conscious lyrics. You can pass a message on in the music."[44]

Upon his return to Nigeria, Fela Kuti recorded constantly with his band, Africa 70. They created a series of blistering twelve- to twenty-minute afrobeat workouts that were palettes for Kuti's diatribes against the Nigerian government and the colonial power structure. In his heyday, Kuti was frequently referred to as "the African James Brown," a designation that connotes the towering scope of each cultural leader.

James Brown and his band visited Nigeria in the fall of 1970. During their visit, members of Brown's band went to Fela Kuti's compound outside of Lagos and caught their performances. Brown did not go. Bassist

William "Bootsy" Collins was a part of the band at the time, and he was transfixed by the experience of meeting Fela and of hearing him play. He recalled in an interview with Jay Babcock:

> Everybody was talkin' about Fela when we got there, and about how he was like the African James Brown. And everybody was tellin' us he was THE man. So after we did one gig in Lagos, Nigeria, we all just went over. Me, Bobby Byrd, Vicki Anderson, Jabo . . .
>
> He was still in the dressing room. And man, we walked in the room and the smoke knocked us down! . . . So we vibed with him, we talked, and we went out to see the show. He came out and did his thing, man, and we had never seen NOTHIN' like that, or FELT anything like that, you know. It was AMAZING, and I guess by going there and seeing that, I kind of absorbed whatever I was hearing and whatever I was seeing. I just brought it back with me, and it became a part of me.[45]

The physicality of African music and the physicality of Brown's funk should not be ignored as parallel developments. Fela and most musicians in the tropics experienced a visceral connection between the sounds of the music and the sensations of the natural body (dance, sweat, sex) as part of their daily activities. For black American artists, this was often a bittersweet reality, as their expressiveness was both their blessing and a curse because it contrasted with the Western notions of polite civility. No small amount of white racism was imparted on black entertainers specifically because of their affectation with the body and their ability to get whites in touch with theirs. Bootsy Collins once explained the funk in the most physical of terms, connecting it to his Cincinnati youth: "Funk was like the way we lived. All of us kids sleeping in one room, it's 105 degrees outside, no air-conditioning. That's funk."[46]

The popularity of the funky, Africanized rhythms of Bootsy Collins and others became a hallmark of early 1970s black party music as an interactive polyrhythmic cross-pollination took place, one which facilitated the rise of funk and disco in the United States. The Cameroonian saxophone player Manu Dibango scored a worldwide hit in 1972 with a James Brown–derived, pulsing dance number, "Soul Makossa." The incessant groove and chanting-babbling of Dibango influenced the Afrocentric New Jersey funk band Kool and the Gang to spin an

African-oriented groove on one of their biggest hits, the hard-driving funk classic "Jungle Boogie."

However, for Fela Kuti, the music was not only about fun and games. Because of his prominent voice against the Nigerian government and the corrupt elites Kuti saw as exploiting his people, Kuti was repeatedly attacked, detained, and harassed by the Nigerian government. After recording the song "Zombie" in 1977, which railed against the Nigerian military, Fela's compound was raided, his mother was thrown from a second-story window (causing fatal injuries), and he and his bandmates were severely beaten. The harassment increased when Kuti announced he would run for president of Nigeria in 1979. However, the government refused to recognize Kuti's party, the Movement of the People. The state repression had a deleterious impact on Kuti's political career and his potential to manifest his larger vision of pan-African liberation. He nevertheless established himself as a singular voice of resistance during an era of postcolonial repression across Africa.

Kuti died of AIDS in 1997. Shortly afterward, more than a million people attended the Fela memorial at his original compound in Lagos. His slogan, "Music Is the Weapon," and his irrepressible body of work would live on.

It is important to note that Bob Marley and Fela Kuti—acknowledged worldwide as political artists—both considered James Brown to be a significant influence on their careers. All three of these men harnessed the power of African rhythms to produce music with a transcendent energy and force for liberation, while each man—both artistically and literally—pushed against the repressive apparatus upholding racial and economic injustice. And all three were subjected to a remarkable level of repression by the state.

The similarities of the artistic activism of each of these men are underscored by the sweeping global milieu of anticolonial agitation and change taking place in the 1960s. In his book, *Fela: The Life and Times of an African Musical Icon*, Michael Veal explains the circumstances surrounding Fela Kuti's political growth:

> African American culture figures crucially among the foreign cultural elements informing Fela's work and radical vision. . . . The 1950s and 1960s were an era of nationalism in Africa and the

Caribbean and civil rights in America. These movements paved the way for what might be called the internationalization of black power during the late 1960s and 1970s—a brief moment in which counterhegemonic protest in these places shared a rhetoric derived from the civil rights and postcolonial struggles.[47]

The "internationalization of black power" was a central element in the re-Africanization of black popular music. The driving, assertive funk beats employed by James Brown, combined with his moralizing and extemporaneous social commentary, all reinforced the conception that Brown's innovations were a part of something larger and not entirely his own.

Brown was recognized around the world as an artist who came from among the people and could identify with common folks. This was related frequently during Brown's visits to Africa, beginning in 1968. Brown was revered as a hero to millions of fans in Africa who appeared to have a special understanding of Brown's work and musical vision. John Miller Chernoff wrote in his 1979 book, *African Rhythms and African Sensibility*, that while he was in Africa studying the highlife music of West Africans, they were constantly querying him about their American music hero, James Brown:

> The tradition of using songs to express philosophical, ethical or satirical themes is so much a part of African musical idioms that it has continued, along with many rhythmic characteristics, within the development of Afro-American styles, and songs continue to serve as guides in practical philosophy to the people who listen to them.
>
> . . . So to a [Ghanaian] fan, James Brown's lyrics in particular are "thick with proverbs comparable to the most philosophical Highlife songs." In fact, many of my friends who were most eager to help me understand their Highlife songs were just as eager for my help in translating James Brown's slang, which they interpreted with no end of enjoyment and delight.[48]

James Brown was popular worldwide because of the virility, the tone, and earnestness of his presentation, and because of his highly polyrhythmic grooves that spoke simultaneously to the past and the future of African people. James Brown and his music stood at a unique crossroads of American social change, black identity formation, and the transformation of American musical traditions.

The Rhythm of Resistance

The long-term impact of James Brown on the popular rhythms of the world is evident in Brown's foundational status in the creation of hip-hop music. Hip-hop, a global phenomenon that many see as a means for members of a voiceless social strata to rediscover their own sense of self and to articulate their issues—through lyrics rhymed over syncopated, funky beats—would not exist if it were not for the work of the Godfather of Soul.

At the end of the 1960s, James Brown's performances and dance-funk recordings focused an energy that encapsulated the black power emanating from the streets. Brown created a space—at his shows and in the minds of his audiences—inhabited by highly charged rhythms, assertive attitudes, and free-form vocal improvisation. With self-aggrandizing titles such as "Superbad," "Sex Machine," "The Payback," and "Papa Don't Take No Mess," Brown's records provided thematic and rhythmic palates for younger disc jockeys to generate dance-floor pandemonium. The edgy and relentless rhythms allowed young dancers to find their own robotic, acrobatic moves within the rhythmic space of the grooves. Brown's charged, syncopated, often improvised lyrics, grunts, and chants became basic ingredients for up-and-coming rappers to personalize their own syncopated deliveries. For the first DJs, the first breakers, and the first rappers, James Brown endures as a founding father of hip-hop.

In the summer of 1973 Clive Campbell, known as DJ Kool Herc, brought the block party to the streets of the South Bronx. He is recognized as the first of the hip-hop DJs. Campbell was a Jamaican immigrant and, like Bob Marley, was also a James Brown fan. He explained the roots of his own craft to Davey D:

> I was born in Jamaica and I was listening to American music in Jamaica. My favorite artist was James Brown. That's who inspired me. A lot of the records I played was by James Brown. When I came over here I just put it in the American style and a perspective for

them to dance to it. In Jamaica all you needed was a drum and bass. So what I did here was go right to the 'yoke.' I cut off all anticipation and played the beats. I'd find out where the break in the record was at and prolong it and people would love it. So I was giving them their own taste and beat percussion-wise, 'cause my music is all about heavy bass.[49]

In the 1980s, when digital sampling technology became available and rap producers compiled their tracks from existing sounds, the choice James Brown beat, grunt, scream, horn riff, or melody became the essential element of hip-hop production. Further, dance music producers tasked with sequencing a segment of music that repeated throughout a song would key into "the One" to keep time. The strong pulse on the downbeat was and remains the timekeeper for Afro-diasporic dance music worldwide. "It all goes back to the Godfather of Soul, James Brown," hip-hop pioneer Afrika Bambaataa has stated.

James Brown helped to internationalize the rhythms of black music, and in the process he helped create a musical movement that has swept the world in the form of rap music, heard and performed on every continent on Earth. This worldwide phenomenon spawned because James Brown was in touch and in tune with the rhythms of the streets when those streets were on fire.

"Revolution of the Mind"

In 1971, on his third *Live at the Apollo* recording, titled *Revolution of the Mind*, James Brown stirred up the audience on his finale by chanting the mantra of the Black Panther Party. With the Apollo crowd in a frenzy, Brown had them shouting, "Soul Power! *Soul Power!* Power to the People! *Power to the People!*" Brown understood the mood on the streets like no other artist of the time.

By forcefully affirming black pride and celebrating black power, James Brown initiated a populist thrust toward black consciousness. As a result, Black Nationalism came home to roost at his doorstep—literally, in the form of black radicals urging Brown forward into a more radical stance toward the black revolution. Brown stood his ground as both an inspiration and a moderating/negating force on elements of change during this tumultuous period.

At the height of the black power era, James Brown saw his role clearly. He knew that an upheaval of black consciousness was taking place, and he believed that he could turn black pride into black economic success. Among his many business ventures, in 1969 Brown collaborated with Donald Warden and former Oakland Raiders football player Art Powell to create "Black and Brown trading stamps" with Brown's face on them. Shoppers in the black community would be able to accumulate stamps with each purchase and redeem them for cash and discounted items later. It was a means to help promote purchasing in the black business community. Brown also invested in a soul food restaurant, the Gold Platter, and engaged in a great deal of publicity in the Macon, Georgia, area. His self-made entrepreneurial success led him toward one of his most controversial decisions.[50]

James Brown would sully his standing as Soul Brother Number One by endorsing Republican president Richard Nixon for reelection in 1972. Brown's self-help mantra overlapped with Nixon's manipulative "Black Capitalism" campaign, and many who followed Brown and regarded him as a figure for social change presumed he was duped or coerced into the endorsement. While he is rarely mentioned among the nation's prominent black Republicans, Brown never wavered in his position on Nixon and even penned a song in 1973 essentially dismissing Nixon's Watergate troubles. "You Can Have Watergate, Just Gimme Some Bucks and I'll Be Straight" sought to give a street-level, stylized dismissal of the Nixon scandal. Despite his ideological contradictions, James Brown never lost the groove. David Hilliard sums up Brown's impact on the Panthers:

> Shit, we danced to James Brown, "Papa's Got a Brand New Bag." James Brown was all right until he started doing these affairs with Nixon. James Brown wasn't really considered a political animal. Remember we came from the community, and politicizing gained our political consciousness out of the necessity of the times, but we were people who came from the community, and James Brown was the consummate entertainer.[51]

The black revolution affected blacks of all walks of life—the activists, the entrepreneurs, the militants, the lovers, the families, the children, the loners, the leaders, the dreamers, and the prisoners—and James Brown could get them all to meet on the dance floor. At the most important moment, James Brown stepped up to the plate, took on the challenges placed upon blacks in the public arena, and did not shy away from them. He may have been "the most important black man in America." Brown's longtime friend Al Sharpton reflected on the gravity of James Brown:

> I think the difference between James Brown and other icons is that he was one of the few—the only one I can think of—who made it on his terms, which is why he was so loved. Because he never changed. There were other entertainers who became the first blacks to go mainstream. He was the first to make the mainstream go black.[52]

4

"People Get Ready"

Civil Rights, Soul Music, and Black Identity

After two roaring upbeat numbers, the band slows things down and performs a ballad. The dancers step and sway in a slow, deliberate motion like their Motown soul music contemporaries.

A velvet-smooth guitar melody brings about the familiar sound of the Impressions' "People Get Ready," a standard of the civil rights movement. Veterans of the integrated marches can easily recite the well-worn lyrics to the original tune by Curtis Mayfield:

> People get ready
> there's a train a comin'
> you don't need no ticket
> just get on board

As the Lumpen's rendition of the song takes shape, the softly moaning background harmonies and horn riffs provide a disarming, peaceful quality to the sound. Clearly this is a group in command of both upbeat and softer numbers. Bandleader William Calhoun addresses the crowd in a somber tone:

It's all right.
Before we, uh, dedicate this song, we make a special dedi-
cation tonight.
As you know we're cutting live here at Merritt College.
We'd like to dedicate our entire album to the minister of
defense, the supreme commander of the Black Panther
Party, Huey P. Newton.

This announcement generates a burst of applause from the audience.

On this particular song we dedicate to Jonathan Jackson,
to William Christmas, to James McClain, to Fred Hampton,
Mark Clark, John Huggins, Alprentice "Bunchy" Carter. And
to the brother that was the beginning, Little Bobby Hutton.

A loud burst of emotional applause follows for Lil' Bobby.

To all revolutionaries . . .
To all revolutionaries that have given their lives to the cause
of freedom throughout the world, we the Lumpen respect-
fully dedicate this song.

(*Applause*)

Yeah sing the song
Freedom wooo freedom
Won't you sing about the most precious thing in this world:
We said people get ready
Revolution's come
Your only ticket
Is a loaded gun

The audience shouts in laughter and approval.

Have courage my people
Have faith be strong
We'll put the pigs
Where they belong—
I believe, oh, I believe
Bobby and the people
Must all be free!

The audience shouts its approval at this verse.

As songwriter William Calhoun recalls: "I liked what he [Mayfield] was trying to say in terms of the message, 'People get ready.' His, of course, was a more spiritual message. I was involved in the revolution. So my thing was 'people get ready for the revolution.' Curtis just gave me entrée to that."[1]

> We said people get ready
> Revolution's come
> In freedom or death
> We will not run—
> Freedom or death
> Let it be known
> We'd rather die free
> Than die one by one—
> I believe oh I believe
> Bobby and the people
> Must all be free

(*Shouts and applause*)

> There ain't no time
> To turn around
> The place for all pigs
> Six feet underground
> We suffer so long
> *Now now now now* we can see
> We must kill those who stop us
> From being free—
> I believe, oh I believe *(Say it loud)*
> Bobby and the people
> Must all be free!

The final verse is sung slowly to a crescendo of applause from the audience.[2]

Part of the soul music aesthetic—which was composed of equal parts gospel morality and rhythm and blues energy—was that the artists to some extent lived the music that they sang, which served to reinforce the integrity of the message. It is in this context that the Lumpen were authentic to their audience as well as to the soul music tradition. One did not invoke a civil rights era standard such as "People Get Ready" unless one was serious about the message one intended to deliver.

The Lumpen paused to commemorate fallen revolutionary comrades on this song by the Impressions, a recording that served as a focal point of nonviolent civil rights movement activism. They acknowledged fallen Panthers in the Bay Area, Jonathan Jackson, James McClain, and William Christmas, killed during a siege of the Marin County courthouse on August 7, 1970; fallen Panthers in Los Angeles, John Huggins and Panther Party Southern California chapter founder Alprentice "Bunchy" Carter, killed by members of the black nationalist group Organization Us at UCLA on January 17, 1969; fallen Panthers in Chicago, Chicago party chairman Fred Hampton and Mark Clark, killed in a raid by Chicago Police on December 4, 1969; and the first recruit of the Party, Lil' Bobby Hutton, killed after surrendering to Oakland police following a shoot-out on April 6, 1968. By acknowledging their fellow revolutionaries, the Lumpen were solidifying their own commitment to the cause they had pledged to support. They appropriated Curtis Mayfield's masterpiece as their own anthem of uprising. This was not an accident. Calhoun recalls: "Anybody who was in support of the struggle was a friend; anybody else was a traitor, Uncle Tom, all the names we could put on people. And Curtis was certainly a friend. James Brown was for a while, until they bought him off. But Curtis Mayfield was somebody that we admired."[3]

This chapter will explore the relationship between the development of soul music, the rise of black consciousness within the community, and the simultaneous explosion of black arts, radical black cultural production, and the transformation of black identities that took place during the late 1960s and early 1970s.

"People Get Ready"

When the Impressions released "People Get Ready" in February 1965, the composition was considered a protest song of the highest order. "You don't need no ticket, you just thank the Lord" is the catchphrase for all who want to join the freedom train. Harmonic and harmonious, the song was familiar and inspirational to all who heard it. The song crossed over that spring, reaching number three on the R&B charts and number fourteen on the pop charts. Craig Werner, in his book *Higher Ground: Stevie Wonder, Aretha Franklin, Curtis Mayfield, and the Rise and Fall of American Soul*, reflects on the impact of Mayfield's soul masterpiece:

> No song bore witness to the movement's trials with greater depth than "People Get Ready," which Mayfield said he wrote "in a deep mood, a spiritual state of mind." . . . From the opening bars—a gospel hum carried along by bells, [Johnny] Pate's beautiful horn chart, and Mayfield's delicately syncopated guitar chording—the song pours a healing vision over a nation poised on the brink of chaos. . . . When the final strains of "People Get Ready" faded to silence, you could almost believe that, despite what was happening on the streets of Chicago and Detroit, the promise of the movement would be fulfilled.[4]

"People Get Ready" was designed to provide inspiration for those seeking to continue the struggle while appearing politically neutral in terms of direct references to the political realities of the day. The song remains a testament to the endurance of the civil rights marchers, as well as a tribute to the sounds of Chicago soul, to the music of the black church, to the blues tradition of coded protest music, and to the rich vein of resistance music within the black community.[5]

Curtis Mayfield and the Movement

Curtis Mayfield had a long and respected career as a socially conscious artist whose work mirrored the state of affairs in black America throughout his thirty-five-plus years as a recording artist. Mayfield's singing group, the Impressions, evolved from a collaboration between Jerry Butler and Mayfield, who both sang as teenagers in their church choir while living in Chicago's Cabrini-Green housing projects. Their friendship led to the formation of a singing group, Jerry Butler and the Impressions, and the hit single, "For Your Precious Love," in 1958. Butler then began a solo career while Mayfield backed him up on guitar, wrote arrangements, and learned the business. In 1960 Curtis Mayfield was ready to run the Impressions himself. At the time, Chicago was the home of the most popular and most polished black American pop singers, such as the legendary jazz crooner Nat "King" Cole, the gritty yet elegant Lou

Rawls, and the former gospel singer turned emergent pop superstar Sam Cooke. Mayfield followed in the footsteps of Cooke, who understood the importance of owning his own music. So in 1961, in an industry rarity, Mayfield formed his own publishing company to protect the rights to his music.

Curtis Mayfield was a stylistic pioneer as well. He fashioned the group with his own gospel-influenced three-part vocal style (new to R&B at the time) of singing featherlight harmonies, backed with his own delicate guitar melodies. Mayfield's subtly expressive guitar work is frequently mentioned as an inspiration for Jimi Hendrix. Despite a reputation for aggressive, dissonant, chaotic solos, Jimi Hendrix was also capable of exquisitely gentle musings, Mayfield's forte.[6]

The new Impressions' first hit singles were pop standards: "Gypsy Woman" in 1961, "It's All Right" in 1963, "I'm So Proud" in 1964, and the uplifting, spiritually oriented "Keep On Pushing." The following year, the group would enjoy pop notoriety with their energetic rendition of the traditional song "Amen," which appeared in the award-winning Sidney Poitier film *Lillies of the Field*. "Amen" would not only win the group wide popular appeal (reaching number seven on the pop charts in early 1965), the song was also utilized as marching music for civil rights demonstrators.

During this time, demonstrators were taking gospel songs out of the churches and onto the streets. In many cases, the activists would transform a traditional gospel song into a freedom song.[7] In 1962, members of the Student Nonviolent Coordinating Committee (SNCC) Cordell Reagon, Bernice Johnson (now Dr. Bernice Johnson Reagon), Charles Neblett, and Rutha Mae Harris founded their own singing group, the Freedom Singers, and toured the country singing freedom songs, expanding their organizing activities, and raising money for SNCC.[8]

Waldo E. Martin Jr., in his book *No Coward Soldiers*, posits that the use of song and the updating of the gospel were essential elements of the daily lives of the civil rights movement workers.

> Throughout the South, "Woke Up This Morning with My Mind Stayed on Jesus" became "Woke Up This Morning with My Mind Stayed on Freedom." "We are climbing Jacob's ladder, Soldiers of the Cross" became "Do you, do you want your freedom, Soldiers of the CORE." . . .

As the Reverend Dr. Martin Luther King Jr. observed at the time, "The freedom songs are playing a strong and vital role in our struggle. They give the people new courage and a sense of unity. I think they keep alive a faith, a radiant hope, in the future, particularly in our most trying hours."[9]

One young Mississippi family of gospel singers during that time played a role in the rise of soul music. Led by Roebuck "Pops" Staples, son Pervis, and daughters Mavis, Cleotha, and Yvonne, the family singing group the Staple Singers began recording gospel numbers in 1952 and were well established gospel music performers by the mid-1960s. But the tenor of the times compelled a move toward the movement and toward movement songs. As Mavis Staples recalled in 2007:

Pops saw Dr. Martin Luther King speak in 1963 and from there we started to broaden our musical vision beyond just gospel songs. Pops told us, "I like this man. I like his message. And if he can preach it, we can sing it." So we started to sing "freedom songs," like "Why Am I Treated So Bad," "When Will We Be Paid for the Work We've Done," "Long Walk to DC," and many others. Like many in the civil rights movement, we drew on the spirituality and strength from the church to help gain social justice and to try to achieve equal rights.

It was a difficult and dangerous time (in 1965 we spent a night in jail in West Memphis, Arkansas, and I wondered if we'd ever make it out alive) but we felt we needed to stand up and be heard.[10]

The Staple Singers were certainly heard over the years. They would later sign with Memphis-based Stax Records and fuse their moral authority of gospel music with the strength of the rhythm sections at Stax to produce some of the most revered soul music of the 1970s, including "Respect Yourself," "I'll Take You There," and many others. For the Staples family, and for a great many others, it was during those watershed years on the terrifying roads in the Deep South that soul music was born.

A wave of inspirational music with a message—which began on the streets as part of the struggle—was incorporated into black popular music recordings. The increasing popularity of black radio also played a role. In 1965 most of what was understood to be "black radio" was a series of small independent radio stations across the country that were typically owned by whites but that frequently featured music sets and playlists compiled by black DJs and black program directors. These radio stations and their on-air DJs were uniquely equipped to present popular black music, lifestyle, and culture, to comment on it, and to respond to community tastes. These stations were still profit-making institutions and as such were not overtly politically oriented. Nevertheless, the defiant, triumphant spirit of black popular music was carried across the airwaves—and across the racial divide.

Curtis Mayfield continued to write songs throughout the late 1960s that were inspired by, or directed toward, the black freedom movement. In early 1968 the Impressions' recording of "We're a Winner" was another breakthrough for Mayfield. The song was a departure from the veiled meanings in soul, as Mayfield sang, "And we're a winner /And everybody knows it too / We'll just keep on pushin' / Like your leaders tell you to." Rumors persist that the song was banned from numerous black radio stations because of its explicitly socially conscious lyrics (Mayfield referred to this on his 1971 live album), yet it still went to number one on the R&B charts and to number fourteen on the pop charts in the spring of 1968.[11] Soon thereafter Mayfield went on to record as a solo artist who wrote, performed, arranged, and financed all of his music. In 1970 Mayfield released *Curtis*, an album of dissonant, extended, adventurous recordings with titles such as "(Don't Worry) If There's a Hell Below We're All Going to Go," "Move On Up," "Miss Black America," and "We People Who Are Darker Than Blue." Mayfield's music at this point had as much in common with the hard black rock and psychedelia of Jimi Hendrix and Funkadelic as it did with Chicago soul. Yet it was, like most of Mayfield's work, eminently appropriate for the times.

Superfly

In 1972 Mayfield produced his modern masterpiece, the *Superfly* movie soundtrack. Mayfield's bittersweet lyrical portrayals of gangster life, along with irresistible hooks and melodies, set new standards for social commentary and solid groove. No longer harmonizing in a pressed blazer with his colleagues in the Impressions, Curtis Mayfield had put together a grooving funk band (à la Sly and the Family Stone) that included a prominent conga player, "Master" Henry Gibson. With Joseph "Lucky"

Scott's rich bass riffs and a tangy, melodic guitar tone supplied by Mayfield, the deep funk groves were irresistible. Mayfield's *Superfly* soundtrack exploded ideas of what a black movie soundtrack was capable of. Mayfield's "Pusherman" was a ghetto superstar who appeared to have no moral compass. Yet the lead character of the film, Priest, struggled to transcend the madness of the situation, as Mayfield captured so vividly.

> Can't be like the rest, is the most he'll confess
> but the time's running out
> and there's no happiness.

After Mayfield, it was no longer possible for an artist to simply support a movie with a soundtrack, the task was to *define* it. Mayfield went on to write and produce many more soundtrack albums.

Despite his status as an icon of soul music, Mayfield did not make the jump to major-label success—or into the superficialities of disco in the later 1970s. Mayfield's staunch independence earned him respect if not financial rewards, and he continued to record thoughtful soul music on independent labels and to perform regularly. On August 14, 1990, he was paralyzed after a stage accident in Brooklyn in which a lighting rig collapsed on him. Paralyzed from the neck down, Mayfield still continued to write and record music. Lying flat for hours just to exhale a verse, Mayfield recorded his final album in 1996: *New World Order.* Mayfield passed away in 1999. His honorable approach to black music is recognized the world over as the gold standard for soul and for social consciousness as an artist.

Chicago Soul to African Jazz

While Mayfield is the preeminent figure in the rise of what was known as *Chicago soul*, he also collaborated with arranger Johnny Pate to create a line of memorable hits for some of Chicago's best soul singers: the Impressions, Jackie Wilson, Jerry Butler, Gene Chandler, the Chi-Lites, Barbara Acklin, and Tyrone Davis. Eugene Record's group the Chi-Lites went on to become one of the most popular soul groups in the 1970s with the popular hits "Have You Seen Her," "Stone Out of My Mind," and "Oh Girl." Their third album, released in 1970, was steeped in social consciousness, as the title song, the hard-driving "(For God's Sake) Give

More Power to the People," was an overture to the well-known slogan of the Black Panthers. "That was the song of the times, that's why we recorded it," Marshall Thompson of the Chi-Lites recalls.[12]

The rich vein of popular music was influenced by the strength of black cultural institutions in Chicago, from the early black-owned jazz clubs in the 1920s to the Nation of Islam, which has been headquartered in Chicago since the 1930s. Chicago was and is the home of some of the most enduring popular black creative and artistic institutions. The Johnson Publishing Company's publications of *Ebony* (since 1945) and *Jet* (since 1951) have informed and entertained black America for generations. The popular, long-running dance program, *Soul Train*, founded in 1970 by Don Cornelius, began in Chicago (with a loan from the Johnson publishers) before moving to Los Angeles in 1972. Chess Records, founded by the Polish émigrés Leonard Chess and his brother, Philip, was the predominant blues label in the 1950s and introduced to the world the great stars Muddy Waters and Howlin' Wolf, along with rock and roll pioneer Chuck Berry. In the 1960s a number of young multi-instrumentalists would take the reins at Chess as musical directors of the label, developing artists such as Etta James, Ramsey Lewis, and Minnie Riperton with a broad range of styles and influences from jazz to psychedelic to soul. Two of these musical directors, Charles Stepney and Maurice White, would have an immeasurable impact on the music of the 1970s, writing and producing for one of the most elaborate yet popular and accessible bands of all time: Earth, Wind & Fire.

Chicago was also the hotbed of some of the most strident Black Nationalist jazz music of the day. Collectives such as Philip Cohran's African Heritage Ensemble, the Pharoahs, and the Art Ensemble of Chicago pushed and reflected the militancy of the streets of black Chicago with a combination of exotic, expansive instrumental music and a fiercely independent business sense. The jazz artists organized themselves into the Association for the Advancement of Creative Musicians (AACM), and, like their soul counterparts Cooke and Mayfield, sought complete financial control of their music. Their vision, encapsulated in their mission statement, was "Great Black Music, Ancient to the Future." The most esoteric jazz musician of all time, Herman Poole Blount, aka Sun Ra, spent the post–World War II years developing his intergalactic afrofuturist worldview while working in Chicago. (Sun Ra would later wind up in Oakland, at the invitation of Bobby Seale, living in a house owned by the Black Panther Party. Sun Ra spent the spring semester of 1971 "lecturing" for a course at UC–Berkeley in the music department titled "The Black Man in the Cosmos.")[13]

Many of the jazz groups, as well as artists of all persuasions, frequented the Affro-Arts Theater, a former movie house on Thirty-Ninth Street and Pershing Road in Chicago. Philip Cohran, who played with Sun Ra until Ra's exodus to New York in 1961, developed the Affro-Arts into one of the most prolific outposts of Black Nationalist cultural production in the region. The center offered art exhibits, film showings, plays, dance classes, lectures, poetry readings, and performances by artists such as Rahsaan Roland Kirk, Oscar Brown Jr., and Gwendolyn Brooks. It billed itself as "the only continuous valid black experience in the midwestern sector of the United States."[14]

Through the AACM and Affro-Arts, the Chicago jazz artists of the late 1960s used the independent, self-contained model of music-business operation that characterized the work of their Chicago predecessors. During the 1920s, before the intrusion of the Chicago mobsters, black jazz club owners provided a prominent social and economic model of independence. The radical artists of the 1960s sought to be similarly self-determined, and they designed youth music-education workshops, produced and performed their own concerts, managed financial collectives, and started up publishing companies for their work. These creative endeavors were inseparably linked to the political life in Chicago, which was equally self-determinist.[15]

Black Power in Chicago

For generations, Chicago politics have been characterized by a succession of bold power consolidations. From Al Capone's gangsters in the 1920s to the Richard J. Daley political machine in the 1960s, power has always been negotiated in plain sight. For years Daley kept control of the city through a tightly organized system of precinct patronage, where street-level vote organizers were given city jobs. His iron grip on Democratic Party politics meant he was rarely challenged in the electoral arena, and his ties to organized crime helped him to establish an impenetrable power base in the streets.

Martin Luther King Jr. had little chance to organize his northern civil rights movement in Chicago. Craig Werner explains how Daley dealt with King's overtures to the established black leadership in Chicago:

> Supported by the black political submachine, Daley simply employed the machine's standard tactics. If a minister offered anything more than rhetorical support to the Chicago movement, the city would dispatch inspectors with the power to condemn church property. If a businessman backed King, city permits or garbage collection would become a problem for him. Faced with a choice between supporting King and accepting grants to continue their programs most neighborhood activists took the money.[16]

The black middle class was beholden to the white power structure, and the entire city was organized in similar fashion. To assert political independence within this context was a radical gesture. As a result, Black Nationalists, from the Nation of Islam to the Black Panther Party, were highly organized within this space. Even the street gangs, such as the Blackstone Rangers and the Vice Lords organized themselves in sophisticated multitiered alliances—among each other, with Black Nationalists such as the Panthers briefly, and with the government in exchange for jobs and community grants. Power was sliced up like raw meat in Chicago, and people organized to obtain it.

Jesse Jackson's organizing efforts were centered in Chicago. After a year of study at the Chicago Theological Seminary in 1964, South Carolina native Jackson marched with and was mentored by Martin Luther King Jr. In 1966 King dispatched the twenty-two-year-old Jackson to head the Chicago chapter of Operation Breadbasket, which was organized to move blacks and their supporters toward "selective buying." This form of boycott was meant to pressure white businesses to integrate and hire blacks, and to eliminate obstacles to black business relationships. Jackson was at the Lorraine Motel in Memphis when King was gunned down on April 4, 1968, and his ambition in the wake of King's death was a concern to older civil rights organizers. Jackson, however, was among the first of the mainstream civil rights leaders to adapt to the black power rhetoric, to don African garb, wear an Afro, and generally ingratiate himself to the youth that adhered to the popular black styles and trends.

Jackson's falling out in 1971 with King's successor Ralph Aberna-thy led to Jackson's formation of his own organization, People United to Save Humanity, or Operation PUSH. The Chicago-based PUSH sought a legitimate claim as an heir to King's national organizational clout by developing similar selective-buying campaigns. However, despite Jack-son's charisma and appeal and the Black Nationalist tenor of the times, PUSH was unable to capture the imagination of mainstream black America (or the working poor, since PUSH was an integrated organiza-tion) to generate an economic impact on a national scale.

The Chicago chapter of the Black Panther Party was founded in late 1967 by Student Nonviolent Coordinating Committee organizer Bob Brown. Early in 1968 Fred Hampton, a young, charismatic NAACP offi-cer fresh out of high school, joined the Party. Within months Hampton was the leader of the organization and had aroused the interest of the national Party offices—as well as the federal government. Hampton was able to internalize and present fundamental elements of the Party plat-form and convince many followers of their value. In addition to develop-ing the People's Clinic, a free breakfast program, and a police-monitoring program, Hampton sought alliances with various black street gangs as well as the predominantly white Students for a Democratic Society. In 1969 Hampton was a key player in organizing the first Rainbow Coali-tion, an activist coalition that included the Puerto Rican Young Lords' Chicago chapter and the predominantly white Young Patriots. It was clear that Hampton could produce results that matched his revolution-ary rhetoric.

With Fred Hampton's dynamic oratory and visionary leadership cap-tivating the black population in Chicago, the Party became a nonne-gotiable threat to the power apparatus of the city. The FBI infiltrated the Chicago Party chapter with an informant who became Hampton's bodyguard. After failed attempts to bribe or coerce Hampton into petty crimes, the order went down to escalate the operation. At 4:00 AM on December 4, 1969, the state and local police raided Hampton's bedroom at the Party headquarters and executed him.

The murder of Fred Hampton, perhaps more than any other single event associated with the Black Panther Party, garnered public sympathy across a broad range of the general society. Such a lawless act commit-ted by law enforcement against someone seen as having such integrity generated a consistent reaction of outrage across the spectrum of the social justice movement. Clayton Riley wrote a postscript to Hampton's death in the *Liberator*, a New York–based black radical magazine that had essentially ignored the Panthers until Hampton's murder:

> The face of Fred Hampton, alive so recently, dead so easily, keeps smiles from many faces. And mine.
>
> One day, if this nation lives long enough, and grows up enough, we will be forced to confront these times and the Panthers. We will have to face them as truly avant heroes. Whom we killed because we had no room in this nation for the heroism of those who sought social change. We will face as well our own mediocrity as a reasoned explanation for the massacre of men and women who were, whatever the nature or soundness of their politics, bigger people than we allow to live here.[17]

Hampton's murder resonated throughout the city and the nation. Popular music responded in kind. Curtis Mayfield's first recording after the death of Hampton was his uncompromising, dissonant, politically charged solo album, *Curtis*, which featured the blistering opening track "(Don't Worry) If There's a Hell Below, We're All Going to Go." The softer tones of Chicago soul were no more. When the Chicago-based Chi-Lites produced their 1970 album title song, "(For God's Sake) Give More Power to the People," only months after Hampton's murder, it was a popular acknowledgment of the leadership and inspiration of the Black Panther Party in Chicago and nationwide.

Soul-singing superstar Chaka Khan was an acquaintance of Hampton's. She recalled Hampton's demeanor in her autobiography, *Chaka*:

> I remember wondering if Fred ever had a good belly laugh, ever cut up and clowned around. For all I know, perhaps he did in private. But whenever I saw him, he was in "movement mode." He was like an army sergeant. Not that I ever saw him be cruel to anyone. He might put a friendly arm around your shoulder by way of encouragement—"Hello, Sister Chaka"—but he wasn't about a lot of chitchat. Fred was all about "the struggle."[18]

For herself, Chaka Khan was also swept into the Black Nationalist milieu. She volunteered for the Black Panther Party in high school, worked the breakfast for children program, and performed at local black cultural centers along with her sister.

> Those were desperate, angry times. We had lived through years of civil rights movement fatalities, with the slayings of Evers, Malcolm, and King at the top of the litany. By the late 1960s, many of us had serious doubts that we would overcome the police brutality and all the other nigger treatment by moral suasion.[19]

Born Yvette Marie Stevens in 1953 in Great Lakes, Illinois, twenty miles north of Chicago, the young Stevens was raised on the South Side of Chicago and spent her spare time reading voraciously and taking singing classes. One day at the Affro-Arts Cultural Center, she was given the name Chaka Adunne Aduffe Yemoja Hodarhi Karifi by a Yoruba priest. At the time, name changes were a part of a coming-of-age ritual that was commonplace among counterculture youth. After a brief marriage to a local musician known as Hassan Khan, she shortened her name to Chaka Khan. She expanded her musical tastes from Motown-style harmonies to eclectic rock and psychedelic-influenced soul music, hooking up with the legendary Baby Huey and the Babysitters. At close to four hundred pounds and intensely expressive, Baby Huey (born James Ramey) emerged as an instant local star but died in October 1970 at the age of twenty-six. Shortly thereafter Khan went on to front the integrated rock-funk band Rufus, which would become her vehicle for obtaining stardom as a lead singer, songwriter, and funk queen. Upon moving to Los Angeles, the group scored years of pop success as Rufus featuring Chaka Khan in the 1970s, and Khan become a household name as a pop singer in the 1980s with songs such as "I'm Every Woman" and "What Cha' Gonna Do for Me."

Chaka Khan, however, was a youth organizer and member of the Black Panther Party back in 1969. As a young activist she faced a turning point in her own black militant career that was perhaps not unlike many other youths of her time. She came into possession of a gun and was tormented by all that it represented. She writes in her autobiography:

> So there I was selling *The Black Panther* on street corners. I was also heading up a free-breakfast program for children in an old South Side church. And one day I was in possession of a gun. It wasn't a

Panther's gun. It belonged to a security guard at Loop [junior college]. . . . I kept that gun for months, toying with the idea of doing something radical. . . .

I was starting to have my doubts that the BPP approach could maintain. I started to see that "The Power," "The Man" grew strong on our anger, on chaos, on divisions—black/white, men/women, old/young. What could my one gun do against that? . . .

I was thinking that maybe I just needed to finish high school and figure out what to do with my life. As for the gun, I hurled that sucker into the University of Chicago's Botany Pond. Immediately, I felt free. Not long after that, . . . I got a call from a BPP comrade. Fred Hampton was dead.[20]

Soul and Black Identity

Chaka Khan was not alone. There were thousands of young people making choices about their role in the movement. Singing superstar Natalie Cole was drawn to the Black Panthers as part of her youth rebellion and worked at the breakfast for children program at the University of Massachusetts. But hers was as a result of a different kind of search: "I totally rebelled. . . . I stole, I drank, I discovered drugs. I discovered a black identity and separated myself from upper-class society. I became a Black Panther advocate and had the Afro and the dashiki—oh yes, all of that. And somehow, in the midst of that, I discovered that I could sing a little."[21] In the case of Natalie Cole, and likely thousands of searching youths, the Black Panthers represented a tangible alternative to the establishment, something they could not simply run away from, but something to run toward.

The life choices of Chaka Khan and Natalie Cole were a result of a particular cultural milieu that provided choices that were filled with idealism and the potential energy of imminent social change. Their generation was afforded the rare privilege of acting upon those ideals. The culture surrounding Natalie Cole's rebellious impulses and Chaka Khan's brush with militancy was a *soul* culture—one that celebrated blackness across classes and regions, which encouraged black youth— and all blacks at this moment—to explore the meaning of their role in social change collectively.

The phenomena of *soul* and *soul music* emerged in the black popular imagination just as the black freedom movement was taking shape. In many ways soul was representative of the growing unity of purpose among black Americans that surged in the post–WWII era. Jazz musicians used the phrases "soul" and "soul brother" as references to their musical and cultural values in the early 1950s. The word was a catchall for what "blackness" supposedly meant for all blacks—urban, hip, and decidedly nonwhite. This emergent new black aesthetic in the jazz community took on a variety of names, including bebop, hard bop, cool, soul, and funk. The notion of soul transcended the music, as LeRoi Jones wrote in *Blues People* in 1963:

> Soul music, as the hard bop style is often called, does certainly represent for the Negro musician a "return to the roots." Or not so much a return as a conscious re-evaluation of those roots. . . . The step from *cool* to *soul* is a form of social aggression. It is an attempt to place upon a "meaningless" social order, an order which would give value to terms of existence that were once not only valueless but shameful. *Cool* meant non-participation; *soul* means a "new" establishment.[22]

The idea that soul brothers—and soul sisters—possessed something unique and special on their own terms was a major shift in consciousness, and it was a public confirmation of a shift in consciousness that was taking place throughout the black American community. Jazz musicians were on the front lines of the black consciousness movement and they initiated the musical movement of soul, but it was the popular performers who brought a new, all-encompassing sense of blackness to the masses.

Soul was as much a part of the movement as marches, speeches, and arrests. In 1965 the Black Arts movement writer Roland Snellings (now Askia Muhammad Touré), writing in the *Liberator*, was inspired to the point that he unabashedly thought to militarize rhythm and blues well before the direct protest song was a common part of the black social justice lexicon.

> This social Voice of Rhythm and Blues is only the beginning of the end. Somewhere along the line, the "Keep On Pushin'" in song, in Rhythm and Blues is merging with the Revolutionary dynamism of

COLTRANE of ERIC DOLPHY of BROTHER MALCOLM of YOUNG BLACK GUERILLAS STRIKING DEEP INTO THE HEARTLAND OF THE WESTERN EMPIRE. The Fire is spreading, the Fire is spreading, the Fire made from the merging of dynamic Black Music (Rhythm and blues, Jazz) with politics (GUERILLA WARFARE) is spreading like black oil flaming in Atlantic shipwrecks spreading like Black Fire. . . .

WE are moving forward, WE are on the move, WE record it all in Rhythm and Blues, New Jazz Black Poetry, WE—the Captive Nation listening to its priests and wisemen; growing stronger; donning Black Armor to get the job done so Rhythm and blues can once again sing about "Love," "mellow" black women and happy children: after it sings this Empire to the grave, after it sings the Sun of the Spirit back into the lonely heart of man.[23]

Through the medium of music, and his own zeal, Snellings was able to capture the spirit of oncoming change that was in the air. His energy and anticipation was high because he could feel a new phase of a people's movement on the horizon. Just as civil rights was transforming into black power, it was becoming clear to many that a movement was heading toward a revolution.

The Black Arts Movement

The Black Arts movement (BAM) was the name given to the explosion of radical black cultural production that emerged from black America in the mid-1960s. Black art created with revolutionary, nationalist ferver was the order of the day. Any opportunity to celebrate and encourage blackness, all things African, and to denounce all things white and Western was taken full advantage of. The goal was a revolution in black consciousness among the people. To accomplish this, young radicals wrote and published plays, poems, short stories, and novels, choreographed dances, designed visual art, produced films, and claimed spaces on the street and in public spaces to do so. They wrote politically incisive (as well as racially inflammatory) articles and prose in black newspapers such as the *Amsterdam News* and upstart Black Nationalist publications such as *Freedomways*, *Umbra*, and the *Liberator*. They sought to create and maintain a black aesthetic in their works and to inspire a rejection of Western constructs of value, relevance, and sophistication.

Although it was a national phenomenon, the Black Arts movement is mostly associated with the New York City–area stable of writers, critics, playwrights, visual artists, scholars, communists, and jazz aficionados that included LeRoi Jones (Amiri Baraka), Roland Snellings (Askia Touré), Larry Neal, Sonia Sanchez, Nikki Giovanni, Calvin Hernton, David Henderson, Harold Cruse, and many others.

They were spurned forward in Harlem by the black pride and discipline displayed by members of the Nation of Islam, and the anticolonial liberation movements such as those of Patrice Lumumba in the Congo, Kwame Nkrumah in Ghana, Nelson Mandela in South Africa, Ho Chi Minh in Vietnam, and Cuba's Fidel Castro (who visited Harlem in 1960). They witnessed the increasingly violent confrontations of the civil rights movement, the incipient urban riots (Birmingham 1963, Harlem 1964), and the daily news of anticolonial warfare. They felt the forceful denunciations of white supremacy and of Negro leaders by Malcolm X; they felt the raw soul music on the radio and the dissonant unbounded sounds of Black Nationalist jazz sweeping through the air. In a few short years, a spirited new generation would pass through the clouds of discontent that would explode into a storm of cultural production.

Many of the young movement writers considered jazz to be their muse. Malcolm X was a key proponent of the jazz aesthetic and was among the many celebrants of the jazz culture who would illustrate how the music could help blacks to free themselves from Westernization and create new directions for their people. He spoke of this at his announcement of the creation of the Organization of Afro-American Unity held at the Audubon Ballroom in Harlem on June 28, 1964:

> I've seen it happen. I've seen black musicians when they'd be jamming at a jam session with white musicians—a whole lot of difference. The white musician can jam if he's got some sheet music in front of him. He can jam on something that he's heard jammed before. If he's heard it, then he can duplicate it or he can imitate it or he can read it. But that black musician, he picks up his horn and starts blowing some sounds that he never thought of before. He improvises, he creates, it comes from within. It's his soul, it's that soul music. It's the only area on the American scene where the black

man has been free to create. And he has mastered it. He has shown that he can come up with something that nobody ever thought of on his horn.

Well, likewise he can do the same thing if given intellectual independence. He can come up with a new philosophy. He can come up with a philosophy that nobody has heard of yet. He can invent a society, a social system, an economic system, a political system, that is different from anything that exists or has ever existed anywhere on this earth. He will improvise; he'll bring it from within himself. And this is what you and I want.[24]

Malcolm X used the metaphor of black musical creativity to fashion a vision of an entirely liberated black civilization. This essential link was the centerpiece of Black Arts ideology. His words inspired a generation of artists and activists to believe in the inherent value and revolutionary potential of their works. If it was black, from black, for black, about black, then it was a part of a greater vision of black liberation. A generation of black cultural workers were transformed by the uncompromising clarity and forcefulness of Malcolm X's love of blackness, and these artists sought to remain true to his word.

Musically, echoes of Malcolm X could be heard at every urban jazz club and dusty juke joint across the country. To a great deal of Black Arts movement aficionados, many confluent movements toward liberation from the constraints and constructs of Western art and culture were taking place on stage and on the records of Albert Ayler, Archie Shepp, Max Roach, Charles Mingus, Cecil Taylor, Ornette Coleman, and John Coltrane. Especially John Coltrane. In his book *Freedom Is, Freedom Ain't: Jazz and the Making of the Sixties*, Scott Saul describes the almost spiritual deification young black radicals gave to both John Coltrane and Malcolm X:

While Coltrane was loath to attach his music to a specific political ideology, preferring a language of universal spirituality, he became posthumously an icon of a uniquely black epistemology. . . .

Although Coltrane and Malcolm X may seem to be opposite figures in disparate universes—the first apolitical and seemingly disconnected from the actual groundswell of the freedom movement, the second firebreathing in his politics and seemingly disconnected from the world of the arts—they did share a broad cultural connection. Both became icons of integrity, figures of an uncompromising and uncolonized black selfhood.[25]

To be able to represent oneself as uncolonized was an important ideal for many of the Black Arts movement practitioners, particularly in the racially stratified and congested urban northeastern cities.

Most of the early Black Arts movement visionaries were college educated, and many were veterans of military conscription. Their hostile, disorienting experiences within the most rigid artifices of the Western social structure (the academy and the military) were both crushing and inspiring in the same way that a repressive Catholic-school upbringing might lead one to a rebellion of hedonism and indulgence. This newest of the New Negro to come out of this milieu was defiantly, obnoxiously, preposterously *Black*.

The revolutionary spirit in the air in 1965 inspired LeRoi Jones to found a uniquely oriented artistic cultural center in Harlem, which he called the Black Arts Repertory Theatre/School (BARTS). BARTS was a watershed because of its unabashed blackness, its vision, and its central geography as a locus of activity and possibility. The focused black culture that was being celebrated was a model for other interested black imaginers, and the model was duplicated all over the country. In Detroit it was the Shrine of the Black Madonna Cultural Center, in San Francisco it was the Black House, in Chicago it was the Affro-Arts Theater, and there were dozens more that were lesser known yet just as functional. Kalamu Ya Salaam, in his book *The Magic of JuJu: An Appreciation of the Black Arts Movement*, clarifies the truly nationwide nature of the Black Arts movement, which he defines as "an artistic manifestation of the collective Black Power–oriented political activity that happened in the sixties and seventies." Ya Salaam explains that there were regional centers of BAM activity that interacted with national trends and then reinvigorated their local centers in a local-national-local process. According to Ya Salaam, the key geographical focal points of BAM were:

The West Coast Bay Area, which produced the seminal journals *Soulbook*, *Black Dialogue*, and the *Journal of Black Poetry*; Chicago/ Detroit, which produced *Negro Digest/Black World*, Third World Press, and *Black Books Bulletin*, as well as OBAC [Organization of

Black American Culture] in Chicago and Broadside Press in Detroit; New York/New Ark (Newark, NJ), which produced BART/S, New Lafayette, and the National Black Theatre in New York, and Spirit House Movers and Jihad Press in New Ark; and New Orleans, home base for the Free Southern Theatre, which traveled throughout the Deep South and influenced the development of BAM activities from Florida to Texas.[26]

Cultural centers sprang up nationwide in homes and offices, church facilities and union halls, in abandoned buildings and on public school and university properties. For these cultural centers to thrive, Black Arts and black artists and black idealists packed the spaces with their wares, their visions, and their energies. In a fundamental way, the Black Arts movement was the cultural dimension to the black power movement.

A Personal Revolution

The artistic production at these sites went hand in hand with the personal transformations taking place individually and collectively in the same spaces. High school and college age black youth were exploring and debating identity in a variety of ways, such as the high-volume debate at Howard University in 1966 when their homecoming queen, Robin Gregory, sported an Afro hairstyle.[27] The exhilarating episode of glamour and aesthetic confrontation was credited with sparking a wave of student activism on the campus.

Assata Shakur, the former Black Panther and steadfast black revolutionary now living in exile in Cuba, described with delight in her autobiography, *Assata*, her early encounters with black cultural organizations during this heady time. Her encounter with the Republic of New Afrika (RNA) was typical. This organization, founded in Detroit by brothers Milton and Richard Henry (now Gaidi Obadele and Imari Obadele), advocated the establishment of a separate black nation within US borders to be made up of South Carolina, Georgia, Alabama, Mississippi, and Louisiana. The premise was both preposterous and at the same time eminently reasonable, considering the radical politics of the day. With the development of a new iconography (the red, black, and green flag, for example) and defiantly African-inspired new cultural practices, the RNA provided a new space to "recover" blackness. Shakur explained her experience:

> The first time i attended a Republic of New Afrika event, i drank in the atmosphere and enjoyed the easy audacity of it all. The surroundings were gay and carnival-like. A group of brothers were pounding out Watusi, Zulu, and Yoruba messages on the drums. . . . Vibrant sisters and brothers with big Afros and flowing African garments strolled proudly up and down the aisles. Bald-headed brothers, wearing combat boots and military uniforms with leopard-skin epaulets, stood around with their arms folded, looking dangerous. Little girls running and laughing, their heads wrapped with galees, tiny little boys wearing tiny little dashikis. People calling each other names like Jamal, Malik, Kisha, or Aiesha.
>
> "Peace, sister," a voice said. "Do you wanna be a citizen?"
>
> "What?" i asked, without the slightest notion of what she was talking about.
>
> "A citizen," she repeated. "Do you want to be a citizen of the Republic of New Afrika?"[28]

The Black Arts movement was as much about cultural production as it was about the lived experience of blackness at the moment of revolutionary change. Another example of this is the way Assata Shakur, born JoAnne Chesimard, came to change her name:

> The name JoAnne began to irk my nerves. I had changed a lot and moved to a different beat, felt like a different person. It sounded so strange when people called me JoAnne. It really had nothing to do with me. I didn't feel like no JoAnne, or no Negro, or no amerikan. I felt like an African woman. From the time i picked my hair out in the morning to the time i slipped off to sleep with Mingus in the background, i felt like an African woman and rejoiced in it. My big, abstract black and white inkblot-looking painting was replaced by paintings of Black people and revolutionary posters. . . . My whole life was moving to African rhythms. My mind, heart, and soul had gone back to Africa, but my name was still stranded in Europe somewhere.[29]

The African Influence

A strong part of the attraction of Africa came from the increasingly visible presence of African culture in black communities. Visits from African dignitaries and celebrities became more frequent at social functions and entertainment venues. An interest in African music created openings for African musicians to take their recreational and ritual activities into the realm of performance and become popular doing so.

In the mid-1950s a Nigerian graduate student named Babatunde Olatunji developed a touring drum ensemble as he was taking breaks from study at New York University. The local performances were so striking that Olatunji was recruited by music executive John Hammond and signed to Columbia records. Olatunji's 1960 release *Drums of Passion*—a drum chorus of raw rhythm—was a defining moment in the growing African influence on black musicians in jazz, soul, and pop. Universally acclaimed, Olatunji performed at President John F. Kennedy's 1961 inauguration and the 1963 March on Washington. His influence was strong on jazz musicians such as Yusef Lateef and, in particular, John Coltrane, whose compositions "Africa," "Gold Coast," "Tunji," and "Dahomey Dance" were all examples of a new worldliness exhibited by the most adventurous of black jazz musicians. Coltrane was an avid Olatunji disciple. "John Coltrane became my number one fan, and didn't hide it," Olatunji recalled in his autobiography, *To the Beat of My Drum*. "He told me in no uncertain terms, 'I really admire what you've been doing. Every chance I get, I come to see and hear you. And when I do, I listen close to every move you make, everything you play. So one day I want to come a little nearer and learn something from you.' "[30] Coltrane's collaboration with and generous financial support of Olatunji led to the foundation of the Olatunji Institute in 1964 in Harlem, where Olatunji taught African drumming, dance, and language to patrons of all walks of life. John Coltrane's final recorded performance took place at the Olatunji Institute in April 1967. The available recording of the performance is somewhat ragged and discordant. Yet the overarching purpose of wedding African rhythms to American jazz improvisation would become a fundamental element in modern black music, particularly funk. According to Olatunji, the two had planned a national tour to initiate "Olatunji Centers" for African cultural learning across the country. Tragically, only months later John Coltrane died of liver cancer on July 17, 1967.

The impact of Babatunde Olatunji and his recording of *Drums of Passion* was enormous. Olatunji summed up the impact of his groundbreaking record:

> *Drums of Passion* played a significant role in all the social change taking place around that time. It was the first percussion album to be recognized as an African contribution to the music of African Americans. It also came right at the beginning of the Civil Rights Movement. This meant we were recognized as pioneers in the "Black is Beautiful" movement. The whole idea of "black power" came along at this time, too. And so did the wearing of the *dashiki* and natural hair.
>
> We found ourselves right in the middle of this, going from one rally to another, sponsored by different organizations fighting for freedom. From the NAACP to CORE to SNCC to the Black Muslims. This era was so full of excitement and challenges to everybody who was alive and part of it, black or white.[31]

The times were ripe for any and all things African to be appropriated and appreciated by a black public lusting for an identity beyond the "Negro." In 1960 the popular South African vocalist Miriam Makeba came to the United States and was instantly swept up in the American pop music world, appearing on such mainstream television vehicles as *The Ed Sullivan Show* and *The Steve Allen Show.* Her lighthearted mix of Western and traditional Xhosa ("click") vocalizing, African dress, and humble style, backed by a familiar-looking, Westernized R&B/pop backup band was an appealing mix for American fans. Makeba's popularity was a point of frustration for her South African government, however, which exiled her. Makeba's engaging presence and comfortably worn natural hairstyle became a cause célèbre among a growing number of style-conscious African Americans in the early part of the 1960s. In her memoir, *Makeba: My Story*, Makeba makes light of the fact that her natural hair influenced a trend that would become a cultural icon in a few short years.

> People wear furs and arrive in fancy cars because they have not seen anything like me. I don't wear any makeup. My hair is very short and natural. Soon I see other black women imitate the style, which

is no style at all, but just letting our hair be itself. They call the look the "Afro."[32]

Makeba's path was influenced by two of the most compelling personalities of the era: the activist leader Stokely Carmichael, whom she married in 1968, and entertainer Harry Belafonte, who sparked her career in the early 1960s. Makeba's marriage to the controversial Carmichael was an inspiration to some who saw the two as a symbol of independent African royalty, but the union caused problems for Makeba's musical career, as venues that once begged her to perform later refused to book her because of Carmichael's defiant black power position and his volatile relationship with the US government. But Makeba's career would have its greatest surge as a result of the universally popular Harry Belafonte.

Harry Belafonte was one of the most important activist-artists of the era. The Harlem-born Jamaican was an early Calypso superstar and an actor who played alongside Dorothy Dandridge in the famous all-black musical *Carmen Jones* in 1954. Belafonte was one of the first post–World War II black superstars, and certainly one of the few African American entertainers to fully engage as an activist as well. Belafonte's iconic 1956 "Banana Boat Song," with its memorable chant of "day-o," was a celebration of Caribbean delights, and it offered Belafonte entrée to the American mainstream, which he has used to maximum effect throughout his stellar career. In the early 1960s, at the height of his influence, Belafonte took Miriam Makeba and black folksinger Odetta under his wing and toured with them, bringing an authentic ethnic presence to the American mainstream. At the same time, Belafonte supported and frequently underwrote Student Nonviolent Coordinating Committee activities, often funding them directly. Belafonte was known to literally fly to SNCC actions with a bag of cash to be deposited in support of their efforts. Belafonte was an outspoken supporter of civil rights and one of the few visible supporters of ostracized entertainer-activist Paul Robeson during Robeson's troubles with the US government. As Belafonte's recording dropped off, he faded from view as a pop icon, but his impact on the culture and the politics of the black revolution was enormous.

The crossover appeal of Belafonte's Caribbean pop music was only the beginning of a growing affection for emerging Afro-diasporic music. Percussion-driven "Latinized" dance music emerged on the pop and

R&B charts in the early sixties with Mongo Santamaria's rendition of Herbie Hancock's "Watermelon Man" and Ray Barretto's "El Watusi," both of which sparked popular dance crazes. A cottage industry of Latinizing popular tunes became profitable for many artists, satisfying audiences of all races. The Afro-Latin fusion of soul in the city was perhaps best celebrated in the summer of 1971 when the Queen of Soul herself, Aretha Franklin, released her tome to the neighborhoods, celebrating "a rose in black in Spanish Harlem," with her delightfully Latinized smash hit "Spanish Harlem."

Aretha Franklin

If one person epitomizes the aesthetics of soul, it is the Queen of Soul herself, Aretha Franklin. The daughter of a well-known Detroit preacher, Reverend C. L. Franklin, Aretha Franklin possessed a trumpet of a voice and a soulful spirit that defined a generation through her songs. Well-established standards such as "Respect," "Chain of Fools," "(You Make Me Feel Like) A Natural Woman," and "I Never Loved a Man (the Way I Love You)" were all chart-topping, soul-stirring smash hits for Franklin in the late 1960s. Her singing had a spiritual strength that sent her audiences into another world of emotional uplift. To witness Aretha Franklin was to experience pure soul at its utmost.

Aretha Franklin's striking sound and dramatic personal evolution parallels the rise and fall of the civil rights and black power movements. Born in Memphis in 1942, Franklin was raised in Detroit in a religious family with an extended network of surrogate parents. She had two children by the age of sixteen. She was nevertheless nurtured in her father's church, where her voice was a siren, and Aretha, it was clear, was headed toward stardom. Seeking to break out of the confines of the church, Aretha quickly signed a recording deal with Columbia Records in 1960 at the age of eighteen. Aretha worked with producers in New York who attempted to craft her into a jazz and pop singer in the mold of Aretha's early mentor, Dinah Washington.

The resulting Columbia output, while reconsidered recently, was out of character for the powerful, gospel-trained, musically skilled young woman. For six years and eight albums, Aretha was told what to sing and how to sing the songs, stifling her unrivaled torch of a voice. In much the same way that the civil rights movement was constrained by benevolent supporters early on, it would take another act of liberation for Aretha to truly find herself.

Upon the completion of her Columbia contract in 1966, Aretha was signed by Jerry Wexler of Atlantic Records. Atlantic was based in New York, though it had strong ties to southern rock, soul, and country recording studios. Wexler took Aretha to the Fame studios in Muscle Shoals, Alabama, gave her a studio full of intuitive (predominantly white) southern session players, and let her loose on the piano, where she found her groove and her voice. Their first recording together, "I Never Loved a Man (the Way I Love You)" was the most guttural and passionate of her recordings to date, and remains a tour de force of soul and personal revelation. "Many of the arrangements were done on the spot, in what we called head sessions," Aretha recalls in her autobiography, *Aretha: From These Roots*, "This was worlds away from how I had worked at Columbia, far more spontaneous and free-flowing, with so much more room to be creative. . . . The enthusiasm and camaraderie in the studio were terrific, like nothing I had experienced at Columbia. This new Aretha music was raw and real, and so much more myself. I loved it!"[33] The remainder of the album was recorded in New York with the Muscle Shoals players in tow, a collaboration that set the stage for one of the most important recordings ever made.

"Respect"

If ever there was a game changer for soul music, it was Aretha Franklin's single "Respect," which hit the stores on May 6, 1967—just days after the Black Panthers visited the California state capitol bearing arms—and soared to number one on the R&B charts. A driving punch to the rhythm and the urgent forceful blast of a voice from Aretha set a tone of redemption, "What you want! Baby I got it!" the power of which was as stirring as anything in black music ever heard to that point. The lyrics are a forewarning from a working partner to her mate, demanding respect when she comes home. A woman demanding respect from her man was a truly radical salvo across the gender divide at the time. The wicked hooks developed by Aretha and her sister Erma, "R-E-S-P-E-C-T / find out what it means to me," put a rhythmic stamp on a soul anthem that sounded like a riff from a girls' jump-rope routine, and it revealed a street savvy that established Aretha as "the Queen of Soul" nearly overnight.

The song burned to number one because it was far more than a dance-inducing cover of a 1965 Otis Redding hit, it was soul and everything anyone ever wanted in soul. It had power—visceral, tangible, physical power—in its sound and an ability to make people act on the ideas in the music. That was Aretha's pure gift: an ability to take that irresistible *umph* that churchgoers get and make it secular, righteous, and real.

With urgent lyrics from a woman demanding respect from her man, Aretha opened up an entirely new discourse across the sexual divide. The vast majority of popular relationship songs dealt with emotional truth, fidelity, betrayal, and honor, but rarely professed a confrontational stance toward the male from the female, and never before with the passion, authenticity, and funky groove of Aretha's rendition. "Respect" was for many a watershed, a revolution in the language of relationships.

Yet "Respect" came to represent far more than a lovers' spat. *Ebony* magazine, in an end of the year commentary, described the summer of 1967 as the summer of "'Retha, Rap, and Revolt"; Aretha did her part by providing a soundtrack to the movement at its most dynamic, driven, and desperate. By this time in the movement, Martin Luther King Jr. had abandoned his silence on US foreign policy and had openly opposed the war in Vietnam. The Black Panthers had "stormed" Sacramento, and SNCC leader H. Rap Brown appeared to be "inciting riots" by endorsing the many urban rebellions that summer. These actions left but a tiny minority of appeasing black leaders for the white establishment to negotiate with. The days of accommodation were over. Not everyone agreed with the black political leaders at the time, but anyone could see that "Respect" represented a shift in the center of the black experience once and for all.

Aretha followed that song with "Natural Woman" and "Chain of Fools," as well as a string of soulful ballads that stirred a collective consciousness in her audience that was both universally appealing and undisputedly black and proud in tone, passion, and soul power. Yet nothing in her later output could match the impact of "Respect," and Aretha knew it. "It is still my biggest song in concert today," Aretha expressed in 1999:

> So many people identified with and related to "Respect." It was the need of a nation, the need of the average man and woman in the street, the businessman, the mother, the fireman, the teacher—everyone

wanted respect. It was also one of the battle cries of the civil rights movement. The song took on monumental significance. It became the "Respect" women expected from men and men expected from women, the inherent right of all human beings. Three decades later I am unable to give a concert without my fans demanding that same "Respect" from me. "Respect" was—and is—an ongoing blessing in my life.[34]

"Young, Gifted and Black"

Aretha would record five more albums for Atlantic as the 1960s progressed, each finding varying degrees of success but none with the social movement resonance of "Respect." However, as the 1970s began, Aretha extracted herself from a failed marriage and decided to once again retool her creative focus, steering her sound in a decidedly more self-conscious, spiritual, and African-inspired direction.

Aretha appeared to be busy in 1970 and 1971, recording the brilliant *Live at the Fillmore West* in San Francisco with guest Ray Charles and releasing a series of singles followed by a greatest hits album. Her fans were continually exposed to Franklin's music, but she went eighteen months between original album recordings, her longest gap since signing to Atlantic in 1967. During this time she was in the studio, carefully crafting one of her most thoughtful albums. The first song Aretha recorded for her new album in August 1970 was "Young, Gifted and Black," a remake of a famous Nina Simone song that had made the R&B charts earlier that year.

To Be Young, Gifted and Black was the name of an unfinished play by the New York essayist, activist, and playwright Lorraine Hansberry, whose 1958 play about a working-class Chicago family, *A Raisin in the Sun,* had been recognized as the first play written by a black woman to have a successful run on Broadway. Hansberry was in fact much more than a playwright. A close confidante of Nina Simone, Hansberry was a political mentor to Simone and helped in the development of Simone's fiery social consciousness.

While Lorraine was a girlfriend . . . we never talked about men or clothes or inconsequential things when we got together. It was

always Marx, Lenin and revolution—real girls' talk. . . . Lorraine
was definitely an intellectual, and saw civil rights as only one part
of the wider racial and class struggle. . . .

Lorraine started off my political education, and through her I
started thinking about myself as a black person in a country run by
white people and a woman in a world run by men.[35]

The impact Lorraine Hansberry had on the black arts of a generation
should not be underestimated. Her body of creative works and fiercely
held beliefs about radical social change were seen as an inspiration across
a broad spectrum of society. Nina Simone was one of her closest followers, and was the most deeply affected. "Before she died Lorraine had
been working on a new play, *To Be Young, Gifted and Black.* I took the
title and wrote a song around it in memory of Lorraine, and of so many
others."[36]

> To be Young, Gifted and black
> Oh what a lovely precious dream.
> To be Young, Gifted and black
> Open your heart to what I mean.

Aretha Franklin chose to remake the Simone classic and give her
1971 album the same name. Aretha's version of the song was structured
in a way very similar to Simone's, beginning with the slow, deliberate pace of a traditional spiritual, and then rising to triumphant highs,
punctuated with dramatic stops and starts. Aretha's version of the song
soars over the highs and lands in a crescendo of church choir celebration. For Aretha Franklin to reference Nina Simone, and by extension
Simone's music (and Hansberry's vision), Aretha deftly acknowledged
her respect for the black freedom movement and solidified her lofty pop
icon status at the same time. The resultant album was one of her most
musically, thematically diverse, as well as one of her most successful,
winning a Grammy Award (her seventh to that point). Franklin also
wrote her funkiest song, "Rock Steady," for the album with the help of
Donny Hathaway on the wickedly swinging organ. Aretha performed
"Rock Steady" on national television on the *Flip Wilson Show* in 1971
and appeared wearing an African-inspired dress and an Afro, with her
backup singers in similar looks.

Aretha was feeling inspired in part because of her new boyfriend, Ken "Wolf" Cunningham, who at the time was developing an African and African-inspired clothing line. In a sense, the two convergent themes of soul music—personal expression and social consciousness— were woven together in 1970 and 1971 as Aretha, the "Natural Woman" and Queen of Soul herself, redefined herself as an African American woman. Aretha Franklin's personal rediscovery was not uncommon at the time. As she explained:

> Well I believe that the black revolution certainly forced me and the majority of black people to begin taking a second look at ourselves. It wasn't that we were all that ashamed of ourselves, we merely started appreciating our natural selves, . . . you know, falling in love with ourselves just as we are. We found that we had far more to be proud of. So I suppose the revolution influenced me a great deal, but I must say that mine was a very personal evolution—an evolution of the me in myself. But then I suppose that the whole meaning of the revolution is very much tied up with that sort of thing, so it certainly must have helped what I was trying to do for myself. I know I've improved my overall look and sound, they're much better. And I've gained a great deal of confidence in myself.[37]

At this point in her life Aretha was not simply talking in generalities about trends and styles. She caused a stir with her support of the black revolutionary Angela Davis. In late 1970 the imprisonment of Davis was national news. Aretha Franklin announced that she was willing to pay the entirety of Davis's bail money to free her.

> Angela Davis must go free. Black people will be free. I've been locked up (for disturbing the peace in Detroit) and I know you got to disturb the peace when you can't get no peace. Jail is hell to be in. I'm going to see her free if there is any justice in our courts, not because I believe in Communism, but because she is a Black woman and she wants freedom for black people. I have the money; I got it from black people—they've made me financially able to have it— and I want to use it in ways that will help our people.[38]

Aretha Franklin's stance in support of Angela Davis was rich in symbolism. (She was out of the country when bail was offered and Davis's attorneys had to use other means, but the offer was genuine.) Her activist awakening reflected the possibilities of mass participation in a movement that has reached the mainstream. Did Aretha become a militant communist revolutionary? No. But she did come closer to an understanding of herself as a complete person—something far more difficult to do in today's climate.

With her newfound confidence, Aretha made yet another move toward independence, recording and releasing a true gospel album. This was one of the boldest moves of her career, as she pulled together all of her resources to produce a live recording in Los Angeles with the Reverend James Cleveland's choir. The high-profile project was a gamble. If it were to fail, it would have set back her career and made it even more difficult for black artists to branch out to secular music and return to their spiritual home. One of the conflicts encountered by church singers branching out into the secular arena was a strong sentiment that one could never go back to the church.

The record, *Amazing Grace*, was an emotional and spiritual tour de force. The Friday night recording session had the energy of a Sunday sermon, and the kinetic spirit was sparked by the soaring voice, as well as the vision and leadership, of the woman in control of the operation. With *Amazing Grace*, Aretha brought soul home to its very roots, full circle. Perhaps her proudest moment as an entertainer, the record sold millions. On the *Amazing Grace* album cover, Aretha is posed in African garb, regal in her complete, natural self.

After *Amazing Grace*, Aretha Franklin appeared to take a break from directing her work and returned to a series of fairly standard productions, almost as if, like Sly Stone, there was little else to be said in as inspired a fashion as she had before. Jazz arranger Quincy Jones produced her next album, *Hey Now Hey (The Other Side of the Sky)*. The luxurious feel of Jones's arrangements recalled Aretha's earlier work at Columbia rather than her ubiquitous raw soul. Lacking the larger vision of Aretha's two previous album efforts, the album was the first in a string of relative commercial disappointments released through the remainder of the decade. Nevertheless, the gold standard of soul was embodied in Aretha, and the black revolution was integral to her emergence.

The idea of soul music and the soul aesthetic—the notion that black culture, black pride, and black enterprise could and should be working together—reached a zenith during this time, 1970 to 1971 (coincidentally, the time the Lumpen were in operation). For some, this was a revolutionary breakthrough of black progress. For others it was not so simple. Lumpen member Michael Torrence appreciated what Aretha Franklin was doing, up to a point:

> She was one of my favorites as far as being a soul singer and the type of music she was making at that time, growing up with it. When she did the *Young, Gifted and Black*, on one hand we kind of felt like, "OK, about time." At the same time, we recognized that we in the Party had moved past the cultural nationalism thing. We heard the message that black is beautiful, which it was all right, but politically speaking we had kind of moved past that. So to that extent, it didn't change how I felt about her as an artist, but it didn't particularly impress me. It seemed more like, "OK, that's the thing to do now, that's the current thing, everybody's getting on board with it"—but they're a little bit behind where we were in terms of the politics of it. The revolutionary politics.
>
> We were very hard-line about that stuff. So we took it for what it was. We looked at it as more of a commercial thing. In terms of her as a singer she was one of the greatest, she is the greatest, she is the Queen of Soul. Later I come to find out, later on, that she was involved in a lot more things than I thought she was at that time.[39]

Though he was a singer himself, for Michael Torrence and the Black Panther Party, the revolution required something stronger than songs to make change. The Panthers were about action.

The mainstream of black America was negotiating these issues on a daily basis and had to contend with assimilation-oriented celebrities such as O. J. Simpson on one hand, and militants such as Eldridge Cleaver on the other. This situation led to a funky mix of popular culture contrasts. But there was one group of black celebrities that could straddle the boundaries between soul power and selling out: the black radio personalities.

Soul Power and Black Radio

A crucial voice in the rise and dissemination of black consciousness during the movement came from the DJs, the radio hosts on black-music-oriented stations. These media savvy men and women captured the explosion of black consciousness on a daily basis during their playful banter between songs and their community announcements, which frequently included protest activities as well as cultural events. The DJ was in the homes of all black Americans and for many was the center of black life. Every major city had at least one black radio station and a stylish, hip, sassy, flashy DJ or two to represent their audience. Many of these DJs took the explosion of black radicalism in stride, and their recognition of the pulse of the people was instrumental in popularizing the black power movement overall, especially in urban areas. Detroit's Martha Jean "the Queen" Steinberg explains what the purpose of radio personalities was in the 1960s:

> We talked like the African drummers used to talk years ago. We talked in a code—"Yes mammy o Daddy, get on down!" We talked about what to do, but some people didn't know what we were talking about. . . . We were the cause of the civil rights movement . . . after it started moving about the nation we let everybody know what was going on, because no one would interview Martin Luther King. No one knew Jesse Jackson. Nobody interviewed these preachers, so we did that ourselves.[40]

Martin Luther King Jr. was well aware of the role of black DJs in the community, and he made specific efforts to cultivate their support as he engaged in civil disobedience around the country. The offices of radio station WERD in Atlanta were directly above King's SCLC headquarters, and he could prepare the radio station for an upcoming announcement through a thump on the ceiling.

In some cases, black radio became black power radio. The militant NAACP leader Robert F. Williams became one of the first and most outspoken movement radio hosts. The Monroe, Louisiana, civil rights leader had developed a black armed guard to police the black neighborhoods in defense against rampant KKK attacks. Williams's principled and public use of guns prompted the NAACP to remove him from leadership.

After a chaotic episode in which a white couple inadvertently found themselves in Williams's home needing protection—Williams aided the couple—Williams was charged with kidnapping and fled the country. In Cuba, Williams wrote the book *Negroes With Guns* and, with the aid of Fidel Castro, began a weekly broadcast, *Radio Free Dixie*, that combined a "voice of agitation and prophesy" with a mix of jazz, blues, gospel, soul, and protest songs. *Radio Free Dixie* could be heard throughout the South and the Eastern Seaboard on Friday nights, setting a standard of what black power radio could accomplish.

In Los Angeles in 1964, the KGFJ DJ Nathaniel "Magnificent" Montague had developed his own signature radio catchphrase, chanting "Burn, baby, burn" whenever a hot song or entertaining banter took place on the air. When Watts exploded in the summer of 1965, the chant was already in use, and the mainstream press conveniently blamed Montague's chant for the melee instead of the conditions facing black Angelenos. Montague continued to use the chant during the days of turmoil, generating a response from his management to desist. At first he refused because, he says, he understood his audience:

> Nobody else was giving them a voice—not the NAACP, not the preachers, not my station's other deejays. But just like a song, you have to give 'em a refrain to make 'em accept it, because they won't do anything they don't want to do. The Negro church was telling them it was wrong to burn. I wouldn't do that. I knew what they were feeling. I knew they felt weak, and I knew the rioting made them feel powerful for once in their lives—that's why, again, we call it a rebellion, not against a certain policy or a particular law, but against weakness. Maybe they didn't know what they wanted. Maybe they only knew what they didn't want, what they would not stand for. It was a start.[41]

After days of resistance and a weekend to cool down, Montague relented and began using the phrase "Have mercy, Los Angeles" as a means of healing the city. A multifaceted collector of black history and a music producer, Montague recorded his own music, wrote black-conscious poems, and designed black-oriented curricula for public schools years ahead of the move to create black studies programs. To say that the singularly popular Montague was in tune with the black power movement may have been an understatement.

In Chicago a stream of stylized DJs such as "Lucky" Cordell, Bruce Brown, Purvis Spann, and Herb Kent "the Cool Gent" ruled the airwaves at WVON. Kent and Spann were civil rights activists as well as on-air personalities, and they would provide appropriate commentary for their audiences when events would take place and often broadcast at civil rights events. The programmers at WVON were instrumental in supporting Jesse Jackson's work on Operation Breadbasket and a number of other local causes. It was a time in black America when the local news was as important as the local music, and the soulful black newscaster was part of the cultural milieu. A fledgling news reporter named Don Cornelius emerged from WVON with a vision to capture black music and dance on his own daily television program, *Soul Train*. *Soul Train* would emerge from the cultural matrix of Chicago soul and become a weekly syndicated program out of Los Angeles that defined black cultural identity for decades.

In New York, the popular WLIB DJ Gary Byrd developed his own brand of black-conscious style and moved from hip banter to making his own music. Byrd recorded a series of R&B music sides that included "If the People Only Knew (the Power of the People)" and "To You Beautiful Black Sister." Byrd's single "Are You Really Ready for Black Power" was a compelling homage to blacks in the movement and a challenge to the average black person:

> Are your really ready for black power?
> Have you thought about where you're at?
> Are your really ready for black power?
> And are you sure your mind is black?

In the modern context, explicitly race-conscious music is hard to find. But at the time Byrd was recording these soul sides, James Brown had established a new tradition of truth-telling in popular music. DJs were playing "Say It Loud—I'm Black and I'm Proud," which reached number one on the R&B charts. In that sense, Byrd's works were direct offshoots of Brown's smash hit single. Gary Byrd's vision, like that of many of the hip, flashy, sassy, black-conscious radio personalities of the day, was tuned directly into the mood of the streets of black America. These DJs offered their audiences a unique combination of universal appeal and race consciousness.

Since the mid-1950s a number of these prolific black DJs had organized into an association, later named the National Association of Television and Radio Announcers (NATRA), led by Jack Gibson, Tommy
Smalls, and a dozen other black media pioneers. The group initially met
to socialize with industry executives, to secure distribution of product,
and to keep business connections intact. However, there was always an
understanding that the forum provided a means of addressing griev-
ances for the members with their predominantly white music industry counterparts. As the group's conventions grew larger in the 1960s,
the voices of dissent became louder. At the 1968 convention, held in
Miami only months after the murder of Martin Luther King Jr., an air of
hostility took over the event and incidents of violence and intimidation
were commonplace. As William Barlow explains, "White record executives, such as Atlantic's Jerry Wexler, and Phil Walden, Otis Redding's
manager, were threatened with violence by roving bands of unidenti-
fied 'militants' unless they paid 'reparations' on the spot. New Orleans
record producer Marshall Sehorn and others were actually beaten up
when they refused to pay."[42] Needless to say, this chaotic event put an
end to the effectiveness of NATRA, but a statement had been made:
the plantation mentality of the R&B industry would not be tolerated
any longer.

Washington, DC, DJ Del Shields is adamant about the impact that
black radio DJs had in general, and he believes the beginning of the end
of their influence came when Martin Luther King Jr. was murdered and
black radio hosts remained on the air through the night to communicate
with their people: "All across the country, the black disc jockey went
to the microphone and talked to his people. . . . It was black radio that
doused the incendiary flames across America. We curtailed the riots.
Had we not been on, and told the people, don't burn baby, and all of that,
it would have been much worse. And somebody sat up and said, 'whoa
this is too much. This is too much power. We can't let them have it.'"
Shields remains convinced that the demise of the stylish, well-connected
black radio DJ was deliberate. "Somebody detected that this was too
much power, it had to be broken up. So one of the ways to break it up
was . . . to get rid of personality radio. . . . Take away the personality of
radio and develop it into a 'format' and you've got the garbage that you
have today."[43]

What Happened to Soul?

Through the first half of the 1970s, soul music enjoyed a zenith of popularity and relevance in terms of the depth and breadth of the music recorded and the credibility and talents of the artists delivering the music. Striking fusions of social statements, love philosophy, and grooving rhythms could be heard from the O'Jays ("For the Love of Money"), Harold Melvin and the Blue Notes ("Bad Luck"), the Main Ingredient ("Everybody Plays the Fool"), Gladys Knight and the Pips ("Neither One of Us"), the Four Tops ("Keeper of the Castle"), the Isley Brothers, and the standard bearers, Stevie Wonder and Marvin Gaye. Yet gradually, and perhaps directly, as the black freedom movement waned, black freedom music faded from popularity.

What happened to soul? A case can be made that soul music survived as long as there was a movement in place to give the music social meaning. Soul music, music from the soul, necessarily involves an emotional involvement in the subject matter. If one produced a love song, one must infuse that song with an element of love from their own soul to give the experience authenticity. In the case of a vibrant social movement, the emotional involvement transcends the personal relationship and reaches out toward a larger set of relationships. Thus, "Respect" and "People Get Ready" are songs that denote a larger love, a love of humanity and of people in motion toward something greater. The requirements of soul music during the black revolution were more deeply ingrained and required a deeper sense of group solidarity and identification. This identification was expressed not only through lyrics but also in the tone, the tension, and the sense of assertiveness and urgency in the delivery.

As the 1970s progressed, there was a marked decline in nationally recognized black activism. At best, one can say that social movement activism was accomplished on a localized basis. There were fervent hot spots of racial confrontation, such as the forced school busing drama in Boston and the stark racially charged local elections in cities such as Atlanta (which elected its first black mayor, Maynard Jackson Jr., in 1973) and Chicago (which elected its first black mayor, Harold Washington, in 1983). In many cities the African American population underwent social changes not reported on the nightly news. The 1968 Fair Housing Act (passed during the crises following the murder of Martin

Luther King Jr.) eliminated one of the barriers to black homeowner-ship outside of traditional black communities and allowed for an exodus of black homeowners leaving (escaping?) the ghettos for safer (whiter?) neighborhoods. Meanwhile, the mean streets of black America became meaner, as many impoverished communities were inundated with illicit drugs, and a sense of bewilderment, confusion, and depression overtook many people, including thousands of traumatized Vietnam veterans. The rise of a black middle class was contrasted with the entrenchment of a dispossessed black underclass that no longer had even the millenar-ian mythos of Martin Luther King's "we shall overcome" to work with. It is in this cultural vacuum that hip-hop emerged as a voice from, and a voice for, the invisible urban underclass.

In the early 1970s, a great many soul songs anticipated a new world of freedom in their message and their moods. Songs like "Move on Up" by Curtis Mayfield, "I Wish I Knew How It Would Feel to Be Free" by Nina Simone, and "Someday We'll All Be Free" by Donny Hathaway reflected this implicit sense of hope and possibility. As the 1970s passed into the 1980s, the hope for a promising future in black America and in black popular music was replaced by a yearning for the better times from "back in the day." A verse from Rick James's 1981 song "Ghetto Life" perhaps best represents the end of those freedom dreams:

> One thing about the ghetto
> you don't have to hurry
> it'll be there tomorrow
> so brother don't you worry.

By 1975 the last of the great movement songs ("Fight the Power" by the Isley Brothers and "Wake Up Everybody" by Harold Melvin and the Blue Notes) were released, yet it might be said that the movement had died years before. It was the premise and the purpose of soul music to represent the unity of purpose in the black experience, even when that unity was rapidly dissolving.

At its height, soul music was the living pulse of the black commu-nity, the conscience of the movement, and a daily inspiration to keep on pushing. When Curtis Mayfield wrote "People Get Ready" in 1965, he was tapping into a collective sense of anticipation of an oncoming social transformation. This is when soul was at its best.

Five years later, those ideas of change had metastasized into something far more confrontational and ominous. When the Lumpen performed the radicalized version of "People Get Ready" in 1970, they were tapping into these palpable energies that were anticipating radical change. They took the optimistic aesthetic of soul and extended its message to the militant extreme.

The Lumpen had crafted a brand of militant soul music, and if that seemed outrageous, theirs was but another domino dropping in the series of revolutionary social changes taking place all around them. Their work was kindling to help inflame the *revolution of the mind* taking place within the souls of black folk in this watershed moment.

5

"For Freedom"

Cultural Nationalism
and the Black Panther Party

As the Lumpen prepare for the next number to follow "People Get Ready," the revolutionary chants are given and the audience responds enthusiastically:

> All Power to the People! *All Power to the People!*
> All Power to the People! *All Power to the People!*
> Free Bobby! *Free Bobby!*
> Free Ericka! *Free Ericka!*
> Free Angela! *Free Angela!*
> Death to the fascist Pigs! *Death to the fascist Pigs!*
> Right on! *Right on!*

The music rolls in slowly. Many in the crowd recognize the gentle ballad and give applause. Earlier that year, the Motown group the Temptations had released their album *Psychedelic Shack*, which became a number one R&B album for the singing superstars, and the album's songs were well known to a typical black audience at the time. "It's Summer" was a lighthearted ballad from the B side of the album, with the sweet melodic chorus, "There's magic in the air / green grass everywhere / it's summer." The softly sung chorus was interspersed with spoken word rhymes such as, "Once again the leaves have returned to the trees / I can just feel that soft summer breeze."[1]

Onstage this night the Lumpen singers begin softly harmonizing, as if in a barbershop quartet. As the disarmingly sweet, harmonic music flows in the background onstage at the Merritt College auditorium, William Calhoun admonishes the Motown Recording Company superstars the Temptations in the following dialogue:

> Y'all heard of the Temptations. Out of the Motown stable. And as singers we relate very strongly to the way the Temptations sound. They are a very polished and very professional sounding group.
>
> There's only one thing wrong with the Temptations, and that is that their message is all messed up. Black people and oppressed people in this country, they live in indecent housing, they don't have proper clothing, they don't have adequate food. And all the Temptations can do is tell you to take to cloud nine, 'cause it's all a ball of confusion. What we've done is we've taken the music of the Temptations and given it a little different message.
>
> This tune features Clark Bailey on vocals. And if you can dig it, the next time you see the Temptations, you tell them, "Look here, brother, you'd be all right to come on down and sing with the people, or get on out of Dodge."
>
> If you know the song, feel free to sing along with us. It goes something like this here:

> All right, easy now / Uh all right
> Now there's bullets in the air
> Snipers everywhere
> For freedom.
> Oo oooo oo

The audience howls with approval at the absurd play on words and the audacity of the delivery. Here is a song, almost comical in its benignity, that the Lumpen have parodied to its extreme. The audience, then expecting the familiar spoken word dialogue of the lighthearted song, receives a different spin:

Outside my window I heard shotguns sing
This is the price that oppression brings
A victory for the people, a pig's blood is in the streets
We've got to move now to make it all complete

(*Applause*)

Now there's bullets in the air
Snipers everywhere
For freedom
Oo oooo ooo

The dialogue continues:

Children, throwing Molotovs
Teenagers, shooting from rooftops
Not even drugs can be found
The brothers, they even put their wine bottles down

Now there's bullets in the air
Snipers everywhere
For freedom.
Oo oooo ooo

Black people, old and wise
Give us shelter
To fight another day
A colony united
All power to the people
That's all we have to say

Now that fall is here
There'll be millions of things for the people to do
Hijackings, bombings, whatever pleases you
Revolution throughout all the land
We'll go and meet them with guns in our hand

There's bullets in the air (everybody say)
Snipers everywhere
For freedom.
Yeaaah, one more time

Calhoun and the group repeat the chorus four times to an enthusiastic crowd response.

> All Power to the People!
> (Audience) *All Power to the People!*

As the mellow melody subsides, the audience is clearly energized by the revolutionary spirit embodied in the music. The Black Panthers were in many ways adept at political theater, and this rendition may be seen as such. As a parody, the send-up of the Temptations was entertaining to the hometown audience that night. As a call to arms, one can only speculate on the effectiveness of the performance. More than any other song in their repertoire, with "For Freedom" the Lumpen brought about the ideology of the Black Panther Party in its most militant form—that of destabilizing the US government through direct confrontation.[2]

It should be noted that in 1970, acts of political violence from black militants were very rare and most often involved acts of sabotage against the state or hijackings for the purpose of escaping the United States. The idea of political violence designed simply to terrorize civilians was unheard of. The audience response to the outrageous lyrics was one of catharsis. The actions imagined in the song were likely seen as a figurative response to relentless state violence in their community.

What is ironic about the message in "For Freedom" is that by late 1970, the Black Panther Party had been distancing itself officially from tactics such as those imagined in the song. By mid-1970 the party had already endured a series of ruptures and internal battles over the role of direct guerilla activity, the role of whites, the role of women, and their relationship with other black radicals. They were also facing a turning point in their relationship with the larger black community.

The issues the Lumpen members expressed with Motown Records were symbolic of a larger complexity of the black freedom struggle. This chapter explores the contradictions that beset the Black Panther Party in relation to groups and ideas that presumed to be in solidarity with Panther party lines, as well as the contradictions that beset the development of soul music, with its unifying ethos, during the racially polarizing times of revolution.

"It's Summer"

If there was a song on black radio in 1970 worthy of parody, the Temptations' "It's Summer" would qualify. The sugarcoated harmony is delivered with apparently no sense of irony or pretense. The first verse of dialogue sets the tone: "Outside my window, a robin builds a nest / At last winter's gone away to rest." One gets the impression right away that the song is not written for those living in the inner city. Yet the song has an irresistible serenity to it. The delicate mood of the song reflects the wide-ranging performance talents of the Temptations at the time, who were at their peak of popularity. "I just liked the song, that's why I chose it," Lumpen songwriter William Calhoun recalls when asked why it was a part of the Lumpen repertoire.[3]

Fans of the Temptations were aware of the sugary song but were also aware that the music of the Temptations had acquired a rather schizophrenic identity. Releasing albums at the rate of more than two a year, this standard bearer for Motown Records was at a creative crossroads in 1970. The group that was known for disarming five-part vocalizing of the highest order had become world famous with gently swinging pop ballads such as "My Girl" in 1964 and "Get Ready" in 1965. As social unrest took center stage for the youth, the music of the Temptations began to evolve, and even their pop songs took on a grittier edge.

Beginning with the album *Cloud Nine* in early 1969, the Temptations began to sing overextended, dissonant, rock-influenced music that often stretched more than eight minutes long and revealed a deeper social consciousness and gritty, realistic themes. Titles such as "Run Away Child, Running Wild," "Take a Stroll Thru Your Mind," and "Ball of Confusion (That's What the World Is Today)" were stark examples of the new direction the group was exploring in 1969 and 1970. Yet not everyone was convinced of the sincerity of their message. The mastermind of the Temptations was staff writer Norman Whitfield, who had no qualms about the directions or misdirections in his music. As Ben Edmonds writes:

> Whitfield made brilliant records, but his primary mission was to have hits, not deliver messages. "I don't like to speculate," Whitfield told Nelson George. "My thing was to revolutionise the sound . . . but without speculating." He wanted the sound of revolution without the messy, unpredictable reality of revolution itself.[4]

"The sound of revolution without the unpredictable reality of the revolution itself" sums up the approach to a great many releases by Motown at the end of the 1960s. Edmonds goes on to compare the less-than-original *Psychedelic Shack* album to one of the long, fake wigs worn by the members of the Supremes. "It was a longhair wig, and not always a convincing one." The accusations of packaged protest music would follow the Temptations, and Motown Records, throughout the era. There were some exceptions, such as Edwin Starr's ferocious rendition of "War" (originally cut rather tamely by the Temptations on *Psychedelic Shack*), but in general the image of Motown Records was of an entity that was following the trends rather than setting them. Nevertheless, Motown Records, and the Temptations in particular, remained a formidable pop commodity throughout the late 1960s black power period.

Dancing in Detroit

The popular music of Detroit rivaled Chicago soul as an expression of the sensibilities of transplanted southerners working in the North. As the center of automobile manufacturing, the Detroit auto industry produced millions of automobiles per year in factories populated by migrating southern blacks (and whites) before, during, and after World War II. The well-promoted image of the city as a destination for working-class successes gave many Detroiters a strong sense that the city played an epic role in becoming a northern multiracial success story. Motown Records played a large part in creating and cultivating that image nationally. Yet the specter of social unrest was ever present.

In September 1964, when the Motown group Martha and the Vandellas released the song "Dancing in the Street," it quickly earned a dubious status as a symbol of urban protest. Riots in Harlem had taken place earlier that summer of 1964, and the upbeat song somehow symbolized the spirit in the streets. "Calling out around the world / are you ready for a brand new beat / Summer's here and the time is right / for dancing in the street" went the first verse with an energetic dance beat. While on tour, Martha Reeves and her singers had to remind clumsy journalists that the song was simply a party song.[5] One could claim certainly that if one were to actually *dance in the street*, the act would likely be a violation of some civic ordinance. But soul music did not require explicit lyrics to reflect the new energy rising up from the streets of black America.

At Motown Recording Co., however, calls to social protest were not a part of the agenda. The successful black-owned label was founded by Berry Gordy Jr. in 1959. Gordy Junior's entire family of siblings had moved north from Georgia and had become college educated and relatively wealthy. Gordy wanted little to do with the radicalism of the black struggle. He sought, from a very early stage, to ally his record company with the upwardly mobile integrationist community of Detroit. In 1963, for example, Martin Luther King Jr. came to speak at Cobo Hall in Detroit as part of a well-planned Great March to Freedom rally that featured civic leaders in full regalia. Gordy secured the rights to record the speech and released it on his Motown label that August. Through recording Dr. King, Gordy and Motown had entered the movement on *their* terms. Six months later, in 1963, Malcolm X came to speak to the Detroit Grass Roots Leadership Conference at King Solomon Baptist Church, just blocks from Motown headquarters. Malcolm X was greeted by a decidedly enthusiastic black audience, but Motown was not interested in recording his "Message to the Grass Roots," one of his most explicitly militant speeches. Motown wanted to transcend the racial strife even as events were taking place that exploded its integrationist ideals.

In the summer of 1967, Detroit exploded in one of the largest urban riots of the decade. Thousands of people were caught up in five days of rioting, looting, and property damage. The carnage left 43 dead, 7,200 arrested, and more than 2,000 buildings burned to the ground. Many accounts of the riots reveal that it was a multiracial affair—whites as well as blacks were addressing their anger at the economic inequalities in Detroit. Suzanne Smith, in her book *Dancing in the Street: Motown and the Cultural Politics of Detroit*, detailed the nature of the upheaval:

> What began as a rather small outburst of violence against the arresting officers—bottles and cans thrown at the paddy wagons—quickly spread, like wildfire, into a citywide disorder characterized by extensive looting, arson, and sniper attacks.
>
> Unlike Detroit's 1943 race riot, in which blacks and whites physically attacked one another, the 1967 uprising had a distinctly different character and objective. As one observer would later

recall, "It was so clear to my own eyes that white people were out there looting too. Not to say that racial tensions didn't exist, but it wasn't black against white. It was the propertied against the non-propertied."[6]

Motown Records stayed open for business during the days of rioting, and the musicians and singers literally had to dodge debris, broken glass, and gunfire to get to and from the Hitsville recording studios, located just blocks from the worst of the melee. Motown Records songwriter Barrett Strong recalled the chaos of those days.

> I came home, and the street I was living on, the whole block was on fire. My mother was outside she was screaming and crying. We were dragging stuff out in the street and stuff like that. I remember all that. And my wife and I we were asleep in our apartment we would hear gunshots. . . . We had to be in the house by six o'clock because there was a curfew. I had little kids to take care of. It was a very scary, scary scary moment in my life. . . .
>
> See a lot of people call it a race riot, but to me it wasn't. It was just a lot of unrest because of the politics that was going on in the city, it was like the people against the system. That's the way it was.[7]

Civic leaders rushed to mop up the damage, proclaiming plans for a "New Detroit," and promoting urban investment and cultural programs with slogans such as "Detroit Is Happening" and "I Care About Detroit." The Detroit establishment sought to present itself as a model city, and civic leaders were all too happy to have an assimilation-minded black business such as Motown Records as a figurehead for its overtures to social equality and black advancement in their city.[8]

Detroit was a major test case for the integration of the industrialized North, as a great many black workers sustained the automotive industry, working long hours in the mechanized factories. Claustrophobic, toxic places to begin with, blacks typically were handed the most dangerous jobs, given the lowest pay, rarely if ever promoted to foreman, and reprimanded or fired first if trouble started. By the 1960s the sheen had worn off the idea that factory labor in the North would provide greater opportunities for blacks migrating from the South.

Out of the 1967 riots emerged a number of black leaders, such as Kenneth Cockrel, John Watson, Chuck Wooten, and General Baker, who

sought to capture the urgency of the moment and create Black Nationalist organizations to sustain their efforts. These men had been student
organizers at nearby Wayne State University, had organized among black
radicals and Marxist groups, and had studied the works of Mao, Lenin,
and Che Guevara. General Baker was one of the first organizers, and
one of the first plant workers fired. Baker and the others went on to
produce a Black Nationalist newspaper, the *Inner City Voice (ICV)*, and
proclaimed it to be Detroit's black community newspaper and "the voice
of revolution."[9]

On May 2, 1968, exactly one year to the day after the Black Panthers marched into the California state capitol building, four thousand
black and white workers at the Dodge Main Plant staged a wildcat strike.
When the Chrysler officials punished the black strikers more harshly
by firing most of them, the workers formed their own organization: the
Dodge Revolutionary Union Movement (DRUM). DRUM utilized the
outlet of the *ICV* paper to regularly announce that "the black working
class would be the vanguard of the revolutionary struggle in this country."[10] Utilizing the methods of study sessions and careful one-by-one
recruiting, the organization slowly but steadily developed a well-read,
dedicated membership.

The DRUM leadership was also in touch with the rhythms of the
street. As Suzanne Smith explains, there was initially a decidedly grass-
roots feeling about the methods and the message of DRUM:

> The DRUM movement relied on cultural expression and indepen-
> dent forms of cultural production to communicate its political mes-
> sage. . . . At one wildcat protest some DRUM activists "danced in
> the street" and beat bongo drums outside the Dodge Main Plant to
> draw attention to their cause and intimidate their opponents.[11]

The leaders of DRUM were serious about their connection to the
plight of workers in Detroit, as well as to a larger union movement
nationwide. They rapidly pushed in both directions. Other plants in the
auto industry formed their own Revolutionary Union Movement organizations and eventually an umbrella organization was formed, the League
of Revolutionary Black Workers (LRBW). The LRBW leaders enlisted
the support of SNCC veteran James Forman, who established ambitious
plans for the organization. Revolutionary Union Movements were going

to be established in industrial sites across the northeast and networked through the Detroit base of operations. However, lateral growth across a national collective of black radical unions was not as important to many as the establishment of a central base of strength in Detroit to fight against the automakers and the Detroit ruling classes. The tactic left Detroit black radicals thin at every front, and by the early 1970s they had lost touch with the rank-and-file workers as well as their leverage to disrupt the industry. Just as the spirit of DRUM faded from the organizations, Motown Records began moving its operations from Detroit to Los Angeles, delivering a double blow to the economic and cultural aspirations of black workers and dreamers in Detroit.[12]

DRUM and the *Inner City Voice* wanted little to do with Motown Records. To them, Motown was little more than another corporation, underpaying and overworking its own rank-and-file. Articles in the *Inner City Voice* offered harsh critiques and little praise for Detroit's own, the largest and most profitable black-owned company in the United States. To the constituency of the *Inner City Voice* and the many union organizers, Motown Records was more interested in its own profits and was far removed from the struggle to improve economic opportunities for workers in Detroit and elsewhere.[13]

Ironically, Motown Records would eventually face the music for faulty treatment of its own workers. In the fall of 1967, shortly after the riots, the songwriting team of Eddie Holland, Lamont Dozier, and Brian Holland—known as the famed H-D-H team, responsible for ten of the twelve number one pop tunes by the Supremes—was among the first to break with the lucrative label and leave over claims of underpayment. Most, if not all, of the well-known artists at Motown were being paid far less than what they were earning for the label. Martha Reeves, the label's first female superstar, is convinced that her career stalled because she was "the first person at Motown to ask where the money was going."[14] Even Eddie Kendricks of the Temptations, during the height of the group's popularity, was ready to take on the label. "Eddie's solution was simpler," original member Otis Williams recalled: "The Temptations would go on strike—no more tours, no more records."[15] Eddie Kendricks would leave the Temptations in 1970 but signed on as a solo artist with Motown subsidiary Tamla and recorded there until 1977 with a moderate string of hits such as "Keep On Truckin'," "Boogie Down," "Shoeshine Boy," and

"He's a Friend." To finally get out of his Motown contract, Kendricks had to abandon the rights to his music publishing—the means of recouping monies for subsequent reissues, covers, and song samples. Clearly Berry Gordy knew how to run his organization like the other successful corporations in Detroit.[16]

Musically, Motown had to be dragged into its message-music phase under the leadership of songwriter Norman Whitfield, who filled the void left by the H-D-H team and introduced the scratch guitar, bongos, psychedelic sound effects, and solo singing verses (à la Sly and the Family Stone) to the music of the Temptations, Gladys Knight and the Pips, the Undisputed Truth, Edwin Starr, and Marvin Gaye. While Berry Gordy Jr. was spending most of his time is Los Angeles by 1969, seeking to expand into film and television, he found that the black radical movement was even stronger there. After the death of Martin Luther King Jr. in 1968, three Motown staffers approached Gordy with the idea of a subsidiary label devoted entirely to social issues. Gordy then authorized the release of a number of radical speeches and poetry on the Black Forum label, including a recording by Langston Hughes entitled *Writers of the Revolution*, and a heart-wrenching anthology of voices of black soldiers in Vietnam, entitled *Guess Who's Coming Home*, in 1972.

The famous battles for creative independence in 1971 that were fought by the label's two giants, Marvin Gaye and Stevie Wonder, wherein each had to threaten to leave the label before their own musical visions would be accommodated, made it clear that Motown would have to adapt to the times.

As the Lumpen announced onstage, the Temptations' music was universally appreciated; however, from the point of view of many radicals—and the Lumpen in particular—Motown's message music was often seen as superficial, cynical, profit-driven, radical-chic populism. In the same way that Motown blazed a trail as the most successful black-owned business of its time, there were strong voices of dissent from certain sides of the black experience. Ironically, the Panthers, as the most "successful" black radical organization of its time, would find a storm of dissenters from among their ranks as well.

The Black Panthers did not play a significant role in Detroit's revolutionary union politics. Two DRUM members, Luke Tripp and John Williams, were members of the initial Detroit Panther chapter. However, the Panthers' base—designed to organize the brothers on the block—drew outside of the black labor community, and the groups did not mesh. As James Geschwender writes:

> [The League] believed that the Oakland-based Black Panther Party was moving in the wrong direction by concentrating on organizing lumpen elements of the Black community. The League did not believe that a successful movement could be based upon the lumpen as they lack a potential source of power. The League believed that Black workers were the most promising base for a successful Black movement because of the potential power derived from their ability to disrupt industrial production.[17]

Further, the black union leaders in Detroit had witnessed many betrayals from white union members so they were not very interested in alliances across racial lines. The relationship between the Panthers and the League of Revolutionary Black Workers continued to deteriorate, and Tripp was purged from the BPP in 1969.[18]

It is likely that Panther leader Huey Newton learned from the example of the drawbacks of the LRBW's nationwide reach. Around the time of the demise of the black radical union efforts in Detroit in the early 1970s, Newton announced the closing of many Panther chapters nationwide and consolidated his resources—and personal control over the organization—in Oakland. It was not mere folly. Based in Oakland, Newton saw the city's resources as within the grasp of his revolutionary organization. When Newton's Party announced in 1972 that Bobby Seale would be running for mayor and Elaine Brown for city council in the 1973 Oakland municipal elections, Newton had his sights set on the lucrative Port of Oakland, which was then administered by the city. The port was one of the leading launching grounds for goods to and from the Pacific Rim to US markets. Newton visualized that Panther control of this central commercial hub would provide leverage for instrumental changes at a municipal level to the benefit of his people.

Huey Newton sought to play on the Black Nationalist and anticapitalist sympathies of Oakland residents in order to initiate a takeover of the city—and, presumably, the economy of the West Coast—through the electoral process. Newton's plan was not an isolated one. Detroit was also a battleground of Black Nationalist–inspired politics through controlled leverage of unionized labor. In Newark, New Jersey, Amiri Baraka sought to implement a race-based project of civic control through hard-fought black electoral leadership in 1970. It can be argued that Black Nationalist ideologies, in certain urban areas where it was strongest, came close to restructuring the apparatus of power in select cities.[19]

Black power meant different things to different people in the late 1960s. Some used the concept to build autonomous black institutions while others used it to advocate the destruction of the white power apparatus and to disrupt business as usual. Still others used the black power concept to help forge a new national identity among blacks, one that could generate a broad new wave of culture and activism that could help bring about social change. The approaches to black consciousness varied, yet were connected through a sense of a collective black ethos and a collective black struggle. At no other time in America's history have so many threads of radical black consciousness been articulated on the national stage at once. The cry was louder than ever, but in practical terms the messages were all variations of a Black Nationalist theme.

Black Nationalism

Robert Allen, in his pathbreaking study, *Black Awakening in Capitalist America*, defines Black Nationalism as an ever-present thread of consciousness within black America that rises to the surface at times of rupture and crisis. The late 1960s was certainly one of these historical moments. "A glance at history suggests that it would be more correct to say that nationalism, and overt separatism, are ever-present undercurrents in the collective black psyche which constantly interact with the assimilationist tendency and, in times of crisis, rise to the surface to become major themes."[20]

The concept of nationalism has existed for centuries and is spawned from the era of colonial rule when European nations conquered and then defined nationhood for their subjects on European terms. As colonized countries sought to reclaim their political independence after World War II, they frequently sought to reclaim their national identity through means both political (i. e., militarily) and cultural. National liberation movements involved more than mere territorial disputes, they were efforts to reclaim (or re-create) a national culture of an indigenous orientation, which was always problematic in a colonized context.

The notion of Black Nationalism also has roots in the US antislavery struggle in the 1800s. Many of the most prominent black antislavery agitators entertained notions of a black return to Africa and various forms of black sovereignty, such as an independent black state. This notion was still strong in the early 1900s when Marcus Garvey developed the Universal Negro Improvement Association (UNIA), the largest Black Nationalist organization in world history. Through black pride and business enterprises, and with much pomp and theater, Garvey, as a Pan-Africanist, sought to develop a sense of nationhood among blacks in the United States, the Caribbean, and worldwide.

Similar to Garveyism, the US–based Nation of Islam (NOI) sought to organize blacks into self-help institutions through strict behaviors and affirmative racial consciousness that was developed through a variant of Islam. Founded by the enigmatic W. D. Fard in Detroit in 1930, the organization played upon the frustrations of recent southern immigrants and attracted a dedicated following with proclamations of a glorious, distant mecca and denunciations of whites and white institutions. Fard transformed a young recruit named Elijah Poole into his first Chief Minister of Islam, Elijah Muhammad. Muhammad would found Temple Number Two in Chicago, where the organization would continue to grow and become nationally prominent.

The NOI saw itself as having a "civilizing" mission upon downtrodden African Americans, and the means toward this redemption were through discipline, hard work, and collective racial self-reliance. The NOI promoted a racial ideology of black supremacy that posited that blacks were the original men and whites (cast as devils) were seen as a genetic mistake and a curse put upon blacks. The most important element of their rhetoric was the steadfast counterpoint to white supremacy that the NOI provided for its followers. The daily work of rehabilitation of blacks in perpetual crisis earned the Nation a significant measure of respect within the community despite their non-Christian beliefs and separatist practices. Amiri Baraka described the essential appeal of the Nation:

> The reason Mr. Muhammad's Nation of Islam has had such success gathering black people from the grass roots is that Mr. Muhammad offers a program that reflects a totality of black consciousness.

Islam is a form of spirit worship (a moral guide) as well as a socio-economic program. . . . It must be a culture, a way of feeling, a way of living, that is replaced with a culture, feeling, way of living and being, that is black, and yes, finally more admirable.[21]

The NOI grew in national prominence in the late 1950s with the popularity of its national spokesman, Minister Malcolm X. In his early recorded speeches as spokesman for the NOI, Malcolm asserted that the best solution to the race problem in America was "complete and total separation" of the races. Malcolm X eventually developed his own ideas that contradicted many of the main precepts of the NOI, and after some intrigues with leader Elijah Muhammad, Malcolm X broke with the NOI in early 1964 and thrived as a national black leader on his own terms.

Malcolm X traveled the world and helped internationalize the plight of black Americans and furthered the growth of an African consciousness among increasingly radicalized blacks in America. Malcolm explored his own faith and went to Mecca to participate in the pilgrimage, or hajj, required of all Muslims. Malcolm became an orthodox Sunni Muslim, with the name El-Hajj Malik El-Shabazz. After experiencing what he saw as the brotherhood of all races during his hajj, Malcolm returned to the United States and denounced his racist presumptions, proclaiming American racism to be a disease that afflicted whites, rather than a genetic predisposition. Malcolm's new position on race served to expand his potential audience and pool of supporters. After his assassination in February 1965 and the publication of *The Autobiography of Malcolm X* later that year, a number of new, radical black consciousness movements began to emerge.

One of the strongest threads of black consciousness to emerge in the later half of the 1960s was cultural nationalism. Black cultural nationalism, as it developed in the 1960s, was a form of Black Nationalism that emphasized a reconstruction of black identity based on an interpretation of African culture and values. It embodied a belief that a process of reclamation of the African/black mind and spirit was a prerequisite to the development of the black revolutionary. Cultural nationalism and the cultural nationalist movement also provided theories of leadership and political strategy, economic organization, and community structure that its supporters felt could sustain revolutionary change. Its most dramatic impact was in the realm of the arts and culture, where a great many blacks from this period adopted the dress, language, and lifestyle of a cultural nationalist; much of the black literature, poetry, music, and visual arts reflected and portrayed cultural nationalist sensibilities in the late 1960s and early 1970s.

The US Organization

The Los Angeles–based US Organization led by Maulana (Ron) Karenga was the prominent cultural nationalist organization on the West Coast in the late 1960s. Like the BPP, the US Organization developed as an outgrowth of the prevailing conceptions of an oncoming black revolution and what the leaders felt were the necessary steps to follow through, to a large degree, with Malcolm X's vision. The US Organization also had a strong influence on Black Nationalist politics in the New York and Newark metropolitan area. The cultural nationalist Amiri Baraka was an avid follower of Karenga's teachings at the time and helped to spread them throughout the eastern United States.

Born Ron Everett in rural Maryland in 1941 as the last of fourteen children, the US Organization leader grew up in a hardworking family that sent a number of siblings to college. Everett followed an older brother to Los Angeles and was a student of anthropology and languages at Los Angeles City College, where he became class president, and later at UCLA where Everett obtained a master's degree in political science. Everett was a frequent visitor to the Nation of Islam events in the early 1960s and worked alongside Donald Warden in the Afro-American Association, the statewide organization that at one time also included Huey Newton and Bobby Seale. The US Organization was developed initially by Karenga and Hakim Jamal, who was a personal friend of Malcolm X, as an outgrowth of the Watts riots of 1965. Originally, US was designed around the legacy of Malcolm in spirit and practice, but Karenga quickly dominated the partnership and changed the emphasis of the organization toward his own ideas, and Jamal left.

Because of his studies of African languages, philosophy, and culture and his immersion into black radicalism, Ron Everett changed his name to Karenga, which is a Kikuyu word meaning "keeper of tradition" (from Jomo Kenyatta's book *Facing Mt. Kenya*). He gave himself the title Maulana, which is an honorific term meaning "master teacher" in Swahili and Arabic. He taught Swahili at a local cultural center and became a prominent Black Nationalist in Los Angeles.

Karenga outlined the premises of black cultural nationalism in his organization as one that sought to cleanse, purify, and reclaim the culture of black Americans, with a specific design for preparing them for the oncoming revolution in America. Karenga believed and preached that the cultural revolution must precede the violent one: "The Revolution being fought now is a revolution to win the minds of our people. If we fail to win this we cannot wage the violent one."[22] He also stressed the centrality of culture to the life of a liberated person:

> Culture is the basis of all ideas, images and actions. To move is to move culturally, i.e., by a set of values given to you by your culture. . . . Everything that we do, think, or learn is somehow interpreted as a culture expression. So when we discuss politics, to US that is a sign of culture. When we discuss economics, to US that is a sign of culture. When we discuss community organization, that to US is a sign of culture. In other words, we define culture as a complete value system and also a means and ways of maintaining that value system.[23]

Karenga developed a massively detailed social organization with myriad concepts and rules to follow, including the Nguzo Saba (the seven principles of blackness) and Kawaida (the philosophy of cultural nationalism). Members were instructed in the language of Swahili and the observation of Karenga-invented rituals such as Kuzaliwa (celebration of Malcolm X's birthday on May 19), Uhuru Day (a commemoration of the Watts Uprising of August 1965), and the most widely known, Kwanzaa, held the week following Christmas.

These activities and rituals were part of a process of decolonization that Karenga and many others felt was necessary to free black Americans of their subjugated, colonized mentalities. Rules of social conduct were extremely strict and had a particular impact on female members. Karenga developed a house system that stated, among other things, "What makes a woman appealing is femininity and she can't be feminine without being submissive."[24] Karenga's house system also allowed for polygamy, although the practice was not well established, and many US women strongly resisted the sexist precepts.

Nevertheless, the presence of the highly disciplined, impeccably dressed (in African-style clothing), knowledgeable Black Nationalists in the US Organization had a great impact on idealistic young blacks at the time. The African aesthetic and the militant stance caught the interest of mainstream media as well, and as early as 1966 US members were photographed practicing self-defense skills on the cover of *Life* magazine.[25]

The impact of US was far-reaching and influenced a great many people who were not members of the organization. UCLA student and journalist Archie Ivy, who would later become a member of George Clinton's Parliament/Funkadelic as a publicist and songwriter, was initially drawn to Karenga's vision. "I was impressed by the theology, by the history, by the sense of purpose, and by the blackness of the whole thing," he recalls. "I was not impressed by the Panthers that brought their guns, their rifles on [the UCLA] campus. I did not think the military thing was going to get us [anything] beyond getting shot up. I agreed with the idea that a strong culture would make us prepared to take any action."[26]

Despite the differences between the black radical groups in Southern California at the end of the 1960s, many were able to work together in the realm of music. The Black Nationalist oriented jazz of Horace Tapscott was one example. Tapscott's avant-garde big band the Pan Afrikan Peoples Arkestra was a driving free-jazz ensemble with many elements of African-inspired rhythm and presentation and was composed of members of the Nation of Islam, orthodox Muslims, independent black radicals, and at least three Black Panther Party members. A great deal of the free jazz being developed by black musicians coast to coast was involved in a continuing process of de-Westernizing themselves and their audiences.

In 1969 James Mtume, an accomplished jazz composer and US Organization member, sought to record an album that linked cultural nationalism and free jazz. (Mtume is best known for his R&B hits with his band Mtume in the 1980s.) Mtume was born James Heath Jr., the son of accomplished reedman Jimmy Heath. The younger Heath got involved with US in 1966 and Karenga gave him the name Mtume, which means "messenger."

In 1969 Mtume used his influence in the jazz community to record a musical tribute to Karenga titled *Kawaida*. The stunning free-jazz collective produced a series of improvisational recordings with chants and poems that celebrated and expressed Karenga's philosophies. The contributions of guest stars such as Albert Heath, Don Cherry, and Herbie Hancock revealed the impact of the movement and the movement's ideas. Mtume however had grown disillusioned with Karenga's organization, just as he was heaping praise on the leader. Mtume recalls that he "had to separate the principles from the person" as he continued to produce Black Nationalist jazz recordings in the early 1970s before signing on to tour with the equally bold jazz-fusion iconoclast Miles Davis.

Mtume influenced other jazz musicians in the exploration of African culture. Around the time of the *Kawaida* album, Herbie Hancock began his lifelong apprenticeship with the electronic synthesizer and began to develop his own free-form flow of electronic-influenced jazz. But instead of a futuristic theme, Hancock's first electronic jazz album was titled *Mwandishi* (Swahili for "composer"). Revealing the cultural nationalist influence, Hancock's entire band gave themselves Swahili names for the record. One highlight of the 1970 album was a complex, thirteen minute, 15/4-time musical tribute to Anglea Davis titled "Ostinato (Suite for Angela)."

In a sense, the work of the free-jazz groups could be seen as principled movement work because of its ideological focus and dedication. Going to see a Black Nationalist jazz concert was often an effort to be part of the movement, not necessarily a chance to party down. Archie Ivy recalls that the black conscious free jazz was performed almost as theater, as a discursive space for forming one's blackness. "Yeah, we were all finding our way, finding ourselves. These shows pushed that on us," he says. Mtume described the purpose of his music in 1969 as "the continuing process of nationalist consciousness manifesting its message within the context of one of our strongest resources." Yet even Mtume warned that "music must not go so far out that it transcends the ability of the people to grasp its meaning and message."[27] As Archie Ivy explains, there were other means for blacks to socialize at the time: "The campus scene had the jazz concerts, and there was parties and the party music where you heard the Motown songs, and then there was the underground parties when the Al Green and the James Brown came out."[28]

Amiri Baraka

Karenga's ideas of cultural nationalism were taken and developed by the playwright and activist Amiri Baraka (formerly LeRoi Jones), who used many of the premises of cultural nationalism to invigorate and organize the blacks of Newark, New Jersey, into a voting bloc that engineered the election of Newark's first black mayor, Kenneth Gibson, in 1970. Baraka's growing organization stood on the threshold of gaining significant leverage in the Newark city infrastructure and had plans to redevelop black housing units and commercial districts based on a Karenga-inspired plan of black community design and control.

Born in Newark, New Jersey, in 1934 to a black working-class family, the articulate LeRoi Jones earned a scholarship to Rutgers, but after experiencing his own "cultural dislocation" he transferred to Howard University. After a stint in the air force, he relocated to New York City. His quick wit, penchant for hyperbole, forceful assertiveness, indefatigable creativity, and political courage made him a leader on many fronts. After his first volume of published poetry, *Preface to a Twenty Volume Suicide Note*, in 1963 Jones wrote the definitive treatment on black music history—*Blues People: Negro Music in White America*—and made a name for himself as a nationalist playwright, author, and poet to be reckoned with. The assassination of Malcolm X was a turning point for Jones. Before the year was out, he had created the Black Arts Repertory Theatre/School (BARTS) and begun a series of programs to provide and produce black art in the community. As he explains:

> The most important things we wanted to do were 1. Create an art that was "Black" in form, feeling and content. 2. We wanted to bring that art "into the streets." We wanted a "mass art," out of the little elitist dens of ambiguity. And so we performed in parks, on the streets and on the sidewalks (literally), in vacant lots, housing projects, playgrounds, in front of bars and supermarkets. The most important point 3. We wanted a Revolutionary Art, not just skin flicks. We were Malcolm's Children, and we wanted a Malcolm Art! One that was itself a call for Black Self-Determination. Self-Respect and Self-Defense, plus W. E. B. Du Bois's "True Self-Consciousness."[29]

The "true self-consciousness" of Du Bois was a prominent theme during the years of the revolution. In 1903 Du Bois, the first "Negro" to receive a doctorate from Harvard, wrote a powerful essay in his book *The Souls of Black Folk* in which he explained the "double consciousness" of the Negro, who was burdened with the deeply ingrained self-knowledge of whites as well as their own Negro identity, rendering "two warring ideals in one dark body." The resolution of this conundrum, specifically for the Black Nationalists, was to purge their white consciousness and to think, act, and dream "black."

BARTS succumbed to power struggles between black radical groups and did not survive its first year, but the impact was felt nationwide. Jones accepted an invitation to teach at San Francisco State as a visiting scholar in the spring of 1967. He found himself in a boiling pot of Black Nationalist activism on the West Coast, working among the Black Panthers and other artists in the Bay Area while developing a relationship with Karenga in Los Angeles.

LeRoi Jones was originally given the Arabic name Ameer Barakat ("blessed prince") by Hajj Heshaam Jaaber, the Islamic priest who eulogized Malcolm X. Jaaber's gesture was essentially an effort to recruit Baraka, as by 1966 Baraka's writing and organizing among the black radical community had inspired the entire Black Arts movement and increased the political consciousness and artistic production among young blacks. In 1968 Karenga would influence Baraka to Africanize the name, changing Ameer to Amiri and Barakat to Baraka. Karenga also gave Baraka an exhalted title, Imamu, which meant "high priest" or "holy teacher," thus Imamu Amiri Baraka was his name and title during this time.

Baraka quickly became enamored of the seriousness of Karenga's plan and presentation, and eventually took many of Karenga's doctrines back to Newark. When Baraka helped to organize a series of Black Nationalist conventions throughout the northeast, Karenga was a keynote speaker at many of them. Gradually Baraka became a steadfast Karenga disciple and demanded that members of his organizations recite Karenga doctrine on a daily basis. As Baraka wrote in his autobiography:

> Because I was so self-critical, especially from a black nationalist perspective, the fact of the US organization—i.e., that it was an organization and not just a bunch of undisciplined people taking up time

mostly arguing with each other about what to do, or what method to use, even about things that most agreed should be done—that I was drawn to the US and Karenga. He was quick-witted, sharp tongued, with a kind of amusing irony to his putdowns of white people, America, black people, or whatever, that I admired. Plus, there was no doubt, when you were around Karenga, as to who was *the* leader, even if you weren't in his organization. And if you were, *all* things revolved around Maulana.[30]

Baraka was among the leaders of the Congress of African People (CAP), which drew delegates from chapters nationwide that were organizing under a Black Nationalist framework. In Newark, Baraka led the Committee for a Unified NewArk (CFUN), which sought to galvanize black outrage at the municipal government's white minority leadership. Baraka held many political coalitions together and was also tied to the political jazz community and the black writers and playwrights in the NYC area. Baraka was able to take the black consciousness raising aspects of cultural nationalism and turn them into political action and community control efforts through CFUN, CAP, and other black radical organizations.

On July 11, 1967, Newark exploded. The simmering heat coupled with outrage from an incident of police brutality, exploding into five days of bottle-throwing, brick-throwing, looting, arson, and sniper fire against the police. In the aftermath, twenty-six deaths, more than one thousand persons injured, and fourteen hundred arrests left the city with a scarred, yet determined, view of itself. Like Detroit two weeks later—and Watts earlier in the decade—the expression of raw anger and emotion created a groundswell of reaction in support of organizing and self-determination for the blacks in the city. The uprising in Newark galvanized the black community against the relatively small white power structure in Newark. Baraka was on the forefront of organizing the street protests and later electoral responses that led to close municipal elections in 1968 (which ended in defeats for blacks) and built a base for the successful election of black mayor Kenneth Gibson in 1970.

Actual civic control meant coalition-building with industrial interests, lobbyists, and financiers that drew on resources far beyond Baraka's reach. Plans to transform rundown city housing projects into the "Kawaida Towers" that would draw and produce income by and for the black community were sabotaged by white *and* black supporters who turned against CFUN. This was one of the grandest attempts of the era to transform black consciousness into tangible results of black community control. By the early 1970s, however, the white-run power structure in Newark had managed to thwart Baraka's political efforts.[31]

By this time, Baraka no longer had Karenga's input due to Karenga's legal and extralegal troubles. Karenga had been so damaged by conflicts with the Panthers and his subsequent paranoid attempts to surround himself with a security apparatus, that by 1970 he was no longer effective in spreading the message of the US Organization. Karenga was arrested, tried, and sentenced to one to ten years for the kidnapping and torture of two women who Karenga suspected had plotted against him. While Karenga maintains his innocence to this day, the momentum of his movement suffered an irreparable blow at the time.[32] Karenga has since reestablished himself as a recognized scholar of African-centered thought as a professor of Africana Studies at California State University Long Beach.

The Black Panther Party versus the US Organization

The Black Panther Party was at odds with Karenga from the beginning. The Black Panthers saw themselves as revolutionary nationalists as opposed to cultural nationalists. The BPP saw itself as a militant organization in solidarity with anticolonial struggles around the world. They were leaning toward socialism and away from Black Nationalism. They did not see culture as the first step toward a revolution, they saw the black man taking up the gun against police brutality as the first step. As many of the original Panther Party members identified with the working classes or lumpenproletariat, they viewed the ornate artifacts and African-inspired rituals with suspicion. With names like Bobby, Huey, David, and Kathleen, the first Panthers were not known to Africanize their names. Typically, US Organization members saw the Panthers as undisciplined street thugs, as ignorant poseurs seeking the radical spotlight and white acceptance. While their goals were similar, the BPP and the US members would find themselves in one tragic conflict after another.

As the Black Panther Party under the leadership of Alprentice "Bunchy" Carter and the US Organization under the leadership of Maulana Karenga grew in significance in Southern California in the late

1960s, the organizations went from coalitions to confrontations over power in the region. Karenga's US Organization sought relationships with organizations that it could control, and the initial Black Student Union at UCLA was one such organization. A "community advisory board" to the BSU selected a Karenga-supported choice to head the BSU without student input. The Black Panthers supported a process that included students. The procedural issue exposed a deeper level of conflict between the two forces, and tensions rose that spilled from the university hallways through the street affiliations of the Panther and US membership. Shortly after one tense meeting that was attended by BPP and US members, guns were pulled and two Party members, including Panther leader Carter, were killed.

The deaths of the two Panther leaders, Alprentice "Bunchy" Carter and John Huggins, at UCLA came as a shock to the entire black radical community. (By most accounts Karenga was shocked to hear the news as well.) There was considerable suspicion of collaboration with government provocateurs, and a number of Panthers were arrested on charges related to the shootings—ostensibly as a means to prevent retribution. As a result, the Panthers, who had obtained the majority of popular support among radicals nationwide, began a relentless propaganda assault against Karenga, the US Organization, and cultural nationalism overall. While the US-Panther conflict did not begin with the UCLA shootout in January 1969, that event marked the beginning of the end of Black Nationalist coalitions, and perhaps of the movement overall.

By 1968 the Black Panther Party was established as the most prominent Black Nationalist organization, and its newspaper the *Black Panther* had a weekly circulation of more than 100,000 copies. When statements about Karenga or cultural nationalism were printed, it served to define cultural nationalism for many who did not know about the distinctions, or about the Panther-US rift. Articles with titles like "Karenga the Number One Bloodsucker" were given prominent space in the Panther paper.

Panther leader Huey Newton described what he saw as the differences between the Panthers and cultural nationalists in an interview published in 1970.

> The cultural nationalists are concerned with returning to the old African culture and thereby regaining their identity and freedom.

In other words, they feel that the African culture will automatically bring political freedom. . . .

The Black Panther party, which is a revolutionary group of black people, realizes that we have to have an identity. We have to realize our black heritage in order to give us strength to move on and progress. But as far as returning to the old African culture, it's unnecessary and it's not advantageous in many respects. We believe that culture itself will not liberate us. We're going to need some stronger stuff.[33]

The "stronger stuff" articulated by Newton was consistent with the theme presented in the *Black Panther* newspaper. Panthers saw themselves as the *real* revolutionaries—revolutionary nationalists—who were determined to stand up to the power structure in no uncertain terms. The Panthers portrayed Karenga and US as little more than poseurs who were unwilling to take on the system when the time came.

It appears that Newton was unaware that Karenga's organization was just as serious about the revolution and was making preparations of its own for an inevitable confrontation with white America. Karenga and US had made proclamations about the oncoming black revolution, and had even declared the final "year of conflict." Scot Brown explains Karenga's long-range plan:

US doctrine advanced its own millenarian-like Seven Year Calendar that Karenga advanced: 1965, Year of the New Generation (Watts Revolt), *Mwaka wa Uasi*; 1966, Year of Black Power, *Mwaka wa Uwezo Mweusi*; 1967, Year of the Young Lions, *Mwaka wa Simba Wachanga*; 1968, Year of the Black Panther, *Mwaka wa Chui Mweusi*; 1969 Year of Reconstruction; 1970, Year of Splitting Apart, *Mwaka was Dabuka* and 1971, Year of the Guerillas, *Mwaka wa Gaidi*.

. . . The Year of the Black Panther, 1968 anticipated the rise of a mass African American independent political party, followed by a year in which African Americans would look inward and reorient their values, sense of identity, purpose and direction. In 1970, Karenga foresaw African Americans separating themselves from White society. This act of autonomy and self-determination would culminate the following year in a guerilla war.[34]

Karenga indeed had a plan for black liberation. To the young, idealistic revolutionary, a long-range vision, a comprehensive vision, no matter how impractical, was enormously appealing. With this in mind, the cultural nationalist line cannot be dismissed as merely an abstract intellectual one, nor one preoccupied with superficial cultural artifacts such as dress and poetry. However, at the time, Karenga's organization was a secretive, primarily underground organization and thrived on the compelling mystique of the secret society in which only a select few are capable and worthy of membership. Many of the details of Karenga's revolutionary visions were shared only within his organization.

In his essays on Black Nationalism in the later 1960s, Amiri Baraka was a staunch critic of the Black Panthers and eschewed their penchant for political theater and their white alliances. He wrote in a 1969 opinion piece published in the *New York Times*: "Frankly the Panthers, no matter the great amounts of sincere but purposefully misled brothers, getting shotup because some nigger was emotionally committed to white people, are extreme examples of PimpArt gone mad."[35]

Bobby Seale was less diplomatic than Newton about cultural nationalism. After watching an Amiri Baraka play in New York in 1968, Seale let his feelings be known about the play and the playwright:

> It kept going over and over, "black, black, black, black, black, black . . ."
> It didn't convey anything. We called Jones and Ron Karenga the high
> priests of cultural nationalism because they didn't really produce any-
> thing except fanatics. They would have been better off, if they were
> going to express anything, to talk about revolutionary culture in a
> way that would change something. Four or five Panther brothers and
> I sat in the audience and ridiculed it among ourselves.[36]

Bobby Seale did not think much of the process of "reclaiming" blackness that the cultural nationalist movement was focused on. It was neverthe- less an important theme of the revolution that was taking place. Seale's enmity toward the cultural nationalists was a popular refrain from the comedian turned black radical leader, but the purpose of the insults served a propaganda purpose, designed to isolate Karenga and US to the margins of the movement. It also set the context for the Black Pan- ther Party's cultural production, in that no artistic production would be emanating from the Party that resembled the Africanized works of cultural nationalists.

The Lumpen and Cultural Nationalism

The Lumpen were on the front lines of the conflict between the Panthers' revolution and cultural nationalism. The band found itself in constant conflict with law enforcement when they performed as Black Panthers, but they were also careful to distinguish themselves from the racially exclusive cultural nationalists. With a blood feud in full force against Karenga and US, the Lumpen were not about to present themselves in dashikis or promote racially exclusive objectives. Their musical milieu at the time was black popular music at its most racially self-conscious. Songs such as "Blackenized" by Hank Ballard, "Message from a Black Man" by the Temptations, "Am I Black Enough for You" by Billy Paul, and "To Be Young, Gifted and Black" by Nina Simone (and remade by Aretha Franklin) all made the black music charts. As a representative of a black revolutionary organization, it might be seen as ironic that the Lumpen did not refer to race explicitly in their works.

The Lumpen did utilize references to the "pig" as the enemy of the people, and the racial designation of the pig was not difficult to determine. However, through their lyrics, the Lumpen did not deal with racially explicit subject matter and primarily sought to unify their audience through a message of a shared (militaristic) revolutionary consciousness. The Lumpen did not need to refer to race in their works because they utilized the shared racial memory inherent in the aesthetics of soul music to further their cause. This was obvious to Lumpen singer Michael Torrence:

> Soul, growing up in the '60s, we used to identify it a lot with James Brown. It was black music. White folks could try to imitate it, but they couldn't really do it. It represented the emotions and the sounds of us as black people, the rhythms that we had, the energy that we had, and it was a black thing. At that point it was something that we had a lot of pride in.[37]

As stage performers the Lumpen were cultural producers, using the culture of the people to help unify and organize their people for action. They were, in a sense, doing the same type of work that the cultural nationalists sought to do: unify the people first, and bring them together toward an agenda of collective action for their own survival and success.

Minister of Culture Emory Douglas was well aware of the specter of cultural nationalism in the perceptions of the Lumpen. He recalls that the distinctions were very clear between Karenga's brand of nationalism and the Panthers when he joined in 1967:

> There were all kind of people in the Party, some who still identified with the cultural nationalists, were sympathetic toward that, but understood what needed to be done. I understood that, but I understood what needed to be done because I worked with Baraka. And Baraka was the one who raised my black consciousness, my black awareness, to the Yoruba culture and all that, when he was wearing the dashikis and the Yoruba beads and the whole bit, about six months before I met up with the Party. When I came in the Party I had a dashiki on. Huey and them told me they were kind of suspect at first. But they seen how I did and what I did and that I was sincere and committed, so they said I was different.[38]

Douglas had earned the trust of the Party as a revolutionary nationalist, so when he advocated for the Lumpen, he was not simply trying to get some singers he knew some visibility. He was serious about their revolutionary mission. Yet he had to navigate the political terrain to advocate for cultural issues. Perhaps seeking to defend the Lumpen against charges of cultural nationalism within their own ranks, Douglas wrote an important support statement for the Lumpen in the *Black Panther* in November 1970, titled "The Lumpen—Music as a Tool for Liberation," where he explained the mission of the group:

> We like the Beat of James Brown, we say the Temptations sound great, but if we try to relate to what they are saying to our conditions we'd end up in a ball of confusion. If we run around saying "It's my thing and I can do what I want to do" We could never be free, or singing "Cloud 9" to help the Mafia launch a new era of drugs, ain't no way. . . .

The Lumpen sing not to make profit or stimulate emotions, but to make revolution and stimulate action. We know action is supreme and only through correct revolutionary action can we transform our oppressive state to a state where freedom is supreme. The Lumpen are revolutionaries they grew out of the oppressive conditions in Babylon. They are the lumpen proletariat, the have-nots, like they sing in their songs "Revolution is the only solution." ALL POWER TO THE PEOPLE! BOBBY MUST BE SET FREE.[39]

Douglas illuminated the complicated relationship between black entertainers and black revolutionaries. He made it plain that Party members were regular people who enjoyed the work of the popular black entertainers of the day. However, Douglas affirmed that what the movement needed was a popular black artist with the revolutionary force of the Black Panther Party, and the Lumpen were presented as the type of group that was needed.

In his book *Just My Soul Responding*, writer Brian Ward discusses the Lumpen and has criticized Douglas's passage and the work of the Lumpen as a production that was too much of an "unrelieved diet of politically correct songs about racial oppression and the coming revolution."[40] Ward implies that the Lumpen performance is a stoic, heavy-handed series of proclamations set to music.

In all these polemics, the Panthers tended to underestimate the politics of pleasure. They neglected the sensual gratification which crucially shapes an audience's potential receptivity to any message in popular music and makes it difficult for any artist to "educate," let alone "mobilize" without first entertaining.[41]

Ward has bought the ruse that the Lumpen's music was not designed to "stimulate emotions." But "stimulate emotions" is exactly what the Lumpen were able to do on that night in North Oakland in 1970. The crowd noises from the live Lumpen concert belie the actual politics of pleasure that the Lumpen employed to full effect. The lush harmonies, the energetic funky rhythms, and the humor and style with which the Lumpen delivered their revolutionary line is evidence of that. The only "strident and didactic" element of the Lumpen performance is their steadfast attack on the power structure, delivered with bombast, hyperbole, and humor.

Ironically, both Ward and Douglas perpetuated the mythos of the revolutionary that won't dance. Ward is convinced that the Panthers are too serious to be soulful, a common and false myth about black radicals, and Douglas, for political purposes, is trying to reinforce the seriousness of what he knows is the soulful experience of the Lumpen group.

It was not a simple thing for revolutionary politics to mesh with the sensuality and materialist aesthetics of black popular music in 1970. How does one sing a love ballad one moment and then sing of overturning the power structure the next? It can be argued that if those sentiments are sincere, and each reflects popular sentiments among the people, then it is possible. By any measure, the Lumpen effectively navigated a storm of political and social contradictions to play their music for the people. And they were the least of the Party's problems.

Black Women and Black Nationalism

The black radical movement of the 1960s experienced fundamental conflicts with regard to the role of women. While the general thrust of black power politics invoked the wartime imagery of the battlefield and involved a male-centered ethos of bravado and bombast—ostensibly to show fearlessness in the face of the forces of repression—the assertion of patriarchal privilege was an ever-present corollary to the challenges to white authority and state violence. It enjoyed an inordinate rise, often at the expense of black women within the organizations. As one former Panther, puts it: "The men were floating on a false sense of heroism, where the women were getting everything together."[42]

At the outset of the civil rights era, black institutions often appeared to operate in concert with prevailing Western gender values. Organizational models for social movements during the civil rights movement of the 1950s and early 1960s were based upon the social structure of the black church, in which the women traditionally did the lion's share of the daily work planning and organizing events while consistently upholding black male figures as leaders and articulators of the vision and mission of the congregation and, by extension, the entire civil rights movement.

The patriarchal social structure of the Jim Crow South circumscribed the organizational behaviors of the earliest black institutions, and when these began to serve as operatives of social change, their organizational models remained intact. This was one reason why there were so few recognized female organizational leaders in SNCC, the Congress of Racial Equality (CORE), the Southern Christian Leadership Conference (SCLC), the NAACP, and the Urban League—the most prominent and respected organizations of the civil rights movement. Brilliant organizers such as Fannie Lou Hamer and Ella Baker of SNCC, the pioneering educator Septima Clark, and even Rosa Parks (NAACP) were frequently marginalized in the male-driven organizations they performed the heavy lifting to build.[43]

In late 1964, a racially integrated group of female members of SNCC presented a statement at their Waveland retreat outlining what they saw as the problems with male dominance in the organization. The authors requested anonymity to avoid reprisals and claimed that "the woman in SNCC is often in the same position as that token Negro hired in a corporation." At the retreat, organized after the grueling Mississippi Summer Project—a street-level effort to generate new black voters in Mississippi—the women participated in a workshop on women in SNCC and made an eloquent case for equal participation within the organization:

> Assumptions of male superiority are as widespread and deep rooted and every much as crippling to the woman as the assumptions of white supremacy are to the Negro. Consider why it is in SNCC that women who are competent, qualified, and experienced, are automatically assigned to the "female" kinds of jobs such as typing, desk work, telephone work, filing, library work, cooking, and the assistant kind of administrative work but rarely the "executive" kind.[44]

Little was done about the complaints made in the position paper at Waveland, and the dismissal of many of the points was related by some to the presence of white women as coauthors. The effort, nevertheless, was a foundational stage for the emergent women's movement and foreshadowed much larger problems within SNCC and the black power movement in the later part of the decade.

Within two years, SNCC had undertaken an ideological transformation toward black power and away from "freedom now" as its theme and was openly agitating for racial self-determination and away from interracial cooperation. In 1966 a new wave of SNCC members began to urge exclusive black participation in all phases of their activities. In what amounted to a purge, the struggle for the leadership of SNCC was increasingly framed in terms of black self-determination and black cultural unity, and against the intrusive "contaminating" presence of white support. The new politics of SNCC were oriented toward a cultural as well as political affiliation with blackness in which SNCC fused identity politics with race-based organizing strategies.[45]

Emerging from the crucible of nonviolent civil disobedience, SNCC had enormous credibility nationwide, which new leader Stokely Carmichael parlayed into a high-profile mandate of black power on the national stage. During the June 1966 March Against Fear through Mississippi, Carmichael first announced the new chant of "Black power!" to exhilarated black Mississippians. The new direction of SNCC appealed to many who had grown weary of Dr. Martin Luther King Jr.'s insistence on nonviolence and its corollary issues of integrationism. Over the summer of 1966, Carmichael's bold strokes reestablished the organization (and himself) as a leader of the more radicalized black power movement.

Under the leadership of Carmichael, the new direction for the organization only served to solidify its patriarchal framework. While a brilliant organizer and courageous advocate for black issues, Carmichael was less of a visionary when it came to women's rights issues, and he was once heard wisecracking that "the only place for a woman in SNCC is prone." Carmichael's remark may have been in jest, but in the context of revolutionary social transformations that had brought so many young activists into the movement, the quip became far more than an after-hours joke. The phrase came to symbolize all that was flawed with the black revolution and has become part of the canon of the women's rights movement.[46]

While the mainstream civil rights organizations were considered integrationist, the black radical organizations, despite their consistently antiwhite and anti-Western rhetoric, were entrenched in their own forms of conspicuously Western patriarchy. The black radical movement drew heavily upon the model of the Nation of Islam, which promoted the idea that women served a functional social role and were to be respected and protected. This idea presumed a strictly enforced male privilege that went with what the members saw as patriarchal responsibility. The logic of this was clear: black women were to be given respect and allowed their dignity as housekeepers and child bearers, with deference in decision-making authority given to the males. At the time, the gender roles in the NOI were not so dissimilar from those in traditional black Christian families, and some black women found the Nation of Islam to be an appropriate outlet for their social and cultural ideals. E. U. Essien-Udom, in his 1962 book *Black Nationalism: A Search for an Identity in America*, claimed that women in the NOI found a place for themselves free of the degradation of sexual advances and insults from outside undisciplined males. He wrote:

> The attraction of the Nation of Islam to women becomes clear if we bear in mind that both men and women in the Nation extend a great deal of deference to each other—something they are unaccustomed to in Negro society. Womanly virtues are respected in the Nation. The Muslim male's attitude toward, and treatment of, Negro women contrasts sharply with the disrespect and indifference with which lower-class Negroes treat them.[47]

The NOI had an emphasis on family and personal responsibility that was absent in the working-class environment of many black women, and the stability of the NOI had a direct appeal. However, the strict codes of behavior and dress, particularly in public, gave the impression to the outside world that women in the Nation of Islam were indeed subordinate, even more so than within the Western Christian context.

The high profile and central leadership role in the black radical movement of onetime NOI national spokesman Malcolm X also sent an implicit message that women were not to be full participants in the revolution. Despite the fact that once he left the Nation Malcolm X was publicly very supportive of black women activists (such as Fannie Lou Hamer, whom Malcolm X once introduced as "the country's number one freedom fighting woman"), a great deal of Malcolm X's rhetoric involved the restoration of the black *man* and, by extension, the return of the black male to what he saw as his proper place at the head of the family. Malcolm X's undisputed image as the patriarch of the black revolution carried the implication that the revolution would be led by black men.

The NOI model of gender roles was a strong influence on Ron Karenga and the house system he developed for the US Organization. A series of restrictive rules and codes of conduct were enacted specifically toward women in his organization, ostensibly to maintain their role as supporters of the men in the revolution. As Scot Brown writes, "The doctrine stipulated that the role of the woman was to 'inspire her man, educate the children and participate in social development.' The role was defined as 'complementary' rather than equal to the supreme status of the Black man."[48] While Karenga may have been typical in expressing the patriarchal viewpoints common to Western males during this time, he was able to effect and generate a far-reaching social policy based upon those beliefs.

Amiri Baraka was often mystified by Karenga's insistence on misogynistic practices. Baraka writes in his autobiography that he could not understand why Karenga insisted on such an unequal social structure for his organization:

> And even though I was heavy influenced by Karenga and Kawaida, there were certain parts of his doctrine which made no sense to me, so I did not impose them on the Newark people. This was especially true of the parts of the doctrine dealing with women. The heavy male chauvinism that I had already suffered from was formally added to. Karenga's doctrine said there was no such thing as equality between men and women. "They were complementary" this was a typical Karenga manipulation of words.
>
> What stopped us from getting too far out in Kawaida was my wife, Amina, who not only waged a constant struggle against my personal and organizational chauvinism, but secretly in her way was constantly undermining Karenga's influence, figuring, I guess, that I would not come up with as much nuttiness disguised as revolution as he, though I did my share.[49]

The tenor of the times and the intense desire among young blacks for a comprehensive plan for black liberation allowed Karenga to pursue his elaborate plans for the social and psychological transformation of blacks on his own terms. The US Organization would endure the black power era as staunch advocates of male privilege.

The Black Panther Party during the same period underwent episodes of growth and reflection upon women in the revolution, and the daily experiences of Panther women encompassed a broad range of views. A number of women in the Panthers experienced harassment, disrespect, and assumptions of their inferiority from Panther men. The New Haven Panther chapter leader, Ericka Huggins, told Phyllis Jackson in the documentary *Comrade Sister*: "There were men that thought that women were to be slept with. I dealt with male chauvinism."[50] Former Panther chairman Elaine Brown went through frustrating and violent episodes with misogynistic Panther men, but she also earned intense loyalty from her subordinates in an environment where violence and misogyny were commonplace. Jeffrey Ogbar asserts that the lumpen nature of the Party was a liability in this context: "Although sexism was ubiquitous in America, the lionization of lumpen behavior encouraged sexism to thrive where it could have been more effectively challenged."[51]

Other women have said that they worked alongside Panther men effectively. Akua Njeri, a former Chicago Panther recalls: "Men did not try to take advantage of sisters in our chapter. We had respect. Men and women both cleaned and cooked for the children. We also trained together. We were all Panthers."[52] The experience of Panther women varied by location, and in places where the leadership was firmly established and Party rules were adhered to, women and men were generally considered revolutionaries first. Phyllis Jackson joined the Oakland chapter, the Panther central headquarters, and found the primary concern was the work that needed to be done: "There was no notion that a revolutionary needed to be either a male or a female. It was about the person willing to stand up against injustice and capitalism."[53]

In the first years of the Party, much of the rhetoric of confrontation involved masculine definitions of power, of the black man "getting his balls back," and a general orientation toward the reclamation of the manhood of black men. While this may have affected the Party's rhetoric of confrontation, it also promoted the false notion that the Party was predominantly male, which, from early on, it was not. By 1969, in public proclamations from both Eldridge Cleaver and Huey P. Newton, the Panther doctrine was to denounce sexism and patriarchy. Analytical writings by Panther women on a range of topics appeared in the *Black Panther*, and the paternalistic language of "protecting our women" by 1969 was no longer a part of the paper's rhetoric.

The BPP grew and changed with the times, due in part to the resilience of strong Panther women and also because of the increasing emphasis on social work, which led to a change in what constituted revolutionary activity. What was typically defined as domestic work, which members of the Lumpen did on a regular basis—cooking, cleaning, obtaining supplies, etc.—was just as important to the revolution as marches, rallies, political education, and security detail. While it was not uniform throughout the Panther offices, the fluid work situation provided openings for black women to emerge as equals and in some cases as leaders. This was in stark contrast to the lack of black female leadership in any of the other black political organizations during those years.

Within the ranks of the black radical movement, some black women were able to organize and theorize about their own liberation. Many found a more appealing voice in the teachings of Marxist philosophers, who equated class equality with gender equality more readily than did black leaders. Published pamphlets of Marxist leaders such as V. I. Lenin presented very appealing prescriptions for women's equality:

> In words bourgeois democracy promises equality and freedom, but in practice not a single bourgeois republic, even the more advanced, has granted women (half the human race) and men complete equality in the eyes of the law, or delivered women from dependence on and the oppression of the male.
>
> Bourgeois democracy is the democracy of pompous phrases, solemn words, lavish promises and high-sounding slogans about freedom and equality, but in practice all this cloaks the lack of freedom and the inequality of women, the lack of freedom and the inequality for the working and exploited people.[54]

Here was a discourse of radical change that implies a fifty-fifty balance between the men and women involved. Lenin's works, and Marxism in general, provided a global ideology of liberation that was more progressive to many women of color in the United States than the views men of color were speaking about or practicing.

In 1969 New York City SNCC veteran Fran Beal had had enough of the behaviors of males in the black radical movement and founded the Black Women's Alliance. The alliance quickly grew to incorporate other women of color and become known as the Third World Women's Alliance (TWWA). Beal's essay "Double Jeopardy: To Be Black and Female" was, for many, a turning point for the black radical women's movement. Beal's analysis incorporates the historical mandate of the present black revolution with a stark proscription of present gender roles:

Those who are exerting their "manhood" by telling black women to step back into a domestic, submissive role are assuming a counter-revolutionary position. Black women likewise have been abused by the system and we must begin talking about the elimination of all kinds of oppression. If we are talking about building a strong nation, capable of throwing off the yoke of capitalist oppression, then we are talking about the total involvement of every man, woman, and child, each with a highly developed political consciousness. We need our whole army out there dealing with the enemy and not half an army.[55]

Beal's organization, the Third World Women's Alliance, and its bimonthly paper *Triple Jeopardy* drew upon the organizing talents of women of color whose skills had earlier been honed as subordinates in male-dominated organizations. The TWWA organized in solidarity with liberation movements worldwide, not merely on "women's issues," and saw itself as anticapitalist, not as a feminist group. The women in the alliance were free to pursue issues of social justice on their own terms. Like many of the early women-of-color organizations that emerged at the time, such as the Combahee Women's Collective and the National Black Feminist Organization, the TWWA was a proactive training ground, establishing a foundation of black women's political leadership that continues to this day.

Angela Davis

Possibly the most iconic and compelling black radical of the period was Angela Yvonne Davis. Davis was born in Birmingham, Alabama, to college-educated parents and lived in an area known as Dynamite Hill for the frequency of Klan attacks. She was acquainted with the four little girls who were killed in the Sixteenth Street Baptist Church bombing in 1963.

Davis's high marks in school allowed her a scholarship to a private high school in New York City, where she developed lifelong friendships with students of all races. She then went to Brandeis University and studied philosophy under Herbert Marcuse and other intellectual giants of the left. She graduated magna cum laude from Brandeis in 1965 and studied and traveled throughout Europe as a graduate student, where she grew stronger in her Marxist political ideology. When she returned to the United States in 1967, she followed Marcuse to San Diego and balanced her time between graduate study in philosophy and organizing the Black Student Union at UC–San Diego.

As the activism and radicalism escalated in Southern California, Angela Davis joined the Black Panther Political Party, which later would become the Los Angeles operation for SNCC. Davis would organize in the streets, lead meetings, teach classes, and do whatever it took to make the movement go.

> For me revolution was never an interim "thing-to-do" before set-tling down; it was no fashionable club with newly minted jargon, or a new kind of social life—made thrilling by risk and confrontation, made glamorous by costume. Revolution is a serious thing, the most serious thing about a revolutionary's life. When one commits one-self to the struggle, it must be for a lifetime.[56]

Davis would later be asked to join the Southern California BPP chap-ter and would get to know Southern California Party leaders John and Ericka Huggins, but she also focused her time with the Che-Lumumba club, the black affiliate of the Southern California Communist Party.

Though her work, Davis quickly emerged as an activist leader, often encountering hostility from her own male colleagues who were jealous and confounded by her levelheaded leadership and organizing abilities. Many of her own black activist allies urged her to denounce her Com-munist ties, fearing that she would bring the red scare of the 1950s down upon the emergent black radical movement.

As a popular and accomplished instructor, writer, and effective theorist, Davis was offered a position as an acting assistant professor in UCLA's philosophy department. When California governor Ronald Reagan heard of the offer, he had it rescinded, vowing that Davis "would never again teach in the University of California system."

In the midst of the turmoil and her growing notoriety, Davis began to organize around the case of the Soledad Brothers, three political prisoners, including the inviolate George Jackson, who were enduring extended terms for the alleged murder of a prison guard. Davis would develop a closeness with Jackson that merged her politics with her per-sonal desires at the time. The revolutionary love story emerged as a subplot in Jackson's published letters from prison in 1970, and Davis's subsequent trial.

On August 7, 1970, George Jackson's seventeen-year-old younger brother Jonathan initiated a raid upon the Marin County courthouse, where three Panthers were on trial, with a goal of taking hostages and earning his brother's release. The resulting chaos that day resulted in four deaths, including his own. One of Jonathan Jackson's guns, taken from Panther storehouses, was registered to Davis. As a result, Angela Davis was charged with murder, kidnapping, and conspiracy as an accomplice to the raid. She became a fugitive and went underground. Davis's most-wanted poster was widely distributed by the FBI, and she quickly became a household name. With her striking frame and towering Afro hairstyle, Angela Davis became a visual icon of the revolution as much as an ideological leader. Her most-wanted posters have since become a part of the enduring imagery and iconography of black power.

While Angela Davis was revered across the progressive movement for her principles at the time and celebrated in song by many artists— including John Lennon and Yoko Ono ("Angela"), Herbie Hancock ("Ostentato [Suite for Angela]"), and Carlos Santana ("Free Angela")— her most enduring pop culture identity continues to be related to her Afro-styled hairdo. Davis has remarked about the reduction of her image to her hairstyle as a double indignity:

> It is both humiliating and humbling to discover that a single generation after the events that constructed me as a public personality, I am remembered as a hairdo. It is humiliating because it reduces a politics of liberation to a politics of fashion; it is humbling because such encounters with the younger generation demonstrate the fragility and mutability of historical images, particularly those associated with African American history.[57]

Despite her national notoriety at the time, Davis remained hidden in plain sight for eight weeks. On October 13, 1970, Davis was captured in Manhattan and put on trial as an accomplice to the Jackson raid. Like many of the earlier trials of black radicals during this period, the use of evidence was secondary to the spectacle of submission that law enforcement was hoping to accomplish.

While Angela Davis was a courageous activist and leader during some of the flashpoints of Southern California's racial violence, it was her radical ideological positions and her refusal to compromise them that led to her designation as an enemy of the state. As a radical black woman activist, communist, Black Panther, and leader of men and women, Angela Davis was a singular figure of defiance and principle. She challenged the white power structure up to and including Governor Ronald Reagan by refusing to denounce her Communist beliefs; she challenged the male chauvinism in the black radical movement by defending her leadership roles in the Los Angeles black power movement; and she challenged the race-based notions from other black radicals that ideologically she could be mentored by white thinkers and lead a black radical movement. She did not abdicate her commitment to a black revolution, and she continues to the present day to advocate for prisoner rights and human rights issues as one of the nation's great activist-intellectuals.

By the time of Angela Davis's acquittal in June 1972, there was a collective exhale from her supporters and yet a growing sense that the movement itself was dissipating and dissolving as well.

White Alliances

One of the most difficult issues for black radicals of all persuasions to overcome was the question of white alliances. As aspiring Marxists who analyzed the oppression of blacks in America through a class lens, the Black Panther leaders appeared to be readily accepting of white radicals and white radical support. It was also apparent to critics of the BPP that male members of the Black Panthers were all too comfortable in their alliances with white women. Karenga, Baraka, and other nationalists denounced these counterrevolutionary activities among the Panthers. However, the cultural nationalists struggled to defend their misogynistic, anachronistic proscriptions for black womanhood.

It appeared that both approaches were flawed in some way. Despite the supposed ideological justification for interracial alliances, personal politics played an important role in the divisions between the groups.

It was clear early on to Newton and other Panther leaders that in terms of organizational politics, white radicals would not be allowed to play a role in directing the Party platform, and so the BPP leadership felt whites posed little threat to the organization. This was unlike earlier civil rights organizations that had to submit their agenda for the approval of white benefactors at crucial turning points in the movement. It was also distinct from the emergent Black Nationalist organizations that specifically and zealously stood by their race-based exclusionism. Komozi Woodard explains:

> The most important disagreement between US and the Black Panthers was over the strategic issue of which groups would be allies for black liberation. For revolutionaries, this is a central question. Karenga and US saw white racism as the main enemy and emphasized the need for a black united front between black radicals and moderates. Although US felt that blacks might enter into *temporary* coalitions with some whites around specific tactical issues, the leading cultural nationalists did not consider any white group a strategic ally of the Black revolution. By contrast, increasingly the Black Panther Party saw capitalism as the main enemy and believed that white radicals and revolutionaries were important allies in the struggle for black liberation.[58]

Much of the appeal of the Black Nationalist support of black unity had to do with a reconstruction of black self-love and the idea that one can and should work with other blacks in any capacity. This meant that it was advisable to patronize black businesses and support black institutions whenever possible. In this way, Karenga and others' vision of black unity necessarily entered into alliances with black capitalists—a group frequently opposed by the BPP as bourgeois pawns of the capitalist empire.

Aside from the common practice of using liberal white lawyers in high-profile court cases, the presence of white allies complicated rather than facilitated almost every action taken by black radicals at the time. The Panthers and other black radicals who sought to work with others outside of their own communities were confronted with the ever-present enigma of white support, white fetishization of the black radical, and for some, the potential presence of the sincere white revolutionary. Further, the masses of middle-class white liberals and conservatives who composed the majority of the American population had a spectrum of viewpoints regarding black radicalism. These issues were not taken lightly. Newton, in support of white radicalism, contended that the white radical was sincere and that the white radical ultimately has a duty to fight the oppressor in the white community:

> I personally think that there are many young white revolutionaries who are sincere in attempting to realign themselves with mankind. . . . In pressing for new heroes the young white revolutionaries found the heroes in the black colony at home and in the colonies throughout the world. . . .
>
> This presents somewhat of a problem in many ways for the black revolutionary especially the cultural nationalist. The cultural nationalist doesn't understand the white revolutionaries because he can't see why anyone white would turn on the system. So they think that maybe this is some more hypocrisy being planted by white people.[59]

Without missing an opportunity to disparage the cultural nationalists, Newton was referencing a dynamic of racial chauvinism within the black radical movement. Black Nationalism, almost by definition, was designed to eliminate whites and white influence on the affairs of blacks. For some it was a simple question of personal preference, and for others it was a necessary political act to exclude whites from any involvement in the operation of a black radical project. For Newton to (rather comfortably) claim that white radicals were allies in the struggle ran counterintuitive to many who were in the throes of a black self-renaissance of their own.

The members of the Lumpen experienced this type of racial crossfire when they went on tour across the country in late 1970. Typically performing on college campuses for Black Student Union–sponsored events, the campus BSU leaders in other cities were surprised to find white members of the Lumpen band on the stage with the Panthers. The Lumpen members recount with pride the fact that when Black Nationalists refused to accommodate their white bandmates, the group as a whole responded in defiance and demanded that their white revolutionary musicians be treated as equals.

Eventually, the presence of white supporters would take its toll on the Black Panther Party. By 1969 the organization was moving away from militant confrontation as a formally stated policy. The Panthers no longer carried guns in public and abandoned the black leather jacket, beret, and blue shirt uniforms in an effort to blend in with the people. The Party was employing a new tack to relate once again to their community. However, the Party had become so popular that enthusiastic radicals (many black and white) could be heard in the press embracing and extolling the militant rhetoric of Panther leaders while appearing to ignore the Party's Survival Programs. By doing so, white supporters contributed to the fetishization of the black militant Panther image, an image Huey Newton tried unsuccessfully to dispel upon his release from prison in August 1970. The presence of white Hollywood movie stars such as Marlon Brando and Jane Fonda at Panther functions only served to complicate the BPP's self-imposed role as the vanguard of a black revolution.[60]

One of Newton's first public appearances after his release from prison was at the Revolutionary Constitutional Convention (RPCC) in Philadelphia in September 1970. The convention, called by Eldridge Cleaver, who was in exile by then, provided an opportunity for thousands of delegates to discuss their practical goals and visions for revolutionary change. Newton, a weak public speaker, struggled at the gathering, which was made up primarily of outsiders to the core Panther community. On the same Labor Day weekend 1970, Amiri Baraka's Congress of African People was holding its own convention in Atlanta that included hundreds of black radicals, effectively siphoning much of the black unity the RPCC might have generated. In one sense, the warnings of other black radicals about the unpredictable and undermining effect of whites, no matter how well intentioned, was bearing fruit and affecting the BPP.[61]

Despite the decrees coming from Oakland headquarters regarding respect for white allies, many Panther chapters outside of Oakland were composed of black radicals who shared the racially separatist position of the cultural nationalists. Conflicts between members in Panther chapters nationwide at the end of the 1960s were fraught with deeply ingrained ideological and personal biases. These conflicts involved race, gender, racial memory, and regional biases that—with the help of government infiltration and disruption—collectively served to render the Black Panther Party ungovernable as a national entity by the end of the 1960s.

Black Nationalism and Popular Music

Despite the demise of the black radical organizations as the 1970s began, their impact on popular culture was just beginning to take shape. Through the Black Arts movement, a venue and a voice for black rage had been given life, and consumers (of all races) were swept up by the urgency, the emotional intensity, and the sense of righteousness in the words. The impulse of Black Nationalism spread throughout black culture and emerged as a central ingredient in all forms of the black arts. To define a new black identity, to explore blackness, to imagine revolutionary change, or just to shape fashion, hairstyle, furniture, or footwear, an emergent black aesthetic thrived, and it thrived as a result of the political insurgency that began to manifest itself in cultural forms. It would not be long before the images were to be co-opted and mass marketed, but at the dawn of the 1970s the spirit of a black awakening in the popular arts was overwhelming.

In a broad sense, the conflicts experienced within the black radical movement in the 1960s were mirrored in the black popular music of the time. It may have been seen as a contradiction, or as merely a coincidence, but the spirit of black power was a central ingredient in the creation of some of the greatest soul music of the day. Many popular songs from the period, from Sam and Dave's "Soul Man" (1967) to the Impressions' "Woman's Got Soul" (1968) to Ike and Tina Turner's "Bold Soul Sister" (1970), carried with them implicit affirmations of a strident racial consciousness. For the most part, the lyrics in the most popular soul music at the end of the 1960s were not overtly racially explicit or exclusionary, but there was an energy, a spirit, fueling the sound like never before. Because the music was directed at a popular audience, there was a necessary negotiation taking place between the inspiration and the final production, one that is typical in any form of popular music. The negotiation, in this case, was between racial hate and racial love, between the desire for personal balance in a relationship and the desire for a greater social justice; between the urgency for black self-expression and the urgency of the day for one's own economic advancement. Without the black revolution, soul music would not have evolved into the classic genre it is today and likely may never have developed into funk or produced the building blocks of hip-hop.

Isaac Hayes, who cowrote "Soul Man" in 1967 along with David Porter for the soul duo Sam and Dave, explained the context of his inspiration for that song:

> That was during the time when there was a lot of racial unrest in this country, and all the black businesses if they write 'soul' on

the businesses [the rioters] they bypass it, will not [burn it]. And I thought about the night of the Passover in the Bible, blood of the lamb on the door, firstborn is spared. I said, 'Oh, soul.' I said, 'That's pride, soul, soul man, soul man!' Yeah, so I called David, I said, 'I got one man.'[62]

In the case of Hayes and Porter, and the huge hit for Sam and Dave, a sentiment was born from the radical times in the streets. "Soul Man" has become one of the most beloved songs in the soul pantheon, in part because it is both universally appealing and applicable to the black cause at once.

Hayes and Porter's masterpiece, "Soul Man" was recorded in Memphis by the interracial rhythm section of Booker T. and the MGs, the standard bearers at the beloved, racially mixed Stax label. Interracial cooperation was commonplace in the recording studios that produced soul and R&B in the otherwise segregated Jim Crow South, but it was also emblematic of a contradiction that would eventually unravel. As Brian Ward has observed,

Even when black nationalism became more prominent within black consciousness and liberation politics in the mid to late 1960s, the widespread interracialism in southern soul endured, only finally crumbling in the face of a particularly reactionary brand of black power militancy around the turn of the decade.[63]

Stax

In Memphis, the renowned celebration of integrated music production at Stax Records, like many southern soul labels, appears to defy the racial exclusionism of life there in the early 1960s. Founded by white siblings Jim Stewart and Estelle Axton, the multiracial social family of musicians had a blast recording soulful, authentic black music on a consistent basis. Their integrated rhythm section of Al Jackson Jr., Steve Cropper, Donald "Duck" Dunn, and Booker T. Jones was a celebration of what was possible through the camaraderie of music. The studio musicians were mixed, the staff was mixed, and the music was eminently soulful, displaying universal emotions of truth with a down-home southern appeal, with country, blues, and gospel sounds hanging on the edges of everything they did. Staff members, writers, performers, and the owners shared a social and cultural scene of mutual respect and affection that worked to everyone's advantage. The camaraderie and collective work ethos portrayed by the Stax family was and remains one of the most uplifting narratives of the 1960s. And the music they created stands the test of time.

The roster at Stax was a who's who of sweet soul music: Carla Thomas ("Tramp" with Otis Redding), The Mar-Keys ("Last Night"), Booker T. and the MG's ("Green Onions"), Rufus Thomas ("Do The Funky Chicken"), Johnnie Taylor ("Who's Making Love"), Jean Knight ("Mr. Big Stuff"), the Staple Singers ("I'll Take You There"), the Bar-Kays ("Soul Finger"), Shirley Brown ("Woman to Woman"), the Dramatics ("Whatcha See Is Whatcha Get"), and Isaac Hayes were among the hitmakers and household names that emerged from the Memphis label.

Black Moses

After the tragic death of the label's leading man, Otis Redding, in a 1967 plane crash and the horrific murder of Martin Luther King Jr. at the Lorraine Motel—the very space where Stax staffers would recreate between recording sessions—a darker tone emerged that eventually overwhelmed the organization. In the bitter and hopeless environment of black Memphis, where Stax headquarters was located, black militants and plain thugs began to harass and confront Stax members, attempting to extort money, steal equipment, or merely undermine the multiracial harmony of the organization. Fences and security guards were installed, the executive offices were relocated across town, and the ambiance of the down-home, integrated, family-owned recording label disintegrated. The label was also in a legal mess regarding its relationship with its one-time distributors Atlantic Records, and Stax was on the verge of dissolution. In a swift move of desperation and genius, label cofounder Jim Stewart hired the multitalented black marketing prodigy and former Washington, DC, DJ Al Bell to rescue the label from financial and social chaos. Bell worked swiftly on all fronts. He brought in a stronger street presence to keep the extreme elements at bay, hiring some trusted street toughs from New York (which in turn helped to create some problems of their own). Al Bell then engineered a new distribution deal and devised a plan to record twenty-seven albums in a span of a few short weeks, the aptly described "Soul Explosion." The high-minded plan would resuscitate the label and by doing so free up many of the artists to take extended musical adventures. Among the most inspired of the acts to record at this time was Isaac Hayes, who's iconic bald head and sultry reserved persona skyrocketed to fame from his album of extended spoken vamps, or "raps" over music, *Hot Buttered Soul*, and the follow up *To Be Continued* in 1969.

Playing on Hayes's image, staff members at Stax convinced Hayes to portray himself as "Black Moses" on a 1971 double album, with a grand album foldout that went six ways (in the shape of a cross) and portraying Hayes as an indomitable Black Moses. Wearing the robe of Moses, and with his tall frame and bald head, Isaac Hayes became an icon of racial pride without having to sing a note. Hayes did, however, sing beautifully over extended ballads, making pillow talk a genre of R&B by himself. Hayes then scored the 1971 film soundtrack to *Shaft*, which earned him an Academy Award for the "Theme from Shaft" and an unforgettable performance at the 1972 Academy Award show in a shirt made of chains. As Rob Bowman writes, "For many African Americans, Isaac's capturing of an Oscar that night was an event comparable to Joe Louis's knockout of Max Schmeling in 1938. It was a victory for all of black America."[64]

Uncomfortable with the religious implications, Hayes initially refused to take on the role of Black Moses. "I had nothing to do with it" Hayes recalled a few years later:

> I was kicking and screaming all the way. But when I saw the relevance and effect it had on people, it wasn't a negative thing. It was a healing thing, it was an inspiring thing. It raised the level of black consciousness in the States. People were proud to be black. Black men could finally stand up and be men because here's Black Moses, he's the epitome of black masculinity. Chains that once represented bondage and slavery now can be a sign of power and strength and sexuality and virility.[65]

At the dawn of the 1970s, despite the tragedies that befell the family-owned label from the southwest side of Memphis, from the ashes emerged a strident, soulful enterprise that reflected the heightened black awareness of its population while never truly losing the universally accessible essence of their sound.

Stax developed a working relationship with Reverend Jesse Jackson and sponsored various events in support of Jackson's Operation PUSH. The label began a spoken-word imprint, Respect, which featured an album of Jackson's speeches titled *I Am Somebody*. Al Bell was adamant about both the cultural and financial success of the label. "In terms of advertising we're pitching black, we're researching black because that's where our product is directed, and we're supported black," Al Bell asserted in 1971. By this time, Estelle Axton was out of the picture, and Stewart and Bell were co-owners of Stax. His construction was seen as simple and proper business sense. The sensibility, however, carried a weight of racial identification that was at a zenith.

Wattstax

By 1972 Al Bell had established an office in Los Angeles and, like Berry Gordy, had his sights set on film and television as well as music. Working with his operatives out West, he put forth a plan to put together a "black Woodstock," an all-day concert of Stax artists to be held at the Los Angeles Coliseum on August 20, 1972. The event would be the culmination of the seventh annual Watts Summer Festival, a weeklong event to commemorate the watershed events of that time, the rebuilding, and the consciousness-raising that emerged in Los Angeles after 1965. With a sponsorship by Schlitz beer, admission was only one dollar, ensuring that the community could attend. Proceeds for the event went to the Sickle Cell Anemia Foundation, the Martin Luther King Hospital, the Watts Summer Music Festival, and the Watts Labor Community Action Committee. Here was a soul music event, by the people and *for* the people. The elaborate plan worked brilliantly and was filmed by David L. Wolper Productions (the film crew responsible for *Roots*). The film and soundtrack were brilliant showcases of black consciousness, black culture, and black capitalism all at once. The richly displayed fashions, the spectacular Afro hairstyles, the improvised dances, the joy of being black were all on display that afternoon, and the money earned went to a black-owned enterprise, and to the community.[66]

This was both the zenith and the crest of the soul music enterprise as a vehicle for promoting a conscious black agenda. There were certainly excellent recordings of conscious soul music that followed, but the combination of spectacle, style, and financial success would not be sustained. The recording industry was consolidating. Major labels were purchasing independents, distribution networks were being centralized, and small-time retailers, record companies, DJs, and promoters would lose their hard-earned prestige in a matter of a few years. The popularity of soul festivals would continue through the decade, typically under the sponsorship of major (white-owned) labels.

The sweet and sour experience of Wattstax was mirrored in the political arena, during the National Black Political Convention of 1972. A gathering of an unprecedented scope of black activists, from members of the Congressional Black Caucus to the Nation of Islam, was represented in a collective effort to determine a "national black agenda." Held in Gary, Indiana—home of the Jackson 5 and one of the first northern cities with a black mayor—the event was bristling with excitement and possibility. The cultural exchanges, the black-and-proud pronouncements, the dazzling fashions, the image of blacks on the advance were unrivaled during those few days in March 1972. The chanting of "It's Nation Time" under the spirited announcement of Jesse Jackson would resonate through the halls of West Side High School Arena, and for a moment, a black nation could see itself, witness the accomplishments of so many generations who had sought political power, and, across the floor, the thrill could be soaked in.

However, the deep divisions within the movement would fundamentally cripple the project from the start. The NAACP, for example, denounced the entire conference as a movement away from mainstream political engagement; the New York representative Shirley Chisolm, was to be the first African American presidential candidate, but she refused to appear at the conference, anticipating that she would be ridiculed by the nationalistic and chauvinistic black men in the arena. Representatives of white-run corporate sponsors attended under the guise of black capitalism, a move that riled members of the Black Panthers and other groups who were steadfastly against such white-power-sponsored intrusions. Deep fissures emerged in the floor debates as well.

The entire conference was held together by Amiri Baraka, whose organizing with the Congress of African People (CAP) had provided the foundation for the large-scale delegate organizing, and during the tense floor arguments over the direction of a black agenda, Baraka had to assert himself into the proceedings with his own soulful inflections to help unify the groups on a cultural level long enough for a political agenda to be determined.[67]

In terms of size and scope, the National Black Political Convention could be seen as the final great achievement of the Black Nationalist movement. It should also be noted that, despite the absence of Maulana Karenga, the NBPC had the imprint of one of his visions. However, a fundamental division emerged in those meetings that could not be resolved. The question for blacks of operating completely independent of whites or of strategic cooperation with whites was an issue in which a consensus could not be achieved.

It appears that Black Nationalism, and in particular the cultural nationalism of Baraka and Karenga, and the militant nationalism of the Panthers would both prove to be essential forces in the overall black revolution that took place at the end of the 1960s. It would be the music that in many ways reflected a unification of the sentiments of both strands of black radicalism. Jazz artists freely borrowed from the imagery and the energy provided by black radicals of the time and produced works that sought to inspire a black nation in their imagination. Soul artists began to advocate—on a culturally framed basis—for social equality based on a deeply ingrained notion of what blackness is all about.

The end result of this ideological upheaval was not an ultimate confrontation with the white power structure. It did not generate a slew of autonomous, exclusively black institutions. But it did generate an explosion in the black arts, an explosion with a force that permeated black popular culture and popular music. One could watch this explosion of black conscious soul every Saturday in the 1970s on *Soul Train*. It did not create a lasting economic base for a black nation, but it was a start, and it was *funky*. As the decade began, soul music, in all of its representations, for a moment, had triumphed.

6

"Bobby Must Be Set Free"

Panther Power and Popular Culture

Deep into their forty-minute set, the Lumpen take control of the audience and deliver the core of their message. Bandleader William Calhoun counts off the time and the band cracks into their hit single, the driving number on the 45 rpm single being sold in the lobby as "Free Bobby Now." Sales of the single were not appreciable, but the group had their own version of a hit, a song that drove the climax of their act, and they played the notion up as any legitimate rhythm and blues act would.

As the groove begins, an intense, chopping rhythm guitar drives against a pulsing bass and drum pattern, while long soaring horn riffs arch above the groove to create a cacophonous high-velocity funk from the bottom to the top. The Lumpen singers, spinning through the first bars of the song, step in rhythm to the mics and begin the background chants, anticipating William Calhoun's lead vocals from his seat by the electric piano.

> Aah, get it
> Woo woo - woo woo / woo woo - woo woo
> woo woo - woo woo / woo woo - woo woo
>
> We say, he walked the streets and carried a gun, *now now*
> To save his people and family, *hear us*

From those who've killed us for four hundred years
Bobby Must Be Set Free,
We're talkin' 'bout
Bobby Must Be Set Free / *yaa—yeah!*

Calhoun and the other singers invoke the time-tested techniques of rhythm and blues performance: the religious invocation; the improvised, ad-libbed, percussive vamps and chants; and the call-and-response techniques. As the background whoops continue, Calhoun ad-libs in-between each background chant:

Woo woo - woo woo / Let me tell the people
Woo woo - woo woo / Good God, now

The dancing singers—Torrence, Mott, and Bailey—take turns on verses that explain their allegiance to their Party chairman and to their cause while reaching out to their audience.

They say that he killed a brother
But this we know it just can't be, yea
He's proven his love for his people
We say, Bobby Must Be Set Free
We're talkin' 'bout / Bobby Must Be Set Free
Good god almighty / *Sing it brother*
How many more brothers must die / Before we all finally see
That the oppressor has no rights we are bound to respect
That's why Bobby Must Be Set Free, *yea yea yea*
We're talking 'bout Bobby Must Be Set Free
One one one more time

Woo woo - woo woo / woo woo - woo woo
We won't sacrifice our chairman
'Cause his life means our destiny, yeah
Cause if we must we'll hold back the night
(group) Bobby Must Be Set Free / We're talking 'bout
Bobby Must Be Set Free / We want our chairman free
BOBBY MUST BE SET FREE / We're talking bout
BOBBY MUST BE SET FREE
Bobby want him home now
Bobby *we're talking 'bout*
Bobby *we're talking 'bout*

BOBBY *bring it on down now*
BOBBY *bring it on down now*
BOBBY *bring it on down now*
BOBBY *bring it on down now*

As the band churns the groove along, William Calhoun takes control of the show and brings the audience inside the message in the music:

Lookit here / *Bobby!*
As we—as you know / *Bobby!*
This song is uh, called "Bobby Must Be Set Free" / *Bobby!*
It's all about our National Chairman Bobby Seale / *Bobby!*
Who is being held as a political prisoner in New Haven, Connecticut, tonight / *Bobby!*
We sing this song in the spirit / *Bobby!*
That we believe the people want Bobby Seale to be set free / *Bobby!*
If you join with us in that feelin' this evening / *Bobby!*
I want everybody in this house to clap your hands / *Bobby!*
Good god, everybody! / *Bobby!*
Want you to sing along with us if you would / *Bobby!*

The audience claps in unison and chants "Bobby" along with the background singers. As party members recall, members of the audience were standing, dancing in the aisles, and moving to the groove of this revolutionary rhythm and blues experience. Calhoun then invites the audience to provide the chorus of the song together:

You've got it so you know the words—all you say is: Bobby Must Be Set Free! Say it now / (*Crowd singing along*) *Bobby Must Be Set Free!*
A little bit louder / *Bobby Must Be Set Free!*
I can't hear ya / *Bobby Must Be Set Free!*
Yea yaeea yea / *Bobby Must Be Set Free!*
Let 'em hear you in Sacramento tonight / *Bobby Must Be Set Free!*
Let 'em hear you in San Francisco tonight / *Bobby Must Be Set Free!*
Let 'em hear you in Winston-Salem tonight / *Bobby Must Be Set Free!*
Let 'em hear you in New Haven, Connecticut, tonight / *Bobby Must Be Set Free!*
Tell the world about it / *Bobby Must Be Set Free!*

The rousing number ends with a crash and an eruption of audience applause, as the audience is awash in the moment and the message of the music. Like any polished R&B act, the Lumpen organized their entire performance around their best-known song, leading songs up to it and gradually winding down their show after the rousing experience.[1]

It should come as no surprise to fans of black popular music, particularly the music of the late 1960s, that the most compelling, most energetic, and most involving song by the group is also the one with the most meaning. All but the most disconnected black entertainer of this time was bound to infuse their performance with some social commentary, and it was expected to come at the climax of their act. At this time, in late 1970, Aretha Franklin was touring with her all-star band, and the climax of her set was—and continues to be—"Respect," while James Brown was working with Bootsy Collins and ending his show with "Soul Power." The ethos, the aesthetic of soul, was to put one's most important point into their most appealing work, and "Free Bobby Now" was an example of that.

The Lumpen were not by any measure the most popular aspect of the Black Panther Party, but they had their moments. This chapter discusses the presence of the Black Panther Party at the flashpoint of black rage in the late 1960s, and its impact on the popular consciousness and the popular culture.

"Free Bobby Now"

The original song the Lumpen performed so adroitly in concert was one of the original two Calhoun compositions the Lumpen played at their first performance on the flatbed truck in the Fillmore District in the spring of 1970. It was side A of the 45 rpm single released by the Party in the summer of 1970 and sold at BPP events. It was also prominently advertised in the back pages of the *Black Panther*, which published the lyrics to the song in the September 26, 1970, issue.

With a record in their hands, members of the Lumpen set about their own promotion and went to both of the black Bay Area radio stations (KSOL and KDIA) seeking airplay. "We went to KDIA, and the DJ—I forgot his name—was sweating like a pig." Michael Torrence recalls. "He told us there was no way that record was going to get played. He would lose his job and all kinds of things would happen." But the group members gave it a shot. "We did the circuit trying to promote that thing," Calhoun says. For an unknown rhythm and blues act to get rejected by a radio station DJ was a common occurrence. However, the Lumpen were trying to bridge two worlds at once, and the stakes of their gambit were far higher.

The lyrics of the song interspersed other Panther-influenced ideas from bandleader Calhoun. When the Lumpen use the phrase "the oppressor has no rights we are bound to respect," a number of historical threads are invoked. The verse is a signifier of the *Dred Scott* decision of 1857, in which the Virginia-born slave Dred Scott sued for his family's freedom on the basis that he and his owner had traveled the frontier and Scott had lived in free states. After a series of appeals, the US Supreme Court rendered a decision far beyond the scope of the case and denied all citizenship rights for African Americans, stating that Negroes were "beings of an inferior order, and altogether unfit to associate with the white race, either in social or political relations, and so far inferior that they had no rights which the white man was bound to respect." It was the *Dred Scott* decision that polarized the nation and rendered inevitable the conflicts that led to the American Civil War four years later. Thus, to turn the phrase on its head is both a timely militant slogan and a recognition of the century-old Civil War resistance that essentially transformed the nation through violent upheaval. The updated phrase was frequently used in Panther discourse. Eldridge Cleaver used the phrase in his speeches. Huey Newton wrote it in an essay, "In Defense of Self Defense," that appeared in the July 3, 1967, issue of the *Black Panther*, where Newton stated:

> The point of departure is the principle that the oppressor has no rights that the oppressed is bound to respect. Kill the slave master, destroy him utterly, move against him with implacable fortitude. Break his oppressive power by any means necessary. Men who have stood before the Black masses and recommended this response to the oppression have been held in fear by the oppressor.[2]

Newton employed the phrase to justify the revolutionary actions of Panther members and to upturn the discourse of the criminalization of black males. "Free Bobby Now" was an exciting song that worked well with a live audience, but writer William Calhoun's words were as serious as his Party leaders' message. The refrain "We won't sacrifice our chairman 'cause his life means our destiny" was delivered as a rallying cry from the Party itself to galvanize its audience members and supporters to sacrifice their lives if necessary for Bobby Seale. "If we must, we'll hold back the night / Bobby Must Be Set Free!" Like an uplifting political speech, the chorus resonated throughout the auditorium, in a crescendo of forceful voices, an explosion of political soul power.

The hard-driving rhythms of "Free Bobby Now" were instantly recognizable as reflections of the James Brown aesthetic of aggressive rhythm and exhilarating shout-singing that was expected of legitimate R&B acts at the time. The Lumpen could chant a revolutionary slogan, chant another one in a different cadence from the first, then repeat the process, with the singers and the band subtly improvising around the rhythms with vocal grunts and accents from the rhythm section keeping the energy level sustained but the sound never feeling repetitive. The horns would lock everything together for a moment, then let go like a fist opening up for the rest of the rhythm to flow through.

It was still somewhat of a contradiction that the Lumpen utilized the many tropes of soul music to further their militant mission. Here was a popular sound and style associated with love, unity, and pride. To some extent, the Lumpen were showing these themes as well. The Panthers sought to convey the love of the revolution, the unity of the community, and pride in the power of the people. They conspicuously avoided the racially explicit approach of black radical jazz contemporaries associated with the cultural nationalists. Other forms, such as folk, rock, or the piano ballads performed by Elaine Brown were not as accessible to their intended audience. Soul worked for the Panthers as an idiom ideally suited to their recruitment needs. Only the lyrics needed to be amended.

The Panthers and Their Public Image

The role and relationship of the Black Panther Party to the larger society was and remains a riddle that has followed the legacy of the Black Panthers. "Free Bobby Now" was a deliberate effort to reach the people on their own terms. On a few occasions, such as Eldridge Cleaver's insistence that he photograph Huey Newton in a rattan chair with a spear in his hand, there were deliberate efforts to popularize the Party. But as it turns out, the Black Panthers, by their actions and public pronouncements, had a spectacular impact on the popular consciousness, one that affected public policy, social discourse, style, fashion, film, and the sensibility of the street.

The Panthers played a social role that had been dwelling in the American imagination since the days of American chattel slavery: the dreams of slaves and the nightmares of slave owners that one day blacks would rise up and free themselves through the very forces of violence that had imprisoned them. There were prophetic renderings of a racial apocalypse from earlier leaders such as Marcus Garvey and Elijah Muhammad, and many believed the time had come to bring the conflagration about. The apocalyptic black art of the day fueled the fires of outrage as folks chanted "Burn, baby, burn" and black radical public figures such as H. Rap Brown and Eldridge Cleaver actively condoned political violence in their speeches.

The Panthers' public image was exhilarating to young blacks in search of a model of resistance that they could participate in. The relentless violence of American government, from forced conscription (the Vietnam War draft that threatened to claim all males over eighteen) to the state-sponsored repression of marchers and rioters gave rise to the Panther, a militant rebel, one that organized in military fashion against the American power structure itself. The Panthers were heady stuff.

Their early image struck nationwide upon news of their disciplined march into the Sacramento capitol in May 1967. By the end of the next year, dozens of Party chapters had been established and more were on the way. After the horrors of 1968 it would become clear that law enforcement had targeted the Panthers. The relentless police attacks on Panther offices and the disciplined and determined responses to police violence earned a measure of respect from others seeking to dismiss the Panthers as a band of California-based hotheads.

Throughout 1969 the Black Panther Party stood for many as a viable counter to the power structure. The Survival Programs were having an impact on a local level. Panther leaders were in the national news, constantly addressing the media and appearing at speaking engagements (typically to drum up money for legal costs). By 1970 the Panthers' image was accomplishing as much as their actions. The Party was providing what many felt was a necessary image of the strong black soldier staring down the gun barrel of his oppressor, but the reality was the organization was fraught with internal dissention and disruption that would not allow it to survive as a national entity much longer. As Safiya Bukhari recalled, "We felt we had two major enemies, we had the other side of the Party and the state apparatus."[3] The Party was struggling to maintain its effectiveness, especially on the East Coast. The work of the Lumpen (mid-1970 to mid-1971) took place at the last moments of the Panthers' effective nationwide operation.

Black Power in New York City

The black power movement in New York City in the 1960s was the epicenter of radicalism on multiple levels. It can best be understood as a whirlwind of conflicting groups, ethnic affiliations, political ideologies, tactics, and historical viewpoints. The city had been at the forefront of black cultural and political activity since the early twentieth century with the founding of the NAACP in 1909 and the emergence of Marcus Garvey's Pan-Africanist organization, the Universal Negro Improvement Association (UNIA) in the 1910s, and the literary and intellectual accomplishments of Harlem Renaissance luminaries such as W. E. B. Du Bois and Langston Hughes as well as entertainers such as Fats Waller and Josephine Baker in the 1920s.

From early in the twentieth century, Harlem was recognized as the black capital of the world because of its great arts, unique opportunities for success, and lasting examples of black brilliance in literature, drama, music, and black radical thought. As the jazz capital of the world, Harlem represented a creative zenith for aspiring black musicians and entertainers pursuing a musical vision of freedom while operating in a segregated musical economy and environment. Thus, great black bandleaders such as Cab Calloway, Count Basie, and Duke Ellington were seen as successful even when they performed in the segregated Cotton Club on 142nd Street and Lenox Avenue.

The emergence of Malcolm X in the 1950s on the streets of Harlem reenergized a process of militant black consciousness raising, one that led to the enormous growth and influence of the Nation of Islam and many other black militant groups that shared the same geographical space. The work Malcolm X and others did to popularize new and defiant ideas of blackness was also a great inspiration to the artists of the Black Arts movement, which led to a storm of black radical activity in the region. Different factions overlapped, complemented, and sometimes competed for the hearts and minds of members of the region's black and brown populations.

The Nation of Islam was the largest Black Nationalist organization in the country, and especially in New York in the 1950s and 1960s. Their years of work rehabilitating blacks, their organizational stability, and their steadfast critique of white institutions and white supremacy were highly respected in the community. However, after the death of Malcolm X and the subsequent conviction of two NOI members for the shooting (despite the strong sense that Malcolm's murderers had not been brought to justice), the NOI suffered a severe image problem in the black radical community. Upon his death, Malcolm X had become the most popular black radical in America, but the Nation and its leaders at the time treated him as an outcast who had met his ignoble fate. Factions, spinoffs, and defections abounded from the phalanx of radicals from this point.

In this respect, the Black Panther Party was not the first, most important, or most popular black radical organization to come to New York. The first Black Panther Party branch in the area was established by David Brothers in Brooklyn in the summer of 1968, and in the fall, Lumumba Shakur set up the Harlem chapter. The New York Panther offices did not enjoy the singular status as vanguards of the revolution. In addition to their typical recruitment of young brothers on the block and idealistic college students and community members, Party membership included veterans of other radical organizations, members of all types of West Indian ethnic groups, African nationals, and a steady supply of agent provocateurs. As a result, Party offices, despite the disciplined activity of many dedicated Panthers, were often hectic and chaotic, and adherence to Party rules and decrees from distant Oakland headquarters were not always followed with regularity.

Eventual popular music superstar Nile Rodgers was a member of the New York chapter. Rodgers recalled his own controversial entrée into the Party:

> The way I got into the Party, I was actually running with renegades.
> I didn't know that they weren't real Panthers. I was running with
> these guys who were shaking down little grocers in the neighbor-
> hood. They would go to the little delis and there would be the old
> mom and pop guys and they would come in and say, "We're the
> Black Panthers, give us some money."[4]

It would not be until Rodgers arrived at the Harlem chapter and met
Jamal Joseph that Rodgers learned that the hustlers he first encountered
were not Panthers. Rodgers was enamored of the way Joseph was able to
recruit youth who were excited about the "equipment" Panthers would
use, and instead of a gun, Joseph would produce a book for them to read.
Rodgers would become a subsection leader of the Lower Manhattan
branch of the Party. "I thought I was going to be a serious revolutionary
à la Che Guevara," he recalls. Rodgers's Panther chapter was a diverse
one (South Asians and Puerto Ricans were members), and eventually
the interethnic friction caused a confrontation between Rodgers and a
nationalistic Party member who did not see the presence of nonblacks
in the same way. The interethnic friction in his Panther chapter and the
general disillusionment toward the movement in 1969 inspired the guitarist Rodgers to move on and start his musical career, which would take
him to superstardom as leader of the disco band Chic and as one of the
greatest popular music producers of all time.

Afeni Shakur, sister of the exiled black revolutionary Assata Shakur
and mother of rapper Tupac, was also drawn to the power of the Panthers in 1968. Her entrée into the organization had more to do with her
own self-reclamation after watching Bobby Seale speak about the Ten
Point Program in Harlem:

> Bobby Seale saying that right there with passion, with intelligence.
> The way he said those ten points made me want that more than
> anything. So there I was wrapped in my Africanness. For the first
> time, loving myself and loving, now that there was something I
> could do with my life. There was now something I could do with
> all this aggression, and all this fear. Because up until this point, I
> wasn't shit.[5]

Afeni Shakur emerged quickly as a leader of the Harlem chapter, and
her "aggression" became legendary in the Party as a Panther and in her

volatile relationship with Party leader Lumumba Shakur. "I needed for people to know I was bad and strong," Afeni Shakur revealed to Jasmine Guy in a 2004 memoir: "I was quick to speak out and volunteer for shit. So I would beg to be sent out on missions. I got sent on one once and I caused complete havoc. I still don't know how I survived. I shot at a man in a tollbooth because I wanted to rob something to show I'm so big and bad. . . . Give me a gun and let me go." Everything would change for Afeni and Lumumba Shakur when they both were arrested in April 1969.

"The New York 21"

By the spring of 1969 law enforcement had developed a working plan against the Panthers and initiated raids on Panther offices, arresting Panther Party officials with regularity in every major city. The process of harassment and taxing use of Party resources in court trials and bail hearings would exact a toll on the organization. The most ambitious law enforcement siege took place on April 2, 1969, two days before the one-year anniversary of the murder of Martin Luther King Jr. In a sweep across the New York region, twenty-one Panthers, including Sundiata Acoli, Michael (Cetewayo) Tabor, Richard (Dhoruba) Moore, Jamal Joseph, Ali Bey Hassan, JoAnne Chesimard (Assata Shakur), Afeni Shakur, and Lumumba Shakur were arrested and charged with dozens of conspiracy charges, alleging that the twenty-one were "plotting terrorist acts" and planning to blow up Bloomingdale's, bomb a local police station, and even target the Bronx Botanical Gardens. The extent of the charges was outrageous. The scope of the charges in a sense was a reflection of the bombast of other Panthers and supporters who often boasted—in bouts of hyperbole—of doing outrageous things to the power structure.

The New York 21 trial would be the longest trial in the state's history, involving more than 150 felony counts for the thirteen Panthers who eventually went to trial. Afeni Shakur was released on bail early in 1970, and in addition to developing her own legal defense, she made the most of her (brief) time on the outside:

> I got pregnant while I was out on bail. I never thought that I wasn't going to spend the rest of my life in jail. I was never getting out and that's why I wanted to have this baby. Because I wanted to leave something here. I was going to jail for three hundred and twelve

years. That's what I was facing. But my sister [Assata] was out. If I
thought I was getting out, I never would have had the baby. I probably would have gotten an abortion.[6]

During a prolonged trial preparation, according to Afeni Shakur,
two Panthers out on bail absconded with the remaining bail money and
left the country, forcing her and others to return to prison until the
entire group of twenty-one was acquitted on May 13, 1971, after forty-
five minutes of jury deliberation. Afeni gave birth to Tupac on June 16.
While the entire trial was a fiasco that humiliated the New York Police
Intelligence Unit (BOSSI) responsible for the arrests, the drain on the
state's resources was minor compared to the drain on the Panther Party's
stability. Huey Newton had purged the Panther 21 in the midst of trial
preparations, and by the end of the trial the Panthers' power in New
York was effectively gutted. This was the context in which Bobby Seale's
indictment in New Haven came about.

The New Haven Case

"Free Bobby Now" was written because Bobby Seale was on trial for
the murder of Alex Rackley in New Haven, Connecticut. Rackley was
a twenty-four-year-old member of the New York Panther chapter who
was kidnapped and taken to the New Haven Party headquarters on May
19, 1969. He was tortured for two days, shot in the head twice, and
dumped into the swamps of Coginchaug River thirty miles north, near
Middletown, allegedly upon the orders of Panther leadership. The insti-
gator of the crime was George Sams, who identified himself to the New
York Panthers as "national field marshal" and claimed the authority to
dispense justice to alleged informants such as Rackley. Many Panthers
have since stated that Rackley was an honest and dedicated rank-and-file
Panther member. But the chaos surrounding the recent roundup of the
New York 21 left doubts swirling around the Black Panther organization
nationwide. Curtis J. Austin explained the in-flux situation surrounding
Sams and how he was able to deceive so many Panthers and infiltrate the
organization:

The New York Twenty-one had recently been arrested and the chapter was in disarray. Sams told unsuspecting New York Panthers,

who did not bother to check his credentials with the Oakland head-quarters, that he had come to straighten out the chapter and to find out who framed the Panther leaders. While he was there, he beat some members, raped a female Panther, and openly carried a loaded weapon while drinking and smoking heavily. All these activities were against party rules. Had the New York Panthers contacted Oakland, they would have discovered that Sams, introduced to the Party by Stokely Carmichael, had been expelled for being the fool he was.[7]

When Sams heard that Panthers were coming from the West Coast to investigate the situation, Sams took Rackley and went to New Haven, perpetrating the same ruse. In New Haven, Sams accused Rackley of being an informant and ordered Rackley to the basement, where he was bound, pistol-whipped, scalded, and tied with coat hangers. After two days of this ordeal, Sams appeared to have relented and released Rackley, only to drive Rackley upstate and order two Panthers—Lonnie McLucas and Warren Kimbro—to shoot him.

Law enforcement was "given a tip," and found Rackley's body on May 21, 1969. The next day they indicted twelve Panthers, including Party leaders Ericka Huggins and Bobby Seale. While McLucas, Kimbro, and Sams testified that they participated in the crime, Sams claimed that he gave the orders to the other Panthers at the request of Bobby Seale. By turning State's evidence, Sams had his conviction reduced to manslaughter and a life sentence. He was later placed under the witness protection program and served only four years of his sentence.[8]

Seale was arrested three months later in Oakland. Seale and Huggins were tried as conspirators. Their trial lasted six months, went through more than fifteen hundred jurors, and was the longest and most expensive in Connecticut history. As Donald Freed wrote: "The Black Panther Party was on trial too, and not just before white people but to the almost 70 percent of the black population (cited in 'white' polls) that supported their program of 'survival pending revolution.'"[9] Massive demonstrations of support for Seale and Huggins took place during the trial in the spring of 1970. A Yale student walkout to protest the Panthers' trial on May 1, 1970, effectively ended classes that semester. Yale president King-man Brewster Jr. issued the statement, "I personally want to say that I'm appalled and ashamed that things should have come to such a pass that I am skeptical of the ability of Black revolutionaries to achieve a fair trial anywhere in the U.S."[10] A Yale law student at the time, Hillary Rodham was one of the courtroom monitors, representing the ACLU.

After doubts about Sams's testimony surfaced, and after months of negative publicity in the local and national press surrounding the obviousness of the faked charges, the government dropped the charges against Seale and Huggins. But the damage had been done. Seale, perhaps the most engaging public speaker of all of the Panthers, had been dragged through the most violent underworld of alleged Panther justice, and by the time he was released in late May 1971, the Party was a shell of its original self.[11]

"You Can't Jail the Revolution"

For Newton and Seale, growing up among the urban underclass—as lumpenproletariat—incarceration was a regular presence in their lives. Once the Black Panther Party became nationally known, constant legal harassment and incarceration was the rule and not the exception. From their May 1967 march through the California state capitol building to the February 1971 party fracture between Huey Newton and Eldridge Cleaver, the Black Panther Party enjoyed its greatest popularity and influence. During those four years, Bobby Seale was incarcerated more than half of that time, and Newton and Seale were only free together for the first three months following the Sacramento event.

Bobby Seale seemed to be targeted for jail once the Black Panther Party made its public demonstration. His was the first name published worldwide as the representative of the Black Panther Party that had "stormed the state capitol." After Watts exploded in the summer of 1965, the general public began to realize that the civil rights movement had not quelled black anger in the cities. The radicalization of SNCC under the leadership of Stokely Carmichael in 1966—under the banner of black power—was openly challenging Martin Luther King Jr. for leadership of the black struggle. In the spring of 1967 Dr. King went public with his opposition to the Vietnam War, connecting the moral imperative of civil rights with the failed morality of the military escapade in Southeast Asia. The action drew Dr. King closer to the position of the popular militants and radicals and solidified his national leadership for a time. Yet there were many candidates capable of becoming the next national black leader, something law enforcement was extremely wary of. Seale was a clear target.

That summer of 1967—the summer of "'Retha, Rap, and Revolt"—would become the most violent in urban America, spurred in part by the Panthers' bold Sacramento display. Within days of that event there were violent antiwar confrontations with civilians and police at Texas Southern University in Houston and at Jackson State in Mississippi, and hundreds of students were arrested. In Newark on July 11, police attempted to arrest a black cab driver on a traffic violation outside of a local precinct house, causing a melee. When a rumor spread that the cab driver had been killed, a mob stormed the police station, and the riot was on. Looters charged into local department stores and black snipers fired at police from rooftops. After five days of chaos, twenty-six people had died, one thousand were injured, and almost fourteen hundred were arrested (among them, LeRoi Jones). On July 23 in Detroit, a late-night police raid on a local bar sparked a disturbance that led to massive riots that left 42 people dead, 386 injured, and over 5,000 arrested. Similar but smaller disturbances took place in more than fifty black communities that summer.[12] The events turned up the rhetoric from the Black Nationalist leaders. Shortly after Detroit, SNCC leader H. Rap Brown spoke to an audience of students in Cambridge, Massachusetts, and said: "Detroit exploded, Newark exploded, Harlem exploded! . . . It is time for Cambridge to explode, baby. Black folks built America. If America don't come around, we're going to burn America down, brother. We're going to burn it if we can't get our share of it."[13] H. Rap Brown's rhetoric was both satirical and scathing. Brown understood the mood of the moment in his community and reflected the desperation and hostility of the times. But he also placed a target on this back.

A sense of seizing the moment was in the air, and black radicals were making their case to the entire nation. The anti–Vietnam War movement took its cue from the black protest movement. An October 15, 1967, series of "stop the draft week" protests in Oakland, California, turned violent as police attacked protestors, bystanders, and media members in downtown Oakland, effectively radicalizing the antiwar movement. Two weeks later, photographs of a wounded and beaten Huey Newton in an Oakland hospital, surrounded by Oakland police officers, set a new tone for the movement.

"Free Huey"

In the foggy early hours of Saturday, October 28, 1967, on the streets of West Oakland, Huey Newton was involved in a fatal altercation with Oakland police officer John Frey, in which Newton was wounded and Frey died of gunshot wounds from a police revolver. Questions abounded about the nature of the altercation, who initiated the gunfire, and who in fact was with Newton in the car at the time. Newton survived the shooting and was taken to the county hospital, but he was chained to the gurney and intermittently beaten by OPD officers on that fateful night.

News of Newton's incarceration and treatment caused a firestorm of outrage, public sympathy for the Panthers, and organizational activity. Bobby Seale, however, was still in jail, and the responsibility for publicizing the case fell on Eldridge Cleaver who, for all his critics (which included Newton), was very media savvy and helped to broadcast Newton's plight worldwide. Cleaver and his brilliant wife, Kathleen, organized rallies, brought together coalitions of rival black organizations, addressed the media frequently and in quotable terms, and publicized the Black Panther Party and the plight of Huey Newton in ways no one else could. Reginald Major explained Eldridge Cleaver's crucial contribution:

> Right up to the moment he left the country, Cleaver was a mainstay of the Party, a leader, an order giver, an organizer with talent, drive and inexhaustible energy, and an orator who combined wit, blasphemy and revolutionary messages in an unpredictable mélange that always made a lot of sense and constantly delights his audiences.[14]

Eldridge Cleaver was enamored of Newton early on. After serving a nine-year sentence at Soledad Prison for a rape conviction in the early 1960s, Cleaver's published prison essays (which would later become his book *Soul On Ice*) made him a black radical celebrity in his own right. Cleaver worked as a writer for *Ramparts* magazine upon his release in 1966 and frequented the Black Nationalist scene in San Francisco. He observed the power struggle between rival black radical organizations that wanted to escort Sister Betty Shabazz, the widow of Malcolm X, to San Francisco for her first public interview since Malcolm's death two years earlier. On February 21, 1967, Newton's Panthers escorted Sister Shabazz from the San Francisco airport to the *Ramparts* office for the interview. As the Panther-Shabazz entourage was leaving the *Ramparts* offices, Cleaver witnessed Newton's confrontation with a San Francisco police officer in which Newton dared the officer to draw his gun. It was clear to Eldridge Cleaver at that point that Newton and the Black Panther Party meant business. Bobby Seale recalled Cleaver's reverence for Newton's nascent organization:

> Eldridge said that when he saw all us brothers with guns, all ready and organized, it didn't take him any time at all to relate to that . . . so he just started moving with the Party, going everywhere, making the scenes. He was relating to it and functioning, but he still had some reservations. . . .
>
> Eldridge just couldn't understand how it could happen—how we pulled this shit off or why niggers would be crazy enough to go out there in the streets. It looked unbelievable. Eldridge said it scared him, that's what it did. Scared Eldridge! He said that when Malcolm was teaching, he was just dealing with rhetoric about how we had to organize a gun club, we had to do this, we had to have these guns, etc. He said it was abstract and he couldn't visualize it. Or if he did visualize it, he visualized a whole army, the black race armed. But then, when he saw us out there in the process of organizing, he saw about ten, twelve dudes with some guns, and he saw all those pigs. It looked like we didn't have a chance, it looked hopeless, but then many times it looked so beautiful and inspiring, that he just had to relate to it.[15]

Both Kathleen and Eldridge Cleaver dedicated themselves to engineering the public cause for the freeing of Huey Newton. They supported an alliance with the fledgling white-led Peace and Freedom Party (PFP), which was seeking signatures to run anti–Vietnam War candidates in the 1968 presidential election. The BPP sought a commitment to their Ten Point Program and other concessions to their leadership of the coalition. While their issues did not entirely overlap, the awkward coalition served each organization greatly at first: the PFP ran candidates in the national election (with Eldridge Cleaver running for president, Jerry Rubin for vice president, and Kathleen for state assembly); the BPP secured thousands of recruits to the "Free Huey" cause.

The Cleavers and other Party leaders also spearheaded coalitions with competing black radical groups. By 1967 the Student Nonviolent

Coordinating Committee (SNCC) had adopted a Black Nationalist stance and was developing a far more militant position under the
guidance of younger leaders Stokely Carmichael, H. Rap Brown, and
SNCC veteran James Forman. Panther leaders sought to merge SNCC
with the Black Panther Party, and on June 29, 1967, in an executive
mandate, Newton drafted Carmichael into the BPP. After some cross-
country negotiations, and with Newton's blessing, the Panthers installed
H. Rap Brown as minister of justice, Forman as minister of foreign
affairs, and Carmichael as "prime minister" of the BPP for a brief time.
All of these fiery orators appeared at the February 17, 1968, "birthday
rally for Huey" at the Kaiser Convention center near downtown Oakland. At the rally, Eldridge Cleaver announced their new titles and the
"SNCC-Black Panther Party merger" to an enthusiastic crowd of thousands. Despite the contradictory statements regarding the role of whites
and the movement, and the fact that the SNCC leaders didn't call it a
merger, the show of solidarity across the black radical movement that
day was striking.

Each black radical leader spoke, trying to outdo the next one with
bravado and confrontational rhetoric. H. Rap Brown claimed: "Huey
Newton is our only living revolutionary in this country today. He has
paid his dues. . . . How many white folks did you kill today?" James Forman took the rhetoric even further:

> We must serve notice on our oppressors that we as a people are not
> going to be frightened by the attempted assassination of our leaders.
> For my assassination—and I'm a low man on the totem pole, I want
> 30 police stations blown up, one southern governor, two mayors
> and 500 cops, dead. If they assassinate Brother Carmichael, Brother
> Brown . . . Brother Seale, this price is tripled. And if Huey Newton
> is not set free and dies, the sky is the limit![16]

"The sky's the limit" carried resonance at this critical moment. Forman's
preposterous challenge became one of the famous Panther chants, which
in light of the Watts, Newark, and Detroit revolts was a chilling echo for
those in fear of a black uprising. After years of urban unrest, the gall-
ing claim to escalate the confrontation captured the imagination of the
country. Huey Newton had reached a mythic status among the restless
and disaffected masses.

It was ironic that the new "SNCC Panthers" out-rapped Panther leaders Cleaver and Seale that afternoon; but pomp and bravado was the order of the day. Newton rose as a symbol of inspired black defiance, as well as a representation of unrelenting white violence against the black community. The potential energy harnessed with Huey's case, the publication of his political analyses from jail, the seemingly constant violence against the Panthers perpetrated by US law enforcement (effectively branded as inept pigs by the Panthers), and the threat of Huey's death by the gas chamber created a moment of well-channeled outrage by the BPP. Their warrior chants during marches and rallies could be heard on the nightly news nationwide:

Revolution has come / *Off the Pigs!*
Time to pick up the gun / *Off the Pigs!*

Black is beautiful / *Free Huey!*
Set our warrior free / *Free Huey!* [17]

"Free Huey" became a black radical rallying cry that swept across a generation of young activists. It also served whites and other supporters who could chant, march, organize, and wear buttons in solidarity with the Black Panthers without any presumption of influence over the organization. White liberals and celebrities, including Hollywood movie stars Jane Fonda, Donald Sutherland, and Marlon Brando, became public Panther supporters. The organization came to symbolize the entirety of the Black Nationalist movement, while by most estimates the BPP never had more than five thousand members.

During the three and a half years Newton was imprisoned, the Black Panther Party enjoyed its greatest rise and its largest influence as the most feared and respected black radical organization in the country. While the Free Huey movement galvanized the Black Panther Party and increased its supporters, Chairman Bobby Seale was developing into a leader in his own right. Seale served four months for the Sacramento event, and when he was released on December 8, 1967, he immediately began to work to free Huey Newton. Seale crisscrossed the country doing speaking engagements and drumming up support for Newton and the Panther cause nationwide. Seale's efficacious demeanor and serious commitment to the Party vision made him an irresistible attraction at college campuses and with the media.

Over the spring and summer of 1968, the country was again gripped by violence. The assassination of Dr. Martin Luther King Jr. on April 4, 1968, in Memphis was followed by a series of shootouts with Panthers even before Dr. King had been buried. King's death had broken the hearts of a generation and caused riots in over one hundred cities across the country. Yet Oakland was relatively quiet. It was as if the city were waiting for a response from the Panthers. Eldridge Cleaver was one of many Panthers who felt that the time had come to take the "confrontation to another level" as a result of Dr. King's murder. "Non-violence has died with King's death," Cleaver told David Hilliard on that day.[18] On April 6 Eldridge Cleaver urged other Panthers, including seventeen-year-old Bobby Hutton, to engage with Oakland police. Cleaver organized carloads of Panthers—many of whom went reluctantly—to search out police and "start something." According to Hilliard, at one point in the awkward caravan, Eldridge "had to pee" and got out of his car. Immediately Oakland police surrounded the group while Eldridge was still outside the car. The shootout that ensued ended with Cleaver and Hutton surrendering from a hiding place in a basement. While unarmed and surrendering, Hutton stumbled and was shot multiple times. Hutton was the first Panther recruit, and was designated as the first Panther killed in action. Cleaver was wounded during the original shootout but survived. Media accounts billed the disorganized confrontation as a Panther assault on the police, and the *Black Panther* announced the failed ambush as a police assault on the Panthers; 1968 was going to be a long year.[19]

By midsummer 1968, mainstream politics had become just as violent. On June 6, the morning after the California Democratic primary election, the winner and presumptive Democratic presidential nominee, Robert F. "Bobby" Kennedy, was shot in the head and back three times during the victory party, ostensibly by a loner named Sirhan Sirhan. The resulting political confusion rendered the popular New Left movement and the Democratic Party's electoral prospects in ruins. The chaos would become evident at the Democratic National Convention that August in Chicago.

Bobby Seale was one of the speakers at a series of rallies and protests that coincided with the Chicago convention. Chicago mayor Richard Daley had announced that there would be no disruptions in his city. Nevertheless, protesters and bystanders were attacked by Chicago police upon orders of Mayor Daley, and the confusion (and tear gas fumes) spilled into the convention hall itself. In the following days, a number of activist leaders were arrested. Bobby Seale was one of the eight arrested and was charged with conspiracy and inciting a riot outside of the convention. Released on bail, Seale was celebrated as one of the Chicago Eight activists that were arrested on inflated charges in order to disrupt their organizing work. Seale's case was separated from the others, who became known as the Chicago Seven.

Seale managed to stay out of jail and serve the Party for almost a year until his arrest in the Rackley case in Oakland on August 19, 1969. Seale posted a $25,000 bond and was then rearrested for the Chicago charge before he left the building. Seale was then tried for the Chicago case while awaiting trial in the New Haven case. It appeared that the government was going to try everything to keep Seale in jail and put him in the electric chair, if possible. In Chicago, Judge Julius Hoffman refused to allow a continuance for Seale's lawyer (Charles Garry, who was having gallbladder surgery), and when Seale demanded to represent himself, the judge again refused. Unwilling to be silenced over the blatant quashing of his rights, Bobby Seale was ordered bound and gagged by Judge Hoffman and forced to watch the proceedings tied to a chair with his mouth taped shut. Eventually both cases would be dismissed. However, the toll taken on the Party and the black radical movement was enormous.

The entire Chicago episode did a great deal of damage to the notion of alliances with whites as well, as Seale found himself isolated from the indicted white protestors who some felt did not commit to his cause of unjust incarceration and treatment in the manner Seale had committed to their antiwar and antigovernment protests. Reginald Major summed up the frustration of many black radicals who saw the folly in Seale's Chicago romp:

> Bobby had been indicted, tried, placed in chains, and was subsequently sentenced to four years in jail for contempt of court as the result of a casual speechmaking excursion into a scene of hippie-involved political mayhem. . . . If . . . his fellow defendants were really the revolutionaries they claimed to be they would have closed ranks and stood on their conspiratorial constitutional rights when Bobby Seale was denied the right to represent himself, and if necessary force the court to chain them all. It didn't happen.[20]

The Panthers had an even greater obstacle than the contradictions involving white allies—the actions of oppressive law enforcement placing the Black Panther Party directly within their sights.

Public Enemy Number One

FBI director J. Edgar Hoover, a well-known opponent of Dr. Martin Luther King Jr., was virulent against the Black Panther Party from the outset. By the summer of 1967, the FBI had the Black Panther Party in its direct line of fire. In February 1968, less than two weeks after the massive Free Huey rallies that brought together the best-known black radical leaders, the FBI produced an internal memo outlining the steps to neutralize the situation. Clayborne Carson discussed the memo in his book, *In Struggle: SNCC and the Black Awakening of the 1960s*:

> An FBI memorandum written on February 29, 1968, bluntly stated the Bureau's intentions regarding "militant black nationalists." It announced that the goals of COINTELPRO were "to prevent the coalition of militant black nationalist groups, prevent the rise of a leader who might unify and electrify these violence-prone elements, prevent these militants from gaining respectability and prevent the growth of these groups among American's youth." To indicate the kind of activities FBI offices might undertake, the memorandum cited the tactics used the previous summer against RAM, a black militant group in Philadelphia. The group's leaders were "arrested on every possible charge until they could no longer make bail" and "as a result [the leaders] spent most of the summer in jail and no violence traceable to [the group] took place."[21]

Within days of the memo, Bobby Seale was arrested in his Oakland home at two o'clock in the morning as police charged into his home on a claim of a "disturbance in the area," pulling their guns on him and his wife, Artie, when the night was quiet and nobody was on the streets. Seale later opined that the entire ruse was to set an exorbitant bail (which was $6,000) in order to drain the Party funds. Oakland judge Lionel Wilson (who would later become Oakland's first black mayor) dropped the charges and had Seale released.

On June 15, 1969, J. Edgar Hoover engaged in his own brand of out-landish rhetoric in a report presented to Congress that stated that: "The Black Panther Party, without question, represents the greatest threat to the internal security of the country."[22] While the threat may not have been as great as Hoover stated, the announcement gave permission for local law enforcement to continue to engage in the further disruption of Party functions, using all means at their disposal to do so.

While the BPP had its share of underground activities, illicit econo-mies, strong-arm activities, and such, their extralegal actions appear to pale in comparison to the methods utilized by the federal government to neutralize the group. The COINTELPRO program shall go down in history as one of the most effective—and lawless—law enforcement pro-grams in modern history. A series of violent assaults on Panther offices, on breakfast for children programs, on classroom students, on individu-als and their families, was backed up by a bewildering array of misinfor-mation, forged letters, incendiary cartoons, false phone calls, and memos designed to foster suspicion, doubt, despair, and incitement to violence that the FBI could then use to discredit and destroy the participants.

Many dedicated Panthers found themselves facing the bleak task of negotiating their release from jail on trumped-up charges simply because they were Panthers. Ward Churchill summarized the impact of Hoover's efforts:

The Black Panther Party was savaged by a campaign of political repression that in terms of its sheer viciousness has few parallels in American history. Beginning in August 1967 and coordinated by the Federal Bureau of Investigation as part of its then-ongoing domes-tic counterintelligence program (COINTELPRO), which enlisted dozens of local police departments around the country, the assault left at least twenty-eight Panthers dead, scores of others imprisoned after dubious convictions, and hundreds more suffering permanent physical or psychological damage. The Party was simultaneously infiltrated at every level by agents provocateurs, all of them har-nessed to the task of disrupting its internal functioning. Completing the package was a torrent of disinformation planted in the media to discredit the Panthers before the public, both personally and orga-nizationally, thus isolating them from potential support.[23]

The US law enforcement community was particularly serious about their engagement with the Black Panther Party. In one COINTELPRO report, it was noted that of the 295 counterintelligence operations conducted against black activists, 233 of them were aimed at the Black Panthers.[24] There were other factions in the black radical movement, and they were targeted as well, but the US government clearly had made its determination as to who was Public Enemy Number One.

How could an organization of poor black youth from inner-city Oakland, California, have induced such a wrath from the state? What set the Black Panther Party apart from the other idealistic and militant black radical groups and individuals in the late 1960s in the United States?

Who's the Man with the Master Plan?

Although the BPP made serious errors, it also gained a considerable measure of success and made several significant new contributions to the BLM [Black Liberation Movement]. The final judgment of history may very well show that in its own way the BPP added the final ingredient to the Black Agenda necessary to attain real freedom: armed struggle and that this was the great turning point which ultimately set the Black Liberation Movement on the final road to victory. —Sundiata Acoli[25]

One reason the Panthers were targeted with such zeal is because they professed a comprehensive plan for black liberation. Their plan was anticapitalist, antiracist, and not owned or influenced by any particular group. Huey P. Newton was the chief theoretician of the Party, as well as its most fearless and ruthless street fighter. Not only did he develop ideas that supported the notion that the poorest of the poor could become the engine of the revolution, he practiced what he preached.

The idea that it was possible for members of the black underclass, the lumpenproletariat, to become leaders of a class revolution was vividly represented by Newton, who like so many other radicalized black youth at the time had looked to Malcolm X for inspiration. Malcolm X was also a member of the lumpenproletariat who had transformed himself (in prison) into a fearless black revolutionary. Newton and Seale, as well as Eldridge Cleaver, saw themselves as direct heirs to the legacy of Malcolm X. The vision and subsequent martyrdom of Malcolm X served as the central inspiration for these black men and others. Eldridge Cleaver was particularly impressed with Newton and witnessed the connection to Malcolm X. David Hilliard wrote of Cleaver's admiration for Huey: "Cleaver saw Huey as the highest personification of Malcolm and his ideas. He saw Huey as the heir and successor of Malcolm's ideology. If Malcolm predicted the coming of the gun to the black liberation movement, then it was Huey who picked up the gun and used it."[26] Huey Newton and Malcolm X shared similar economic backgrounds and both came from large families, which provided stability and various types of support over the years. In addition to family, both men found a home on the streets. Huey Newton found strength in his associations with the brothers off the block and had little problem associating with them and their cultural priorities. Bobby Seale wrote of Huey's preferred brand of Panther:

> Huey wanted brothers off the block—brothers who had been out there robbing banks, brothers who had been pimping, brothers who had been peddling dope, brothers who ain't gonna take nothing, brothers who had been fighting pigs—because he knew that once they get themselves together in the area of political education (and it doesn't take much because the political education is the ten point platform and program), Huey P. Newton knew that once you organize the brothers he ran with, he fought against, who he fought harder than they fought him, once you organize those brothers, you get niggers, you get black men, you get revolutionaries who are too much.[27]

Huey's predilection for the street-tough brothers is what set the Black Panther Party in motion, yet his intellectual and theoretical imagination proved uniquely suited to the environment from which he came and to where he took the black struggle. To be sure, a combination of forces contributed to the rise of the BPP, not the least of which was the charisma and energy of Bobby Seale and Kathleen and Eldridge Cleaver. They early on championed Huey's cause and rose above the fray to portray the myriad ideals of the Black Panther Party to the nation and the world when Huey Newton was still a mystery and a myth.

Black Thought and the Black Revolution

Early on in their development as Black Nationalists, Newton and Seale frequented black study groups and Black Nationalist organizations in the Oakland area. During their formative period of study at Merritt College in the early and mid-1960s, they explored the many theories and rationales for revolution being enacted throughout the world. They did their homework.

They studied the works of Robert F. Williams (*Negroes With Guns*) of North Carolina, who advocated the use of armed self-defense against white terror in the South and was expelled from the NAACP for his position. Williams would leave the country and continue to write in exile in support of armed resistance in the United States. Seale and Newton studied the works of Che Guevara (*Guerilla Warfare*) of Cuba, who clarified many of the tactics and theoretical advantages of guerilla warfare employed by an outnumbered group. They studied Kwame Nkrumah's philosophical and economic ideas that fused indigenous ideas of communalism with the prevailing Marxism-Leninism and Maoism that was being spread by white radicals at the time. They read Marx, Lenin, and Mao. And they read Fanon. They wanted to follow along with other movements for national liberation calling for freedom for the black nation. They understood that black people needed to unite in their cause, thus the blacks-only caveat for the Black Panther Party. However, they saw a larger picture in their revolutionary vision.

Newton and Seale initially saw socialism as the correct approach to their work, as it challenged the capitalist apparatus of industry and profit that put blacks at the bottom and created an impoverished working class and a lumpenproletariat unable to contribute to the economy. Huey Newton and Bobby Seale had a unique understanding of the ideas of Marx and Lenin and applied their own experience to the class-based analysis of traditional Marxism. Newton and Seale understood that beyond the Marxian notion that there are going to be vagrants and social outcasts who simply "can't function" within the economic organization of industrial capitalism, there is also the fact of racism creating a new form of lumpen, someone socially outcast due to race as well as economically outcast due to lack of work prospects. And they understood that this dual combination creates a subclass of social outcasts placed upon the fringes of society essentially on account of their race. They felt the words of Fanon resonated with their own experience:

> It is within this mass of humanity, this people of the shanty towns, at the core of the *lumpenproletariat*, that the rebellion will find its urban spearhead. For the *lumpenproletariat*, that horde of starving men, uprooted from their tribe and from their clan, constitutes one of the most spontaneous and the most radically revolutionary forces of a colonized people.[28]

Newton and Seale saw the political transformation of the lumpenproletariat as their unique mission and the most practical approach for reaching the final victory.

The primary example used by Newton and Seale of their position was that of Malcolm X. Born Malcolm Little, Malcolm X was a top student in middle school in Lansing, Michigan, and was elected class president in the eighth grade. According to Malcolm X's autobiography, things unraveled when he told his teacher, Mr. Ostrowski, of his ambition to become a lawyer. As Malcolm X recalled, Mr. Ostrowski's response was: "You've got to be realistic about being a nigger. A lawyer, that's no realistic goal for a nigger. You need to think about something you *can* be. You're good with your hands, making things. Everybody admires your carpentry shop work. Why don't you plan on carpentry?" Malcolm X struggled with the meanings of those words at the time, although it wasn't entirely clear to him. "The more I thought about it afterwards the more uneasy it made me. It just kept treading around in my mind," he recalled. Malcolm X mused repeatedly on that moment, as if everything he was unconsciously trying to make out of himself was deflated in that instant.[29]

As he explained in his autobiography, his subsequent spiral into socially deviant behavior resulted from his disillusionment with the social system imposed upon him and was not a result of some innate nihilistic tendency or psychological inability to behave responsibly. It was rather as a result of a racial caste system enforcing itself directly upon his being, upon his self-worth, and upon his aspirations as a human being. If one extrapolates that this type of enforced "lumpenization" was and is still taking place a thousand times a day upon unsuspecting and ambitious black and brown youth who are regularly confronted with rejections of their humanity and the enforced limitations of their natural ambitions, then their reactions can and will fall into the ever-so-familiar path of self-destructive lumpen behavior.

Newton and Seale understood that blacks coming out of prison had been hardened to withstand the rigors of life under those circumstances, and they reasoned that if these new recruits could reclaim their humanity, the subject's innate sense of worth and justice would emerge, just as Malcolm X's had. To Newton and Seale this involved a transformation in which one's natural survival instincts were harnessed and put to use in a political context. It also involved a social transformation into the behaviors required of a Panther. Thus, the Party initiated a set of codes of conduct for the daily behavior of Panther members. This was done in concert with the political education, self-defense training, and daily work regimen that was imposed upon new recruits.

In the abstract, this approach made sense to Newton and Seale. With many new recruits coming from the discipline of a military background (due to the Vietnam War draft), the socially conforming nature of other black cultural nationalist groups such as the Nation of Islam, or even the self-regulating environment of prison, Newton and Seale saw revolutionary potential in every ex-convict, Vietnam veteran, and unemployed brother or sister on the block.

To say the Black Panther Party, even in its early stages, was an organization composed entirely of lumpen would be inaccurate. Despite their emphasis on the gun early on, the difficulties they had with student groups, and their initial efforts at patrolling the police, the Party membership included young blacks of all walks of life from the very beginning of the Party's existence. As former New York Panther Sundiata Acoli recalled,

> It can be safely said that the largest segment of the New York City BPP membership (and probably nationwide) were workers who held everyday jobs. Other segments of the membership were semi-proletariat, students, youths, and lumpen-proletariat. The lumpen tendencies within some members were what the establishment's media (and some party members) played-up the most. Lumpen tendencies are associated with lack of discipline, liberal use of alcohol, marijuana, and curse words; loose sexual morals, a criminal mentality, and rash actions. These tendencies in some Party members

provided the media with better opportunities than they would otherwise have had to play up this aspect, and to slander the Party, which diverted public attention from much of the positive work done by the BPP.[30]

"Lumpenism" and the Party

In many appraisals of the Panthers, "lumpenism" is frequently examined as a primary cause of the organization's demise. In *The Black Panther Party (Reconsidered)*, Chris Booker wrote an essay titled "Lumpenization: A Critical Error of the Black Panther Party," in which he stated that "Panther leaders emphasized the revolutionary potential of the Black lumpen as a whole without giving adequate attention to the dangerous tendencies of various sectors within this class. This crucial oversight would prove detrimental for Party fortunes."[31] Booker asserted that the Panthers "Lumpen behavior also made the organization susceptible to government repression":

> The Black Panther attitude and practice with respect to violence stands out in their uniqueness from all preceding organizations in African American history. On the one hand, the Panthers announced that they opposed spontaneous violence, including rioting, and called for disciplined tactical use of violence within the framework of a long term strategy. However, in reality, as evidenced by their own documents, the Black Panther party, generally indirectly, encouraged spontaneous violence against representatives of the government, especially the police.[32]

The Panthers, for all of their disciplined behavior, reveled in their rhetoric of confrontation. This was part of the process of demystifying the power of the gun—the gun possessed by the white man in power—and as such, brazen affronts such as "off the pigs" were part and parcel of destroying blacks' fear of the police and of "the Man." The brash, in-your-face rhetoric was the raw material that attracted so many young, aggressive, and dedicated (and perhaps not-so-dedicated) new members to the Party in the early years.

Newton in particular was a diligent wordsmith, and understood the power of words and images. The party developed the term *pig* as a deliberate means of demystifying the power of the police in uniform. It would be easier, Newton reasoned, for Party members to shed their fears of "the Man," and stand up to a "filthy farm animal," as opposed to a potential killer in uniform. The appellation was a success, and *pig* became one of the most popular additions to the lexicon of the movement.

Much of the over-the-top rhetoric of the Party invoked a degree of "tricksterism," an element of black language in which the bombastic statement must be seen in the outrageous context in which it is presented. Eldridge Cleaver had a little bit of "signifying monkey" in him when he stated that if he were elected president, he would not have entered the White House but "would have burned it down and turned it into a museum of a monument to the decadence of the past." In black vernacular, this was not seen as a literal threat to the White House. Indeed, the Panthers saw much of their rhetoric as political theater. Law enforcement did not. NAACP leader Roy Wilkins elaborated: "A bunch of black guys sitting around drinking in the middle of the night, yelling about how mean white folks are and what they'd like to do to them, is part of the catharsis. But the [FBI] was not equipped to deal with black hyperbole."[33]

The confrontational rhetoric of the Black Panthers often served as justification for law enforcement harassment. The Panthers' lumpen tendencies were then played up in the media as examples of the typical nature of Party members. This was the image that remained in the public consciousness. Booker summarizes by stating:

> The experience of the Black Panther Party strongly suggests that its survival, development, and institutionalization were undermined by the ascendancy of the criminal element of the lumpen of the Party. The reckless, erratic, and often violent behavior associated with this sector served to alienate many people from the organization, chronically destabilize it, and render it more vulnerable to the FBI-police onslaught. . . .
>
> Abandoning its lumpen emphasis would have been necessary for the organization to resume its initial development and growth. Instead, the Black Panther Party declined as a national political formation by mid-1971.[34]

To a certain extent, Huey Newton's decision to emphasize the Party's Survival Programs and community service after his 1970 release from prison can be construed as an attempt to do just as Booker suggested: retreat from the lumpen orientation of the organization. As Newton and his followers would discover, this would ultimately prove more difficult than expected.

The organizational approach of the Black Panther Party strode a delicate balance between tapping into the outrage and aggressiveness of young urban blacks and harnessing the social energy for the essential needs of the black community. Newton and Seale understood their task regarding their lumpen recruits. They understood that it involved a political transformation as well as a social transformation into the behaviors required of a Panther. This was not unlike the requirements of the Nation of Islam or the US Organization, which required a great deal of sacrifice and discipline and a total transformation of the subject. Newton and Seale saw themselves as providing a more direct and accessible method of transformation, one that did not directly negate or deny many of the cultural aspects of a recruit's pre-Panther lifestyle.

"Survival Pending Revolution"

The most labor-intensive aspect of Black Panther life was the maintenance of the Survival Programs that the Party began in 1969. Early on in Newton's writings, the idea of serving the people was part of the organizational structure, and it expanded exponentially as the organization exploded. Newton made it clear that

> the original vision of the Party was to develop a lifeline to the people by serving their needs and defending them against their oppressors, who come to the community in many forms, from armed police to capitalist exploiters. We knew that the strategy would raise the consciousness of the people and also give us their support. Then, if we were driven underground by the oppressors the people would support us and defend us.[35]

The idea was that the Party would initiate "Survival Programs pending revolution." This enabled diverse aspects of the black community to participate in the real work of sustaining and supporting the people. The first was the breakfast for children program. Utilizing donations from local merchants and labor from Panther members and their supporters, neighborhood children were fed a hot breakfast before going to school. Saint Augustine's Episcopal Church, on Twenty-Ninth Street in Oakland, under the pastorship of Father Earl Neal, was the location of the first breakfast for children program, which began on January 20, 1969. The idea spread rapidly. As a result of his time spent with Bobby Seale, James Mott brought the idea to Sacramento and instituted what he claims was the second breakfast for children program initiated in the country.

> And I know we were feeding quite a few children here in Sacramento, and everything we got were donations from the businesses in the community. And they would donate willingly, and the premise was, you give back to your community, its going to increase your business. White businesses or Asian business, mom-and-pop operations. You draw churches together, you draw businesses together behind a common goal.[36]

In addition to the breakfast for children program, the Party established "Liberation Schools" in many chapters. There was also the People's Free Medical Clinic in Oakland, and in various cities free clothing programs, free food giveaways, free busing to prisons programs, sickle cell anemia testing programs, free shoe programs, a free pest-control program, and, in 1974, a free ambulance program. These activities were administered by Party members, with professionals donating their time and nonprofessionals dedicating their labor. In many cases these programs were huge successes and a point of contention for law enforcement, which looked shameful setting fire to boxes of breakfast cereal during raids on Panther offices.

The Survival Programs were an integral component of the history of the Black Panther Party and constituted its greatest liaison to the greater community. Thousands of people worked in these organizations, and even more in the community were served by them. The workload was immense on Panther regulars, but they took it on. Contrary to the issues of black masculinity and gender divisions within the BPP, rank-and-file men and women in the major Party chapters participated in all of the "Serve the People" projects. All of the Lumpen members spent hours cooking for the children, cleaning up, driving people around, and generally doing what might be considered domestic work. In the central locations, men and women both shared the risks and duties of security, guarding the party offices and facilities at night. Clark Bailey recalls a typical day as a Lumpen member and BPP revolutionary:

> Let's see: wake up, first off we always had breakfast program, that started at like four thirty in the morning. We had to get up, start preparing food for the kids. They would start getting in there from six to about nine. Then we had to get out and start selling papers because that was the basic way that we were able to function. That would be maybe four or five hours worth of work, selling papers. Then we would come back to the office and feed the kids that were there and then off to practice, where we would practice and shower and braid our hair up and get ready for the show. And then when we finished, we had to go back to the office and pull security.[37]

Despite the glamorous recitations of the militant black revolutionary in popular accounts, as far as the daily life in the Black Panther Party was concerned, there was a great deal of taxing, unrecognized labor required of all organizational members. The Party would have lasted only a few months at best were it not for the sacrifices of many people from all walks of life engaging in mundane service as rank-and-file Party members.

As a social organization, the party continued to evolve as well. In August 1970, only days after his release from prison, Huey Newton published one of his most far-reaching decrees. In the essay "The Women's Liberation Movements and the Gay Liberation Movements," he declared that "homosexuals are not the enemy of the people." Newton decreed that "when we have revolutionary conferences, rallies, and demonstrations, there should be full participation of the gay liberation movement and the women's liberation movement. Some groups might be more revolutionary than others. We should not use the actions of a few to say that they are all reactionary or counterrevolutionary, because they are not." Newton did not simply decree that homophobia did not belong in the revolution, he communicated it in a direct way to his audience, in the *Black Panther* on August 15, 1970, that dealt with their misgivings about the issue:

> As we very well know, sometimes our first instinct is to want to hit a homosexual in the mouth, and want a woman to be quiet. We

want to hit a homosexual in the mouth because we are afraid we might be homosexual; and we want to hit the woman or shut her up because we are afraid that she might castrate us, or take the nuts that we might not have to start with.[38]

Newton's proclamations had a far-reaching impact on the New Left and drew many new supporters to Party fund-raisers and rallies. Just weeks after Newton's statement, the Party sponsored a massive conference in Philadelphia to "draft a new constitution providing authentic liberty and justice for all." Thousands of delegates from progressive organizations worldwide came to the Revolutionary People's Constitutional Convention (RPCC) to participate and to draft forward-thinking visions of a just society. The white activist George Katsiaficas could not contain his praise for the event: "Although seldom even mentioned in mainstream accounts, this self-understood revolutionary event came at the high point of the 1960s movement in the United States and was arguably the most momentous event in the movement during this critical period in American history."[39] (Katsiaficas was equally as disappointed when the follow-up convention in Washington, DC, in November ended in failure, as a venue could not even be secured, and the most the delegates got was a performance of the Lumpen outdoors on the Howard University campus.)

In essence, the RPCC, the Survival Programs, and, to a degree, the emergence of the Lumpen band were all examples of how far Newton's Party had gone to distance itself from the paramilitary actions and rhetoric of their early years. Newton was, in effect, "abandoning the lumpen emphasis" of the Party in order to change with the times. While the Party earned a degree of respect in the community, it also created a tremendous amount of internal dissention that eventually ruptured the Party.

The Eldridge Rift

At the time of Huey Newton's release from prison after the charges for manslaugher in the killing of Officer Frey were dismissed on August 5, 1970, Bobby Seale had been in prison defending himself in two trials since August 1969 and Eldridge Cleaver had been in exile since November 1968. During Newton's incarceration, the Party witnessed the killings of two Los Angeles chapter leaders, Alprentice "Bunchy" Carter and

John Huggins in January 1969, and the murders of two Chicago chapter leaders, Fred Hampton and Mark Clark in December 1969. Newton's choice to run the Party during this time was childhood friend David Hilliard, whom Newton gave the title of chief of staff. Hilliard, however, was not the charismatic speaker or compelling leadership figure that Panther followers had come to expect. In the absence of Newton, Seale, and Cleaver, the Party had difficulty maintaining the tenuous relationships between disparate Party chapters, other social-service groups, other black militants, white radicals, mainstream white supporters, and the media.[40] Despite the fact that the Black Panther Party was a household name, or perhaps because of it, at the end of the 1960s the BPP struggled to provide leadership to the black radical community.

When it was announced that Huey Newton would be released in early August 1970, the excitement was tempered by the realization that the Party Newton founded was in shatters, and Huey's mythic status as a fearless guerilla warrior was already being contradicted by his many decrees from prison. Nevertheless, the August 5 release of Huey Newton was a remarkable event. Never at a loss for political theater, Newton emerged from the Alameda County Courthouse in downtown Oakland to a phalanx of disciplined Panthers and thousands of joyous community members. Newton stood upon a car and addressed "his people"—and removed his shirt to the delight of the crowd—yet there was nothing he could say or do that could have filled their revolutionary expectations. Not the fiery orator like Eldridge, nor the sassy humorist like Bobby, Huey's voice was high pitched and his language contained abstractions that didn't play on the rhythms of the audience he and his mythos had generated. The revolutionary hero Huey was out of jail, but it appeared to some that the revolution was no closer than the day before.

On August 7, two days after Newton's release, Jonathan Jackson, the younger brother of incarcerated BPP member George Jackson, initiated an assault on the Marin County Courthouse to demand the release of his brother. Jonathan Jackson freed BPP members William Christmas and James McClain and held Judge Harold Haley and two female jurors hostage, demanding his brother's release. All four men, including Judge Haley, were killed by police as the Panthers attempted to drive away from the courthouse.

The aftermath of the Jonathan Jackson assault sent deep emotional rifts through the organization. The younger Jackson was martyred by many supporters as a man-child of the highest revolutionary spirit, garnering praise from those who saw such activity as a necessary action of the times. Elaine Brown wrote a song in praise of Jackson's spirit, "Jonathan," on her second album in 1973. Other Panthers and their supporters believed that Jonathan Jackson's actions should be met with an escalation of guerilla activity. A month after Jackson's Marin County Courthouse raid, members of the white radical group the Weathermen bombed the same courthouse, claiming solidarity with Jackson.[41]

Jonathan Jackson's actions in support of his brother were an inspiration to those who felt that the time for the use of the gun for black liberation had arrived. However, the repercussions for the organization were profound that summer of 1970. The brazen raid damaged the reputation of the Party within the mainstream black community and reinforced the Party's public reputation among frightened whites and others as a terrorist organization bent on lawlessness.

Newton had to navigate his Party's need to publicly honor and commemorate the courage of Jonathan Jackson while steering the organization away from such activities, which Newton calculated would only serve to cause more death and isolate his Party further from the mainstream black community. Newton believed that the broader community was not prepared to engage in or support guerilla activity for their liberation and that a level of sustained support and education to alleviate their suffering was a necessary step before any presumed action against the state could take place.

The organization had reached a turning point. On February 26, 1971, Panther Party leaders Huey Newton and Eldridge Cleaver (still in exile in Algeria) agreed to speak by phone on a local television program broadcast, ostensibly as a show of Party unity. However, instead of providing a public show of solidarity, the two wound up denouncing one another, exposing and cementing the divide that had been festering behind the scenes for some time. Newton and Cleaver expelled each other from the Party. That fateful phone call was the public acknowledgement of the growing rift between Newton's notion of a socialist-leaning, politically engaged Panther Party and Cleaver's notion of a guerilla warfare oriented Party. Within hours, Newton expelled Eldridge Cleaver and his followers from the Party, pushing a large number of committed revolutionaries underground from the very organization that had sustained them and their revolutionary dreams.

The resulting internal warfare damaged the organization even further and a regional rift developed, with many New York Panthers aligning with the Eldridge Cleaver faction and West Coast Panthers aligning primarily with the Huey Newton faction. The roots of the conflict involved far more than just tactics. Personalities, egos, COINTELPRO-fueled suspicions, cocaine-driven paranoia, and strategic desperation all played a role.

Because Huey Newton had the purse strings, access to white financial and structural support, the massive propaganda outlet of the weekly *Black Panther* paper, and the loyalty of hundreds, if not thousands, of dedicated Panthers and supporters doing the daily work of the Survival Programs and party business, the organization lived on, although the revolution did not.

The Lumpen were planning a second tour of the East Coast when the split went down. All of a sudden, what was shaping up to be a triumphant event for the Lumpen members became another example of the hazardous duties of Panther life. James Mott recalls:

> I remember I was at central [headquarters] and I got a call from some of our people in New York that were still loyal to the Party. People called it a Party civil war. They said, "James, James, you guys can't come back here right now. They have your pictures on a target and they're shooting holes in the Lumpen's pictures." These were people candidly calling us from home. "Man, you guys can't come back now." We were just about to kick off the second tour. Everything had been lined up. It was going to be bigger and better than the first one. Everything fell apart at that time.[42]

The crises that befell the organization were not conducive to the production of rhythm and blues concerts, no matter how ideologically aligned they may be. But it wasn't because the group did not have supporters. As William Calhoun recalls, there were plans in the works for more tours: "There almost was three [tours] until Eldridge and Huey split up. Eldridge was going to bring us to Algiers, but then that blew up."[43]

A Lumpen performance in Africa might have been an event worth attending. African national politics and culture were in full bloom on the continent at this time. In August 1969 the government of Algeria sponsored the first Pan African Cultural Festival in Algiers, which included a massive display of revolutionary spirit and pomp. With state-level proclamations of the efficacy of African culture and the presence of the "international wing of the Black Panther Party," the US black power delegation was formidable. Eldridge Cleaver, in hiding for almost a year, chose the event of the festival to announce his location publicly. Other Party leaders made the trek to Africa, including Minister of Culture Emory Douglas, Party Chief of Staff David Hilliard, and former SNCC leader Stokely Carmichael and his wife, South African singer Miriam Makeba. Iconoclastic jazz greats Archie Shepp and Clifford Thornton performed there with their groups, as well as with African musicians on the same stage. It would have certainly been an interesting scene if the Lumpen were able to perform at one of these festival events. The Lumpen, however, and the Party in general, were dealing with myriad conflicts at home, both ideological and personal, that were becoming increasingly difficult to overcome.

The Black Panther Party never recovered from the split that took place in February 1971. A tragic sequence of factionalized violence resulted from the rift, and the Party disintegrated over the split allegiances of those involved. Some Eldridge faction Party members went underground to join the Black Liberation Army (BLA) and continue the guerilla war they had joined the Panthers in order to fight. The BLA was an underground black radical guerilla organization with goals to destroy the American government and liberate blacks. If the practical goals appeared unreachable, some of the most determined and disciplined Panthers, such as Elmer "Geronimo ji-Jaga" Pratt and Assata Shakur, joined the BLA and continued to follow their revolutionary dreams.

Huey Newton saw the massive dissention in his organization as unmanageable and initiated a nationwide purge of membership. Newton ordered many Panther offices closed and consolidated operations in Oakland with those whom he believed were loyal. The purges, the sweeping proclamations, the lush penthouse apartment he was given upon his release, the cocaine addiction, and Newton's late-night carousing around the city became problematic even for Newton's most ardent supporters. (Eventually Newton's cautious tactics and cocaine-driven paranoia merged, and even Bobby Seale was eventually expelled from Newton's operation in 1974.)[44]

Ultimately, the chaos of the Party activities on a national scale; the infiltration, disinformation, detainment, and disruption by law enforcement; and the subsequent disillusionment of so many who had vested in radical change took its toll on the Panthers and the black radical movement in general. Many people retreated to lives of disengagement, drug addiction, and quiet sacrifice for family and the causes they still believed in. Meanwhile dozens of former Panthers and other black radicals remain in prison as political prisoners—still prisoners of a time.

"The Supreme Servant"

The rift with Eldridge Cleaver was only the beginning of a breakdown of the Panther Party as the 1970s began. The primary issue revolved around Huey Newton's cult of personality and how it became solidified in Oakland, if nowhere else. After his release from prison, Newton was given a penthouse apartment overlooking Lake Merritt, the downtown lake that is part of Oakland's secret charm. The penthouse caused a great deal of consternation from the faithful, who understood and believed Huey Newton to be their selfless guerilla warrior. Outside critics justifiably labeled the luxurious apartment as an ideological, materialist contradiction and capitulation to a self-absorbed cocaine addict, not a selfless revolutionary. Despite the contradictions, or perhaps because of them, Newton was able to maintain ties across a broad spectrum of society, from the drug dealers on the streets to public officials and wealthy entertainers and supporters. Elaine Brown, Newton's lover and lieutenant at the time, described the unique talents displayed by the Supreme Servant:

> A visit to the penthouse had become an awesome experience. It was where truth was both explored and extracted, the house of redemption or damnation. When the men with cocaine came, Huey laughed with them and snorted with them, for as long as they could stand it. When the intellectuals came, he wound them up with hours of debate. When the women came, he addressed their loneliness and his. When the rich came, he gave them absolution in return

for their contributions to the party. When the few party members came, he offered enlightenment, sometimes with the back of his hand, or worse.[45]

Most confounding for many was Newton's penchant for cocaine and irrational behavior, frequently resulting in violence, and the obligatory rationales dispensed upon the Party faithful and the waning public. When Newton appeared in public in the 1970s it was with an aura of a larger-than-life force of nature, still revered and still feared, like a local mob boss. "When Huey would come into my father's shoe store," Oakland resident Kevin Foster recalls, "the customers would separate like the parting of the Red Sea, and give Huey the run of the place." It happened in business after business, throughout black East Bay. Huey had the cache and comic/tragic/fearsome credibility of a Mafia don. It appeared to many that in a few short years Huey P. Newton, the visionary, the urban guerilla unafraid to use the gun against his oppressors, had devolved into a maniacal godfather of sorts, dispensing decrees at his whims. "He kind of got a vision of making the Black Panther Party into some sort of black mafia," Lumpen singer Michael Torrence recalls. "You know, he had made it mandatory for all Party members to go see *The Godfather.*"

> You know, they'd set up operations at the Lamppost where they had some of the sisters working the bar and then they were going around leaning on the drug dealers and sticking up after-hour joints and he's beating people up and I'm out there trying to sell papers and I got people running up on me talking about, "Your chairman's in the penthouse and he beat up my cousin last night," and I don't know nothing about it, you know.[46]

It was around this time that Newton became a popular party guest for the entertainers. To be seen around Newton was the height of radical chic for some and an inspiration for others seeking to redefine themselves as allies to a revolution. The legendary black comedian Richard Pryor was one of Newton's cohorts for a brief time. Pryor lived in Berkeley in 1970 and 1971 and soaked up the radical politics as well as the extreme recreational lifestyles of the black Bay Area. In his memoir *Pryor Convictions*, Pryor tells of sharing cocaine and women with Huey Newton. In the 1973 documentary film *Wattstax*, Pryor refers to his years in Oakland

and Berkeley when he "got ultra-black for a while." Newton provided the inspiration for both extremes.

The Party and "Blaxploitation"

The Panthers' image as gun-toting black revolutionaries has remained with the organization despite Newton's efforts to abandon the lumpen emphasis. As black power engendered the growth of cultural productions that reflected and responded to the black militant identities that emerged from black radical movements, a new genre of entertainment emerged: fictionalized cinematic narratives of working-class black antiheroes from the streets, with varying stages of social consciousness, sticking it to "the Man" or just getting over by themselves. Some films were insightful explorations of the black underclass, while others were shallow fetishizations of black anger, sexuality, and emotion. In terms of technique, they were not cinematically sophisticated, yet they were extremely popular.

The first wave of blaxploitation films can be seen as variations on a Panther theme of giving agency to blacks, but with a twist. In the spring of 1971 Melvin Van Peebles released his tome to survivalism in the ghetto entitled *Sweet Sweetback's Baadasssss Song.* The central character, "Sweetback," utilizes his guile and his inherent bond with his community to evade a series of legal and extralegal snares. Newton himself wrote a lengthy praise for the film for its "revolutionary qualities":

> It is the first truly revolutionary black film made and it is presented to us by a Black man. . . . *Sweet Sweetback* blows my mind every time I talk about it because it is so simple and yet so profound. It shows the robbery which takes place in the Black community and how we are the real victims. Then it shows how the victims must deal with their situation, using many institutions and many approaches. It demonstrates that one of the key routes to our survival and the success of our resistance is unity. . . .
>
> *Sweet Sweetback* does all of this by using many aspects of the community, but in symbolic terms. That is, Van Peebles is showing one thing on the screen but saying something more to the audience. In other words he is signifying, and he is signifying some very heavy things.[47]

What is also fairly visible in the film is that the character of Sweet-back, played by Van Peebles, in terms of his look, his language, his dress, style, and vocabulary, bears a strong resemblance to the public image of Bobby Seale. That a Panther can be placed into the narrative of the black antihero that is freed by the community served to ingratiate and inspire Newton.

Similarly, the next two most famous blaxploitation films, *Shaft* (1971) and *Superfly* (1972), appropriated the iconography of the Panther leadership for their own respective characters. The rough and rugged black cop, John Shaft, played by Richard Roundtree (and reprised by Samuel L. Jackson in 2000), with his dark, slender, foreboding physique, is a signifier on Eldridge Cleaver. Cleaver, the menacing Panther in dark shades and black leather, was a skilled orator who was capable of inciting fear, excitement, or humor as he verbally confronted the power structure. However *Shaft*, the film that offers us a tall, dark, mysterious, sexually promiscuous crime fighter with a gun, shrewdly depicts an "Eldridge" working for "the Man." The lead character is the enigmatic loner John Shaft, who is an undercover policeman operating in the streets of New York. Similarly, the streetwise drug dealer "Priest," played by Ron O'Neal in the 1972 film *Superfly*, has the fair skin, effeminate features, and mysterious, menacing aura of potential violence that Huey Newton became famous for in the public presentation. It was as if the Panthers became the imagistic template for black street narratives in Hollywood. The imagery of black women was similar. In her essay "Restaging Revolution," Leigh Raiford asserts that the lead female character in *Foxy Brown* (1973) played by Pam Grier is a depoliticized representation of Angela Davis and Kathleen Cleaver. As Raiford writes:

> Blaxploitation simultaneously championed and cartooned Black Power; it made use of the language and impulse of Black Power while containing its force. . . . Furthermore, this transition reduced black feminist activist-intellectuals like Angela Davis and Kathleen Cleaver to the hypersexual, constantly dressed and undressed, body of Pam Grier in particular.[48]

The reduction of black radicals into mere fashion statements, or even worse, enemies of their own causes, was a tragic counterpoint to the impression made by black radicals on the national psyche in the late 1960s. Before the advent of black action films, a dazzling array of vibrant, authoritative, charismatic black activists capable of putting forward insightful social critiques were commonplace in the public discourse, in the news, at public events, and to an extent, in the music. Their efforts—those of the Panthers and all of the other black radicals—to assert themselves onto the national scene, the national body politic, and the national culture, with a few memorable exceptions did not translate into filmic representations in a meaningful way.

The Mack

The 1973 film *The Mack*, filmed in Oakland, California, features the story of the pimp "Goldie," played by Max Julien, who navigates the urban terrain of Oakland by overcoming rival pimps, a crime lord, two white cops, and Goldie's brother "Olinga," played by Roger E. Mosely, who is a black activist trying to rid the streets of Goldie's trade. Some of the scenes, including the infamous "Players Ball" involving a series of pimps and players strutting in high ghetto style, involved many real pimps and prostitutes playing themselves.

The actual production of the film carried its own intrigue. According to the film's producers, they sought permission from local black crime boss Frank Ward to film parts of the urban street life in their own setting. Because of the friction between the Ward brothers and the efforts of the Panthers to clean up the community, the filmmakers were caught in the crossfire. The producers claimed that the Black Panthers threatened them and harassed their efforts to make the film. Frank Ward was killed, shot in the head while sitting in his Rolls-Royce shortly before the film was completed, leading to speculation that Newton's Panthers were somehow involved.[49]

The Mack also showcased a lead character with very Newton-like facial features and demeanor. Quiet and passive to a point, and then unabashedly violent at a moment's notice, Goldie is the epitome of street savvy. Goldie is seen as the hero of the streets, while his own brother, the revolutionary, while seen as a sympathetic character, is in many ways a lost idealist. In the film, Olinga, Goldie's brother, asks his brother to give up the drugs and pimping life, and is rebuked.

OLINGA: You really don't understand, do you? Hey man, don't you realize in order for us to make this thing work, man, we've got to get rid of the pimps and the pushers and the prostitutes and then start all over again clean.

GOLDIE: Hey look, nobody's pushing me anywhere; not you, not the cops, nobody, man. I mean, you want to get rid of the pushers I'll help you. But don't send your people after me.

OLINGA: Come on, John. Can't you see that we can't get rid of one without getting rid of the other? We got to come down on both of them at the same time in order for this whole thing to work for the people.

GOLDIE: Look, nobody's closing me out of my business.[50]

In this process, the Hollywood culture machine addresses and yet negates the work of the black activists, the ones who had literally opened up the door to the struggles of the black underclass only to watch them become commodified aspects of popular entertainment. Hollywood managed to neutralize the most potent counterhegemonic black male images into apolitical, accommodationist operatives of the state or greedy thugs content to live on the margins of society as unrepentant lumpenproletariat. The immense popularity of these films cemented their imagistic permanence in the American imagination. Generations later, the West Coast G-funk or gangsta rappers went out of their way to celebrate the aesthetic qualities of these film characters, further solidifying their space in the American imagination.

Many of these iconic characters were taken from the pantheon of Panther imagery, in which young men and women gave their lives to create an image of strength and defiance against the dehumanizing situation facing their people. Within a few years of the popular medium of film, the Panthers had been overrun—not by "the Man," but by Hollywood.

The valorization of lumpen lifestyles had come full circle, to the point where by 1973 the idea of a politicized lumpen was no longer legitimate, no longer cool, and no longer imaginable. Are the Panthers to blame for this? Or did they capture a recurrent theme—white America's fetishization of the black body, black sex, and black death—and turn it on its head for a brief moment?

Within a few short years the Party was decimated by internal and external pressures and its own ideological contradictions. Yet their presence in the American imagination continues to be a compelling element of the black experience. The nature of the legacy of the Panthers is subject to constant debate. Their militarism, their social consciousness, their lawlessness, their street associations, and their impact on the popular culture continue to swirl as each generation posits a new revision to the narrative.

7

"Ol' Pig Nixon"

The Protest Music Tradition, Soul, and Black Power

The Lumpen at this point "own" their audience. Any solid rhythm and blues act worth its salt would, after five songs, now have the crowd in the palms of their hands. This is when they can play their most iconoclastic music—songs that may require the devotion and patience of the listener. It is at this point that the Lumpen perform their version of "Ol' Man River," a widely popular American standard recently reprised by the Temptations.

The Lumpen start with their familiar political chants, and by this time the audience is fervent it its response:

> All Power to the People! / *All Power to the People!*
> All Power to the People! / *All Power to the People!*
> Free Bobby! / *Free Bobby!*
> Free Ericka! / *Free Ericka!*
> Death to the fascist Pigs! / *Death to the fascist Pigs!*
> All right . . .

William Calhoun introduces the song with another dialogue and another reference to the Temptations, letting the audience know that the version the

Lumpen is about to play is in reference to the Temptations' rendition of the song, which was well known to R&B fans at the time.

> Once again we'd like to get into the Temptations our way.
> We're gonna feature Clark Bailey once again on vocals.
> It's a little thing, goes like this.

The band plays a very slow, rolling melody, and the tone of a traditional hymn fills the room. It is familiar yet unfamiliar, and probably not expected at a revolutionary gathering like this one. A soft, low voice produces the opening, followed by the gentlest of harmonies sung collectively by the group:

> (Voice 1) Here we all suffer / in the hands of fascists
> (Baritone voice 2) Here we are pained / while the rich pig plays
> (Voice 1) Getting no rest / from the dawn til the sunset
> (Voice 2) Getting no rest / until freedom day

There is something oddly familiar about the softly sung notes, and the rich contradiction is only beginning to emerge on the audience. If there is one hit by the Temptations that represents the best and worst of Motown records for many, it is the Temps' rendition of "Ol' Man River." The original was much more than a slow ballad with a melancholy theme of endurance and toil. It was a controversial showcase of "the plight of the Negro" in America. "Ol' Man River" was a popular show tune throughout the mid-twentieth century and had been performed and recorded by artists such as Frank Sinatra, Bing Crosby, Ray Charles, Sam Cooke, Judy Garland, and even Aretha Franklin. The towering harmonies and heartfelt tones of the song had resonated across generations. The Lumpen's artistic foils, the Temptations, had recorded a live version of the song on October 3, 1966, at Roostertail's Upper Deck in Detroit that appeared on the 1967 album *Temptations Live!* The song was included on a later compilation, *The Temptations in a Mellow Mood*, in 1968, which was their best-selling album to that point. Motown Records founder Berry Gordy Jr. was adamant during the early years of the record label that his acts perform the most sugarcoated pop standards in an effort to gain a larger audience. It was one of many contradictions surrounding the group and label that was nevertheless so successful.[1]

The Lumpen seize upon this contradiction and make their audience aware of it. For their 1970 performance in Oakland, the Lumpen structure their rendition of "Ol' Pig Nixon" with precisely the same stanzas and cadences as the Temptations' version. The audience is primed to recognize and follow the song note for note. Yet the message, three years after the Temptations recording, is altogether different:

> (*Forcefully sung chorus*) They chained us up they shot us down!
> They spread our blood all through the ground!
> (*Spoken*) Well lift that gun and show no fear
> (*Sung very slowly*) We'll shoot those pigs until they're dead

The audience at the Lumpen performance screams with delight at this verse as the richly sung harmonies—so reminiscent of sadness and submission—are sung with a spirit of defiance and militancy. It should be noted that the song "Ol' Man River" has a controversial history of its own that many music fans are likely aware of, and the sheer delight of the audience upon hearing the melodies of that song can be in the catharsis of witnessing that composition spun on its head. No one has heard the tones or the texts of this pop standard expressed in this manner.

> (*Sung slowly in the high range*) Never be free while Agnew breathes
> Lift up our guns / to end this madness
> Lift up our guns / and run the pigs along
> (*Sung in the low range*) Ol' Pig Nixon, that ol' Pig Nixon
> He don't know nothing / We all should do something
> For ol' pig Nixon / He just keeps on oinking along

At this point in the Lumpen performance, the audience appears hysterical with delight, as the traditional song has been skewered and President Richard Nixon has been revealed as the source of the song's derisive subject matter. By the time the Lumpen reach the extended notes of the final verse, hoots can be heard from the audience as the crowd appears to be consumed by the rich rendering of the vision and the quality of the music.

> For ol' pig Nixon, he just keeps oinking
> Ol' pig Nixon, he just keeps oinking
> Ol' Pig Nixon, he won't be oinking *too lonnng!*

A crescendo of applause follows the final line of the song, along with the enthusiastic Panther Party chants.

> All Power to the People!
> (*Audience*) *All Power to the People!*
> All Power to the People!
> *All Power to the People!*[2]

For the Lumpen to appropriate a traditional song in their revolution-ary performance speaks volumes about their approach to their work as musicians as well as black revolutionaries. The many representations of "Ol' Man River" resonate with controversies that date back to the original performances of the song in the 1920s. This chapter will explore the relationship between black musical traditions and social change, and in particular the music recorded in the revolutionary moment of the Lumpen's existence.

The Ebb and Flow of "Ol' Man River"

The radical rendition of "Ol' Man River" performed by the Lumpen in 1970 was a timely revision to an American standard, although the song itself has been anything but static over the years. The song had survived for generations as a show tune and pop standard, and the Lumpen were certainly not the first to remake the traditional song on their own terms. The lyrics to "Ol' Man River" were originally written by the American songwriter Oscar Hammerstein II for the 1927 Broadway stage musi-cal *Show Boat*. Hammerstein is recognized as one of America's great lyricists, with a number of famous compositions ("Oklahoma," "Some Enchanted Evening") that have become firmly established in the Ameri-can narrative. The melancholy and dramatic music was written by the noted American theater composer Jerome Kern, who collaborated with Hammerstein on the score for the musical. The meticulously arranged score has remained eminently recognizable over the years. However, the lyrics to "Ol' Man River" have taken as many turns as the Mississippi.

Show Boat was a massive, groundbreaking Broadway stage show uti-lizing 160 performers and grand stage props. The production is often credited as a turning point in American theater, in which the story and the songs were thematically woven together, as in an opera, but the music was of contemporary form. Based on a 1926 novel by Edna Ferber, the story revolves around a traveling musical troupe on the Mississippi River in the postbellum South. The initial stage production of the musi-cal showcased its own liberal sympathies for the suffering of Negroes at the time. The story tells two interwoven narratives, that of the enter-tainers on the show boat and that of the tribulations of the black service workers.

The experience of *Show Boat* was a striking one. As the production begins, a festive tone surrounds the primary characters as their relationships and potential conflicts are established in the first act. As the second-act curtain rises, a burly black tenor (frequently played by Paul Robeson in the original run) sings "Ol' Man River" to typically stunned audiences. One critic described the show as "an overwhelming feast of spectacle, melody and drama." Because of Robeson's impact, the musical was extremely popular and ran for three years until the stock market crash of 1929.[3]

"Ol' Man River" was written to be a lament of slavery and the suffering of blacks who lived and worked near the Mississippi river. The original opening lines to the song, intended to be delivered slowly as the curtain rose on act two were: "Niggers all work on de Mississippi / Niggers all work while de white folks play . . ." Hammerstein II insists that he deliberately chose those lyrics to emphasize the degradation inflicted upon blacks at the time.

The harsh lyrics drew immediate controversy, which increased as the popularity of the song "Ol' Man River" transcended the stage show. The song's abject sadness and emotional depth—so well represented throughout the song—contributed to the controversy. From its earliest inception, there were two starkly divergent opinions regarding the lyrics. The white authors and stage show producers generally supported the use of the phrase "Niggers all work" in the song as a dramatic device, while the black cast members understandably resisted the use of the demeaning slur, despite the realism it was purported to convey.

Oscar Hammerstein's son William directed and produced *Show Boat* over the years and frequently encountered resistance from the blacks in his cast:

> Every time I've staged the show, I've had a talk with the cast; they all agree, but eventually they come to me separately and say, "I can't sing that." "Colored folks" was brought in 1946 when I was the stage manager. "Here we all work" is Paul Robeson's awkward addition. My father hated it, and I hate it.[4]

As a result of the controversy, the lyrics were frequently revised to represent the established racial and cultural norms of the time. In the 1936 film version of *Show Boat* (which Hammerstein II supervised), the lyrics were revised to: "Darkies all work on de Mississippi / Darkies all work while de white folks play." When the musical was revived in 1946, the opening lines were changed again to: "Colored folks work on de Mississippi." Later in 1946 a film biography of the "Ol' Man River" songwriter, Jerome Kern, was produced, and the opening lines were revised once again, to the point where the meaning—and certainly the graphic reality—was obscured: "Here we all work 'long the Mississippi / Here we all work while the white folk play."[5]

This "cleaner," less racially charged opening stanza has become for all intents and purposes the standard version of the song, popularized on recordings by Frank Sinatra, Ray Charles, and Sammy Davis Jr., among others. The verses would alternate from striking shouts—"Don't look up / An' don't look down / You don' dast make / De white boss frown!"—to solemn singing moans—"Dat ol' man river / He mus' know sumpin' / But don't say nuthin' / He jes' keeps rollin' / He keeps on rollin' along." One aspect of the durability of the song is that it had an ability to convey an awareness of racial injustice to a predominantly white audience, both through the lyrics and through the music itself. This occurred in part because the popular song had the tonality of a black religious song, or spiritual. The song also invoked a well-established trope in black cultural memory, that of using the river as a passage onward and as a passage to freedom from bondage.

Paul Robeson

A series of significant revisions of the song were popularized by the indomitable African American artist and activist Paul Robeson. Robeson was a towering figure of American popular culture and a leader of a mid-twentieth-century black renaissance. Robeson's presence on the American popular cultural scene in the 1930s and 1940s cut a new path for the black activist-artist at the time. Born in 1898 in Princeton, New Jersey, Robeson's father was a Methodist minister who had been born a slave. His mother died from a stove fire accident when he was six, yet Robeson pushed on; he went to Rutgers as an athlete, where he lettered in four sports, and earned a Columbia Law School degree. He then entered the theater and became famous in the mid-1920s for his dignified lead roles (for the time) in plays and subsequent films such as *The Emperor Jones* and *Othello*. Robeson was also a hugely popular singer who would perform spirituals, traditional folk songs, and later union songs and political protest songs with his thunderous baritone voice.

As Robeson toured the world from the mid-1920s through the 1940s, he studied the languages and folk songs of local people and would sing their songs in their own languages. Said to be fluent in twenty-five languages, his primary affiliation was with the working-class people he met on his journeys. Robeson spoke with admiration for the humanity he experienced while overseas and his affection for the working-class-oriented culture of the Soviet Union. The USSR was of particular interest to Robeson and, in subsequent years, to the US government. As he once stated: "I have spoken many times about my first trip to the Soviet Union in 1934. For the first time as I stepped on Soviet soil, I felt myself a full human being, a full human being."[6]

Robeson determined that the suffering of people in the working classes worldwide was no different from those in the United States, and that if the workers in the United States could transcend their racial divide, they could organize against the ruling classes. Robeson also realized that his ability to entertain could be used as political leverage in the causes he espoused. This was perhaps his greatest threat. He realized that the ability to convey messages through the singing voice had a potentially deeper impact than merely speaking for a cause.

In 1936 Robeson performed and sang "Ol' Man River" in the film version of *Show Boat*, and he remained true to the standardized lyrics for the play and the film. The film version afforded Robeson another level of worldwide popularity. However, when he performed the song in concert, which was a fan favorite, he rearranged many of the lyrics to give the black subject more agency. Robeson revised the original standardized lines: "Dere's an ol' man called de Mississippi / Dat's de ol' man dat I'd like to be" and replaced them with the lyrics: "There's an ol' man called the Mississippi / That's the ol' man I don't like to be." Similarly, a later verse—"Git a little drunk, an' you land in jail"—was changed to—"You show a little grit and you lands in jail." Robeson's revisions of the final verses of the song are perhaps Robeson's crowning blow to the steeped misery of the song:

> But I keeps laffin' instead of cryin'
> I must keep fightin'
> Until I'm dyin'
> And Ol' Man River
> He just keeps rollin' along![7]

Robeson was a triumphant artist, orator, and leader of people during the decades of the between war years (mid-1920s to early 1940s). He was by far the most significant African American known to the world at the time. Robeson's physical stature, highly educated demeanor, and personal charisma made him a natural-born leader. However, when his working-class politics began to clash with American foreign policy, his demise would become a national spectacle. In 1947 Robeson was charged with being a communist and was called to testify before Congress. Robeson refused to cower to the inquisition and claimed his own artistic and political independence. During testimony, he claimed that he was "violently antifascist" and that if he was antifascist overseas, then he "should be allowed to be antifascist in the U.S."[8]

"I Am Going to Only Sing for Causes"

Robeson made another principled leap, perhaps even more courageous, to become and to remain a political artist. He used his ability to entertain, enrapture, and envelop an audience for political and social purposes. In 1947 Robeson "retired" from the stage with the following proclamation:

> I am today, giving up my concerts for two or three years, to enter into this struggle, for what I call getting into the rank and file of my people, for full citizenship in these United States. So I won't be singing, except for the rights of my people, for the next couple of years. No pretty songs, no pretty songs.[9]

On his own, Robeson had advanced ideas later propagated by black radical theorists such as Harold Cruse, Amilcar Cabral, and Frantz Fanon, that a revolutionary *culture* is part and parcel of revolutionary change. As Harold Cruse wrote in 1967, "No social movement of a protest nature . . . can be successful or have any positive meaning unless it is at one and the same time a *political, economic and cultural movement.*"[10]

The friction Robeson received as a result of his interpretation of "Ol' Man River" was minor compared to the crushing career blows that came as a result of his public sympathies with the Soviet Union at the time. During a 1949 speech in Paris in which Robeson expounded upon the folly of war and the role of American blacks in it, his words were reconfigured to imply that he wanted black Americans to defy the US government and refuse to fight against the USSR should a conflict arise. As nebulous as the claim was, the entire weight of the American popular culture apparatus was targeted on Robeson. Shortly after Robeson's Paris comments, the popular black baseball star Jackie Robinson was summoned to speak to Congress and publicly denounced Robeson's (misrepresented) claims and, by extension, Robeson. Robeson refused to publicly criticize Robinson, claiming "it is just what they want us to do."[11]

The resultant chilling effect on the activism of black entertainers from that point was devastating. Robeson was the most prominent black celebrity of his era, and certainly the most prominent celebrity of his time to attempt to bring about social change through his status as an entertainer. Robeson stood by his beliefs and defiantly claimed his right to speak and to sing out in the ways he felt were consistent with those beliefs.

In 1950 the United States entered into a military conflict in Korea. As part of the anticommunist hysteria of the times, the US government revoked Robeson's passport, and many of his associates within the entertainment industry blacklisted him, preventing him from performing in the United States. Aside from a series of concerts sung at the Canadian border to listeners in Canada in the early 1950s, Robeson was effectively silenced for nearly a decade. Nevertheless, his principles and his understanding of the significance of the cultural front in social change were indisputable. When Robeson died in 1976, his tombstone read: "The artist must first elect to fight for Freedom or for Slavery. I have made my choice. I had no alternative."[12]

Paul Robeson represented the most accomplished example of the activist-artist that the African American community had produced in the twentieth century. His uncompromising stance, however, served to accelerate his isolation from his peers and his personal downfall into depression and despair. The most significant end result of the Robeson experience for African American artists, however, was the strong and stark division fostered between the entertainer and the activist. After Robeson, it was clear that the American public (and members of the African American population desperate to enter the mainstream) would only accept its blacks as one or the other. Therefore, activists such as Martin Luther King Jr. and entertainers such as Sammy Davis Jr. got the harsh message that they should remain politely outside of each other's view.

The pressure was severe on black entertainers during the 1950s. They saw themselves as embarking on their initial steps into the American cultural mainstream, and the colossal scorn and scrutiny heaped upon Robeson left no room at all for expression of the slightest alliances. Robeson's grand overture to revitalize "Ol' Man River" was quietly ignored by his contemporaries. Artists such as Sammy Davis Jr., Duke Ellington, Sam Cooke, Ray Charles, Judy Garland, and Frank Sinatra all recorded "Ol' Man River" and did not venture out of the "accepted" lyrical range of the song. One might expect an African American artist to show solidarity with Robeson at some point and use his version of the lyrics. The absence of this symbolic support is telling. The Lumpen may have been the first African American singers to dramatically alter the lyrics of the song in any way since Robeson, and certainly the first to repoliticize it.

Black entertainers during the WWII period were focused on eking out a living in a steadfastly racist and segregated industry within a racist and segregated society. In this respect, black entertainers were engaging with Jim Crow almost every night, frequently as the only blacks their white audiences would ever come to know, often facing up to stereotypes of the foulest nature, and nightly inducing the emotionalism of their own musical traditions to engage with, and salve the guilty hearts of, their white patrons. For a great many black entertainers, from big band performers such as Count Basie and Duke Ellington to singers such as Lena Horne and Billie Holiday, it was a bittersweet road to a stilted version of stardom in white America.

"Strange Fruit"

One song during the pre–World War II period that resonated directly with a message of injustice for African Americans was "Strange Fruit," recorded by Billie Holiday in 1939. No popular song from a black entertainer contained such stark references to the suffering of blacks at the time.

> Southern trees bear strange fruit
> Blood on the leaves and blood at the root
> Black bodies swinging in the southern breeze
> Strange fruit hanging from the poplar trees.

Sung slowly and methodically, the song seems to embody the terror and despair felt by the victims of the thousands of lynchings—those racist mob murders that occurred with such brazen regularity in the South. The "black bodies swinging" are no longer dancing the jitterbug or lindy hop, they are corpses, physical examples of the raw race hate unleashed by whites upon blacks in this country. This was Billie Holiday's triumph.

"Lady Day" was born Eleanora Fagan in Philadelphia in 1915 and had endured rape, neglect, and a life of prostitution by her teenage years. Her temper was legendary and she could spit tobacco with the best of the sailors who stumbled through the seedy clubs she performed in during the early parts of her career. Yet she transformed her trials into a searing sound of blues that transcended time and place. Billie's expressive, somber sounds reflected upon the collective blues people regardless of the lyrics to her music. One heard the suffering of her people in anything she played. But "Strange Fruit" would take it to another level.

Like "Ol' Man River," "Strange Fruit" was written by a Jewish American who wanted to bring a focus to the injustices afforded blacks. However, where Oscar Hammerstein II was himself an American songwriting institution with a lineage of iconic songs and musicals to his credit, "Strange Fruit" was written by a little-known radical Jewish poet named Abel Meeropol, who went by the pen name of Lewis Allan. Meeropol, who had seen a horrific photo of a lynching in a teachers' union magazine, was moved to write about the injustice and performed the song in leftist circles in New York City. Barney Josephson, the founder of New York's self-proclaimed "first integrated nightclub," Café Society, urged Meeropol to play the song for Billie Holiday, who was playing at the club at the time. (Café Society was often referred to as the first truly integrated nightclub in the United States when it opened in 1938. There were, however, many black-owned nightclubs in major cities before 1938 that did not have racially exclusive codes.)[13]

Reports differ on just how receptive Holiday initially was to the request to sing a song with such stark lyrics. Holiday claims in her autobiography that she jumped on the idea immediately, while other accounts state that she was more circumspect. Nevertheless, Holiday performed the song in concert regularly until her death in 1959. "Strange Fruit" would become her definitive recording due to her ability to convey the horrors of lynching through both lyrical clarity and emotive force. Rarely are the two elements of music so starkly and effectively combined. Unlike "Ol' Man River," the essence of "Strange Fruit" was not diluted over the years, and the song has remained as an anthemic clarion call to announce the horrors of black life in America.[14]

For Holiday, it cemented her status as an icon of black jazz and blues. It also opened up larger questions of the role of popular music in the dissemination of topics involving social justice, particularly from the black music tradition. Most black artists recording at the time were content to produce safe lyrics in their music and typically avoided the direct language of rage, violence, or racial enmity in their works. This does not mean the sentiments were not prevalent. It is interesting to note that both Holiday and Robeson were already established artists with a white audience—and that each recorded music that was designed to shock and challenge their listeners with provocative words, words that an unknown singer would not dare risk a career on. One may argue that established artists not only has the potential to dramatically change their public image, but also possesses an ability to alter the sensibilities of a large audience of listeners. This is one reason why popular protest music has such value as a potential force for social change.

The Protest Song Tradition

Paul Robeson was not the first prominent artist to utilize popular music for political purposes. From the earliest days of the nation, periods of social upheaval have given rise to protest songs. Labor activists were prolific at creating workers' anthems out of popular refrains. The Civil War–era patriotic song "Battle Hymn of the Republic" was rearranged by Ralph Chaplin, songwriter for the Industrial Workers of the World, for the workers' anthem "Solidarity Forever" in 1915. In 1947 John Handcox wrote the song "Roll the Union On" from the foundation of the 1937 gospel song "Roll the Chariot On."[15] To take a gospel song or a patriotic anthem and transform it into rebel music is like taking a snapshot of a moment in time, from past to present, in which an accepted rendition from a previous era is transformed, made new and relevant to the present in a different context, sometimes a dramatically different context.

During the Great Depression and post–World War II period, the modern protest song was commonly associated with the folksingers of the day. Singers such as Woody Guthrie and Pete Seeger were consistent authors of protest songs who wrote and performed with a simple voice and guitar accompaniment. Guthrie, a hardscrabble vagabond and prolific writer who lived and wrote amidst the poverty of rural America, is best known for his 1940 composition "This Land Is Your Land," which was a response to what he saw as the shallow message of the Irving Berlin standard "God Bless America." Guthrie's triumph was to reimagine a standardized song and style into something representative of the dispossessed people of his time. This approach survived down the years and found new life in the 1960s amid the youthful, roots-inspired counterculture. Bob Dylan's stark guitar ballads of the early 1960s kept the traditions of Woody Guthrie and Pete Seeger alive and foreshadowed a decade of deep discontent.

The Lumpen were accidental heirs to a tradition, ones who applied a new spirit to musical arrangements, lyrics, performances, rituals, and commemorations that were in the process of being transformed by the social movements of the day. The selections of traditional songs and established popular black music that the Lumpen chose to record, reprise, and parody reveals them to be active agents in the deep tradition of resistance music that centered on the "updating" of popular songs.

The Blues Tradition and Black Protest Music

The secular party music of African Americans from the mid-nineteenth to the mid-twentieth centuries centered around the leisure time performances of vocalist/guitarists, fiddlers, and brass and piano players who played to their working-class audiences with a tone and timbre that was as rough and raucous as their lives were. "The blues" was the central ethos, sound, and style of the black working class, those whom LeRoi Jones called the "blues people." From rural Delta juke joints to urban jazz and swing clubs, black revelers could hear the rhythms, the moans, and the screams that turned sadness and sorrow into celebration—if only for a night. Angela Y. Davis explains:

> The blues idiom requires absolute honesty in the portrayal of black life. It is an idiom that does not recognize taboos: whatever figures into the larger picture of working-class African-American realities—however morally repugnant it may be to the dominant culture or to the black bourgeoisie—is an appropriate subject of blues discourse.[16]

Under the weight of second-class citizenship, black Americans have consistently used the blues as their own form of resistance music. It spoke to their collective experience, yet was intimately personal. It spoke in humorous puns and twists essentially as a way to laugh to keep from crying. "Blues is the devil's music and we is his children," one of the characters in Walter Mosley's blues novel, *RL's Dream*, explains. The blues is both survival and sorrow, life force and death wish, God and the devil's music rolled all into one collective expression of historical memory. Mosley's character Soupspoon speaks of his recollection of the value of the blues in the daily life of Delta sharecroppers:

> He remembered the cotton field and all the men and women lumbering off to work from the plantation barracks. Hollers and calls came from the fields even before the sun was up. But it was silence he heard at the end of the day.
>
> *I'm way past tired to almost dead,* [he] would say. But by midnight on Saturday he was dancing full out.
>
> A Negro didn't own too much back then, but he had the ears to hear music and the hands and mouth to make it. Washboards, washtubs, and homemade guitars. Mouth harps from the dime store and songs from deep down in the well. . . .[17]

All social movements have utilized the celebratory music of the masses and aligned them with the politics of pleasure in order to unify their group members. Many of the lyrics of black music have affected the use of implied meanings and coded messages of resistance. Many spirituals, the songs of hope wailed by slaves, allowed for shrewdly delivered visions of freedom. One such traditional song, "Follow the Drinking Gourd," in fact veils a reference to the Big Dipper, the star formation that pointed the way north during slavery. "Wade in the Water," ostensibly a song about baptism, was also used as a call to cross the river to freedom. From the outset of the black experience in America, a dual language of music was employed to allow subversive communication to occur through the established work songs and Christian spirituals that black slaves were allowed to sing. As Stokely Carmichael so aptly put it: "We are an African people, so it was natural that from the beginning, from the spirituals right on up, music would be our weapon and our solace."

The spirituals, the blues, jazz, and rhythm and blues have provided means of sustenance and subversion through a complex matrix of call-and-response collective exhortations, of strained and intense yet controlled vocal inflections, of collectively improvised harmonizing, scatting, sing-talking, and outright preaching over a tune. The tone and texture of blues songs, ballads, stompers, and personal laments were all imbued with a collective expression of both sorrow and hope that reflected the collective mood of a people. The songs as a whole were radical by virtue of their defiance of hopelessness, thereby supplying strength to the community through a common understanding.

"Oh My Lawd They Done Killed the Blues"

In the mid-1960s, no sound of black music was more popular than Motown Records. "The Sound of Young America" had taken over the country. The syrupy doo-wop vocalizing of Smokey Robinson, the breathtaking harmonies of the Temptations and the Four Tops, and the glamour spectacle that was Diana Ross and the Supremes established Motown as a symbol of African American success and an element of American folklore almost instantly.

Pop music, Motown, and other elements of soul music in the early and mid-1960s represented the sounds and signposts of a new generation that was looking forward, not back. The breeding ground for a break from the blues tradition was set in place, ironically, by the most mainstream of black popular music institutions.

The rise of Motown Records as a northern soul label with an affinity toward pop melodies and crossover appeal was taken with a degree of irony as well as pride from all quarters. The upwardly mobile ethos of Motown was both a source of pride and polite derision for African Americans of all persuasions, including young musicians in the Bay Area. William Calhoun of the Lumpen has his own theory about the Motown sound and what it was all about:

> I wanted to do a book back in the early '60s and I wanted to title it "Oh My Lawd They Done Killed the Blues." It's really just the story of the emergence of Motown and the Motown sound, because they related to the first generation of black folks that were totally urban and had no connection to the Deep South. So the music, the blues, was over. The Delta blues that had kind of made its migration, and even the more citified blues out of Chicago, the Motown thing was away from that.[18]

Motown music was, in many ways, revolutionary in that it broke away from the prevailing forms, techniques, and methods of black music making. Beyond just the personal appeal of their youthful and vibrant lead singers, these artists were developing a sound that was indeed removed from the siege mentality and survivalism of the Jim Crow experience.

Certainly, the younger performers such as Little Stevie Wonder and the Jackson 5 would emerge almost entirely detached from the apartheid experience of the South. Stevie Wonder's astonishing and jubilant performance on the harmonica on his first hit record, "Fingertips Part 2" in 1963, recast the use of that instrument almost overnight. As a well-established tool for propagating the feel of the blues, the rolling, moaning tones of the harmonica had wailed for release from the misery of poverty and Jim Crow for generations. Stevie Wonder brought the sound out of the South and into the sound of young America. The spirited steps and youthful exuberance of the Jackson 5 were uplifting showstoppers when they hit the pop scene in 1969 with four consecutive number-one pop hits. The entire Motown apparatus, which was quite literally organized around the assembly-line approach to music making, steered clear of the blues.

Motown founder Berry Gordy Jr. was a jazz aficionado. He appreciated the jet-setting jazz-influenced high life. He couldn't and wouldn't stand for working in the automobile factories. He was, at that time, out of step with working-class Detroit. As Nelson George writes:

Detroit's favorite performer was not jazz giant Charlie Parker, but John Lee Hooker, a foot-stomping, one beat boogie bluesman from Clarksdale, Mississippi. Hooker shared the same values and background as the older black masses of Detroit. His songs catalogued his life, especially the transition from rural to urban living, and, in doing so, created a verbal portrait of life as seen by Detroit's black immigrants. And Hooker's metallic guitar strokes were the perfect stimulant for house parties and gin drinking.

Hooker's blues, and that of the other urban bluesman, was a crude, vital music that didn't move Berry the way jazz, or even the smoother sound of Nat "King" Cole or Detroit native Della Reese, did.[19]

Gordy was also adept at recruiting singers with a touch of polish who didn't bring "the church" to the session with them. As Gerald Early writes:

The three major early groups of the company—the Supremes, the Temptations, and the Miracles—were put together and rehearsed at their high schools. They were not church groups; in fact, the members did not attend the same church, and in various autobiographies there is little talk about the influence of the black church in their music.[20]

By creating an operation that utilized talented songwriters, jazz-trained musicians willing to follow directions, and worldly, charismatic personalities to sing the songs, Berry Gordy Jr. created the bourgeois black world he wanted to inhabit. He eventually found a means of creating a music that combined the emotional vitality of the blues yet kept the sound and the style upwardly mobile and accessible to people outside of the blues experience. Black music was changing in subtle and unsubtle ways, and Motown was a bright (white?) beacon of that change.

The breeding ground for a rupture with the blues tradition was set in place by a convergence of crosscurrents of black culture. From the pop idols of the Motown stable to the Black Nationalists in urban battle zones, the idea of moving forward essentially left little space for a celebration of the blues impulse at the moment of revolution. Maulana (Ron) Karenga, writing in 1967, took the revolutionary transition to its logical conclusion and sought to retire the blues. In his essay "Black Cultural Nationalism," he concludes his discussion with the following:

> Art will revive us, inspire us, give us enough courage to face another disappointing day. It must not teach us resignation. For all our art must contribute to revolutionary change and if it does not, it is invalid.
>
> Therefore, we say the blues are invalid; for they teach resignation, in a word acceptance of reality—and we have come to change reality. We will not submit to the resignation of our fathers who lost their money, their women, and their lives and sat around wondering "what did they do to be so black and blue." . . .
>
> Perhaps people will object violently to the idea that the blues are invalid, but one should understand that they are not invalid historically. They will always represent a very beautiful, musical and psychological achievement of our people; but today they are not functional because they do not commit us to the struggle of today and tomorrow, but keep us in the past. And whatever we do, we cannot remain in the past, for we have too much at stake in the present. And we find our future much too much rewarding to be rejected.
>
> Let our art remind us of our distaste for the enemy, our love for each other, and our commitment to the revolutionary struggle that will be fought with the rhythmic reality of a permanent revolution.[21]

To make an outright challenge to such a fundamental aspect of the lived experience of African Americans was a bold move on Karenga's part. Yet it was reflective of the times in many ways. Karenga saw himself as a leader of a cultural revolution that would change the hearts and minds of black people, who he determined were in search of cultural references that would sustain their revolutionary struggle.

Karenga's comments were unpopular to members of a generation that was sustained by the blues, those who understood the "infrapolitics" of survival—what Robin D. G. Kelley in *Race Rebels* calls the "hidden transcripts" of resistance that the blues so eloquently transmitted across generations every Friday and Saturday night at juke joints from Rochester to Waco, and infused the Sunday morning church sermons and songs with resplendent fire and spirit as well.[22]

Yet Karenga was on to something. On the streets of black America in the mid to late 1960s a new rhythm was emerging, one that resonated along with the "black and proud" stance promoted so effectively by James Brown years before he penned the song that contained the phrase. Many black youth, Black Nationalists, and black revolutionaries in the late 1960s had a visceral experience of being drawn toward the radical new rhythms and led away from the traditional framework for black music. As James Brown and his band began the process of "re-Africanizing" black American music, the cultural isolationism of "the so-called Negro" began to break down. The new black music was changing the cultural landscape of the world. The blues was not a part of the Black Panther Party's musical repertoire either. A new era, a new time, required a new approach to music making.

"Mississippi Goddam"

It would take a great deal of courage for an established black musical entertainer to break from the norms of the industry and produce direct social commentary in her music during the early 1960s. It would take Nina Simone to break that mold, as she had always done. A trailblazer of her own, a gifted pianist and classically trained performer, her career was marked by fits of outrage and improvisational genius. It would be the events of 1963 that would take Nina Simone over the edge:

> The bombing of the little girls in Alabama and the murder of Medgar Evers were like the final pieces of a jigsaw that made no sense until you had fitted the whole thing together. I suddenly realized what it was to be black in America in 1963—it came as a rush of fury, hatred and determination. In church language, the Truth entered into me and I "came through."
>
> . . . I had it in my mind to go out and kill someone, I didn't know who, but someone I could identify as being in the way of my people getting some justice for the first time in three hundred years. . . .
>
> I sat down at my piano. An hour later I came out of my apartment with the sheet music for "Mississippi Goddam" in my hand. It was my first civil rights song, and it erupted out of me quicker than I could write it down. [23]

The end result was a blistering rant against Jim Crow segregation, with a twist of dark comedy. During her first performance, Simone announced the song as "a show tune . . . but the show hasn't been written for it yet." With a bouncing melody that might anticipate a lighthearted frolic, Simone pours her anger out like never before:

> Picket lines, school boycotts
> They try to say it's a communist plot
> All I want is equality
> For my sister my brother my people and me!

Simone slices up the contradictions of southern life, and by the end of her rant, Simone's outrage explodes beyond the use of rhymes

> Everybody knows about Mississippi
> Everybody knows about Alabama
> Everybody knows about Mississippi God-damn!

Prefiguring the protest movement style of the latter part of the decade, Nina Simone, like the Lumpen a few years later, would work from a familiar form—in her case show tunes, in the Lumpen's case soul music—and turn the purpose and the production on its head.

Like Paul Robeson, Nina Simone's bold foray into message music was not immediately followed up by her peers. Simone was not imitated in part because she had no peers in the industry, and, once again, African American artists deliberately addressing a social movement in direct language risked their entire careers. It typically required an artist at the top of his or her craft to make such an attempt and not be wiped from the scene.

A Change Is Gonna Come

Sam Cooke was one of the few artists in the position of Nina Simone, with a massive white and black following in the early 1960s. Cooke, despite his smooth persona and lighthearted pop music fare, was a radical activist-artist in his own right. Cooke sought to organize black musicians into their own union, similar to the white-run unions that regularly kept black musicians out of hired studio work. Cooke was among the few who would publicly claim, "If this is our music, why don't we own it?" In New Orleans he created the All for One Executives organization (AFO) to pool the best of local black talent and to basically "own the sessions" their musicians played in. In Los Angeles Cooke set up Soul Station #1, a recording studio through which he had planned to invite local black musicians to audition and record on their own terms. Cooke had plans to expand Soul Stations in other cities along the lines of the Black Muslims who were utilizing the resources of the community on their own terms.[24]

By 1963 the contradictions between civil rights, Jim Crow, and his own celebrity had taken their toll. In October, shortly after the Birmingham church bombing, Cooke and his entourage attempted to check in to the all-white Holiday Inn in Shreveport, Louisiana. After being rebuked (despite his confirmation) and complaining to the hotel staff, Cooke and his entire party left—and were later tracked down at the Negro hotel across town and arrested for disturbing the peace. The incident had a lot to do with Cooke's inclusion of the phrase "I go to the movies and I go downtown / somebody keep telling me, 'Don't hang around'" in the lyrics to his upcoming song. On December 21, 1963, Cooke went into the RCA Studios in Los Angeles with his trusted arranger Rene Hall and completed his masterpiece.

With an incessant pull on the heartstrings and a towering vocal authority, the normally laid-back Cooke wails intensely on the recording, putting as much blues into the song as he can. The ever so intimately felt lyrics resonated with movement workers and mainstream sympathizers alike. Daniel Wolff explains how "A Change Is Gonna Come" brought about a synthesis of many musical styles, foregrounding the stylistic changes that were to come:

"Change" opens in a wash of strings with a French horn calling, then [drummer Earl] Palmer finds an easy beat, and Sam comes in testifying—his voice up high in its range and urgent. He was born by the river in a little tent. If that sounds like gospel—born again in some tent-revival baptism—when he adds that he's been running ever since, we're into the blues. [Chuck] Badie's heartbeat of a bass line gives an undertone of sadness as Sam hits the chorus for the first time: a change is gonna come. Next, he borrows a line

from "Ol' Man River"—afraid of living, scared of dying—and, in
one phrase, the Reverend's son passes out of the realm of gospel,
announcing that he doesn't know what's up there, "beyond the sky."
Still, a change is gonna come.[25]

In a single stroke, Sam Cooke had transcended gospel and yet honored the tradition; he delivered the blues like he had never done before,
yet he pointed forward, toward an emerging new world that he himself
was tirelessly helping to engineer.

The song emerged slowly on the scene, as the last song on Cooke's
1964 album *Ain't That Good News*, with the record company releasing
upbeat singles from the disc at first. As 1964 wore on, and wore on Sam
Cooke, it became clear that the song deserved more visibility, and Cooke
insisted that it be released as a single. He would not live to see it released
as a single or become an anthem of a generation's hopes and dreams. He
was shot by a motel manager in Los Angeles on December 11, 1964.
The song saturated the black-music radio waves throughout the spring of
1965, through the wake of Malcolm X's murder, through the Watts riots
in August, and through a decade of tumultuous change.

The soul music of the mid-1960s managed to exude an energy that
belied its formal structure. A spirit thrived in the recordings that was
revolutionary in a great many ways, despite the fact that the songs were
typically in the three-minute range and designed for mainstream radio
airplay. They nevertheless were part of the landscape of revolution in the
air. Los Angeles–based DJ Magnificent Montague provides the following
commentary on the soul sounds of the mid-sixties:

> Now get your old turntable out and listen to the soul music of 1966.
> Listen to Slim Harpo sing "Baby Scratch My Back" and Sam and
> Dave sing "Hold On! I'm Comin'" and Lee Dorsey sing "Working in
> the Coal Mine" and Stevie Wonder sing "Uptight" or "I Was Made
> to Love Her" and Percy Sledge sing "When a Man Loves a Woman"
> and Wilson Pickett sing "634-5789" and Junior Walker sing "Road
> Runner" and Eddie Floyd sing "Knock on Wood" and Otis Redding
> sing "Try a Little Tenderness" and the Capitols sing "Cool Jerk."
> Listen to how, even though the melodies stay in church, rapturous,
> the pressure is rising, as though the performers are testing you—
> challenging you, demanding you listen. The horn arrangements are

even sharper, a little more forceful. The rhythm, out of the box, is a little faster, more dramatic. The combined effect is overwhelming. You can't sit still. The singer and the arrangement are tugging at you, wanting to make your head explode. The song builds and builds until the singer comes back after the chorus and hits the third stanza with a scream, a desire to release, to crawl out of the tensions that imprison him, to take you with him. It's like a riot, a controlled, melodious riot that is just about to break. It would break, by '68, the year that James Brown let the funk machine run wild and released "I'm Black and I'm Proud" and turned our music away from church. We weren't at that point in '66 but we were close to the edge, closer than we realized.[26]

In the mid-1960s a pungent scent of anticipation could be sensed in the popular music of the day, but it would not last. The calamitous end of the decade would offer sights and sounds that would compel the most cautious black music artists to expand their lyrical range, and their musical visions, to accommodate the chaotic new world that they were living in.

Marvin Gaye

One artist who transcended his own boundaries to become a signpost for the movement was the iconic Marvin Gaye. As the social changes around him swirled, the revolution was pushing Marvin toward a personal and social artistic triumph. Born and raised in a strict Pentecostal religious home in Washington, DC, Gaye was a troubled genius from day one. His father beat Marvin regularly and shamed the young man for having aspirations outside of the church. Marvin eventually left home and became a secular singer and drummer. Branching out into secular performance much like Sam Cooke, Gaye found his niche as an appealing young pop singer and quickly rose to the forefront of Motown Records once he was introduced to Berry Gordy by singer Harvey Fuqua.

After sparkling early success with singles such as "Hitch Hike" and "Pride and Joy," Gaye's triumphant duets earned him another level of pop adoration as his playful banter with partner Tammi Terrell reinforced his appeal as the most desirable Motown male artist of the 1960s. But tragedy was right around the corner. After complaining of headaches before a show, Tammi Terrell collapsed in Gaye's arms onstage at a concert at a small Virginia college on October 14, 1967. After a two-year-long convalescence, Terrell passed away in March 1970 of a brain tumor at the age of twenty-four.

Moody and depressed from the steady decline of Tammi Terrell, Marvin took to his brother Frankie's letters of war in Vietnam. Frankie returned from a harrowing three-year tour of duty in Vietnam that spring of 1970. The joy of his brother's return was tempered by the stark realities of the war recounted nightly by Frankie Gaye to his brother. It would take months of seclusion and introspection before Marvin would reemerge and began a reappraisal of his craft. It would take the movement and the music working upon one another to bring Marvin back.

People's Park and "What's Going On?"

In 1969 the Motown standard-bearers the Four Tops were performing in the San Francisco Bay Area. Bass singer Renaldo "Obie" Benson found himself riveted to the televised accounts of the local protests taking place over People's Park in Berkeley. The People's Park "riots" were some of the most chaotic domestic disturbances in the country. Because of the fixed location—a small block of unused land three blocks south of the UC–Berkeley campus—the series of street confrontations that took place over the land could be witnessed by the media unabated. The Bay Area had already seen its share of violent antiwar confrontations, and earlier that spring the University of California at Berkeley had weathered a disruptive student strike in demand of a Third World College. Tensions were high. In April 1969 a group of students and community activists (some veterans of the 1964 Free Speech Movement at Berkeley) decided to rebuild the abandoned lot by planting trees and developing a free public-use park. Local officials, however, saw the effort as an attack on the property rights of the university. While local officials tried to negotiate with the young trespassers, Governor Ronald Reagan saw the event as an insurrection and ordered hundreds of police and later National Guard troops to destroy the park—and to use tear gas and open fire with deadly buckshot to repel the protestors. The conflict had reached a point

Superstars of Black Power Soul Music

James Brown in 1971.
Getty Images

Sly and the Family Stone in 1970—Larry Graham, Jerry Martini, Greg Errico, Freddie Stone, Sly Stone, Cynthia Robinson (below, left to right).
Getty Images

Soul Queens of the Black Power era

Nina Simone in 1970 (right) and
Aretha Franklin in 1972 accepting
her Grammy Award (below).
Getty images

Curtis Mayfield and the Impressions, 1969—Curtis Mayfield, Fred Cash, Sam Gooden (left to right). *George Livingston Collection*

Soul superstar Chaka Khan was a Black Panther supporter in Chicago while in high school in 1969. She worked in the breakfast for children program and knew Fred Hampton. *Photofest*

Mississippi-bred gospel stars turned soul icons: the Staple Singers—Pops, Cleotha, Yvonne, Mavis (left to right). *Getty Images*

Soul superstars utilizing a black power theme

Isaac Hayes *Black Moses*, Stax 1971.

Diana Ross and the Supremes *Love Child*, Motown 1968.

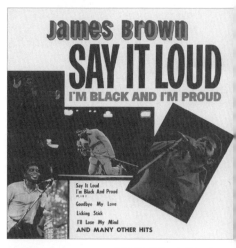

James Brown *Say It Loud—I'm Black and I'm Proud*, King 1968.

The Temptations, *Cloud Nine*, Motown 1969.

The iconic Huey Newton chair was utilized in popular soul music. George Clinton used the image in 1979 on the Funkadelic album on Warner Brothers, *Uncle Jam Wants You.*

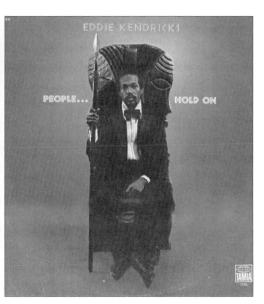

Former Temptations singer Eddie Kendricks's second solo lp for Tamla/Motown Records, *People... Hold On,* in 1972, referenced the image in a new form.

The 1967 photo of Huey Newton was taken by Eldridge Cleaver to help the Party promote the image of the Black Panther as a fearless warrior.

Courtesy of the Dr. Huey P. Newton Foundation

Jimi Hendrix regularly gave credit to the Black Panthers during his final months of 1970–71. His black rock trio the Band of Gypsys performances featured his seminal songs "Machine Gun" and "Power of Soul."

Elaine Brown's first album of revolutionary songs in 1969, *Seize the Time*, was a groundbreaking work of soul and substance, with artwork from Panther artist Emory Douglas.

Douglas (at right) designed many of the promotions for the Lumpen, such as the one shown here. © 2013 Emory Douglas/Artists Rights Society (ARS), NY

Stephen Shames/Polaris Images

Elaine Brown, the original "Song-writer for the Black Panther Party" performs during her campaign for Oakland City Council in 1973.
Stephen Shames/Polaris Images

A rare performance of Mott, Torrence, and Bailey with Elaine Brown in 1971.
Courtesy of It's About Time Archives

Bob Dylan was deeply affected by the death of George Jackson and wrote a single in his memory.

This famous photograph of Huey Newton holding Bob Dylan's lp *Highway 61 Revisited* is emblematic of the influence of Dylan and the charisma of Newton. *Stephen Shames/Polaris Images*

New York Panther leader Afeni Shakur in 1971 shortly after acquittal in the New York 21 case. She is holding her baby Tupac, wearing Panther buttons.

Courtesy of Its About Time Archives

where National Guard troops were guarding vacant plots of land in the city in case someone tried to *plant something* there.[27]

The unprecedented violence during those days was striking. It moved Obie Benson to reconsider everything.

> All the kids up there with the long hair and everything. The police was beatin' on them, but they weren't bothering anybody. I saw this and started wondering what the fuck was going on. What is happening here? One question leads to another. Why are they sending kids so far away from their families overseas? Why are they attacking their own children in the streets here? And so on.[28]

It was as a result of these chaotic Bay Area events that Benson penned the first version of "What's Going On?" Benson first offered the song to his own group, the Four Tops. The Four Tops, while not known for explicit message music, were standard-bearers for relevant soul songs about dignity in relationships and were quite respected Motown superstars in their own rights. The group, however, rejected Benson's composition. Benson continued on with his song and claims that on a tour in London he offered the song to folksinger Joan Baez, who turned him down as well.

Back in Detroit, Benson developed the song further with Al Cleveland, and Cleveland approached Marvin Gaye with the song. Gaye initially offered to produce the record for one of his side projects, the singing group the Originals. Benson then had to enlist the help of Gaye's wife, Anna, who literally forced Marvin to claim the work for himself. Gaye was finally driven to record the song, on his terms, and crafted a soul masterpiece in the process.

> Father, father
> We don't need to escalate
> You see, war is not the answer
> For only love can conquer hate.

The original single was recorded in June 1970 and was released in January 1971, around the same time the Lumpen were in operation. The success of the song inspired Gaye to pen an entire album of music around the same theme, lamenting, cherishing, and worshipping at the altar of life in a turbulent, post-movement world. In a sense Marvin Gaye was capturing a eulogy for the movement, as so many issues he dealt with—endless war, police brutality, drug abuse, environmental destruction, and the long-lost chance at spiritual redemption—were presenting a hopeless landscape of the post-movement world. Yet as he was depicting these harsh realities, the music, *the music* was transcendent; it was an exaltation of what precisely was possible in the human spirit to overcome these obstacles. As lush and orchestrated as the *What's Going On* album is, the purpose served was closer to some of the greatest blues music—the tone, the feel, the spirit, the hope embedded in the sound rose above all of the melancholy to provide a spiritually transcendent moment.

Marvin Gaye was a fan of the Black Panthers, to a degree, as his brother Frankie Gaye explained in his memoir *Marvin Gaye, My Brother*:

> At one point during his stretch of songwriting, Marvin took a break to do interviews . . . in support of the Black Panthers and the Black Power movement. Marvin loved the Panthers even though he never completely agreed with their policies. "What I like, I really like," he admitted. "The brothers need waking up because so many of us are being killed and hurt. There's no need for the beatings and shootings that go on in the inner city. And too many of our people are homeless and going hungry. The Panthers go door-to door for donations of food or money to help the poor. I support that."
>
> What Marvin didn't support, actually despised, was the Panthers' militant and often violent actions, along with their antigovernment stance. Nor could he tolerate what he called "the pig thing," the Panthers' attitude toward the police. We had been brought up to respect the police, not to mess with them. We knew there were things they didn't always do right. . . . We knew about the shootings and beatings, but we were taught to believe that the majority of cops were good, and only a few gave them a bad name.[29]

Marvin Gaye became in many ways an icon of social soul music: music with a message that possesses all of the sincerity and moral authority of earlier blues and soul music, but was now invested in a relationship with the larger world. Gaye's intimate approach to soul was far more complex, and it would be bared for all the world to see.

You're the Man

After the robust success of *What's Going On*, Marvin Gaye had initially considered a subsequent message-music album as a follow-up. Recording in the same format as the *What's Going On* album sessions, Marvin Gaye went into the studio with a detailed message song and recorded a diatribe against the power structure with a level of detail not heard on the previous album:

> Politics and hypocrites
> Is turning us all into lunatics
> Can you take the guns from our sons?
> Right all the wrongs this administration has done?

On "You're the Man" Marvin Gaye sought out civic involvement in the form of the vote, claiming, "If you've got a plan, if you've got a master plan, I got to vote for you." It would not be a stretch to imagine Gaye's reference to "the master plan" was influenced by the Panthers' Ten Point Program. In the Ten Point Program, well known to all who read about the Party, was a master plan for black liberation. It was a relevant question for the start of the decade—"Who's the man with the master plan?' The history of black politics in the 1970s reminds us that as a result of Hoover and Nixon's COINTELPRO program, there were few people with a master plan for black liberation remaining by the time of Gaye's composition.

Despite Gaye's vivid detail of his social awareness—rhymed over a streetwise funk groove—the approach did not take off as his single "What's Going On?" had a year before. Sales for the single "You're the Man" were marginal. Facing rejection again, Gaye abandoned the social-commentary album idea, turned away from direct message music, and turned inward. He next arranged an instrumental album for the film *Trouble Man*, an apropos name if there ever was one for an artist. The melodic instrumental work was quintessentially Marvin at the moment and served to establish him as an arranger with impeccable credentials. Gaye then plunged full force into bringing his own hedonistic fantasies to life through music. The resulting album-length works, *Let's Get It On* and *I Want You* were easily as popular as *What's Going On*. In a certain way, Marvin Gaye had become more of a rebel with *Let's Get It On*, as he was going on his own, regardless of the critics or the social values; he was going to express himself on his own terms.

The black music tradition had reached a zenith with *What's Going On*. All of the pain and suffering, all of the blues, all of the conflicts, all of the funk, all of the screams from the streets, and all of the sophistication of black art had come together in one moment. Black music could now aspire to be elegant and streetwise at once. Black sophistication did not mean social aloofness, and street consciousness did not have to mean desperation or demeaning self-images. An epiphany of black liberation was achieved by *What's Going On*.

Larger social issues were becoming a part of the lexicon of black popular music. The impact of the Vietnam War on the rock music world remains a part of the American social fabric, and the many twists the music and the performers and the audiences took those crucial 1969 to 1971 years has provided an indelible stamp on the history of popular and protest music in America. An equally robust and radical impact was felt on black musicians and could be heard in their music as well. In many cases the artists were responding to their own personal experiences as well as the explicit nature of the war on television, not yet censored by government propagandists as it would be in later US military conflicts. In fact, it could be argued that the explicit violence and social contradictions that were exposed and articulated by popular performers in response to the Vietnam War provided the opening for black artists to dispose, once and for all, with the tradition of implication and innuendo and start to tell their own harsh, bitter truths in lyrically explicit terms.

Soul Apocalypse

Some of the most dramatic turns in black music took place from 1969 to '71, the time the Lumpen were performing. The epic performances of Jimi Hendrix and Sly and the Family Stone at Woodstock in 1969, the jazz fusion experiments of Miles Davis's *Bitches Brew* and *Jack Johnson* sessions, the first recordings by Mandrill, Kool and the Gang, Earth, Wind & Fire, Ohio Players, and Funkadelic sparked a decade of black musical innovation. The goal for many was no longer the three-minute 45 rpm single, it was to make a statement with their craft.

The radical times of the day were reflected in the extreme reactions by some established soul artists to expand far beyond the established standards of the sound as the new decade beckoned. "Progressive soul" was an industry term for music that connected the genres of rock, jazz, blues, and gospel into something never before heard. The beloved Curtis Mayfield surprised many with his turn to psychedelia on his first solo album, released in October 1970, with the eight-minute opening track "(Don't Worry) If There's a Hell Below We're All Going to Go." The reorganization at Stax Records in Memphis allowed artists such as Isaac Hayes to stretch out and record extended ten-plus-minute bedroom vamps over music, redefining a freeform sound of soul. The Isley Brothers fled Motown in 1969, tired of their standard pop fare, and began to produce stronger groove-oriented funk such as "It's Your Thing" and "Get Into Something." They let loose youngest brother Ernie Isley to mimic their onetime sideman Jimi Hendrix, and as a result produced some extended powerhouse rock songs delivered with their trademark affecting vocalizing. In 1971 they went against their type once again and recorded an entire album of soulful covers of rock tunes. The album, *Givin' It Back*, features covers of Neil Young's "Ohio," Bob Dylan's "Lay Lady Lay," and Steven Stills's "Love the One You're With." It was clearly a bold statement across the racial divide, done with a soulful approach. This was done on the heels of the emerging psychedelic soul of the Temptations, Billy Paul, the Undisputed Truth, and Stevie Wonder's plunge into electronics and atmospheric moods on his 1971 album *Where I'm Coming From.*

The established midwestern soul singer Gene McDaniels had earned a reputation with his vocal clarity, articulate and yet passionate delivery, and thoughtful lyrics on ballads such as "Tower of Strength" and "A Hundred Pounds of Clay" in 1962. After enduring the turbulent sixties, he reemerged as the iconoclastic "Eugene McDaniels, the Left Reverend McD," penning the well-traveled tome to despair "Compared to What?" and two of the most esoteric and visionary albums of the era, *Outlaw* and *Headless Heroes of the Apocalypse. Headless Heroes* is a mélange of folksy rock, extroverted jazz and soul, bitter Dylan-esque irony, lighthearted whimsy, and deep discontent. McDaniels's twisted turn earned him the wrath of Vice President Spiro Agnew, who was informed of McDaniels's harsh critique on *Headless Heroes* and contacted executives at Atlantic Records, urging them to remove the record. The album was shelved.[30]

Eventually bizarre became the norm for soul singers on the edge. The Florida-based soul singer Clarence Reid was a marginal yet feisty rhythm and blues talent, churning out such kicking fare as "Nobody But You Babe" and "I'm Your Yes Man" in the late 1960s. Working out of the studios that turned out Latimore, Betty Wright, and KC and the Sunshine Band, Clarence Reid could have continued along a career of moderate mainstream soul music success. Instead Reid donned a costume, cape, and mask and turned his career inside out by taking on the filthy rhyming persona of Blowfly. In 1971 Reid employed the same Florida-based band that backed up Betty Wright's top-selling hit "Clean Up Woman" and produced the album *The Weird World of Blowfly*. This session featured such absurdity as a send-up of "Soul Man" called "Hole Man," "Spermy Night in Georgia," and "Shitting on the Dock of the Bay." *Blowfly* pushed the pop music parody to the limit, yet it somehow reflected the radical nature of the times. Reid's *Blowfly* was by no means the first of its kind, and his contemporaries Redd Foxx, Rudy Ray Moore, and Pigmeat Markham were all adept at the quick-witted raunchy rhyme. Reid, however, built his act almost entirely around X-rated parodies of soul music.

In 1967 a little known doo-wop outfit from Plainfield, New Jersey, called the Parliaments, led by an obscure industry hustler named George Clinton, scored a top five R&B hit with "(I Wanna) Testify." For their first tour in 1967 the group recruited local Plainfield musicians Billy Nelson (bass) and Eddie Hazel (guitar), then undertook a 180-degree turnabout and morphed into the black rock band Funkadelic. Funkadelic shows featured black performers in outrageous costumes and exaggerated stage behavior, punishing guitar chords and eerie keyboard sound effects, and "the Parliaments'" vocalists harmonizing amidst their psychedelic brethren. For some, Parliament/Funkadelic was evidence that soul had reached its apocalypse. For Clinton, it was just a sign of the times. "We couldn't keep our ties alike, couldn't keep our shirts clean, hair was always undone, you realize the reality of that was really silly, especially when the hippies had just hit the scene and it was hip to be, you know, funky looking. We didn't have a whole bunch of hit records to do it anyway, so it was natural for us to become hippies," George Clinton recalled. "We found out the vibe was more important than them actually hearing us. But I knew then that it was more about making faces, jamming and having a good time."[31] On their song "Wars of Armageddon" from their 1971 *Maggot Brain* album, members of the band could be heard chanting, "More power to the pussy / more pussy to the power," an edgy twist to the prevailing black radical milieu.

At the end of 1969, the great black rock guitarist Jimi Hendrix took a radical turn of his own. As a result of a contract dispute, Hendrix was obligated to produce a onetime album for another label. The new album involved his army buddy and bass player, Billy Cox, and the living mountain of a drummer, Buddy Miles. The all-black power-rock trio—the Band of Gypsys—produced a never-before-heard amalgam of punishing guitar riffs over crisp rhythm and blues grooves along with soaring soul vocalizing from R&B veteran Miles. The funk-rock sound would change the face of black music, setting a template for the spectacular glam-funk of the 1970s. One of the original songs debuted during those sessions was the Hendrix composition "Power of Soul," which encapsulated the ideals of these black rock and rollers from their soul roots:

> With the Power of Soul
> Anything is possible!
> With the power of you
> Anything you wanna do![32]

The impact of Jimi Hendrix on black popular music and black artists was enormous. Bootsy Collins, collaborator with George Clinton's Parliament/Funkadelic (P-Funk), credits Hendrix with changing the entire social and musical landscape for his generation:

> Jimi Hendrix was the cat that said not only can you play guitar, I want you to come up front and do the wild thing. Back in that day, brothers wasn't cool with being freaky and being out there like that. We hadn't caught up to that yet. . . . It was in a time when we didn't even want to be called black. And James Brown came through and made "Say it loud I'm black and I'm proud"—and that's when we started to like being black. . . . And I think that's why me getting with George [Clinton] helped bring the black people on board as to what Jimi was really doing.[33]

Jimi Hendrix and the Black Panther Party

There are a number of accounts of the popular black rock star and his relationship to the Black Panther Party. Hendrix was asked to perform at a number of benefits for the Party, but Hendrix's managers were adamant about canceling them, double booking, rumor spinning, and avoiding all public exposure of the Hendrix-Panther connection. While his public statements about the Party were often cryptic, implying that there needed to be no need for them, Jimi Hendrix nevertheless often held court regarding the Panthers, and according to biographer David Henderson, "Jimi was acquainted with Black Panthers on the East and West coasts. Several high-ranking Party members had had discussions with Jimi about a benefit performance." Hendrix biographer Charles Shaar Murray provides an account of how Jimi's white bass player, Noel Redding, was caught in the black radical crossfire:

> Hendrix was, after all, the only black rock star with a massive white audience, and he was correctly perceived by the Black Panther Party and others as having a vast influence on the young whites who followed him. He was thus courted by the Panthers—Noel Redding was once highly miffed to find himself virtually excluded from the Experience's dressing room by a Panther delegation with whom Hendrix was having a meeting.[34]

Jimi Hendrix appears to have taken advantage of many opportunities to express his solidarity with the Panthers. On the final set of his groundbreaking New Year's Eve/New Year's Night 1969/70 concerts at the Fillmore East in New York City, Hendrix anounced: "We're going to do this song, the Black Panthers' national anthem," and proceeded into a thundering rendition of "Voodoo Chile (Slight Return)." On May 30, 1970, in Berkeley, Jimi Hendrix proclaimed his solidarity with the Panthers after performing his own rendition of "The Star-Spangled Banner": "Now we're going to play our American anthem. . . . This is especially dedicated to People's Park, and especially the Black Panthers."

Aaron Dixon, captain of the Seattle Black Panther Party chapter, recalled that Jimi asked the Panthers to handle security for him during his 1970 concert in Seattle, the last performance in his hometown.

> Whenever he performed in Seattle he always dedicated a song to the Black Panther Party. And so we were really elated when he asked us to provide the security for his last concert in Seattle. The management called our office and told us that Jimi wanted us to do the

security for him. It was an outdoor concert, in Seattle, Seattle Six stadium. I remember it was a light rain coming down. I remember he burned up a couple of guitars, and he was his old self.

Jimi Hendrix did more than simply give shout-outs to black radicals. Jimi himself was a radical black, a living example for some of what a completely liberated black man could be. Aaron Dixon recognized this even as he was standing guard representing the Black Panthers at Jimi's concert.

> There was so much great music at that time, so much great music from the white community, from the black community and Jimi Hendrix just brought the two together. . . . Jimi really represented this whole rebellious nature of young America. When he passed away, that was kind of a changing of this whole thing that had been taking place in the late '60s.[35]

In a poetic sense, Hendrix and the Panthers were flip sides of the same revolutionary coin. The Panthers gave a generation the courage to demand freedom, and Hendrix was able to allow that generation to imagine what freedom looked and sounded like.

The Black Panther Party inspired rock artists of all persuasions to indulge in their outrage at the system, their outrage at racial injustice, and simply to let the world know of their angst at the loudest possible volume. The Michigan-based hard-rock quintet MC5 (Motor City Five) was a noise machine that is considered a forerunner of the punk movement in the United States. In October 1968 the group performed an eighteen-minute swamp blues blowout called "I'm Mad Like Eldridge Cleaver" live at the Grande Ballroom in Detroit. Their one-time manager and activist John Sinclair was inspired by Huey Newton to create the "White Panthers," a cultural group that advocated free love, rock and roll, the legalization of marijuana, and the "abolishment of capitalism."

Other established rock artists, most notably John Lennon and the Grateful Dead, pursued positive relationships with the Black Panther Party. After a chance meeting with Huey Newton on a cross-country airplane flight, members of the popular Bay Area–based Grateful Dead engaged in a lengthy conversation with the Panther cofounder. Shortly afterward, the Grateful Dead performed at Revolutionary Intercommunal Day of Solidarity for Bobby Seale, a benefit for the Black Panther Party on March 5, 1971, at the Oakland Auditorium Arena in downtown Oakland. The Lumpen also performed at the daylong event. Another Grateful Dead concert at Wesleyan University during the Bobby Seale/Ericka Huggins trial in nearby New Haven, Connecticut, was promoted as a Panther benefit by the local Black Student Union, lending credence to the popularity of the Dead and their connection to the Panthers.[36]

The rock and roll superstar John Lennon emerged as a vocal social critic on the American scene once he was removed from the obligations of his original band. The Beatles delivered their share of pithy social critiques on their irreverent and beloved pop singles such as "Revolution" and "Back in the USSR." As a solo artist, Lennon recorded the rousing rock and roll single "Power to the People" that went to #12 on the American pop singles chart in the spring of 1971—just as the Lumpen were using the chant on every song of their weekly performances. (The Lennon song was interpolated by Michael Franti on his popular chant "Power to the Peaceful" during the early 2000s.) Later that year Lennon spoke publicly of his friendship with Bobby Seale, and introduced Seale to a daytime syndicated television audience of *The Mike Douglass Show* during Lennon's week as guest host.[37] John Lennon and his wife, Yoko Ono, were publicly involved in social issues at the time and were aware of their potential as artists to bring this change about. Their impact was given an injection when the two headlined (along with Stevie Wonder) a concert in Detroit to free MC5 manager John Sinclair, who had been imprisoned for handing two joints to a female undercover officer. Three days after the concert, Sinclair was released.

The Panthers were part and parcel of the counterculture of resistance and antiwar activism associated with rock music culture at the time. The cultural front of black power was the last battleground of the Black Panther Party.

Elaine Brown

The highest-profile Party member to be associated with music was eventual Panther Party chairman Elaine Brown, who recorded two albums of defiant protest music in the midst of her BPP tenure. Her first album, *Seize the Time*, was recorded in 1969 for Vault, and the second (for Black Forum/Motown in 1973) was recorded with the help of Motown executive Suzanne de Passe, who became personal friends with Brown. Brown's two albums' worth of self-penned messages of black pride and Panther power were artistic renderings in a class by themselves. The structure of her music was decidedly different from that of the Lumpen. Her musical style was aesthetically closer to the traditional ballad-driven protest music of Paul Robeson than the rowdy rhythmic aesthetics of rhythm and blues. Lumpen member William Calhoun explains the differences between their respective forms of revolutionary music:

> Elaine had been doing some music with the Party before, but Elaine's stuff was more jazz kind of oriented, I guess is the best way to put it. My musical roots came from James Brown and Ray Charles. So, we were a little closer to the funk. And people reacted a little differently to us. We were a little funkier I guess.[38]

Elaine Brown's passionate revolutionary ballads were a favorite of Huey P. Newton, who encouraged her work. Brown and Newton's personal relationship undoubtedly played a role, as did the fact that Newton was a classical music fan and was not known as a good dancer, and as such was perhaps inclined to prefer her music to the jumping and shouting at Lumpen shows.

Elaine Brown was raised in the tough working-class neighborhoods of Philadelphia, but her mother provided her with a number of upscale opportunities to attend private schools, take ballet and music classes, and learn the trappings of wealth, all the while growing up in poverty. She began to write songs as a youth, generally about teenage angst and relationships. Once out of high school, Brown moved to Los Angeles to pursue an entertainment career. After struggling as a cocktail waitress at the infamous Pink Pussycat club, she enrolled in Los Angeles City College and developed as a student activist. Brown began to write poetry and music for the revolution. The night of one of her poetry readings, at which she chastised black men in the movement, she became an inaugural member of the Southern California chapter of the Black Panther Party.

Los Angeles was one of the most violent locales for Party activity. Brown was on the UCLA campus when the infamous shooting occurred between Panthers and members of Karenga's US Organization on January 17, 1969, which resulted in the murders of Alprentice "Bunchy" Carter and John Huggins. On the night of Bunchy Carter's funeral, Chief of Staff David Hilliard was told about Brown's revolutionary songs. Brown discusses that evening in her autobiography.

> Masai [Hewitt, Panther leader and minister of education] had told him I wrote revolutionary songs. David wanted to hear them before going back to Oakland. He ordered Geronimo to find a piano and to gather everyone in the area together to listen. There had been too much pain for me to be embarrassed about it. I sang him the song for Franco, "The Panther," and the one for Eldridge, "The Meeting." I sang the one written at Sybil Brand for Bunchy and John: "Assassination." David cried and ordained that the one for Eldridge become the Black Panther National Anthem.[39]

According to Brown, Hilliard then ordered that copies of the "Black Panther National Anthem" be distributed around the organization and that Elaine record an entire album of her songs. Brown and her musical director, the accomplished jazz artist Horace Tapscott, recorded her first album, *Seize the Time*, under constant police surveillance. Brown states in her autobiography: "The joy I felt in making the music was undercut by the presence of the police, who followed us every day, who sat outside the Vault recording studio during the sessions, who stopped and delayed us going to and from the studio. They were omnipresent."[40]

While the music didn't play on black radio, it did not go unnoticed. Tapscott arranged the horns, strings, and piano accompaniment that stretched the dramatic tension of Brown's voice. She displayed command of her tone and could sustain impassioned notes at a feverish pitch. Brown combined her piano recital training with her radical politics to write compelling music for the revolution. On "The End of Silence" she makes clear what is necessary for the revolutionary fight:

> You know that dignity, not just equality
> Is what makes a man a man . . .
>
> Well then believe it my friend that this silence can end
> We'll just have to get guns and be men.

Brown wrote with a reverence for black men that went far beyond typical romantic lyrics. It is illustrative of the male-centered thrust of Brown's revolutionary politics that she would implore her listeners to "get guns and be men." Certainly the figurative methods of music making are fair game for metaphorical license, and Brown was a skilled poet and lyricist. In terms of the prevailing conceptions of patriarchal strength, courage, and militancy, Elaine Brown meant what she said.

On "The Meeting," Elaine Brown wrote and sang about the dynamic and controversial Minister of Information Eldridge Cleaver as a representation of black manhood that people had been waiting for.

> I said, Man, where have you been for all these years
> Man, where were you, when I sought you
> Man, do you know me as I know you
> Man, am I coming through?

In her commentary about the album, Elaine Brown was candid about the point of her work:

> I used to write about flowers and butterflies and love. That kind of bullshit. But now since I've joined the Panthers, my words are hard and concrete and there's no abstract, esoteric message. Things are laid out clearly, so that people can understand how we feel.[41]

"The Panther" was another example:

> He is a hero, he walks with night
> His spirit's beauty, his soul is right . . .
>
> His face is black and he would die for you
> To get your freedom back.

Elaine Brown's music stands as a window into the workings of a black radical organization at its social, political, and cultural zenith. She was referred to then as "the Songwriter for the Black Panther Party." However the Party was not stable enough to develop their cultural apparatus much further beyond the production of her albums and the Lumpen's performances. In many ways, Elaine Brown's musical work, much like her work in Party leadership in the 1970s has been overshadowed historically by the glare of the gun in the hands of the Panther.

There were other musical ventures by Panther Party members. Other chapters in other cities had singing groups, and volunteer entertainment was a staple of Panther social events and recruitment throughout the Party's lifetime. But the entire Party design was implemented in Oakland. In the 1970s the Black Panthers' liberation school developed into a successful charter school in Oakland, originally called the Intercommunal Youth Instutute and later the Oakland Community School. Ericka Huggins directed the institute through most of its existence, and it had its own choir and an Intercommunal Youth Band directed by Charles Moffeit. The Panthers' award-winning work lasted nearly a decade and educated hundreds of Oakland students while requiring no tuition. Veteran Panther Huggins served on the Alameda County Board of Education while directing the institute. She endured some of the most tumultuous periods in Panther history and established a lasting legacy as an educator. Legendary soul singer Lenny Williams knew many of the Panthers well in the 1970s and explains the unique circumstances of the female leadership of the Party as only he could:

> Ericka is just a sweetheart, you know, but a very strong woman. I mean, you look at those women like Ericka and Elaine Brown, I mean, those women, when Huey was gone they controlled the party. And you know, these are women that are controlling men that are carrying guns and men that'll fight and men that'll lay down their lives and die for a cause, so these weren't the ordinary women that's going to kowtow to what a man says and, you know, that you could just, I mean shoot, they were women so they loved to be touched and loved and cared for as women might like, you know, but you couldn't shuck and jive them, that's one thing for sure. So it took a hell of a man to be involved with Ericka and Elaine and some of the other women that were there at the party.[42]

Huey Newton and Bob Dylan

Among the most intriguing intersections of Panther politics and popular music was Huey Newton's affection for the works of Bob Dylan, the enigmatic folksinger and iconic social commentator of the 1960s. Dylan's ability to pierce the soul of the listener with his poignant, stark, and often surrealistic narratives of bleak times and impending social upheaval skyrocketed him to the center of the rebel rock generation's search for meaning through the medium of music. Born in Minnesota as Robert Allen Zimmerman in 1941, the young singer patterned himself after the great depression–era folksinger Woody Guthrie, and many of his fans saw him as a modern-day troubadour of the contemporary disillusioned youth of America. In terms of his stark renderings of life on songs like "The Times They Are A-Changin'," Dylan could easily be compared to Woody Guthrie or Guthrie's political mentor, the left-leaning Pete Seeger. Playing a twangy guitar and singing with an equally twanging voice, Dylan presented lyrics that were the unique feature of his appeal, and for Dylan, the overwhelming social changes in the United States during the early 1960s were captured with a brilliance unmeasured. Songs like "The Times They Are A-Changin'" and "Only a Pawn in Their Game" revealed issues and brought to life characters with a deep dislocation from American mainstream mores and values. His first major hit, "Blowin' in the Wind" was a major inspiration for Sam Cooke's foray into message music. Dylan's ideas resonated with a generation of youth just facing the Vietnam War draft and the moral torrent of the civil rights movement.

Dylan's ability to dislodge himself from the prevailing tenets of society and yet signify on many deeply held literary themes and ideas made him an irresistible social force—and an overnight celebrity in 1963 when his second full-length album *The Freewheelin' Bob Dylan* was released on Columbia. Just as Malcolm X was solidifying his hold on the disillusionment of black Americans at the dawn of the 1960s, Dylan was the accomplished voice of the distraught and disoriented white rebel youth. The stark messages in "Masters of War" and "A Hard Rain's a-Gonna Fall" provided a strong appeal for a dislocated generation. Robbie Robertson summed up the tenor of Dylan during this dangerous period:

> I could hear the politics in the early songs. It's very exciting to hear somebody singing so powerfully, with something to say. But what struck me was how the street had had such a profound effect on him: coming from Minnesota, setting out on the road and coming into New York. There was a hardness, a toughness, in the way he approached his songs and the characters in them. That was a rebellion, in a certain way, against the purity of folk music. He wasn't pussyfooting around on "Like a Rolling Stone" or "Ballad of a Thin Man." This was the rebel rebelling against the rebellion.[43]

Huey Newton played Dylan's music regularly and ordered it played at various times around Party functions. Dylan's album *Highway 61 Revisited* could be heard routinely during the Panther paper shipping night. Every Panther in the inner circle was aware of Huey's affection for Dylan, and Huey made sure they all knew of the symbolism and messages in Dylan's work. Dylan showed a deep respect for the blues and blues forms and understood the passion and nuance of blues standards. Blues lyrics are generally circumspect, open to interpretation, and full of metaphor. Dylan's lyrics, however, are often either painfully direct or disorientingly abstract.

Early in his career, however, Dylan performed a withering treatment of the Emmett Till case. Emmett Till was a fourteen-year-old Chicago boy who during a 1955 visit to Mississippi was accused of "sassing" a white woman in a store and was subsequently lynched by her acquaintances. The perpetrators of the crime freely admitted their deeds and were still acquitted by an all-white Mississippi jury. The case was significant because of both the courage of the black Mississippians to accuse the whites of the crime in court—a major breakthrough of resistance at the time—and the media coverage of the event, one of the first televised trials in the United States, as well as due to the recurring publishing of the photograph of young Emmett Till's misshapen head in the casket at his Chicago funeral, deliberately left open by Till's mother, so "everyone could see what they did to my baby."

Bob Dylan's rendition rolls like a coal miner tragedy or other Depression-era account of folk-song despair, and his lyricism is as biting as ever: "This boy's fateful tragedy you should all remember well / The color of his skin was black and his name was Emmett Till" went the introduction. The details of the deed were not missed by Dylan:

> They tortured him and did some things too evil to repeat
> There was screaming sounds inside the barn, there was laughing
>   sounds out on the street.

It was a rarity at the time for any artist (and especially rare for black artists) to address such a painful topic with the amount of realism in the words.

In 1964 Dylan traveled to the South, along with Joan Baez and Pete Seeger, where he witnessed the courage of SNCC workers firsthand and, as Mike Marqusee put it, "was awed by their courage and commitment, suffering and directness." He performed his song "Only a Pawn in Their Game" for the sharecroppers there, who undoubtedly appreciated his efforts if they did not fully appreciate the aesthetics of his style.[44]

Perhaps Dylan's most significant work in terms of the Panthers was the surrealistic "Ballad of a Thin Man" from his 1965 album *Highway 61 Revisited*. The slow, foreboding tension of the song backgrounds a harrowing visit by a "Mr. Jones" to a freakshow, in which he horrifyingly realizes that in some way the freaks he came to see are reflections of himself.

> You hand in your ticket and you go watch the geek
> Who immediately walks up to you when he hears you speak
> and says, "How does it feel to be such a freak?"

The layers of meaning in "Ballad of a Thin Man" have been debated extensively over the years by followers who claim, among other possibilities, that Mr. Jones is a naive journalist confronted with the spectacle of Dylan's genius/madness or is a series of allusions to a gay strip joint, which he walks into with a "pencil" and is confronted by a "one-eyed midget" and other curious characters. While some Dylan followers dismiss the record as nonsensical, some have clung to the lyrics of "Thin Man" with a zeal. Huey Newton was captivated by "Ballad of a Thin Man" and insisted that his fellow Panthers listen carefully to the symbolism and meaning within the song. Bobby Seale, in his memoir, *Seize the Time*, recounted his encounter with Huey and the "Thin Man":

> Huey P. Newton made me recognize the lyrics. Not only the lyrics of the record, but what the lyrics meant in the record. What the lyrics meant in the history of racism that has perpetuated itself in this world. . . . The point about the geek is very important because this is where Huey hung me.
>
> . . . He doesn't like eating raw meat, or feathers but he does it to survive. But these people who are coming in to see him are coming in for entertainment, so they are the real freaks. . . .
>
> Huey says that whites looked at blacks as geeks, as freaks. But what is so symbolic about it is that when the revolution starts,

they'll call us geeks because we eat raw meat. But the geek turns around and hands Mr. Jones a naked bone and says, "How do you like being a freak?" And Mr. Jones says, "Oh my God, what the hell's going on?"[45]

Dylan, through a sense of the dramatic and flirtation with the surreal, penetrates with an incisive linkage between the oppressor and the oppressed and how each defaces and dehumanizes the other. As Newton saw it, Bob Dylan managed to implicate all parties involved in the ruse that was America's self-image, as tattered as it was in the 1960s.

The fact that the Black Panthers were adept at producing revolutionary theater in many of their proclamations speaks to the insights that Newton had been developing, influenced in part by the "Thin Man." Much of the Panthers' rhetoric was both literal and figurative at once, such as "The Sky's the Limit" or "All Power to the People." Their language could be taken at face value or interpreted on an in-depth level. The Ten Point Program, with its initial declarations followed by more detailed explanations of each point, is an example of how the Panthers attempted to deal on multiple levels with their audience. Yes, the Panthers sought to reach the brothers on the block, the hardened street toughs, on their terms, but there was another level of connection that Huey Newton was convinced he could impart to his followers. It is not an exaggeration to say that he gained some of these insights from listening to Bob Dylan.

Dylan's most dramatic association with the Black Panthers was a song he wrote in 1971 after the death of George Jackson in the San Quentin prison yard. Jackson had joined the Party in prison after acquiring a one-year-to-life sentence for robbery in 1961. Jackson studied Marxism while in prison and was one of the founders of the Black Guerilla Army in 1966. While in Soledad Prison in 1969 Jackson was charged—along with two others, Fleeta Drumgo and John Clutchette—with the murder of a prison guard, and the Soledad Brothers became a cause célèbre. Jackson's published letters from prison in 1970 reveal him to be among the most resolute and articulate of the many incarcerated rebels of the time. Jackson, for many (including Dylan), was seen as a pure revolutionary, one completely dedicated to the cause of revolutionary change, and in that sense, incorruptible. To his followers Jackson was as noble and rational as one could become, trapped in the cage that he was. This was perhaps his appeal to Bob Dylan.

In an assault that remains in dispute to this day, a prison "riot" took place on August 1, 1971, in which officials claim that Jackson "acquired" a gun, ordered or took part in the murders of prison guards and prisoners, and ran onto the prison yard, where he was shot by the prison guards from above. The circumstances of the prison riot and the means by which Jackson obtained a firearm in the middle of a maximum security federal prison are still unclear. As James Baldwin remarked at the time, "No Black person will ever believe that George Jackson died the way they tell us he did."[46] Nevertheless, George Jackson died that day, and his disturbing death sent a shock wave through those who saw him as perhaps the last of the pure revolutionaries of that era. Dylan certainly was one.

His lyrics were deeply personal, as Dylan sings of waking up with tears in his bed, after learning that a man he "really loved" had been killed, shot in the head. The chorus to the song was as sorrowful as any of Dylan's work, as he wails to "the Lord" that "they cut George Jackson down" and reliving the funeral, he appears to be moaning as Jackson's body is put to rest. In typical Dylan fashion, he delved deeper into the complex relationship of a political prisoner, as he rebuked the prison guards, who watched him from above and were "frightened of his power" and "scared of his love."

Bob Dylan captured the sentiment of Jackson's followers vividly in a way that only he could. While not a participant in the movement per se, Dylan was terribly moved by Jackson's death and recorded two versions of the song, an acoustic and a full-band version, and demanded that his label release the single immediately with the lyrics on the single sleeve cover. In his own way, Bob Dylan directly addressed the revolution and revealed how deeply he was affected by it.

Dylan's final verse to the song sums up his own despair and a somber global consciousness that harbors a stark resonance in modern times:

> Sometimes I think this whole world
> Is one big prison yard
> Some of us are prisoners
> The rest of us are guards.

The world as one big prison yard. Once again Dylan is quick to implicate everyone involved. Yes, many are imprisoned by the poverty and
social misery of life at the bottom of society, but to frame the rest of
the population as prison guards implicates everyone else as complicit in
the literal economic incarceration of the world's underprivileged. Once
again, this time in an act of pure despair, Dylan had struck one of his
master strokes.

While Dylan, like the Beatles and Jimi Hendrix, had an immense
impact on black artists, he failed to gain traction in the black mainstream. But many black artists sparked their careers doing covers of
Dylan songs, including soul artists such as Sam Cooke, Stevie Wonder,
the Staple Singers, Bobby Womack, and the Isley Brothers. By the end of
the 1960s and the start of the 1970s, the entirety of America's musical
traditions were up for grabs, in flux, and open to anyone with the courage and foresight to manipulate them. Blues, gospel, jazz, show tunes,
soul, rock, funk, everything was undergoing change, and the black revolution was a primary source for the upheaval in the music.

Soul Day at San Quentin

One of the final events that the Lumpen performed as a group was an
appearance at San Quentin Prison in May 1971, along with Curtis Mayfield and the guest of honor that day, Muhammad Ali. A prisoners' organization within the federal prison had put together what was called "Soul
Day at San Quentin," and with the help of the newly formed San Quentin chapter of the Black Panther Party, the daylong event was a success.
With speeches, dancers, and songs, the spirit was understandably lively,
and the setting was rich in cultural symbolism and solidarity with the
black movement. The San Quentin chapter of the Black Panther Party
appropriated the populist Soul Day at San Quentin that was approved
by the prison officials and transformed it into a tribute to Malcolm X,
renaming the event "Malcolm X Day at San Quentin."

Some Panther women had formed a dance troupe that performed
with the Freedom Messengers, the backing band to Lumpen, to entertain the inmates. Prison officials and a local radio host brought in to
coordinate the event were adamant about preventing a performance by
the Lumpen—the band followed the dancers' performance and only

managed to get through a portion of one song before they were hastily removed from the stage by prison officials. William Calhoun recalls the events of that day:

> Curtis Mayfield was there, Muhammad Ali was there, we were there, and believe me they didn't know we were coming. They cut us off almost as soon as we got started. They didn't know who we were. We were there, at any rate. And I did get a chance to tell him [Curtis Mayfield] what I had done. Him and Ali were the stars of the day. It was the only time I met Muhammad. He was incredible, just incredible. Curtis was . . . very open, very giving, very generous with us, or at least with me, and what we were trying to accomplish.[47]

For Calhoun to recount that Curtis Mayfield empathized with the radicalization of his work explains a great deal about the depths of respect Mayfield had for the black radical community. Mayfield sought to make protest music in the context of his own values and traditions, yet he was clearly in solidarity with the struggles of the Black Panther Party at the time. Ali was in a similar situation. Ali was considered the people's champion, based upon his conversion to Islam, his prior relationship with Malcolm X, and his steadfast refusal to serve in Vietnam. "Ali was the initiator of black consciousness for us," Mumia Abu-Jamal explained in the documentary *Long Distance Revolutionary*. Ali was an icon of black pride as an athlete, and was an articulate and uncompromising leader of an entire cultural movement of black consciousness and resistance.[48]

That day at San Quentin was symbolic of the overall disruption that the Lumpen caused upon the premises and the paradigms of black music at the time. The Lumpen had asserted themselves directly into the revolution in music and culture that was taking place in their community. Just as Soul Day represented an evolution of the prison reform movement, the Lumpen represented the latest transformation of the rich traditions of black protest music.

The enjoyment of that day would be short-lived. The San Quentin chapter of the Black Panther Party was created by George Jackson with a vision of organizing the entire US black prison population. Only three months later, George Jackson would be gunned down by prison guards. Two weeks after Jackson's death, prisoners in Attica State Prison in upstate New York staged a high-profile takeover of the institution, which captured the attention of the nation and exposed the humanity of those imprisoned and the brutality of the US prison system. The brutality was further exposed when state troopers raided the prison and shot and tortured the surviving prisoners in the process of retaking the institution.

In a way, the collision of culture and politics that took place that day at San Quentin was inevitable. The soul revolution and the black revolution were taking place together. An explosion of soul music has the ability to destroy boundaries imposed on the psyche by Western civilization. Soul Day was an attempt to provide popular entertainment for the prison population, but it was politicized by the prisoners themselves. Who is to say what the "Power of Soul" may have done to "liberate" those in the yard that day?

8

"Revolution Is the Only Solution"

Protest Music Today and the Legacy of the Lumpen

The evening's performance is about to wind up. The Lumpen have delivered the message and the show they came to present to their audience. Only one task remains: to groove the audience all the way home. Like any strong R&B act of the day, the Lumpen band starts its finale with a percussive groove jam that makes people feel the music and soak in the message that has been delivered for the past thirty-five minutes.

The JB-style groove was unmistakable and irresistible. Then came the scat-singing vamps of Calhoun that brought together the vibe over the background chants of the group:

> 1,2, 1, 2, 3 get it / ahhh get it
> Revolution is the only solution
> what you say
> Revolution is the only solution
> now if you want to be free
> Revolution is the only solution

> say pick up that gun and walk like me
> Revolution is the only solution
> say it now
> Revolution is the only solution
> Say it say it now
> Revolution is the only solution
> Say if you want to be free
> Revolution is the only solution
> say pick up that gun and walk like me

William Calhoun addresses the crowd with a dialogue spoken in the rhythm of the music, not unlike R&B headliners of the day:

> Brothers and sisters as we close, we would like to thank everyone for coming out tonight / because without the spirit of the people, the Lumpen don't exist.
> And we're going to take that spirit with us across the country, as we'll be leaving tomorrow.
> Before we go though, we want to say we love you. All Power to the People! (*Audience replies*) "All Power to the People!"
> Lookie here, we're going to leave with the spirit, everybody clap your hands one more time, everybody in this room, good god, we want you to sing with me now, everybody would you sing with us, everybody sing "revolution," "revolution" everybody, good god, bring it on up . . .

As the audience chants *revolution* and claps along with the band, the Lumpen singers work the stage with dance steps and induce crowd participation in the form of soul claps (double-time clapping on the beat) and a variety of time-tested dance-routine techniques. The ad-libbing and audience chanting goes on for more than five minutes, as the extended song drives a rhythm home for the listeners. As the song crashes to an end to sustained applause and the chant "All power to the people," the audience is energized and politicized in ways unlike any other rhythm and blues performance before or since.[1]

The Show Ends

While their message was one of a kind, the Lumpen were a rhythm and blues act, and the show was not going to end mildly. Fans of black popular music know that a classic rhythm and blues performance typically concludes with as much energy and enthusiasm as it begins. Michael Torrence understood the purpose of a finale:

> My uncle Bobby McClain sang doo-wop in the '50s and he always said, "If these people come to see you, make sure they're glad they came." So that was the same thing, we wanted that by the time you left that program, or Lumpen show, that you knew that you had seen something; that it was something you could feel, that you would talk about.
>
> So it was all about leaving it all out there, don't even give them a chance to catch their breath. Every now and then we slow it down. Calhoun had that experience too about how to pace a show, slow it down every now and then, but when you slow it down, the next time, bring you right back up on it.
>
> So by the time we get to "Revolution Is the Only Solution" you always take them up on a big high on that one. We'd be stepping very hard on "Revolution Is the Only Solution," we'd be high kicking and everything. It used to almost get dangerous if the stage was too small.
>
> It was a lot of high energy a lot of hard work. We wanted everybody that came out of that to be talking about it. Be talking about it four days later. Telling people, "You should've been there; if you see they'll be playing again, go see them, go see them."[2]

If they performed their duties as rank-and-file Panthers properly that night, the Lumpen would have energized their audience, excited them, and introduced them to a new and visceral way to internalize the mission of the Black Panther Party. If the Lumpen members did their jobs, many new potential recruits would take seriously the opportunity to join the Party and sustain the revolution. Perhaps some would stay and read the literature, talk to the Panthers there, and get to know the soul brothers and soul sisters that made up the rank-and-file of the Party. Perhaps others would be strictly entertained by a righteous slice of Bay Area funk and keep with them an unforgettable experience. Regardless, for James Mott, Clark Bailey, Michael Torrence, and William Calhoun, the next day would be another day in the Black Panther Party.

As the program on this night concluded, the Lumpen members turned around and took down their equipment, loaded it, and prepared for their East Coast tour, which was about to begin. After the rousing concert, the group members were afforded little fanfare before taking on their Panther duties. No autographs, no interviews with interested media representatives, and certainly no money came their way. "We never saw a penny for what we did," James Mott recalls.[3]

That night, a recording console was in the building and a truck was parked outside with recording equipment for the purpose of recording a state-of-the-art live performance of the Lumpen for public sale. They even announced, "We're recording live tonight at Merritt College," which was typical for bands to do at the time. (None of the Panthers I interviewed could recall who was recording the show or what happened to that concert tape.) The group then went on their chaotic national tour, after which most of the Freedom Messengers, the all-volunteer backup band, called it quits. Weeks later, the Lumpen singers, along with a new group of backing musicians, went to the Golden State Studios in San Francisco to record overdubs and rerecord some of the songs. The existing tape of the live concert features elements of live and studio-recorded songs. Mysteriously, the master tapes of that concert have disappeared and only a grainy cassette of the event has been recovered to this point.

With their high musical standards, and their effectiveness at their revolutionary mission, why were the Lumpen not afforded more status within the organization? "Some people didn't want us to succeed," James Mott recalls. Emory Douglas was in the mix when things began to unravel.

> They were committed to the Party and the work that they were doing. But certain people didn't want it to flourish or didn't think it was gonna flourish the way it did, and when it did, they wanted to dictate to us how it was gonna go. And that was a frustration there.
>
> You got people who felt they were getting too big, and they needed to put it [the band] in its place, or they felt that the Lumpen felt that they needed to practice too much and they needed to show their control by saying they had to come do this and do that, and do

this work and do that work. I don't get into names but that was the reality of the environment.[4]

The Lumpen, for some, had become too big for its place within the Black Panther Party. Structurally they were a traveling act with at least seven regular members that required upkeep. Ideologically, it appears that the BPP was struggling with a unified position toward the band's very existence.

With the internal fissures throughout the Black Panther Party in late 1970, the public rift between Huey Newton and Eldridge Cleaver in February 1971, and with Bobby Seale still on trial in Connecticut, the Party was in its deepest crisis. Many projects were put on hold or eliminated. Huey Newton's principled stances against violent confrontation were being challenged by many who wanted to start the revolution immediately and by those who wanted to simply watch the carnage. Newton himself had begun his personal dissolution, retreating into cocaine addiction, dispensing decrees by day and roaming the streets by night.

At his best, Huey Newton steered the Party into an enlightened new direction for the new decade. He issued proclamations denouncing sexism, denouncing homophobia in the revolution, and advanced social theories of intercommunalism and collective economic development. His loyal followers (including the Lumpen singers) followed his orders diligently. By mid-1971, however, things were unraveling, and it took a great deal of loyalty to continue to operate for a fractured leader in a fractured organization.

By the end of May 1971, William Calhoun had had enough. The pressures of Party life and the growing recognition that he actually had his own life responsibilities to consider had begun to change his outlook.

Sukari, my woman in the Party, was pregnant with Jamil, with James. And I was beginning to think about that. I had been on duty one night—on guard duty—one night at national headquarters. And there was a practice vamp. The police used to just do that all the time. About three or four o'clock in the morning they just come out of nowhere, be three or four rows deep, in their riot gear and the FBI patrol up and down in front, just trying to intimidate us. But one night when they did a practice vamp, I'm sitting there, my AK in my lap, looking at them looking at me and thinking about the fact that I have a baby coming. The thought came to me, *What good would it do for me to die here tonight? What does that accomplish? What does that change?* And that's the first time I had a thought like that. A couple of months later, something came in my head and said leave, and I left.[5]

The Lumpen performed their final concert in Sacramento on May 23, 1971. Days later, Bobby Seale returned from New Haven to be reunited with Huey Newton and the Panthers. Bobby had been set free. But for Calhoun, it was time to move on.

After a few years, Calhoun, through his music industry connections, got a job at local radio station KSOL and became somewhat of a local celebrity as "Billy King." By the mid-1970s KSOL was the number one FM radio station playing black music, and Billy King was one of their most popular radio hosts. Few if any of his fellow DJs knew of his past as a Black Panther.

William Calhoun continued on his life path of principle, and shortly after leaving the KSOL gig he pursued organized religion. "I don't do anything casually. If I'm into something, I'm into it all the way."[6] In 1980 the Reverend William E. Calhoun, along with Minister Timothy Sowell, founded the Wo'Se community church in Oakland. The ministers were ordained Baptist, and the church community reflected the East Oakland neighborhood it was based in. The church was also involved in a number of efforts to support African-centered thought and helped to develop the African philosophy of *Ma'at*, which was an important method of giving black youth a sense of an ancient lineage of moral codes and higher consciousness that one could apply to the modern world.

Years later, Calhoun expanded his role as a counselor and advisor and took on a job it seemed that no one would take. He took on the task of helping some of the most troubled youth in Sacramento: violent sex offenders.

I was working with at-risk teenagers. Teenage sex offenders. The worst of the worst as far as society is concerned. Kids that people just throw away. And I don't believe any human being should be thrown away. So yeah I spent ten years working with those kind of kids, training the staff, hiring the staff that works with those kids. So I taught the staff that worked with those kids, I saw that as a ministry; I saw that as a way to serve. . . . Because these were kids that had nothing. Many of them had nobody. So the only human contact they had was us. Their only contact with the world was us.[7]

Calhoun was working at the center when I first located him for this project in 2004. He has revealed himself to be a multifaceted individual, one who took on issues of social conscience throughout his days, and the black revolution was no exception.

Cal-Pak

In May 1971 Huey Newton, as the unquestioned leader of the Black Panther Party in the Bay Area, challenged a large black-owned business consortium to donate more goods for the breakfast program. The California State Package Store and Tavern Owners Association (Cal-Pak) had established itself in the East Bay as a successful black-owned operation that "was responsible for the creation of nearly 500 jobs for blacks in the beverage industry throughout California."[8] The group offered a one-time donation, but Newton demanded regular services in return for continued Panther support. Cal-Pak was resilient, and their leadership refused to capitulate to Newton. Newton replied by stating that "we can take you down" and set up a round-the-clock picket line outside one of the Grove Street liquor stores of Bill Boyette, then president of Cal-Pak. While the daily actions in front of the store provided some entertaining street theater, the taxing use of rank-and-file membership to maintain the picket line was enormous. The boycott lasted nearly a year, and it took the efforts of newly elected Congressman Ron Dellums to negotiate a deal whereby donations could be distributed to a variety of Oakland social work organizations, including the Party. While the entire affair put the business community on notice about its perceived one-way relationship with its patrons, the damage done to the relationship of the Party and local black-owned businesses was considerable.

Rank-and-file members pulled shifts at the picket line, continued to sell papers, made the breakfasts, and pulled security for BPP officers. They were then given the task of setting up the election campaigns of Bobby Seale for Oakland mayor and Elaine Brown for Oakland City Council. The enormous workload on the tested rank-and-file was taking its toll, and after the close elections, Michael Torrence felt it was time to leave the Party.

Michael Torrence had a harrowing experience trying to get out of the Party in 1973. As a trusted confidante, his loss would be felt by the inner circle of Panther leadership. At that time he was head of the Black Student Union at Laney College (formerly Oakland City College). Torrence, like Calhoun, had a child on the way, and determined that his work for the revolution had run its course. By 1973, however, everyone was wary of Huey's mood swings. Torrence recalls that he approached Bobby Seale at the Panther after-hours club the Lamppost about leaving, and after a heartfelt discussion, Seale bid him well. However, before he could leave the building, Torrence was asked upstairs by Newton, who made a dramatic attempt to keep Torrence in the fold:

> "Do you want to leave bad enough to die?" I said, I don't understand the question. He said, "Brother, do you want to leave bad enough to DIE!" And I said, "Well—" and he said, to one of the other brothers, "Hey, show him what I mean," and the guy pulled out a .357 and put it to my head. And at that point, you know, ain't no shame in my game, I went down and I said, "No, brother, I don't want to die." I went down to my knees because, see, I knew these guys would do it. I had been trained to do it.
>
> So I went to my knees and I said, "No, I don't want to die." He said, "Well, then you stay." And then I said, "Yeah, but my daughter—" and he said, "Brother, you know, show this brother not to talk when I'm talking to him," so the brother kicked me in the mouth. And I said, "I stand corrected." He said, "Good, now this is what's going to happen. We're going to send your daughter fifty dollars a month and you going to stay. A'ight? So OK, all power to the people, right, OK, and that's it."[9]

Despite the madness in Huey's brand of communication within the Party, Michael Torrence stayed on for about a year, until he was told by another Party member that the money for his daughter was going to stop and that he could leave the party.

For Michael Torrence, as it was for many of his age, it was time to move on and think about a career instead of a revolution. Torrence had experience in rhythm and blues, and he kept his networks together over the years. He started singing in a local group called Ladies Choice. On a tour through Oakland in late 1973, the legendary Motown singer Marvin Gaye's group auditioned backup singers for an upcoming concert. Michael Torrence and Ladies Choice successfully passed the audition. Torrence was signed on and performed onstage with Gaye on the famous *Marvin Gaye Live*, recorded at the Oakland Alameda County Coliseum Arena on January 4, 1974. This live album was one of Gaye's most successful, and that night's rendition of "Distant Lover," with the female audience screaming in pure passion throughout the song, is recognized as one of the greatest live soul music performances ever recorded. "That was an amazing night," Torrence recalls. "To be on the stage with legendary musicians, and to touch so many people in that way. It was a powerful experience."

However, the role of a backup singer on the road was anything but glamorous. Despite the fame of Marvin Gaye, or perhaps because of it, the backup singers were not treated with a great deal of respect. The singers were hastily shuttled to and from shows during tours and forced to wait on-call for weeks between gigs. Torrence effectively went from rank-and-file in the revolution to rank-and-file in rhythm and blues. From the daily struggle of the Black Panther Party to the nightly routine of R&B, Torrence went through both ends of it. After the Oakland concert, Ladies Choice had to audition yet again for the national tour:

> Marvin's brother [Frankie], he liked us. We locked up in a motel room, and he would come in with us every day. We were just working on choreography and learning all the songs and stuff off the records and stuff, and he would tell us, "Well, Marvin would like this, Marvin wouldn't like this, and Marvin might like this, he might like that." And so by the time we got a shot to see him, we had a full routine, steps and everything—and Frankie advocating for us—and we got the gig. So we toured with him for about a year and a half.[10]

Torrence toured and recorded with Marvin Gaye through 1976. The backup performers weren't paid very well, and Marvin rarely spoke to the band. On the few occasions that he did, it involved keeping the supporting musicians off balance and dependent on the star rather than nurturing their talents. Torrence and the others were told repeatedly that at the end of the tour, their own group would be given the chance to record, but that did not come about. "He liked to play a mind game with you, which I found out later when I got to work with his wife and met Berry Gordy that this is what they're teaching at Motown—you never tell a guy how good he is."

Through a contact on the tour Torrence obtained a contract as a Motown staff writer, and for two years he wrote songs for Motown Records, some of which wound up on albums for Rare Earth and the little-known Motown girl group High Energy. Torrence also crossed paths with Elaine Brown once again, who was also writing and recording for Motown at the time. Relocating to Los Angeles in the late 1970s, Michael Torrence left the music industry and, through his contacts with the former Party minister of education, Ray "Masai" Hewitt, obtained work as a counselor for at-risk youth in urban Los Angeles. It is a job he has to this day.

James Mott continued to work at the Oakland Community School, the Panthers' school, until 1978. After ten years of service, he felt it was time to get a "real job" and went into real estate, insurance, and other financial ventures. In the early 2000s he went to New Orleans to help start a progressive land-development project, but the project was washed out by Hurricane Katrina. He relocated to Oakland, and has reestablished himself as assistant pastor of Agnes Memorial Christian Academy in East Oakland, doing much of the community-based social work he did in the Party.[11]

Clark Bailey remained with the Party through the late 1970s, ostensibly working for the Panther Community School. However Bailey had other duties that involved maintenance of some of the Panther storehouses of weapons, equipment that was kept in preparation for the revolution that would never come. Bailey was lieutenant to Flores Forbes, a meticulous organizer who kept the Panther storehouses maintained, while also working at the Panther school. Panther work in the late 1970s took its toll on the rank-and-file: Aaron Dixon, in his memoir, *My People Are Rising*, muses upon the loss of Clark "Santa Rita" Bailey from the Party.

> Flores called one morning to tell me that Santa Rita had left. Santa Rita, a member of the party's vocal group the Lumpen, was a singer, a coordinator, an administrator, and a gunman; whatever needed

to be done, he would try to accomplish it. And if he couldn't, he would tell you so. We didn't have too many brothers like him left. At one time we'd had scores of comrades like Santa Rita all across the country, but losing him just put more pressure on those remaining.

Santa Rita's departure planted a seed in my mind. He had left because he was just plain tired and disenchanted, and I think many of us who had been working so long and so hard were quietly feeling the same way, despite the recent accomplishments [Panther supported candidate Lionel Wilson was elected Oakland mayor in 1977]. But the prospect of leaving something we'd devoted our lives to was extremely complicated, and there always some new development, some unexpected challenge to test and renew our commitment.[12]

After leaving the Party, Bailey settled in Sacramento and worked for the Regional Transit Authority, driving a public transit bus for twenty-five years.

It may be mere coincidence, but each of the leaders of the Lumpen engaged in their life pursuits while remaining consistent with their values and principles of public service and the uplift of their community. This is noteworthy in light of the tragedies that befell other dedicated rank-and-file members: Alex Rackley, Robert Webb, Samuel Napier, Lil' Bobby Hutton, and others who were murdered; or Elmer "Geronimo" Pratt, Mumia Abu-Jamal, Sundiata Acoli, and the countless other political prisoners whose commitment to Party principles led to the tragedy of decades of incarceration. Further, the tales of drug addiction, ideological confusion, and self-destruction displayed by Party leaders Newton, Cleaver, and others left for some an unshakable impression that a commitment to the Panthers was destined for destruction and for some was a great, hollow mistake.

What the Panthers represented to a great many from all walks of life was that it was possible to live according to one's own beliefs and that one's ideals need not be crushed by the oppressive economic and social system afflicting so many in urban America today. One might say that the members of the Lumpen, rank-and-file dedicated revolutionaries, stand as an example of what a humble life lived upon these principles is all about.

"You Become What You Sing"

The Lumpen members produced music that represented their values and beliefs at the time and were able to act on those beliefs through their dedicated participation in the revolutionary organization the Black Panther Party. They were not parroting a line for corporate consumption, nor were they seeking personal gratification through superstar stage dynamics. The essence of their dedication came through in their work.

It is not very often that black musicians are able to express their ideas without the constraints of an industry dictating that they compromise, tone down, or radically retreat from their own personal sensibilities simply to sell records. The implications for this are far-reaching on a personal and a societal level. Jazz vocalist Abbey Lincoln perhaps put it best when she said, "I discovered that you become what you sing. You can't repeat lyrics night after night as though they were prayer without having them come true in your life."[13] One might imagine that artists, at their best, write and perform the music that they most sincerely believe in. The current climate of corporate-controlled black popular music frequently dictates that artists must do just the opposite.

At the time of the Lumpen, black popular music was reaching a zenith in terms of its clarity in its portrayals of the state and the aspirations of black America. Much of the black popular music of the day was produced by artists who were writing and performing works that they themselves could believe in—redemption songs, love songs, songs of spiritual salvation, songs of revolutionary aspiration—and the range was broader than at any other time in the history of black American music and culture. This creative freedom was enabled, in essence, because of the level of street protest that made it clear that black aspirations, no matter how contradictory, would not be limited by white constraints.

Authenticity was a significant part of the ethos of black artistic expression at the time, and the musicians were engaging this ideal at its extreme. By engaging and beseeching their audience to take action—James Brown's 1970 recording of "Get Up, Get Into It, Get Involved" as one such example—radical-minded musicians challenged both the artist and the audience to take action on behalf of the black community. For a brief moment, black musical entertainers were in large numbers invested in social issues and were beginning to be seen as artist-activists themselves.

At this flashpoint of outrage, one would find the radical jazz artists and poets who sought to spark the flame of uprising through their words and sounds. As revolutionary artists they took on an identity that transcended aesthetics as their art reached into the realm of activism. Abiodun Oyewole, one of the original Last Poets, found himself at a crossroads between his radical music and his personal politics:

> I wasn't happy being a poet. I began to feel that being a poet was a pitiful example of being a revolutionary. So, you write a poem, you get up onstage and you say it, you're a revolutionary. Wow, I mean come on, give me a break. Especially when somebody down the block just fed about ten kids with food stamps. Come on, give me a break, there's more to do here. So I decided to do more. I joined the Harlem Committee for Self-Defense, which was one of the many offshoots of the Black Panthers. My association with them led to the cops harassing me and caused me to leave New York City. I left tired of violence and fear, and fled to North Carolina where I got deep into Afrocentricism and African culture.[14]

Oyewole's experience represents one of the fundamental conflicts of cultural activism. He makes clear an important issue of this book, that at some point it is ridiculous to speak of an artist simply rolling over in a loft, penning some stanzas of indignation, while others are risking their lives nightly with police mandates to harass and kill them with impunity. Yet at some level, there is a common motivation between the artist and the activist, between the radical artist and the revolutionary fighter, that moves each forward toward a change that may or may not come.

Another serious question emerges from Oyewole's experience: how does one reconcile revolutionary fantasy with revolutionary work? To advocate for social change as an artist while performing and recording in pursuit of personal gain is a contradiction every conscious artist eventually must come to terms with. During the black power era, the situation was magnified. To advocate the militant overthrow of the US government while simultaneously seeking its bourgeois trappings was an insoluble contradiction that eventually served to drain the spirit of the struggle. Oyewole eventually "grew up" and out of his militancy. Yet the issues remained:

I was truly in line with my reality back then, which was that there was going to be a revolution and that all of this stuff was going to be ashes and we were going to have a brand-new world. I was truly on a mission in terms of just dealing with what I felt I must be about, and monetary things didn't have very much to do with it. Now I'm grown, I've got children. I've got responsibilities, and I must try to fulfill them.[15]

Black power was a transformative movement in the lives of many young people. A spirit of change overtook a generation, as Oyewole recalled. Life went on, yet the issues that sparked the revolution remain. To what extent is the revolution a lifetime process? Angela Davis has stated that "when one commits oneself to the struggle, it must be for a lifetime." If one were to look at the overall arc of Abiodun Oyewole's career, his life has been oriented toward social justice in some way. One does not need a political organization nor a musical group to work for social change.

The Revolution Will Not Be Transmitted

In the current climate, there is another generation of young people seeking a radical restructuring of society, though they are living in a world entirely different from the one discussed here. While the daily lives of working-class youth of color today are fraught with the stark realities of economic oppression, police brutality, hostile health-care and educational institutions, and the emotional burdens of despair and constant danger, the sense of hope—the millenarian mythos of redemption so eloquently presented by Dr. Martin Luther King Jr.—remains for many a distant wisp of idealism.

Is there a concurrent creative musical response to the injustices occurring in modern times? Is there another Bob Dylan, another Marvin Gaye, another Lumpen laying in the wings? If so, it is likely to be a localized, decentralized phenomenon, as the corporate media market operatives have effectively hijacked the discourse of social justice, replacing it with a parade of the trivialities of pop culture.

The youth of today are not exposed to high-profile volunteer racial-justice organizations, such as the Student Nonviolent Coordinating Committee, the US Organization, or the Black Panther Party for Self-Defense. The Nation of Islam remains an established and respected institution of black self-help and community building, but its role and influence have diminished from its zenith in the 1960s. The youth today do not experience the cohesion of a geographically or economically self-contained black community. Class fractures and the glorification of individualism and "getting mine" have driven deep fissures into the once-salient notion of a black community. "We Shall Overcome" has succumbed to "Get Rich or Die Tryin'." The increase of ethnic heterogeneity in urban areas has coerced many people into defensive self-definitions, into spurious claims of what type of community they are *against*, as opposed to what inclusive visions they are *for*.

The youth of today are also deprived of a sympathetic media, which no longer romanticizes the antiestablishment "rebel without a cause" as it had done in the past. Privileged children of the rich are given vast amounts of air time, reality television shows and endless gossip channels proliferate, while struggling, working-class rebel youth are caged, rendered invisible, or, in the case of rappers, are trivialized or demonized as sociopaths. Rebel youth of today must assert their own images into the world.

For young people who wish to find a channel for their natural inclination toward humanity, peace, and community, finding their own image in the media means in essence turning off the radio and the television and seeking out or creating their own progressive, interactive spaces. For the millions involved in the 2011 Arab Spring and Occupy movements, young people worldwide chose to build their own institutions of communication, and their actions have had an impact on global politics. For the African American community to build a collective consciousness, to build a foundation of resistance against their collective forces of submission, a marked change in the culture might be as important as economic reforms.

There have been moments when the methods of social control (now effectively operationalized as cultural control) are temporarily ruptured. During the rise of rap music in the mid-1980s, emergent cable companies did not exert sophisticated control over the messages that surfaced in rap videos. Consequently, there was a time in the late 1980s when conscious rap music had high visibility and the national cable companies gave time and space to Afrocentric, politically astute, positive rap videos. As a result, organizations such as Louis Farrakhan's revamped Nation of

Islam were given new prominence, as well as Afrika Bambaataa's Zulu Nation, X-Clan's Blackwatch, and other black political formations who were included in the chorus of rap voices witnessed on mainstream rap outlets such as Music Television (MTV), Black Entertainment Television (BET), and Video Hits One (VH1).

When Boots Riley of the rap group the Coup was starting his career in 1993, he discovered that he could get his edgy, anticapitalist rap videos aired on BET nationwide by producing on a shoestring budget and shipping his videos on a VHS tape directly to BET. In today's climate of intense industry control, the radically anticorporate rap group, which consistently packs houses worldwide and ships records in the hundreds of thousands, has virtually no chance of being heard or seen on corporate-controlled radio or television.

As rap labels and artists went national, they gradually gave in to bottom-line ethics, and, whether deliberate or not, each appears to have conspired to eliminate all but their most superficial party music from their repertoire. To enjoy a mix of music with a variety of messages is one of the hallmarks of effective cultural production. However, the mainstream musical menu has eliminated nearly all vestiges of social critique. If but a few samples of antiestablishment music surfaced, they would go a long way toward balancing the thematic range of popular music, allowing people to make their own judgements about social consciousness, sacrifice, social change, or accommodation. If one were to eliminate 99 percent of the critical perspectives that one might be exposed to in the media environment, one's own moral muscles would begin to atrophy. This is what has happened to the black popular music industry in its hegemony over the minds and aspirations of unsuspecting generations of party people. The rapper Paris made this explicitly clear in an April 2007 essay:

> If Def Jam or Interscope or any of these other large culture-defining companies issued a blanket decree that they would only support material and artists with positive messages then 99% of those making music now would switch up to accommodate. That's real talk. I'm not saying these labels should (or would), but if they did, gangstas would stop being gangstas and misogynists would stop being misogynists at the drop of a DIME. Many artists are like children, and most will say and do what is expected of them in order to

benefit financially. And although there is definite self-examination that needs to take place within the artist community, the lion's share of the blame falls on the enablers who only empower voices of negativity. Record labels and commercial radio often use the excuse that they are "responding to the streets" and that they are "giving the people what they want." BULLSHIT. They dictate the taste of the streets, and people can't miss what they never knew. The fact is that there are conscious decisions made by the big business and entertainment elite daily about what to present to the masses—and it is from those choices that we are allowed to decide what we do and do not like. Who presents the music that callers are invited to "make or break" on the radio? That callers are invited to "vote on" on T.V.? Who decides on what makes it to the store shelves or the airwaves at all? Like I said, life imitates art, and pseudo-black culture is determined by those other than us every day. Walk into any rap label or urban radio station and you can count the number of black employees on one hand.[16]

The dearth of industry executives with a working sensitivity to the realities and sensibilities of the working-class African American community has become a source of great frustration, miscommunication, and outrage in recent years. In 2007 the child star, actress, and recording artist Keke Palmer signed a major music deal with Atlantic Records. The African American teenager was already a veteran of film and television, with the lead role in the critically acclaimed Oprah Winfrey–produced 2006 film *Akeelah and the Bee* among her credits. However, once she was signed to the music label, she was told that her market was "urban" and that she would have to sing, dress, and perform in a sexually provocative way. As Palmer recalled, "From the very beginning Atlantic's A&R representative tried to get me to record inappropriate music, and my parents and I resisted." Palmer and her family were told by the label, "We will not promote her unless she records urban music." As Bruce Banter wrote in a commentary on the subject, "Atlantic Records Tries to Pimp Out 14yr Old Actress": "They knew her age when they signed her, they came to her after seeing *Akeelah and the Bee* and begged her to sign, so why did they not think that she could really be like Akeelah, a good girl?" As Palmer put it: "I am only a kid, my parents would kill me if I sang stuff like that." Yet Atlantic A&R executive Mike Caren claimed that he knew what Keke Palmer's market was, and refused to promote her teen-friendly, positive approach to pop R&B music. Her album's worth of polished pop and R&B music has since died on the vine.[17]

The Palmer experience sheds light on the plight of so many younger entertainers of color who do not have the pedigree of Palmer yet would have preferred a more wholeseome (read: accurate) image in their media presence. They are subject to a pernicious process of artistic control based on narrow stereotypes of the behavior and priorities of people in communities of color. The established power brokers in the entertainment industry have little to worry about from outraged artists and their supporters, because the negative, violent, uncritical, materialist images of African Americans are selling so well. This has prompted one commentator to claim that "BET Has Become the New KKK" because of its incessant promotion of artists that advocate violence and self-destructive behavior in the black community. As Dr. Boyce Watkins, a self-proclaimed "hip-hop insider" writes about the 2011 BET Awards:

> The executive committee for the BET Awards made the interesting decision to give the greatest number of award nominations to Lil Wayne, the man who said that he would (among other things) love to turn a woman out, murder her and send her dead body back to her boyfriend. Oh yea, he also said that he would kill little babies, have sex with every girl in the world, carry a gun on his hip and "leave a ni**a's brains on the street."
>
> The music might be considered simple entertainment were it not for the fact that millions of Black youth who had their history stolen during slavery actually look to Hip-Hop music to tell them how to dress, talk, think, act and live. There is no high school speaker more popular than a Hip-Hop star.
>
> The Ku Klux Klan has been regularly criticized for encouraging violence against African Americans and terrorizing our community. But the truth is that the Klan doesn't have much power anymore, and their thirst for African American blood seems to have waned a bit. At the same time, Lil Wayne and artists like him have made a habit of encouraging Black men to shoot one another, to abuse or murder women, to consume suicidal amounts of drugs and alcohol and to engage in irresponsible, deadly sexual behavior.[18]

Dr. Watkins is making an important point about how out of touch the mass producers of African American culture have become from the communities that they serve. Until a popular movement—"a Resistance Culture"—emerges in which serious critiques of the process emerge in the mainstream, and strong, positive images of youth of color with morality, dignity, and courage are sustained, more and more Lil' Waynes will be celebrated and more and more Keke Palmers will be pimped out. It may take a social movement on the scale of the late 1960s black awakening before such changes take place.

The whitewashing of the black entertainment industry of critical perspectives was done with a COINTELPRO-like efficiency. Clouded by the euphemisms of "market driven" and "regional tastes" and "freedom of speech," negative music in the form of overused stereotypical black gangsterism has long since passed a point of minstrelsy. Young, ambitious blacks (and others) gleefully perform gangsta-face in order to procure marginal monies from corporate benefactors who thrive on perpetuating the adolescence of black cultural forms. Was black popular music deliberately whitewashed and left devoid of critical content by some racialist agenda to keep blacks perpetually disenfranchised and dysfunctional? Or was it simply a result of the market forces of capitalism? Often these two appear to be one in the same.

"Change It All"

Some of the most charismatic and dedicated activist-artists are doing the work of entertaining as well as serving their community. Despite their millions of record sales and potential for sustained mainstream popularity, they do their political work under the mainstream radar.

In the contemporary context, the urge for antiestablishment music is as strong and articulate as it has ever been. The theme of an oncoming social revolution is described vividly by a number of artists who have dedicated themselves to a life of consciousness, culture, activism, and social change. Michael Franti has earned a reputation as one of the leaders of a new wave of courageous artist-activists who are seeking a new way for people to visualize themselves in a just world. He made the following observations on the title track of his 2005 album, *Yell Fire*:

> A revolution never come with a warning
> A revolution never sends you an omen
> A revolution just arrive like the morning
> Ring the alarm, we come to wake up the snoring.

While Oakland native Michael Franti has been belting verses similar to this ever since his metal thrashing days in the Beatnigs back in the 1980s, one does not need to rock out to share his sentiments. The Bay Area–based R&B singer Goapele became well known for her haunting, sublime love songs on her first national hit record *Even Closer* in 2002. Once she obtained a recording contract from Sony, Goapele took a bold step and wrote the title song of her Columbia album, *Change It All*. Arranged with the subtle complexity and beguiling sensuousness of most of her music, her impassioned lyrics and lush tone recall music from Marvin Gaye's *What's Going On* album:

> Basically there are people left out
> From living comfortably can't we figure it out
> I've been waiting restlessly for the words to a song
> That could change it all, change it all, change it all.

Goapele's sentiments are not uncommon. To hear these sentiments on a larger scale was and remains the hope of some of the greatest artists who ever lived. When Billie Holiday sang "Strange Fruit" in 1939, she undoubtedly hoped that she could curb the scourge of lynching that was so prominent in the South; when John Lennon and Yoko Ono sang from their bedroom "Give Peace a Chance," they were pleading in the most personal way for a change from the heart from within. When Stevie Wonder produced the song "Happy Birthday" and toured in support of his *Hotter Than July* album in 1980, it was to promote his vision of making Dr. Martin Luther King's birthday a national holiday (a campaign for which he was successful). When KRS-One and his massive crew of New York rappers produced their "Self-Destruction" video in 1989, they were clearly seeking—through the song and all it symbolized—to stop the violence in hip-hop. Similarly, the West Coast Rap All-Stars sought to check their own violent lifestyles in their 1990 collaboration "We're All in the Same Gang."

What if a song could in fact change it all? If only there truly was a method that could rally a generation to take action in their own

interests. The sentiments for a youth-based movement of major propor-
tions already exist in the United States and in many places around the
globe. Can a cultural movement become the spark for a sustained surge
of social justice?

One might conclude that economic and political inequality and privilege are so entrenched that people can only turn to the cultural front
to imagine a large-scale swing of the political pendulum. But waiting
on the world to change is not going to do it. Perhaps Boots Riley was on
to something when he came up with his 2007 album title: *Pick a Bigger
Weapon*. Or as Talib Kweli put it in a 2007 rap, "Bushonomics," "Revolution requires participation."[19]

Obama and the Change Generation

The year 2008 represented a generational shift in national politics as
well as the nature of participatory electoral politics, as the most diverse
generation in the nation's history participated in the election of the first
African American president of a majority white country, Barack Hussein Obama. To a large degree, many of the issues that had ripped apart
the social fabric of the United States in 1968 were still in play and were
symbolically confronted and woven together in the watershed events of
2008. The bitter racial divide of the 1960s that compelled so many African Americans to actively engage in armed self-defense of their communities also spawned a generation of activity in the realm of community
activism and local electoral politics. While Obama tactically avoided the
representation of the black radical era and the black radical movement,
he was clearly a product of it.

While Obama's message of racial transcendence was and is drawn from
Martin Luther King's laudable vision of equality for all, Obama's direct
speaking style does not imitate the southern Christian church dialect.
Obama does not speak like a southern Baptist preacher. In fact, Obama's
oratorical technique borrows directly from the cadence and syntax of the
veteran Harlem street orator Malcolm X. Obama captured the imagination of a nation that was desperate for change. He rallied those who desired
a respite from the famously incompetent George Bush administration, as
well as those who sought a complete, total change in America's political landscape. Obama presented himself as a new-era Abraham Lincoln,

bringing right and left together while seeking to demolish the racial caste system. Obama may have succeeded in making a leap around the race mountain, but inequality exists, and the fallout from his failed "change" mantra could result in a backlash that goes on for further generations.

It is interesting to note that during the Obama campaign, a number of rappers and black entertainers produced tributes and performed in support of his candidacy. Once he was elected, however, the music retreated (much like Obama's policy promises toward the working class) back to the shallow status quo. Further, the television and movie industry dropped the ball on the opportunity to reflect the racial diversity seen in the White House every day, and there remains a palpable dearth of characters, television hosts, and leading men and women of color on the airwaves. Despite the monumental social transformation of electing an African American to become the president of the United States, a cultural movement that acknowledges the diversity and humanity of the people in the United States has not materialized. It will take more than politicians to generate lasting social change in America.

Occupy and Arab Spring

A worldwide protest movement that involved nonviolent expressions of a collective desire for human equality took place in 2011. That spring an "awakening" swept through a number of Middle Eastern countries— Tunisia, Egypt, Bahrain, and others—that involved what appeared to be spontaneous mass mobilizations of thousands. They were typically peaceful human expressions of a collectively expressed hope for basic freedoms and demands for the removal of totalitarian rulers. The repressive reactions of the governments, and intrigues by foreign empires, have thwarted the initial thrust of these movements. Nevertheless they are worthy of discussion.

The movements were spawned by youth who utilized modern technology—social networking—to form alternative communication networks that forged an imagined community based on shared humanity and a shared quest for basic respect and personal freedoms. Massive nonviolent protests served to oust the decadent, outdated authoritarian leaders in Tunisia and Egypt, which inspired millions more across the region to act, with varying results.

A case can be made that this process began when Barack Obama spoke in Cairo in 2009, reaching out to the Muslim world and affirming the basic humanity of a quarter of the world's population, providing a pathway for millions to envision a global community devoid of the outdated barriers constructed by warmongers, profiteers, racists, and colonialists. A case can also be made that this movement was taking place regardless of the actions of any civic or national leaders, and that the people—connected horizontally as equals on a global scale like never before—were doing this entirely on their own.

In the fall of 2011 a group of protestors gathered at the steps of the New York Stock Exchange and began a sustained sit-in to express their outrage at the vast inequality that exists between corporate owners and workers in the United States. The dual economic crises of millions of home foreclosures and financial-industry meltdowns—banks that were bailed out by the US government but crippled the finances of millions of workers—have caused what many see as a permanent rift between the moneyed and the labor classes. A broad cross-section of America's workers, not as racially stratified as before and increasingly economically unstable, have found a voice in what was termed the Occupy Movement. The Occupy Wall Street protests spawned similar actions across the country and worldwide in solidarity with Occupy and Arab Spring civil protests.

In addition to organizing events that emphasized the human face of the economic oppression taking place, many of the groups sought to de-emphasize the idea of centralized leadership. Some peculiar aspects of the movement included the fact that most of the events took place without leaders and often came together through consensus meetings held in public, on public grounds occupied by the protestors. Often, recently laid-off middle-class workers and people who had been homeless for years were choosing to share the same space and admit that they shared many of the same issues, as "the 99 percent" shared similar hopes for basic respect and economic opportunity. Many of the Occupy sites developed their own forms of personal services, food services, health services, and sanitation services that allowed the people, all the people, to be treated with dignity in the absence of corporate, profit-driven constrictions. In many ways, the methods of the Occupy protestors were revolutionary, not simply as strategic sites of protest but in the cultural transformation of daily interactions, as they were providing a deeper critique of the power apparatus than any chant or sign or police tear-gas canister thrown. Occupy was creating "free space" for a generation of people to envision and imagine an entirely new type of liberation, one free of hierarchical, corporate control.

The corporate media initially tried to ignore the phenomena, then when some cases of police excess made national news, the media tried to ridicule and marginalize the protestors. When the movement grew to more than nine hundred cities worldwide, action was taken to seize control through brute-force police activity to quell the nonviolent, civil, public protests. In one case in Oakland, California, OPD threw tear gas canisters on peaceful occupiers of the downtown plaza in front of city hall, late in the evening of October 25, 2011, spawning a graphic melee that went viral on social media within minutes.

In response, city officials retreated in embarrassment, and the Occupiers announced a general strike, in which the entire population was invited to spend the day in downtown Oakland on November 1, to take children out of classes, to skip work, and occupy the central city with an all-day festival, followed by a march to the nearby Port of Oakland to protest the economic exploitation taking place at the commercial freight transportation hub. The day was a spectacle, as free food, free music, and free people thrived in the streets of the city for hours, without police presence or a profit motive to contain the revelers. For a moment, a free space had been created. The loudspeakers at the central plaza blasted James Brown's "The Payback" (an anthem of the Occupy Movement if there ever was one) in rotation with other celebratory dance songs. Angela Davis was at the event, along with thousands of others:

> The general strike—I think that when we experience such moments, we have to preserve them for the revolutionary promise that they offer. Obviously revolution is not going to happen in a single day or a single year but there are moments that inspire us. And I can remember on that day and looking around at the people at that gathering, the march. . . . It was multiracial, it was multiethnic, it was multigender, it was multigenerational, and there was something very palpable about the community of resistance that we were forging.[20]

Davis referred to a community of resistance that was growing in size, intensity, and clarity. She was acknowledging that a new generation is beginning to believe that it is capable of a generating new type of human revolution. If one were to study closely the rhetoric of the rebels of the 1960s, many of their demands were similar to those of the Occupiers, who sought human dignity and the ability to live lives free of discrimination and free of corporate economic and social controls.

On Revolution . . .

During the early years of the Black Panther Party, Minister of Defense Huey Newton made unequivocal statements about the necessity of political violence in the challenge to the power structure. "Kill the slave master, destroy him utterly, move against him with implacable fortitude. Break his oppressive power by any means necessary." This was the rhetorical forge that sharpened the spearhead of Panther politics and garnered the attention of the young masses—and the wrath of the state. A revolution required revolutionaries, ready and willing to take on the awesome power of the Western ruling classes. Young people by the thousands followed the call. The Lumpen members all answered this call as well, long before the order to perform songs about the revolution was given to them. The Party's long-term results, as we have seen, were mixed.

In the 1990 documentary *Eyes on the Prize*, former Black Panther Party chairman Bobby Seale explained the purpose of the organization in terms of revolution: "Now a lot of people call revolution, a confrontation. Really, what Huey and I meant by revolution was the need to revolve more political power, more economic power, back into the hands of the people, that's really what revolution is."[21] While this larger view may not jibe with some of the militant rhetoric used by the Panthers during their heyday, the idea remains that Bobby Seale and the Panthers were addressing social inequalities through the means that were at their disposal at the time. The times required a fearless challenge to the power structure, one that told the world that their humanity would not be denied and that they were prepared to fight for their freedom "by any means necessary."

Over the years, both Seale and the tenor of the times have changed, and the nature of the forces against the masses of underprivileged people have changed. In the way that Huey Newton grew to understand that Black Nationalism was but a starting point for his organizational philosophy, he constantly redefined the Party's vision as events steered the Party. Newton's ideas of social change evolved to the point where he could foretell many global shifts generations hence:

> In 1966 we called ourselves a Black Nationalist Party because we thought that nationhood was the answer. . . . Shortly after that we decided that what we really needed was revolutionary nationalism, that is, nationalism plus socialism. After analyzing conditions a little more we found . . . we had to unite with the peoples of the world so we called ourselves Internationalists. . . . But then . . . we found that everything is in a state of transformation. . . . These transformations . . . require us to call ourselves "intercommunalists" because nations have been transformed into communities of the world.[22]

Huey Newton, at a speech at Boston College in 1970, was beginning to move the Party toward a recognition of a global community some forty years ahead of the people's uprising worldwide sparked by the Arab Spring. Newton's concept involved the sharing of resources on a community level, in a post-national society that values all members equally, decentralizes power, and emphasizes the interconnectedness of all people. In a sense, the collective people's movements of 2011 and their imagined remaking of social movements can be thought of as a variation of Newton's idea of intercommunalism.

While short-lived movements at the time, the opening of the Occupy movement and Arab Spring events had set in motion some larger, greater opportunities to rethink the meaning of radical social change, a redefinition of community that transcends the traditional modes of protest and demands. As Grace Lee Boggs has stated:

> We are at the point of a cultural revolution in ourselves and in our institutions that is as far reaching as the transition from hunting and gathering to agriculture eleven thousand years ago, and from agriculture and industry a few hundred years ago.
>
> The time has come for us to reimagine everything. We have to reimagine work, and go away from labor, we have to reimagine revolution and get beyond protest, we have to reimagine revolution and

think not only about the change in our institutions but the changes we have to make in ourselves.[23]

In a far-reaching panel discussion between Boggs and Angela Davis in March 2012, the two embarked on a discussion of how to go about reimagining a world in which humans are not fractured by the obligations of work only to be forced to find fulfillment by demanding higher wages rather than demanding a better way to live and work. They spoke of the need to rethink not just environmental destruction, but food politics and how what we eat and how the way we obtain our food reflects upon who we are as human beings; to not just rethink health-care reform, but to remake how we care for people and how we link generations with our elders in a mutually helpful form. These human questions have the possibility of transforming how we deal with trivialities of political contests and economic mandates. How does one begin this reimagining process? Davis said:

> Of course we find ourselves in a period with rising unemployment. The tendency is simply to demand more jobs. Also with education, the tendency is to demand greater access to education, but we don't necessarily ask ourselves what needs to be transformed about education, and what needs to be transformed in the way we conceive of work.
>
> Through our labor we externalize our own creative impulses. And that actually, work should be fulfilling. Workers should possibly be able to have the same relationship to that which they produce as artists have to their art.[24]

Could workers truly have a relationship to their work as viable as artists have with their art? Could the muse of the artist help to frame the nature of work, of society, of civilization? This has been part of the premise of rock and roll since the 1960s.

Carlos Santana explored this in a conversation with Brian Copeland in 2011:

> But one thing that I knew [in the 60s] was that things were not going to be the same between young people and the United States government, because we realized that we have a different kind of power than the Pentagon. We have the power to put the pressure

on the United States government and we got them out of Vietnam. We the hippies. When I say hippies I mean conscious people. Some people try to stereotype the hippies as people who just get loaded, and wear rainbow shirts and they don't know nothing. Hippie people are conscious people. In Hitler's time it was the beatniks and bohemians in the French Resistance. The hippies are the ones, along with the Black Panthers, who made a change in the United States forevermore.

I like to see the young people be a little more passionate about putting pressure on brother Barack Obama, and promise what he said he was going to do, which is to stop the war, and spend more money on education than incarceration. Because as brother Marvin Gaye said, "War is not the answer, only love can conquer hate."

I would invite brother Barack Obama to listen to *What's Going On* by Marvin Gaye from beginning to end, and don't be so concerned about what the Republicans be thinking. Follow the voice of your heart who got you there in the first place, and before they kick you out, or you stay there, fulfill the promise that you made.[25]

It is perhaps a reach to imagine that a song or some music could transform a collective consciousness of a people, or of a leader. Of the far-reaching visions put forth by the people in this book, many harbored ideals that were just as far-fetched, and because masses of people saw their viability, the ideas took hold. The ideas went beyond Marxist or capitalist, they were seeking a greater connection, a connection to humanity, to the Earth, to their lives and families that was and is free of oppression. During the black power years, those ideas were revolutionary, and the revolutionaries were from all walks of life.

A new vision of human relationships is evolving that is post-capitalist and post-Marxist and is growing daily on the basis of a shared humanity. Che Guevara, writing "On Socialism and Man in Cuba" in 1965, wrote: "At the risk of seeming ridiculous, let me say that the true revolutionary is guided by great feelings of love. It is impossible to think of a genuine revolutionary lacking this quality."[26] Guevara may have been seeking that connection that inspires and unites all of humanity in a shared struggle for coexistence based on mutual respect. One day, perhaps, the inspiration of the artist, the musician, the source of their muse will be studied as a methodology for structuring a society never before seen, or heard.

Conclusion

Every song tells a story. Some songs not only reveal stories and provide storytelling narratives, but they generate stories—legends—of their own making. Curtis Mayfield, Aretha Franklin, James Brown: they were a part of the movement, of an awakening, of a revolution. Their songs tell a story of a people in motion. Soul music tells us a story of social change in America.

The Black Panthers were a part of a cultural revolution in America, in which a dispossessed and disheartened population redefined itself and staked a claim to self-determination. The Lumpen group is a crystallization of the revolutionary culture that the Party helped to create. Through music, the potential for cultural memory always exists, so that the power of soul music may one day take form again in the manifestation of a people's movement.

To write a book about the Black Panther Party is no simple task. The organization was far too vast an enterprise to be properly captured in one study. There are, however, a number of worthy volumes that have successfully captured the nature of various elements of the Party, and my hope is that there will be many more. This work was only partially about the Black Panther Party; it has sought to merge the important research being done on the Party as a political organization with an examination of the popular culture that was profoundly affected by the Panthers in the late 1960s.

There should be further serious study of the Black Panther Party because the efforts of the leadership, the rank-and-file membership, and their nonblack supporters resonate with many of the present-day struggles people are undertaking to restructure society on terms that the masses deserve. The strategies, tactics, commitments, and countermeasures engaged in by the Party, while perhaps anachronistic in today's political climate, are certainly worthy of analysis and reflection.

Furthermore, one should realize that the Black Panthers have been studied in depth by their opposition. Those generating the forces of social control have gone the extra mile to study everything the Party leadership ever thought about doing, let alone what the Panthers were able to put into action or introduce into the public discourse. Some of the Panther Party operations may look frivolous today, such as their constitutional convention, their erratic forms of internal discipline, and their near-extortion of local businesses for donations. However, other projects were very foresighted, such as their police patrols, sickle cell anemia testing, their free busing to prisons, and their breakfast for children programs. Their fearless public presence was a watershed of cultural capital that was a necessary and perhaps inevitable outgrowth of the evolution of the black power ethos within the black community. The sharp social critique put forward by the leadership has stood the test of time as a rigorous analysis of the failings of the American enterprise. In addition, these young people from the streets had the bombast to produce an action plan for doing something to change the situation.

Perhaps most prominent, and most essential to this study, was the humanity of the Party membership, in all of its various quarters, various camps and factions, class divisions, fractious gender dynamics, infiltrations, and betrayals. It is indeed that humanity that remains a testimonial to the endurance of the human spirit and desire for justice. The sacrifices some have made for this cause are too great to mention in one volume.

To that extent, this book is dedicated to all of those Black Panther Party veterans—especially the political prisoners—and so many other like-minded spirits who are still being harassed, dehumanized, and subjected to the law enforcement apparatus for the crimes of associating with the Black Panther Party and for sharing their dreams of a just society with people with the audacity to try to bring those dreams into reality.

Acknowledgments

My family has sustained me through the entire process of this project, from graduate school to grinding out the publication. My lovely wife, Tess, and sons, Marcus and Gary, have grown along with me throughout this process and I would not have made it this far without them. My ethnic studies doctoral program classmates, in particular Jordan Gonzales, Debora Nyere da Silva, Victor Rios, Sylvia Chan, Loan Dao, Erinn Ransom, Tamara Orozco, Marcie Chin, Roberto Hernandez, Jose Palafox, Eli Barbosa, and Maristella Huerta, readily invested in my success and my gratitude to them is unbounded. I have been privileged to enjoy editorial support and encouragement from Blanche Richardson, and Professors Cornel West, Ronald Takaki, Robin D. G. Kelley, Donna Murch, Ula Taylor, Jason Ferreira, Leon Litwack, and my coconspirator in this pursuit of black power culture, Pat Thomas. I am also grateful for the guidance of my dissertation committee members, professors Robert Allen, Elaine Kim, Waldo Martin, and Leigh Raiford. To the funky and righteous writers who kept me focused and inspired: Tony Bolden, Scot Brown, Thomas Sayers Ellis, Patrick Jones, Adam Masbach, Kalamu Ya Salaam, Daphne Brooks, Darius James, DeAngelo Stearnes, and Greg Tate, keep on keepin' on. To the journalists Dennis McNally, Alec Palao, Jeff Kaliss, and Lee Hildebrand for their vast knowledge of Bay Area music and culture, to Charles Blass for his New York connections, to Harry Weinger and Alan Leeds for each sharing their knowledge of music history, to Davey D for everything he does, to the DEF Professor Dawn-Elissa Fischer for her steadfast support, to Jeff Chang for his generous time and energy, and to my homie Dr. Scot Brown, who always put the fire under me for this project, I am very grateful.

Thanks to Weyland Southon and the folks at Hard Knock Radio, and the 2000s' crew at KPFA: the late Andrea Lewis, Deverol "Syntax Era" Ross, Anita Johnson, Esther Manilla, Aimee Allison, Greg Bridges, Dennis "Spliff Skankin" Bishop, Walter Turner, Gary Baca, LapuLapu "Bruddah K" Kayumanggi, Tomic "T-Kash" Lenear, Joy Moore, Gary Niederhoff, David Gans, JR Valrey, Ken Pruitt, Pedro Reyes, Ventura "Mr. Chooch" Longoria, Sandra "Giggles" Lemus, Frank Sterling, Mickey Mayes, Norma "La Brava" Scheurkogel and Gabriel Mireau, Luis Medina, and Noelle Hanrahan. Thanks to the funkateers that sustained me through the madness: Funkyman, Marlon "Dr. Illinstine" Kemp, Anthony "Dave-id K-os" Bryant, Phil "PTFI" Jones, Sam "Zootzilla" Brown, Phil LaMoureaux, Donte Harrison, "Kashif the Number One James Brown Fan," Calvin Lincoln, Mark McLemore, Ryan "Grizzly" Scott, Neil Austinson, Lisa Bautista, Bobby Easton, Seth Neblett, Steve Arrington, Genevieve McDevitt-Mauldin, Femi Andrades, Tamika Nicole, Chiedza "Lady Chi" Kundidzora, Ronald "Ronkat" Spearman and his Katdelic band, Gina Hall, and the good doctor, George Clinton.

I am grateful also for the many musicians—Danny Ray Thompson of Sun Ra's Arkestra, Marshal Thompson of the Chi-Lites, Alfred "Pee Wee" Ellis, William "Bootsy" Collins, Fred Wesley, Jabo Starks, Dawn Silva, Chuck D, Gil Scott-Heron, Oscar "Paris" Jackson Jr., Archie Ivy, Richie Havens, Juma Sultan, Billy Cox, Charles Wright and the late Jimmy Castor; to Mack Ray Henderson, Minor Williams, David Levinson and Thomas Wallace of the Lumpen band—and local artists—Lenny Williams, Michael Cooper, Rodger Collins, Rustee Allen, Vaetta "Vet" Stewart, Skyler Jett, Ken Pruitt, Larry Vann, and Andre Russell—who shared their recollections with me. I am truly grateful.

I am extremely thankful to former Black Panther Party members Emory Douglas, David Hilliard, Ericka Huggins, William "Billy X" Jennings, Elbert "Big Man" Howard, and Walter Turner for their generous insights. My deepest respect goes out to Mumia Abu-Jamal, who took the time to read my dissertation "The Lumpen: Music on the Front Lines of the Black Revolution" and stepped to the plate and advocated for the project. Much gratitude to Greg Morozumi, Boots Riley, Justin Richmond, Nishat Kurwa, Jessica Damian, George Livingston, Susan Betz, Michelle Williams, Frances Goldin, and the ever-so-patient Sam Stoloff.

And my deepest gratitude goes to the members of the Lumpen: William Calhoun, Clark Bailey, Michael Torrence, and James Mott. As talented and bold as they were in their youth, their integrity and quiet commitment to their people stands out beyond the beats. In their humble yet principled ways they are some of the most impressive men that I have ever met.

In memoriam: this book is dedicated to Professor Ronald Takaki, who was my first and greatest scholarly influence as an undergraduate at UC–Berkeley in the 1980s. His dedication to the education of the people had a deep impact on my professional identity.

Finally, my late father, Ted Vincent, author of five books about black history and culture, was an unofficial guide for this entire work. While he was able to read the dissertation, his hand has been on all of my writing, and I trust this will make him proud.

Sources

Books and Periodicals

Abu-Jamal, Mumia. *We Want Freedom: A Life in the Black Panther Party.* Cambridge, MA: South End Press, 2004.

Ahmad, Muhammad. *We Will Return in the Whirlwind: Black Radical Organizations 1960–1975.* Chicago: Charles H. Kerr Publishing Company, 2007.

———. "The League of Revolutionary Black Workers: A Historical Study." *History Is a Weapon,* www.historyisaweapon.com/defcon1/rbwstudy.html.

Alkebulan, Paul. *Survival Pending Revolution: The History of the Black Panther Party.* Tuscaloosa: University of Alabama Press, 2007.

Allen, Robert. *Black Awakening in Capitalist America.* Trenton, NJ: Africa World Press, 1990 (1969).

Apthecker, Bettina. *The Morning Breaks: The Trial of Angela Davis* 2nd edition. Ithaca, NY: Cornell University Press, 1999.

Austin, Curtis J. *Up Against the Wall: Violence in the Making and Unmaking of the Black Panther Party.* Fayetteville: University of Arkansas Press, 2006.

Awkward, Michael. *Soul Covers: Rhythm and Blues Remakes and the Struggle for Artistic Identity (Aretha Franklin, Al Green, Phoebe Snow).* Durham, NC: Duke University Press, 2007.

Bailey, Clark. Telephone interviews with author, November 24 and 29, 2004.

Baldwin, James. *The Fire Next Time*. Austin, TX: Hold, Rinehart and Winston, 1990.

Ballard, Hank. "Cliff White Jacket Notes." In *James Brown: CD of JB II*. Polydor 831-700-2, 1992.

Baraka, Amiri. *Raise, Race, Rays, Raze: Essays Since 1965*. New York: Random House, 1971.

———. *The Autobiography of LeRoi Jones*. New York: Lawrence Hill Books, 1997 (1984).

Baraka, Amiri, and Larry Neal, eds. *Black Fire: An Anthology of Afro American Writing*. Baltimore: Black Classic Press, 2007 (1968).

Barbour, Floyd, ed. *The Black Power Revolt: A Collection of Essays*. New York: Collier Books, 1968.

———. *The Black 70s*. Boston: Porter Sargent, 1970.

Barlow, William. *Voice Over: The Making of Black Radio*. Philadelphia: Temple University Press, 1999.

Bass, Paul and Douglas W. Rae. *Murder in the Model City: The Black Panthers, Yale, and the Redemption of a Killer*. New York: Basic Books, 2006.

Beal, Frances M. "Black Women's Manifesto; Double Jeopardy: To Be Black and Female." New York: Third World Women's Alliance, 1969.

Bego, Mark. *Aretha Franklin: The Queen of Soul*. New York: Da Capo Press, 2001.

Belafonte, Harry with Michael Shnayerson. *My Song: A Memoir*. New York: Alfred A. Knopf, 2011.

Bennett, Lerone. Introduction to *Tradition and Conflict: Images of a Turbulent Decade 1963–1973*, curated by Dr. Mary Schmidt Campbell. New York: Studio Museum in Harlem, 1983.

The Black Panther, Black Community News Service, September 26. 1970.

The Black Panther, Black Community News Service, October 24, 1970.

The Black Panther, Black Community News Service, October 31, 1970.

The Black Panther, Black Community News Service, November 7, 1970.

The Black Panther, Black Community News Service, December 26, 1970.

The Black Panther, Black Community News Service, March 20, 1971.

The Black Panther, Black Community News Service, March 27, 1971.

The Black Panther, Black Community News Service, May 23, 1971.

The Black Panther, Black Community News Service, May 29, 1971.

Bloom, Joshua, and Waldo E. Martin Jr. *Black Against Empire: The History and Politics of the Black Panther Party.* Berkeley: University of California Press, 2013.

Booker, Chris. "Lumpenization: A Critical Error of the Black Panther Party." In *The Black Panther Party Reconsidered,* edited by Charles E. Jones. Baltimore: Black Classic Press, 1998.

Bowman, Rob. *Soulsville, U.S.A.: The Story of Stax Records.* New York: Schirmer Books, 1997.

Bratcher, Melanie E. *Words and Songs of Bessie Smith, Billie Holiday and Nina Simone: Sound Motion, Blues Spirit and African Memory.* New York: Routledge, 2007.

Brown, Elaine. *A Taste of Power: A Black Woman's Story.* New York: Anchor Books, 1992.

Brown, H. Rap (Jamil Abdullah Al-Amin). *Die Nigger Die! A Political Autobiography.* New York: Lawrence Hill Books, 2002.

Brown, James. *I Feel Good: A Memoir of a Life of Soul.* London: New American Library, 2005.

Brown, James. Telephone interview with author, August 1993.

Brown, James, and Bruce Tucker. *James Brown: The Godfather of Soul.* New York: Macmillan, 1986.

Brown, Scot. *Fighting for US: Maulana Karenga, the US Organization, and Black Cultural Nationalism.* New York: New York University Press, 2003.

Brun-Lambert, David. *Nina Simone: The Biography.* London: Arum, 2009.

Bukhari, Safiya. *The War Before: The True Life Story of Becoming a Black Panther, Keeping the Faith in Prison & Fighting for Those Left Behind.* New York: The Feminist Press at the City University of New York, 2010.

Burns, Peter. *Curtis Mayfield: People Never Give Up.* London: Sanctuary, 2003.

Cabral, Amilcar. *Unity and Struggle: Speeches and Writings.* New York: Monthly Review Press, 1979.

Calhoun, William. Telephone interviews with author, November 9, 2002, and July 21, 2007.

Carmichael, Stokely with Ekwueme Michael Thelwell. *Ready for Revolution: The Life and Struggles of Stokeley Carmichael (Kwame Ture).* New York: Scribner, 2003.

Carson, Clayborne. *In Struggle: SNCC and the Black Awakening of the 1960s*. Cambridge, MA: Harvard University Press, 1981.

Chaifetz, Ashley. "Introducing the American Dream: The Black Panther Party Survival Programs, 1966–1982." Master's thesis, Sarah Lawrence College, 2005.

Chang, Jeff. *Can't Stop, Won't Stop: A History of the Hip-Hop Generation*. New York: St. Martin's Press, 2005.

Cheney, Charise L. *Brothers Gonna Work It Out: Sexual Politics in the Golden Age of Rap Nationalism*. New York: New York University Press, 2005.

Chernoff, John Miller. *African Rhythm and African Sensibility*. Chicago: University of Chicago Press, 1979.

Churchill, Ward, and Jim Vander Wall. *The COINTELPRO Papers: Documents from the FBI's Secret Wars Against Domestic Dissent*. Boston: South End Press, 1990.

———. *Agents of Repression: The FBI's Secret Wars Against the Black Panther Party and the American Indian Movement*. Cambridge, MA: South End Press, 2002.

Citron, Stephen. *The Wordsmiths: Oscar Hammerstein 2nd and Alan Jay Lerner*. New York: Oxford University Press, 1995.

Cleaver, Eldridge. *Soul on Ice*. New York: Ramparts, 1968.

———. *Post Prison Writings and Speeches*. London: Compton Printing, 1969.

———. *Soul on Fire*. Waco, TX: World Books, 1978.

———. *Target Zero: A Life in Writing*. New York: Palgrave Macmillan, 2006.

Cleaver, Kathleen, and George Katsiaficas, eds. *Liberation, Imagination and the Black Panther Party*. New York: Routledge, 2001.

Coffey, Dennis. *Guitars, Bars and Motown Superstars*. Ann Arbor: University of Michigan Press, 2004.

Cohen, Robert. *Freedom's Orator: Mario Savio and the Radical Legacy of the 1960s*. New York: Oxford University Press, 2009.

Collins, William ("Bootsy"). Interview with the author.

Collins, Patricia Hill. *Black Feminist Thought: Knowledge, Consciousness and the Politics of Empowerment*. New York: Routledge, 2000.

———. *From Black Power to Hip-Hop: Racism, Nationalism, and Feminism*. Philadelphia: Temple University Press, 2006.

Corbett, John. *Extended Play: Sounding Off from John Cage to Dr. Funkenstein*. Durham, NC: Duke University Press, 1994.

Coyote, Peter. *Sleeping Where I Fall: A Chronicle*. Washington, DC: Counterpoint, 1998.

Cruse, Harold. *The Crisis of the Negro Intellectual*. New York: Quill, 1984 (1967).

Danielsen, Anne. *Presence and Pleasure: The Funk Grooves of James Brown and Parliament*. Middletown, CT: Wesleyan, 2006.

Darden, Robert. *People Get Ready! A New History of Black Gospel Music*. New York: Continuum, 2004.

Davis, Angela Y. *Women, Race and Class*. New York: Random House, 1981.

———. *An Autobiography*. New York: International Publishers, 1988 (1974).

———. *Blues Legacies and Black Feminism*. New York: Pantheon Books, 1998.

Davis, Miles with Quincy Troupe. *The Autobiography*. New York: Simon & Schuster, 1990.

Dixon, Aaron. *My People Are Rising: Memoir of a Black Panther Party Captain*. Chicago: Haymarket Books, 2012.

Dobkin, Matt. *I Never Loved a Man the Way I Love You: Aretha Franklin, Respect, and the Making of a Soul Music Masterpiece*. New York: St. Martin's Press, 2004.

Doggett, Peter. *There's a Riot Going On: Revolutionaries, Rock Stars, and the Rise and Fall of '60s Counter-culture*. New York: Canongate, 2007.

Douglas, Emory. "The Lumpen: Music as a Tool for Liberation." *The Black Panther*, November 7, 1970.

Douglas, Emory. Telephone interview with author, March 18, 2004.

Drake, St. Clair, and Horace R. Cayton. *Black Metropolis: A Study of Negro Life in a Northern City*. Chicago: University of Chicago Press, 1993 (1945).

Duberman, Martin B. *Paul Robeson*. New York: Alfred A. Knopf, 1988.

Durant, Sam, ed. *Black Panther: The Revolutionary Art of Emory Douglas*. New York: Rizzoli, 2007.

Dyson, Michael Eric. *Mercy, Mercy Me: The Art, Loves and Demons of Marvin Gaye*. New York: Basic Civitas Books, 2005.

Early, Gerald. *One Nation Under a Groove: Motown and American Culture*. Ann Arbor: University of Michigan Press, 2004 (1995).

Easlea, Daryl. *Everybody Dance: Chic and the Politics of Disco.* London: Helter Skelter Publishing, 2004.

Ebony. *The Black Revolution: An Ebony Special Issue.* Chicago: Johnson Publishing Company, 1970.

Edmonds, Ben. *What's Going On: Marvin Gaye and the Last Days of the Motown Sound.* Edinburgh: Mojo Books, 2001.

Edwards. Harry. *The Struggle That Must Be: An Autobiography.* New York: Macmillan, 1980.

Elbaum, Max. *Revolution in the Air: Sixties Radicals Turn to Lenin, Mao and Che.* London: Verso, 2002.

Essien-Udom, E. U. *Black Nationalism: A Search for Identity in America.* New York: Dell, 1964.

Eyerman, Ron, and Andrew Jamison. *Music and Social Movements: Mobilizing Traditions in the Twentieth Century.* Cambridge, UK: Cambridge University Press, 1998.

Fanon, Frantz. *The Wretched of the Earth.* New York: Grove Press, 1963.

———. *Black Skin, White Masks.* New York: Grove Press, 1967 (1952).

———. *Toward African Revolution (Political Essays).* New York: Grove Press, Inc, 1967.

Foner, Philip S., ed. *Paul Robeson Speaks; Writings, Speeches, Interviews 1918–1974.* New York: Brunner/Mazel Publishers, 1978.

———. *The Black Panthers Speak.* Cambridge, MA: Da Capo Press, 1995 (1970).

Fordin, Hugh. *Getting to Know Him: A Biography of Oscar Hammerstein II.* New York: Random House, 1977.

Forman, James. *The Making of Black Revolutionaries.* Seattle: University of Washington Press, 1997 (1972).

Forman, Murray. *The Hood Comes First: Race Space and Place in Rap and Hip-Hop.* Middleton, CT: Wesleyan University Press, 2002.

Fox, Ted. *In the Groove: The People Behind the Music.* New York: St. Martin's Press, 1986.

Franklin, Aretha and David Ritz. *Aretha: From These Roots.* New York: Villard Books, 1999.

Freed, Donald. *Agony in New Haven: The Trial of Bobby Seale, Erika Huggins and the Black Panther Party.* New York: Simon & Schuster, 1973.

Friedwald, Will. *Stardust Memories: A Biography of 12 of America's Most Popular Songs.* Chicago: Chicago Review Press, 2002.

Gaye, Frankie with Fred E. Basten. *Marvin Gaye, My Brother.* San Francisco: Backbeat Books, 2003.

Gayle, Addison Jr., ed. *The Black Aesthetic.* Garden City, NY: Anchor Doubleday, 1972.

Georgakas, Dan and Surkin, Marvin. *Detroit: I Do Mind Dying: A Study in Urban Revolution.* Cambridge, MA: South End Press, 1998.

George, Nelson. *Where Did Our Love Go? The Rise and Fall of the Motown Sound.* New York: St. Martin's Press, 1985.

———. *The Death of Rhythm and Blues.* New York: Penguin, 1997.

———. *Hip-Hop America.* New York: Penguin, 1999.

———. *Buppies, B-Boys, Baps and Bohos: Notes on Post-soul Culture.* New York: Da Capo Press, 2001.

George, Nelson with Alan Leeds, eds. *The James Brown Reader: 50 Years of Writing About the Godfather of Soul.* New York: Plume, 2008.

Gilroy, Paul. *The Black Atlantic: Modernity and Double-Consciousness.* Cambridge, MA: Harvard University Press, 1993.

Giovanni, Nikki. *Black Feeling, Black Talk, Black Judgement.* New York: William Morrow, 1970.

Goldman, Vivien. *The Book of Exodus: The Making and Meaning of Bob Marley and the Wailers' Album of the Century.* New York: Three Rivers Press, 2006.

Guillory, Monique and Richard C. Green, eds. *Soul: Black Power, Politics, and Pleasure.* New York: New York University Press, 1998.

Guralnik, Peter. *Sweet Soul Music: Rhythm and Blues and the Southern Dream of Freedom.* New York: Harper Collins, 1986.

Guridi, Lauryn. "Occupying Culture: A Look into the Occupy Movement." Senior thesis, Mills College Sociology Dept., 2011.

Halasa, Malu. *Elijah Muhammad: Religious Leader (Black Americans of Achievement Series).* New York: Chelsea House Publishers, 1990.

Hamilton, Linda. "On Cultural Nationalism." In *The Black Panthers Speak,* edited by Philip Foner, 51. Cambridge, MA: Da Capo Press, 1995.

Hampton, Sylvia with David Nathan. *Nina Simone: Break Down and Let It All Out.* London: Sanctuary, 2004.

Haralambos, Michael. *Soul Music: The Birth of a Sound in Black America.* New York: Da Capo Press, 1974.

Harding, Vincent. *There Is a River: The Black Struggle for Freedom in America.* New York : Harcourt Brace Jovanovich, 1981.

————. *Hope and History: Why We Must Share the Story of the Movement.* Maryknoll, NY: Orbis Books, 1990.

Haskins, James. *Profiles in Black Power.* Garden City, NY: Doubleday, 1972.

Haskins, Jim. *Power to the People: The Rise and Fall of the Black Panther Party.* New York: Simon & Schuster, 1997.

Heath, Louis G. *The Black Panther Leaders Speak: Huey P. Newton, Bobby Seale, Eldridge Cleaver and Company Speak out through the Black Panther Party's Official Newspaper.* Metuchen, NJ: Scarecrow Press, 1976.

————. *Off the Pigs! The History and Literature of the Black Panther Party.* Metuchen, NJ: Scarecrow Press, 1976.

Henderson, David. *'Scuse Me While I Kiss the Sky: The Life and Times of Jimi Hendrix.* New York: Bantam Books, 1981.

Hildebrand, Lee. Telephone interview with author, February 16, 2012.

Hilliard, David. Telephone interview with author, April 27, 2004, and November 15, 2004.

Hilliard, David, and Donald Weise, eds. *The Huey P. Newton Reader.* New York: Seven Stories Press, 2002.

Hilliard, David, Keith Zimmerman, and Kent Zimmerman. *Huey: Spirit of the Panther.* New York: Thunder's Mouth Press, 2006.

Hilliard, David, and Lewis Cole. *This Side of Glory: The Autobiography of David Hilliard and the Story of the Black Panther Party.* Chicago: Lawrence Hill, 1993.

Hinkle, Warren. "Metropoly: The Story of Oakland, California." *Ramparts Magazine,* February1966, 25.

Horne, Gerald. *Fire This Time: The Watts Uprising and the 1960s.* New York: Da Capo Press, 1997.

Howard, Elbert "Big Man." *Panther on the Prowl.* Baltimore: BCP Digital Printing, Inc., 2002.

Jackson, George. *Blood in My Eye.* Baltimore: Black Classic Press, 1990 (1972).

Jackson, George. *Soledad Brother: The Prison Letters of George Jackson.* Chicago: Lawrence Hill Books, 1994.

Jamal, Hakim A. *From the Dead Level: Malcolm X and Me.* New York: Random House, 1972.

Jeffries, Judson. *Huey P. Newton: The Radical Theorist.* Jackson: University Press of Mississippi, 2002.

Jennings, William (Billy X). Telephone interview with author, April 18, 2004, and November 22, 2004.

Jones, Charles E., ed. *The Black Panther Party Reconsidered*. Baltimore: Black Classic Press, 1998.

Jones, LeRoi. *Blues People: Negro Music in White America*. New York: Morrow, 1963.

———. *Black Music*. New York: William Morrow, 1970.

Jones, LeRoi, and Larry Neal, eds. *Black Fire: An Anthology of Afro-American Writing*. New York: William Morrow, 1968.

Joseph, Jamal. *Panther Baby*. Chapel Hill, NC: Algonquin, 2012.

Joseph, Jamal. *Tupac Shakur: Legacy*. New York: Atria Books, 2006.

Joseph, Peniel E., ed. *The Black Power Movement: Rethinking the Civil-Rights Black Power Era*. New York: Routledge, 2006.

———. *Waiting 'Til the Midnight Hour: A Narrative History of Black Power in America*. New York: Henry Holt and Co, 2007.

Karenga, Ron. *The Quotable Karenga*. Los Angeles: US Organization pamphlet, 1967.

———. "On Cultural Nationalism." In *The Black Aesthetic*, edited by Addison Gayle Jr. Garden City, NY: Anchor Doubleday, 1972.

Kelley, Robin D. G. *Race Rebels: Culture, Politics, and the Black Working Class*. New York: Free Press, 1996.

———. *Freedom Dreams: The Black Radical Imagination*. New York: Beacon Press, 2002.

Kempton, Murray. *The Briar Patch: The Trial of the Panther 21*. New York: Da Capo Press, 1997 (1973).

Khan, Chaka, with Tonya Bolden. *Chaka! Through the Fire*. Emmaus, PA: Rodale, 2003.

Kitwana, Bakari. *The Hip-Hop Generation: Young Blacks and the Crisis in African American Culture*. New York: Basic Civitas Books, 2002.

Knight, Michael Muhammad. *The Five Percenters: Islam, Hip-Hop and the Gods of New York*. Oxford. England: One World Publications, 2007.

Kofsky, Frank. *Black Nationalism and the Revolution in Music*. New York: Pathfinder Press, 1970.

Kuumba, M. Bahati. *Gender and Social Movements*. Walnut Creek, CA: Alta Mira Press, 2001.

Lazerow, Jama, and Yohuru Williams, eds. *In Searth of the Black Panther Party: New Perspectives on a Revolutionary Movement*. Durham, NC: Duke University Press, 2006.

Levinson, David. Telephone interview with author, December 14, 2004.

Lewis, George. *A Power Stronger Than Itself: The AACM and American Experimental Music*. Chicago: University of Chicago Press, 2008.

Lipsitz, George. *Dangerous Crossroads: Popular Music, Postmodernism and the Poetics of Place*. London: Verso, 1994.

Major, Reginald. *A Panther Is a Black Cat*. New York: W. Morrow, 1971.

Makeba, Miriam, with James Hall. *Makeba: My Story*. New York: New American Library, 1987.

Marable, Manning. *Malcolm X: A Life of Reinvention*. New York: Viking, 2011.

Marcus, Greil. *Mystery Train: Images of America in Rock and Roll Music*. New York: Dutton, 1990 (1975).

———. *Invisible Republic: Bob Dylan's Basement Tapes*. New York: Henry Holt and Company, 1997.

Margolick, David. *Strange Fruit: Billie Holiday, Café Society, and an Early Cry for Civil Rights*. Philadelphia: Running Press, 2000.

Marine, Gene. *The Black Panthers*. New York: New American Library, 1969.

Marqusee, Mike. *Redemption Song: Muhammad Ali and the Spirit of the Sixties*. London: Verso, 1999.

Martin, Bradford D. *The Theater Is in the Street: Politics and Public Performance in the Sixties America*. Amherst: University of Massachusets Press, 2004.

Martin, Waldo E., Jr. *No Coward Soldiers: Black Cultural Politics in Postwar America*. Cambridge, MA: Harvard University Press, 2005.

Marx, Karl, and Friedrich Engels. *The Communist Manifesto*. New York: Penguin Books, 2002 (1845).

McNally, Dennis. *A Long Strange Trip: The Inside Story of the Grateful Dead*. New York: Broadway Books, 2002.

McNally, Dennis. Telephone interview with the author, January 21, 2008.

McTaggart, Ursula. *Guerillas in the Industrial Jungle: Radicalism's Primitive and Industrial Rhetoric*. Albany: State University of New York Press, 2012.

Minton, Torri. "Race Through Time." *San Francisco Chronicle*, September 20, 1998, SC-4.

Miyakawa, Felicia M. *Five Percenter Rap: God Hop's Music, Message, and Black Muslim Mission*. Bloomington: Indiana University Press, 2005.

Montague, Magnificent (Nathaniel), with Bob Baker. *Burn, Baby! BURN! The Autobiography of Magnificent Montague.* Urbana: University of Illinois Press, 2003.

Mooney, Paul. *Black Is the New White: A Memoir.* New York: Simon Spotlight Entertainment, 2009.

Moore, Natalie Y., and Lance Williams. *The Almighty Black P. Stone Nation: The Rise, Fall, and Resurgence of an American Gang.* Chicago: Lawrence Hill Books.

Moseley, Walter. *RL's Dream: A Novel.* New York: WW. Norton, 1995.

Moten, Fred. *In the Break: The Aesthetics of the Black Radical Tradition.* Minneapolis: University of Minnesota Press, 2003.

Mott, James. Telephone interview with author, July 20, 2007.

Muhammad, Basheer. Telephone interview with author, February 23, 2012.

Muhammad, Elijah. *Message to the Blackman in America.* Chicago: Muhammad's Temple No. 2, 1965.

Munro, Martin. *Different Drummers: Rhythm and Race in the Americas.* Berkeley: University of California Press, 2010.

Murch, Donna Jean. *Living for the City: Migration, Education, and the Rise of the Black Panther Party in Oakland, California.* Chapel Hill: University of North Carolina Press, 2010.

Murray, Charles Shaar. *Crosstown Traffic: Jimi Hendrix and the Post-War Rock 'n Roll Revolution.* New York: St. Martin's Press, 1991.

Nadell, James. *Bob Marley, Jimi Hendrix and Black Music: Profiles in Fanonist National Culture.* (unpublished galley proof) Nashville, TN: Winston-Derek, 1995.

Neal, Larry. "And Shine Swam On." In *Black Fire: An Anthology of Afro American Writing,* edited by Amiri Baraka and Larry Neal. Baltimore: Black Classic Press, 2007 (1968).

———. "The Social Background of the Black Arts Movement." *The Black Scholar* 18, no.1 (1987): 19.

———. *Visions of a Liberated Future. Black Arts Movement Writings.* New York: Thunder's Mouth Press, 1989.

Neal, Mark Anthony. *Soul Babies: Black Popular Culture and the Post-Soul Aesthetic.* New York: Routledge, 2002.

———. *Songs in the Key of Black Life.* New York: Routledge, 2003.

Newton, Fredrika. Telephone interview with author, November 17, 2004.

Newton, Huey P. *Revolutionary Suicide*. New York: Ballantine Books, 1973.

———. *To Die for the People: The Writings of Huey P. Newton*. New York: Writers and Readers Publishing, 1999 (1972).

Nkrumah, Kwame. *Towards Colonial Freedom*. London: Heinmann, 1962.

———. *Consciencism; Philosophy and Ideology for De-Colonization*. New York: Monthly Review Press, 1970.

Nyerere, Julius. *Ujamaa: Essays on Socialism*. London: Oxford University Press, 1971 (1968).

Ogbar, Jeffrey O. G. *Black Power: Radical Politics and African American Identity*. Baltimore: Johns Hopkins University Press, 2004.

Olatunji, Babatunde, with Robert Atkinson. *To the Beat of My Drum: An Autobiography*. Philadelphia: Temple University Press, 2005.

Olsen, Jack. *Last Man Standing: The Tragedy and Triumph of Geronimo Pratt*. New York: Doubleday, 2000.

Omi, Michael, and Howard Winant. *Racial Formation in the United States*. New York: Routledge, 1994.

O'Reilly, Kenneth. *"Racial Matters": The FBI's Secret File on Black America, 1960–1972*. New York: The Free Press, 1989.

Oyewole, Abiodun, and Umar Bin Hassan. *On a Mission*. New York: Henry Holt, 1996.

Packard, Jerrold M. *American Nightmare: The History of Jim Crow*. New York: St. Martin's Griffin, 2002.

Pambeli, Mzuri. "The Black Panther Party . . . from a Sister's Point of View: An interview of Dr. Phyllis Jackson." *Positive Action*. (March–April 2007):8.

Paris. "Are You a Hip-Hop Apologist?" www.guerrillafunk.com, April 18, 2007.

Pearson, Hugh. *The Shadow of the Panther: Huey Newton and the Price of Black Power in America*. Reading, MA: Addison-Wesley Publishing Company, 1994.

Pinderhughes, Dianne M. *Race and Ethnicity in Chicago Politics*. Urbana: University of Illinois Press, 1987.

Pohlman, Marcus D. *African American Political Thought. Volume 2: Confrontation vs. Compromise: 1945 to the Present*. New York: Routledge. 2003.

Pond, Steven F. *Head Hunters: The Making of Jazz's First Platinum Album*. Ann Arbor: University of Michigan Press, 2005.

Porter, Eric. *What Is This Thing Called Jazz? African American Musicians as Artists, Critics and Activists.* Berkeley: University of California Press, 2002.

Pryor, Richard. *Pryor Convictions, and Other Life Sentences.* London: Revolver Books, 2006.

Racism Research Project. *Critique of the Black Nation Thesis.* Berkeley: Racism Research Project, 1975.

Radmin, Ron. *Paul Robeson: The Man and His Mission.* London: Peter Owen Publishers, 1987.

Raiford, Leigh. "Restaging Revolution: Black Power, *Vibe* Magazine, and Photographic Memory." In *The Civil Rights Movement in American Memory*, edited by Renee C. Romano and Leigh Raiford. Athens: University of Georgia Press, 2006.

Raines, Howell. *My Soul Is Rested: Movement Days in the Deep South Remembered.* New York: Bantam Books, 1978.

Ramsey, Guthrie P., Jr. *Race Music: Black Cultures from Bebop to Hip-Hop.* Berkeley: University of California Press, 2003.

Reed, Teresa L. *The Holy Profane: Religion in Black Popular Music.* Lexington: University Press of Kentucky, 2003.

Rexroth, Kenneth. "The Making of the Counterculture." www.bopsecrets .org/rexroth/essays/counterculture.htm, 1969.

Rhodes, Jane. *Framing the Black Panthers: The Spectacular Rise of a Black Power Icon.* New York: The New Press, 2007.

Riley, Clayton. "Assault on the Panthers." *Liberator.* (January 1970), 7.

Ritz, David. *Divided Soul: The Life of Marvin Gaye.* New York: Da Capo, 2003.

Robeson, Paul. *Here I Stand.* Boston: Beacon Press, 1988 (1958).

———. *Paul Robeson Speaks: Writings, Speeches, and Interviews, a Centennial Celebration.* New York: Citadel, 1998.

Robinson, Cedric J. *Black Marxism: The Making of the Black Radical Tradition.* Chapel Hill: University of North Carolina Press, 2000 (1983).

Rogers, Nile. *Le Freak: An Upside Down Story of Family, Disco, and Destiny.* New York: Spiegel & Grau, 2011.

Rose, Cynthia. *Living in America: The Soul Saga of James Brown.* London: Serpent's Tail, 1990.

Rosen, Ruth. *The World Split Open: How the Modern Women's Movement Changed America.* New York: Viking Press, 2000.

Royko, Mike. *Boss: Richard J. Daley of Chicago.* New York: Plume, 1998.

Saul, Scott. *Freedom Is, Freedom Ain't: Jazz and the Making of the Sixties.* Cambridge: Harvard University Press, 2003.

Schanche, Don. *The Panther Paradox: A Liberal's Dilemma.* New York: Mc Kay, 1970.

Schoonmaker, Trevor, ed. *Fela: From West Africa to West Broadway.* New York: Palgrave MacMillan, 2003.

Schwerin, Jules. *Got to Tell It: Mahalia Jackson, Queen of Gospel.* New York: Oxford University Press, 1992.

Scott-Heron, Gil. *Now and Then: The Poems of Gil Scott-Heron.* Edinburgh: Canongate, 2000.

———. *The Last Holiday: A Memoir.* New York: Grove Press, 2012.

Seale, Bobby. *Seize the Time: The Story of the Black Panther Party and Huey P. Newton.* New York: Vintage, 1973.

———. *A Lonely Rage.* New York: New York Times Book Co., 1978.

Self, Robert O. *American Babylon: Race and the Struggle for Postwar Oakland.* Princeton, NJ: Princeton University Press, 2003.

Selvin, Joel. "The Top 100 Bay Area Bands 1–50." *San Francisco Chronicle*, December 19, 1999.

Senghor, Leopold. *On African Socialism.* New York: Praeger, 1964.

Sexual Freedom League. *The Records of the Sexual Freedom League.* London: Olympia Press, 1971.

Shakur, Afeni, with Jasmine Guy. *Evolution of a Revolutionary.* New York: Atria, 2004.

Shakur, Assata. *Assata: An Autobiography.* Chicago: Lawrence Hill Books, 2001.

Sharpton, Al. "The Godfather and Dr. King." *Rolling Stone*, January 25, 2007, 48.

Sidran, Ben. *Black Talk.* New York: Da Capo Press, 1981.

Simone, Nina, with Stephen Cleary. *I Put a Spell on You: The Autobiography of Nina Simone.* New York: Da Capo Press, 1991.

Smethurst, James Edward. *The Black Arts Movement: Literary Nationalism in the 1960s and 1970s.* Chapel Hill: University of North Carolina Press, 2005.

Smith, RJ. *The One: The Life and Music of James Brown.* New York: Gotham Books, 2012.

Smith, Suzanne E. *Dancing in the Street: Motown and the Cultural Politics of Detroit.* Cambridge: Harvard University Press, 1999.

Smith, Tommie. *Silent Gesture: The Autobiography of Tommie Smith*. Philadelphia: Temple University Press, 2007.

Snellings, Rolland (Askia Toure). "Keep On Pushin': Rhythm and Blues as a Weapon." *The Liberator*, October 1965.

Springer, Kimberly. *Living for the Revolution: Black Feminist Organizations, 1968–1980*. Durham, NC: Duke University Press, 2005.

Stewart, Gary. *Breakout: Profiles in African Rhythm*. Chicago: University of Chicago Press, 1992.

Szwed, John. *Space Is the Place: The Lives and Times of Sun Ra*. New York: Da Capo Press, 1998.

Tapscott, Horace. *Songs of the Unsung: The Musical and Social Journey of Horace Tapscott*. Durham, NC: Duke University Press, 2001.

Tate, Greg. *Flyboy in the Buttermilk: Essays on Contemporary America*. New York: Simon & Schuster, 1992.

———. *Midnight Lightning: Jimi Hendrix and the Black Experience*. Chicago: Lawrence Hill Books, 2003.

Thomas, Pat. *Listen Whitey: The Sights and Sounds of Black Power, 1965–1975*. Seattle: Fantagraphic Books, 2012.

Thompson, Heather Ann. *Whose Detroit? Politics, Labor and Race in a Modern American City*. Ithaca, NY: Cornell University Press, 2001.

Torrence, Michael. "The Lumpen: Black Panther Party Revolutionary Singing Group." www.itsabouttimebpp.com/lumpen.htm, 2004.

Torrence, Michael. Interview aired on KPFA Radio, October 16, 2006.

———. Interview with author at KPFA Radio studios, February 23, 2007.

———. Telephone interview with author, December 8, 2008.

Trouillot, Michel-Rolph. *Silencing the Past: Power and the Production of History*. Boston: Beacon Press Books, 1995.

Ture, Kwame (Stokeley Charmichael), and Charles Hamilton. *Black Power: The Politics of Liberation in America*. New York: Vintage, 1992 (1967).

Tyson, Timothy B. *Radio Free Dixie: Robert F. Williams and the Roots of Black Power*. Chapel Hill: University of North Carolina Press, 1999.

Van Deburg, William L. *New Day in Babylon: The Black Power Movement and American Culture, 1965–1975*. Chicago: University of Chicago Press, 1992.

———. *Modern Black Nationalism: From Marcus Garvey to Louis Farrakhan*. New York: New York University Press, 1997.

Veal, Michael. *Fela: The Life and Times of an African Musical Icon*. Philadelphia: Temple University Press, 2000.

Vincent, Rickey. *Funk: The Music, the People and the Rhythm of The One*. New York: St. Martin's Press, 1996.

Vincent, Theodore G. *Black Power and the Garvey Movement*. Oakland: Nzinga Publishing House, 1988 (1970).

Vincent, Ted. *Keep Cool: The Black Activists That Built the Jazz Age*. London: Pluto, 1995.

Vincent, Toni. Telephone interview with author, April 13 and 27, 2003.

Ward, Brian. *Just My Soul Responding: Rhythm and Blues, Black Consciousness and Race Relations*. Berkeley: University of California Press, 1998.

———. *Radio and the Struggle for Civil Rights in the South*. Gainesville: University Press of Florida, 2004.

Watkins, Craig S. *Hip-Hop Matters: Politics, Pop Culture, and the Struggle for the Soul of a Movement*. New York: Beacon Press, 2006.

Watts, Daniel H. "The Eve of Revolution." *Liberator*, September 1967, 3.

Werner, Craig. *A Change Is Gonna Come: Music, Race and the Soul of America*. New York: Plume, 1999.

———. *Higher Ground: Stevie Wonder, Aretha Franklin, Curtis Mayfield, and the Rise and Fall of American Soul*. New York: Crown, 2004.

Wesley, Fred. *Hit Me Fred: Recollections of a Sideman*. Durham, NC: Duke University Press, 2003.

Whitall, Susan, with Kevin John. *Fever: Little Willie John's Fast Life, Mysterious Death and the Birth of Soul*. London: Titan Books, 2011.

Whitburn, Joel. *Billboard's Top Rhythm & Blues Singles 1942–1988*. Menomonee Falls, WI: Record Research, 1988.

———. *1999 Billboard's Top Rhythm & Blues Albums 1965–1998*. Menomonee Falls, WI: Record Research, 1999.

White, Armond. *Rebel for the Hell of It: The Life of Tupac Shakur*. New York: Thunder's Mouth, 1997.

White, Timothy. *Catch a Fire: The Life of Bob Marley*. New York: Henry Holt, 2000 (1983).

Widener, Daniel. *Black Arts West: Culture and Struggle in Postwar Los Angeles*. Durham, NC: Duke University Press, 2010.

Wiener, Jon, ed. *Conspiracy in the Streets: The Extraordinary Trial of the Chicago Eight*. New York: New Press, 2006.

Williams, Otis. *Temptations: Updated*. Lanham, MD: Cooper Square Press, 2002.

Williams, Robert F. *Negroes with Guns*. Detroit: Wayne State University Press, 1998 (1962).

Williams, Yohuru. *Black Politics / White Power: Civil Rights, Black Power, and the Black Panthers in New Haven*. St. James, NY: Brandywine Press, 2000.

Winston, Henry. *Strategy for a Black Agenda*. New York: International Publishers, 1973.

Wolff, Daniel. *You Send Me: The Life and Times of Sam Cooke*. New York: William Morrow and Co., 1995.

Womack, Bobby. *Midnight Mover: The True Story of the Greatest Soul Singer in the World*. London: John Black Publishing Ltd., 2006.

Woodard, Komozi. *A Nation Within a Nation: Amiri Baraka (LeRoi Jones) and Black Power Politics*. Chapel Hill: University of North Carolina Press, 1999.

X, Malcolm. *By Any Means Necessary*. New York: Ballantine, 1992 (1970).

X, Malcolm, and Alex Haley. *The Autobiography of Malcolm X*. New York: Ballantine, 1965.

X, Malcolm, and George Breitman. *Malcolm X Speaks: Selected Speeches and Statements*. New York: Grove Weidenfeld, 1990.

Ya Salaam, Kalamu. *The Magic of Ju Ju: An Appreciation of the Black Arts Movement*. Unpublished manuscript, 2007.

Discography

Brown, James. "Sex Machine Live," CD Polydor 517984 (1993); originally released as: lp King 1115 (1970).

——. *Revolution of the Mind (Live at the Apollo Volume Three)*, CD Polydor 517983 (1993); originally released as: lp Polydor 3003 (1971).

——. *CD of JB II*, CD Polydor 831-700-2 (1987).

——. "Star Time," 4CD Polydor 849108 (1991).

Brown, Elaine. *Seize the Time*, CD Water 183 (2006); originally released as: lp Vault 131 (1969).

——. *Elaine Brown*, LP Black Forum 458L (1973).

Chi-Lites. "(For God's Sake) Give More Power to the People," LP Brunswick B-754170 (1971).

Cooke, Sam. *The Wonderful World of Sam Cooke*, CD World Star Collection 99001 (1987).

Dylan, Bob. *Masterpieces*, Columbia 3CD 462448 (1998).

Franklin, Aretha. *Soul Sister*, LP Columbia 9321 (1966).

———. *30 Greatest Hits*, CD Atlantic 81668-2 (1990).

Franti, Michael. "Yell Fire," CD Liberation 22 (2006).

Gaye, Marvin. *The Very Best of Marvin Gaye*, 2CD Motown 5302922 (1994).

Goapele. "Change It All," CD Sony 92910 (2005).

Last Poets. "Last Poets," LP Douglas Z-30811 (1970).

———. "Right On," CD Collectables 6500 1 (1991).

Lennon, John. *John Lennon/Plastic Ono Band*, CD Capitol 28740 (2000).

———. "Some Time in New York City / Live Jam," CD Capitol 18372 (2007).

The Lumpen. "Free Bobby Now/ No More," 45 rpm single, Black Panther Party Productions, 1970.

The Lumpen. "Live," recording from Merrit College, Oakland, CA. Taped November 10, 1970; from Huey P. Newton collection, Stanford University, Palo Alto, CA.

Mayfield, Curtis. *People Get Ready: The Curtis Mayfield Story*, 3CD Rhino/WEA 72262 (1996).

McDaniels, Eugene. *Headless Heroes of the Apocalypse*, Water Music Records CD 150 (2005).

Robeson, Paul. *Ballad for Americans: and Great Songs of Faith, Love and Patriotism*, CD Vanguard Records VCD 117/18 (1989).

———. *The Peace Arch Concerts*, 2CD Folk Era Records FE1442CD (1998).

Gil Scott-Heron. "Small Talk at 125th St and Lenox," LP Flying Dutchman 10131 (1969).

———. "The Revolution Will Not Be Televised," CD Bluebird 6994-4-RB6 (1990).

Simone, Nina. *Nina Simone Anthology*, CD RCA 82876530152 (2003).

Sly and the Family Stone. *The Essential Sly and the Family Stone*, 2CD Sony 86867 (2002).

Temptations. "In a Mellow Mood," LP Gordy 924 (1967).

———. *My Girl: The Very Best of the Temptations*, CD Motown 017298 (2002).

Various Artists. *Motown Classics Gold*, CD 312002.

Watts Prophets. *Things Gonna Get Greater: The Watts Prophets 1969–1971*, CD Water 157 (2005).

West, Cornel. *Never Forget: A Journey of Revelations*, CD Hidden Beach Forum 44 (2007).

Videography

Eyes on the Prize. Directed by Louis Massiah and Terry Kay Rockefeller. PBS / Blackside, 1990, VHS.

41st & Central: The Untold Story of the L.A. Black Panthers. Directed by Gregory Everett. Ultra Wave Media, 2010.

The Last Poets. Provocateur/First Drum, 2002.

The Last Poets, Made in Amerikkka. Directed by Claude Santiago. La Huit, 2009.

Lords of the Revolution: The Black Panthers. Written by Martin Torgoff. VH1, 2009.

The Mack. Directed by Michael Campus. Cinerama, 1973.

Mackin' Ain't Easy. Directed by Laura Nix. New Line, 2002.

Marley. Directed by Kevin McDonald. Magnolia Pictures, 2012.

The Night James Brown Saved Boston. Directed by David Leaf. VH1, 2008.

Public Enemy: Reflections of the Black Panthers. Directed by Jens Meurer. Real Fiction, 1999.

Respect Yourself: The Stax Records Story. Directed by Robert Gordon and Morgan Neville. Concord Music Group, 2007.

Scandalize My Name: Stories from the Blacklist. Directed by Alexandra Isles. Unapix Entertainment, Inc., 1998.

Speak of Me as I Am: The Story of Paul Robeson. Directed by Rachel Hermans. BBC Wales/New Jersey Public Television, 1999.

The U.S. vs John Lennon. Directed by David Leaf and John Scheinfeld. Lionsgate, 2006.

Wattstax. Directed by Mel Stuart. Columbia Pictures, 1973.

Notes

Introduction

1. Stokely Carmichael with Ekwueme Michael Thelwell, *Ready for Revolution: The Life and Struggles of Stokely Carmichael (Kwame Ture)* (New York: Scribner, 2003), 529.

2. Craig Werner, *A Change Is Gonna Come: Music, Race & the Soul of America* (New York: Plume, 1999), 121.

3. James Brown and Bruce Tucker, *James Brown: The Godfather of Soul* (New York: Macmillan, 1986), 173.

4. Nina Simone with Stephen Cleary, *I Put a Spell on You: The Autobiography of Nina Simone* (New York: Da Capo Press, 1991), 100.

5. Ibid., 112.

6. Mumia Abu-Jamal, *We Want Freedom: A Life in the Black Panther Party* (Cambridge, MA: South End Press, 2004), 176.

7. NAACP activist Benjamin Hooks recounts the story of Mahalia and Dr. King in Jules Schwerin, *Got to Tell It: Mahalia Jackson, Queen of Gospel* (New York: Oxford University Press, 1992), 169.

8. Waldo E. Martin Jr., *No Coward Soldiers: Black Cultural Politics in Postwar America* (Cambridge, MA: Harvard University Press, 2005), 77.

9. Chanting could be heard in footage from *Eyes on the Prize*, directed by Louis Massiah and Terry Kay Rockefeller (PBS/Blackside, 1990), VHS.

10. Martin Luther King Jr., "I Have a Dream," August 28, 1963.

11. Malcolm X speech in Malcolm X and George Breitman, *Malcolm X Speaks: Selected Speeches and Statements* (New York: Grove Weidenfeld, 1990), 9.

12. Bennett, Introduction to *Tradition and Conflict: Images of a Turbulent Decade 1963–1973*, curated by Dr. Mary Schmidt Campbell (New York: Studio Museum in Harlem, 1983), 9–10.

13. Michael Omi and Howard Winant, *Racial Formation in the United States* (New York: Routledge, 1994), 99.

14. Jeffrey O. G. Ogbar, *Black Power: Radical Politics and African American Identity* (Baltimore: Johns Hopkins University Press, 2004).

Chapter 1: "Party Music": The Story of the Lumpen

1. Michael Torrence, interview with author, December 12, 2008.

2. Torrence, author interview, 2008. It should be noted that the aborted student walkout occurred only weeks after Smith and Carlos's Olympic games action. The situation was very volatile for all involved.

3. William Calhoun, interview with author, July 21, 2007.

4. Ibid.

5. Clark Bailey, interview with author, November 24, 2004.

6. Torrence, author interview, 2008.

7. Michael Torrence, interview on KPFA radio, October 16, 2006.

8. Ibid.

9. William Calhoun, interview with author, November 9, 2002.

10. William Calhoun, interview on KPFA radio, October 8, 2010.

11. Torrence, KPFA interview, 2006.

12. Calhoun, KPFA interview, 2010.

13. Bailey, author interview, 2004.

14. Calhoun, author interview, 2002.

15. Ibid.

16. Karl Marx, *The 18th Brumaire of Louis Bonaparte* (Rockville, MD: Wildside Press, 2008), 37.

17. Karl Marx and Friedrich Engels, *The Communist Manifesto* (Oxford and New York: Oxford University Press, 1992), 14.

18. David Hilliard, interview with author, April 27, 2004.

19. Bailey, author interview, 2004.

20. Michael Torrence, interview with author, March 12, 2012.

21. Calhoun, author interview, 2002.

22. James Mott, interview with author, July 20, 2007.

23. Torrence, KPFA interview, 2006.

24. Mack Ray Henderson, interview with the author, March 10, 2012.

25. Calhoun, KPFA interview, 2010.

26. The Lumpen, "The Lumpen Theme," written by W. Calhoun (Calhoun Music Group/ASCAP, 1970), transcription from recording housed at Stanford University Huey P. Newton Foundation archives.

27. Mack Ray Henderson, author interview, 2012.

28. Basheer Muhammad, telephone interview with author, July 12, 2012.

29. Lenny Williams, telephone interview with author, June 18, 2011.

30. Torrence, KPFA interview, 2006.

31. Calhoun, author interview, 2002.

32. Bailey, author interview, 2004.

33. Bailey, author interview, 2004; Michael Torrence, interview on KPFA radio, February 23, 2007.

34. The Lumpen, "Free Bobby Now," written by W. Calhoun (Calhoun Music Group/ASCAP, 1970), transcription from 45 rpm record courtesy of Walter Turner.

35. The Lumpen, "No More," written by W. Calhoun (Calhoun Music Group/ASCAP, 1970), transcription from 45 rpm record courtesy of Walter Turner.

36. Billy Jennings, telephone interview with author, March 11, 2013.

37. Calhoun, author interview, 2002.

38. Emory Douglas, interview with author, March 18, 2004. Most later Lumpen performances were advertised in the *Black Panther* paper. Many were full-page advertisements with artwork, animation, and photos designed by Emory Douglas. Douglas designed the majority of the Lumpen layouts. The Lumpen members said they did not meet the Grateful Dead, as the Lumpen performed early in the day-long event, while the Dead played later.

39. David Levinson, interview with author, December 14, 2004.

40. Mott, author interview, 2007.

41. Ibid.

42. Calhoun, author interview, 2007.

43. Levinson, author interview, 2004.

44. Bailey, author interview, 2004.

45. Ibid.

46. Fredrika Newton, in an impromptu telephone conversation with author, 2006. The Lumpen members confirmed the names of Newton's associates.

47. Torrence, author interview, 2012.

48. The Black Panther Party Central Committee was modeled on the organizational modes of democratic centralism developed by Mao and Lenin, and it organized and allocated the resources for all Party activities.

49. Douglas, author interview, 2004.

50. Torrence, KPFA interview, 2006.

51. Calhoun, author interview, 2002.

52. Vivid descriptions of the cases surrounding the Panther internal conflicts and disintegration can be found in Curtis J. Austin, *Up Against the Wall: Violence in the Making and Unmaking of the Black Panther Party* (Fayetteville, AK: University of Arkansas Press, 2006) and Peniel E. Joseph: *Waiting 'Til the Midnight Hour: A Narrative History of Black Power in America* (New York: Henry Holt, 2007).

53. Calhoun, author interview, 2007.

54. From previously listed interviews with all the Lumpen members.

55. Bailey, author interview, 2004.

Chapter 2: "Power to the People": Bay Area Culture and the Rise of the Party

1. The Lumpen, "Power to the People," written by W. Calhoun, 1970, transcription from recording housed at Stanford University Huey P. Newton Foundation archives. Published by Calhoun Music Group / ASCAP. A live rendition of Sly and the Family Stone's "Dance to the Music" can be heard on *The Woodstock Experience* Epic/Legacy CD 748241 (2009).

2. Joel Selvin, "The Top 100 Bay Area Bands 1–50," *San Francisco Chronicle*, December 19, 1999.

3. Frederick "Freddie Stone" Stewart recounted details of the family's quick exodus out of Texas during an on-air interview on KPFA radio, March 15, 2002.

4. *Coming Back For More*, directed by Willem Alkema (Netherlands: Dwarsproducties, 2008) film.

5. Greil Marcus, *Mystery Train: Images of America in Rock and Roll Music* (New York: Dutton, 1990), 91. Also Rickey Vincent, *Funk: The Music, the People and the Rhythm of The One* (New York: St. Martin's Press, 1996).

6. Savio had spent the previous summer in Mississippi as a part of the dramatic voter registration efforts of the Student Nonviolent Coordinating Committee's "Freedom Summer." Savio survived threats from the Ku Klux Klan in Mississippi and returned to Berkeley fearless in his moral commitment to human rights. See Robert Cohen, *Freedom's Orator: Mario Savio and the Radical Legacy of the 1960s* (New York: Oxford University Press, 2009).

7. Vincent, *Funk*, 56–7.

8. Torri Minton, "Race Through Time," *San Francisco Chronicle*, September 20, 1998.

9. Important studies of black activism in the Bay Area before the Black Panther Party include Robert O. Self, *American Babylon: Race and the Struggle for Postwar Oakland* (Princeton, NJ: Princeton University Press, 2003), and Hugh Pearson, *The Shadow of the Panther: Huey Newton and the Price of Black Power in America* (Reading, MA: Addison-Wesley, 1994). A chronology of the desegregation of the armed forces can be found at the Harry S. Truman Library and Museum website, www.trumanlibrary.org/whistlestop/study_collections /desegregation/large/index.php?action=chronology.

10. Self, *American Babylon*, 223.

11. Interviews with multiple local musicians and historian Lee Hildebrand.

12. Warren Hinckle, "Metropoly: The Story of Oakland, California," *Ramparts* magazine, February 1966, 25.

13. Bobby Seale, *Seize the Time: The Story of the Black Panther Party and Huey P. Newton* (New York: Vintage, 1973), 8.

14. Ibid., 12.

15. Ibid., 3.

16. David Hilliard, Keith Zimmerman, and Kent Zimmerman, *Huey: Spirit of the Panther* (New York: Thunder's Mouth Press, 2006), 23.

17. Bobby Seale's role in the founding of the Party is discussed in detail in Seale, *Seize the Time*.

18. Huey P Newton, *Revolutionary Suicide* (New York: Ballantine Books, 1973), 17–18.

19. Newton, *Revolutionary Suicide*, 19.

20. Hilliard, Zimmerman, and Zimmerman, *Huey*, 7.

21. Hilliard, Zimmerman, and Zimmerman, *Huey*; Roger Guenveur Smith discusses Newton's alternatives to dancing in his performance of Newton in *A Huey P. Newton Story* (directed by Spike Lee, 2001).

22. Newton, *Revolutionary Suicide*, 92–93; also see *The Records of the San Francisco Sexual Freedom League* (London: Olympia Press, 1971).

23. Discussion of the Diggers and their relationship to the Black Panthers can be found in Peter Coyote, *Sleeping Where I Fall: A Chronicle* (Washington DC: Counterpoint, 1998). Further information from Dennis McNally, interview with author, January 21, 2008; McNally is the author of *A Long Strange Trip: The Inside Story of the Grateful Dead* (New York: Broadway Books, 2002).

24. Scot Brown, *Fighting for US: Maulana Karenga, the US Organization, and Black Cultural Nationalism* (New York: New York University Press, 2003), 28–29.

25. Newton, *Revolutionary Suicide*, 71.

26. Seale, *Seize the Time*, 66–7.

27. Newton, *Revolutionary Suicide*, 120.

28. Elbert "Big Man" Howard, *Panther on the Prowl* (Baltimore, MD: BCP Digital Printing, 2002), 30.

29. Hilliard, Zimmerman, and Zimmerman, *Huey*, 58.

30. Seale, *Seize the Time*, 162.

31. "Gunmen Invade West Coast Capitol," *Chicago Tribune*, May 3, 1967; "Armed Negroes Enter California Assembly in Gun Bill Protest," *New York Times*, May 3, 1967; "Armed Gang Invades State Capitol," *Guardian* (London), May 3, 1967.

32. Amiri Baraka, *The Autobiography of LeRoi Jones* (New York: Lawrence Hill Books, 1997), 353.

33. James Mott, interview with author, July 20, 2007.

34. William Calhoun, interview with author, November 9, 2002.

35. Ibid.

36. William Calhoun, interview with author, July 21, 2007.

37. Clark Bailey, interview with author, November 24, 2004.

38. Ibid.

39. Ibid.

40. Michael Torrence, interview with author at KPFA studios, February 23, 2007.

41. Ibid.

42. Ibid.

43. Mott, author interview, 2007.

44. Ibid.

45. Ibid.

46. Ibid.

47. Ibid.

48. Ibid.

49. Ibid.

50. Bailey, author interview, 2004.

51. Minor Williams, interview with author, October 23, 2008.

52. Despite repeated queries, the Lumpen leaders had difficulty recalling the specific names of band members.

53. David Levinson, interview with author, December 14, 2004.

54. Curtis J. Austin, *Up Against the Wall: Violence in the Making and Unmaking of the Black Panther Party* (Fayetteville, AK: University of Arkansas Press, 2006), 250.

55. Ibid., 250–251.

56. Kenneth Rexroth, "The Second Post-War, the Second Interbellum, the Permanent War Generation" in *The Alternative Society: Essays from the Other World* (Herder & Herder, 1970), available as "The Making of the Counterculture" at www.bopsecrets.org/rexroth/essays/counterculture.htm.

57. Sly Stone interviewed in *Coming Back for More*, directed by Willem Alkema (Netherlands: Dwarsproducties, 2008) film.

Chapter 3: "The Lumpen Theme": James Brown, the Rhythm Revolution, and Black Power

1. The Lumpen, "The Lumpen Theme," written by W. Calhoun, 1970, transcription from recording housed at Stanford University's Huey P. Newton Foundation archives, published by Calhoun Music Group / ASCAP.

2. William Calhoun, interview with author, July 21, 2007.

3. Michael Torrence, interview with author, March 12, 2012.

4. Larry Neal, "Black Art and Black Liberation," *The Black Revolution: An Ebony Special Issue* (Chicago: Johnson Publishing Company, 1970), 42.

5. Joe Tex attempted a competition for "Soul Brother Number One" that some might have taken seriously as a publicity stunt, but not as a legitimate claim.

6. Leroi Jones, *Black Music* (New York: William Morrow, 1970), 186.

7. Ben Sidran, *Black Talk* (New York: Da Capo, 1983), 147.

8. Mark Deming, "Review: James Brown *Live at the Apollo*," allmusic.com, accessed 2006.

9. Mott , interview with author, July 20, 2007.

10. James Brown, *I Feel Good: A Memoir of a Life of Soul* (London: New American Library, 2005), 80.

11. James Brown, interview with author, August 1993; also see Rickey Vincent, *Funk: The Music, the People and the Rhythm of The One* (New York: St. Martin's Press, 1996), 60.

12. William "Bootsy" Collins, in "James Brown—Say It Proud," *CNN: Special Investigations Unit*, aired May 5, 2007, transcript available from http://transcripts.cnn.com/TRANSCRIPTS/0711/22/siu.02.html.

13. James Brown and Bruce Tucker, *James Brown: The Godfather of Soul* (New York: Macmillan, 1986), 158.

14. Brown, *I Feel Good*, 81.

15. Brown and Warden, see RJ Smith, *The One: The Life and Music of James Brown* (New York: Gotham Books, 2012), 179–80; "didn't like singing and dancing" was from my mother, Toni Vincent, a former AAA member.

16. James Brown, "It's a Man's Man's Man's World," written by James Brown and Betty Newsome, *Star Time*, 4CD Polydor 849108 (1991).

17. Brown and Tucker, *James Brown*, 169.

18. Ibid., 181.

19. Ibid., 181–2.

20. Ibid, 187.

21. Alfred "Pee Wee" Ellis, interview with the author, November 15, 2010.

22. The Hank Ballard quote about "machine-gun-toting Black Panthers" can be found in the Cliff White 1987 jacket notes to *James Brown: CD of JB II* Polydor 831-700-2; Brown discusses openly his relationship with black power radicals in both of his memoirs.

23. Fred Wesley, *Hit Me, Fred: Recollections of a Sideman* (Durham, NC: Duke University Press, 2003), 107.

24. Mack Ray Henderson, interview with author, March 10, 2012.

25. Al Sharpton in "James Brown—Say It Proud," *CNN*.

26. James Brown, "Say It Loud—I'm Black and I'm Proud," written by James Brown and Alfred James Ellis, *Star Time*, 4CD Polydor 849108 (1991).

27. Al Sharpton, "The Godfather and Dr. King," *Rolling Stone*, January 25, 2007, 48.

28. Linda Harrison, "On Cultural Nationalism," in Philip Foner, ed. *The Black Panthers Speak* (Cambridge, MA: Da Capo Press, 1995), 151.

29. Brown and Tucker, *James Brown*, 200.

30. Abiodun Oyewole, *The Last Poets, Made in Amerikkka*, directed by Claude Santiago (La Huit, 2009).

31. Purdim, ibid.

32. Thomas Barry, "The Importance of Being Mr. James Brown," *LOOK* magazine, February 2, 1969, 62.

33. "James Brown—Say It Proud," *CNN*.

34. Larry Neal, "The Social Background of the Black Arts Movement," *The Black Scholar*, 18, no. 1 (1987): 19.

35. Brown, *I Feel Good*, 187–89.

36. Brown discusses his IRS harassment in both of his memoirs. An October 25,1975, *Jet* magazine article explicitly named James Brown as one of the victims of illegal government persecution; info on the Special Services Committee found in *Time* magazine article "Keeping a Little List at the IRS," *Time*, August 13, 1973, available at www.time.com/time/magazine/article/0,9171,907662,00 .html?iid=chix-sphere.

37. Vivien Goldman, "Dread, Beat and Blood," *Observer Music Monthly*, July 16, 2006, www.guardian.co.uk/music/2006/jul/16/urban.worldmusic.

38. Aston Barrett, *Marley*, directed by Kevin McDonald (Magnolia Pictures, 2012).

39. Timothy White, *Catch a Fire: The Life of Bob Marley* (New York: Henry Holt, 1983), 20.

40. Leroy Jodie Pierson and Roger Steffens, 1997 jacket notes to *Black Progress: The Formative Years, Vol. 2*, JAD-CD-1003.

41. Ibid.

42. Gary Stewart, *Breakout: Profiles in African Rhythm* (Chicago: University of Chicago Press, 1992), 118.

43. Michael Veal, *Fela: the Life and Times of an African Musical Icon* (Philadelphia: Temple University Press, 2000), 69.

44. Sandra Isadore interviewed in Jay Babcock, "Fela: King of the Invisible Art," in *Da Capo Best Music Writing 2000: The Year's Finest Writing on Rock, Pop, Jazz, Country, and More*, Peter Guralnick, ed. (Cambridge, MA: Da Capo Press, 2000), 19.

45. Jay Babcock, "Bootsy Collins on Fela Kuti," *Arthur* magazine, November 7, 1999, www.arthurmag.com/2009/11/02/bootsy-collins.

46. "James Brown—Say It Proud," *CNN*.

47. Veal, *Fela*, 247.

48. John Miller Chernoff, *African Rhythm and African Sensibility* (Chicago: University of Chicago Press, 1979), 73–74.

49. Davey D, Interview with DJ Kool Here, 1989 New Music Seminar. *Davey D's Hip Hop Corner*, www.daveyd.com/interdirect.html.

50. Smith, *The One*, 224–225; also see "Retailing: Soul Stamps," *Time*, Friday, July 11, 1969.

51. David Hilliard, interview with the author, 2004.

52. Sharpton in "James Brown—Say It Proud," *CNN*.

Chapter 4: "People Get Ready": Civil Rights, Soul Music, and Black Identity

1. William Calhoun, interview with author, July 21, 2007.

2. The Lumpen, "People Get Ready," written by W. Calhoun, 1970, transcription from recording housed at Stanford University's Huey P. Newton Foundation archives. Published by Calhoun Music Group / ASCAP.

3. William Calhoun, interview with author, November 9, 2002.

4. Craig Werner, *Higher Ground: Stevie Wonder, Aretha Franklin, Curtis Mayfield, and the Rise and Fall of American Soul* (New York: Crown, 2004), 125.

5. Curtis Mayfield, "People Get Ready," in *People Get Ready: The Curtis Mayfield Story*, 3CD Rhino/WEA 72262 (1996).

6. The best treatments of Jimi Hendrix and his relationship to soul music are *Crosstown Traffic: Jimi Hendrix and the Post-War Rock 'n' Roll Revolution* by Charles Shaar Murray (New York: St. Martin's Press, 1991), and David Henderson, *'Scuse Me While I Kiss the Sky: The Life and Times of Jimi Hendrix* (New York: Bantam Books, 1981).

7. Michael Haralambos, *Soul Music: The Birth of a Sound in Black America* (New York: Da Capo Press, 1974), 138–9.

8. Clayborne Carson, *In Struggle: SNCC and the Black Awakening of the 1960s* (Cambridge, MN: Harvard University Press, 1981), 63–64; also see www.bernice johnsonreagon.com/freedomsingers.shtml.

9. Waldo E. Martin Jr., *No Coward Soldiers: Black Cultural Politics in Postwar America* (Cambridge, MA: Harvard University Press, 2005), 47–48.

10. Mavis Staples, liner notes to *We'll Never Turn Back*, Anti, 2007.

11. Curtis Mayfield, "We're a Winner," in *People Get Ready: The Curtis Mayfield Story*; Craig Werner, *Higher Ground*; Mayfield refers to the attempted silencing of "We're a Winner" in a dialogue during a performance of the song on his 1970 *Curtis Live* album.

12. Marshall Thompson, interview with author, February 25, 2012.

13. Sun Ra's relationship with Bobby Seale and the Black Panther Party is discussed in John Szwed, *Space Is the Place: The Lives and Times of Sun Ra* (New York: Da Capo Press, 1997); Recently recovered tapes of Sun Ra at UC–Berkeley are available on Transparency Records.

14. Documentation of the Chicago Black Arts movement can be found in James Edward Smethurst, *The Black Arts Movement: Literary Nationalism in the 1960s and 1970s* (Chapel Hill: University of North Carolina Press, 2005); For a narrative of Chicago black power cultural activity, see Chaka Khan with Tonya Bolden, *Chaka! Through the Fire* (Emmaus, PA: Rodale, 2003), 40.

15. A discussion of black club owners in Chicago can be found in Ted Vincent, *Keep Cool: The Black Activists That Built the Jazz Age.* (London: Pluto Press, 1995).

16. Werner, *Higher Ground*, 124.

17. Clayton Riley, "Assault on the Panthers," *Liberator* (January 1970): 7.

18. Khan, *Chaka!*, 44.

19. Ibid, 45.

20. Ibid, 45–6.

21. Natalie Cole, *Love Brought Me Back: A Journey of Loss and Gain* (New York: Simon & Schuster, 2010), 75.

22. LeRoi Jones, *Blues People: Negro Music in White America* (New York: Morrow, 1963), 218–9.

23. Ibid., 8; Askia Muhammad Touré (as Roland Snellings), "Keep on Pushing (Rhythm & Blues as a Weapon)," *Liberator* 5 (October 1965): 6–8.

24. Malcolm X, *By Any Means Necessary* (New York: Ballantine, 1992), 63–64.

25. Scott Saul, *Freedom Is, Freedom Ain't: Jazz and the Making of the Sixties* (Cambridge: Harvard University Press, 2003), 248, 260.

26. Kalamu Ya Salaam, *The Magic of JuJu: An Appreciation of the Black Arts Movement* (Unpublished manuscript of second edition, provided by author, 2007), 9.

27. Robin Gregory's Afro caused an enormous controversy, discussed in Kathleen Odell Korgen, *From Black to Biracial: Transforming Racial Identity Among Americans* (New York: Praeger, 1999), 21.

28. Assata Shakur, *Assata: An Autobiography* (Chicago: Lawrence Hill Books, 2001), 183–84.

29. Ibid., 185.

30. Babatunde Olatunji with Robert Atkinson, *To the Beat of My Drum: An Autobiography* (Philadelphia: Temple University Press, 2005), 155.

31. Ibid., 157.

32. Miriam Makeba with James Hall, *Makeba: My Story* (New York: New American Library, 1987), 90.

33. Aretha Franklin and David Ritz, *Aretha: From These Roots* (New York: Villard Books, 1999), 109.

34. Ibid., 112.

35. Nina Simone with Stephen Cleary, *I Put a Spell on You: The Autobiography of Nina Simone* (New York: Da Capo Press 1991), 87.

36. Ibid., 88.

37. Mark Bego, *Aretha Franklin: The Queen of Soul* (New York: Da Capo Press, 2001), 145.

38. "Aretha Says She'll Go Angela's Bond If Permitted," *Jet*, December 3, 1970.

39. Michael Torrence, interview with the author, March 12, 2012.

40. William Barlow, *Voice Over: The Making of Black Radio* (Philadelphia: Temple University Press, 1999), 210.

41. Magnificent Montague with Bob Baker, *Burn, Baby! BURN! The Autobiography of Magnificent Montague* (Urbana: University of Illinois Press, 2003),134–5.

42. Barlow, *Voice Over*, 224.

43. Brian Ward, *Radio and the Struggle for Civil Rights in the South* (Gainesville: University Press of Florida, 2004), 344.

Chapter 5: "For Freedom": Cultural Nationalism and the Black Panther Party

1. The Temptations, "It's Summer," *My Girl: The Very Best of the Temptations*, CD Motown 017298 (2002).

2. The Lumpen, "For Freedom," written by W. Calhoun, 1970, transcription from recording housed at Stanford University Huey P. Newton Foundation archives. Published by Calhoun Music Group / ASCAP.

3. William Calhoun, interview with author, July 21, 2007.

4. Ben Edmonds, *What's Going On: Marvin Gaye and the Last Days of the Motown Sound*. (Edinburgh: Mojo Books, 2001), 212.

5. Martha and the Vandellas, "Dancing in the Street," *Motown Classics Gold* CD 312002, 2005; Suzanne E. Smith discusses the depth of symbolism of the song in *Dancing in the Street: Motown and the Cultural Politics of Detroit* (Cambridge, MA: Harvard University Press, 1999).

6. Smith, *Dancing in the Street*, 186.

7. Barrett Strong in the documentary series *Soul Deep: The Story of Black Popular Music* (BBC, 2005).

8. Insightful commentary on Detroit's public image can be found in Smith, *Dancing in the Street*, and Heather Ann Thompson, *Whose Detroit? Politics, Labor and Race in a Modern American City* (Ithaca, NY: Cornell University Press, 2001).

9. Dan Georgakas and Marvin Surkin, *Detroit: I Do Mind Dying: A Study in Urban Revolution* (Cambridge, MA: South End Press, 1998).

10. Smith, *Dancing in the Street*, 221; Also see Georgakas and Surkin, *Detroit*.

11. Smith, *Dancing in the Street*, 222.

12. See Smith, *Dancing in the Street*, Georgakas and Surkin, *Detroit*; Also, James Forman discusses his unsuccessful national union organizing strategies in *The Making of Black Revolutionaries* (Seattle: University of Washington Press, 1997).

13. Smith, *Dancing in the Street*, 223; Georgakas and Surkin, *Detroit*.

14. Martha Reeves, quoted in Nelson George, *Where Did Our Love Go? The Rise and Fall of the Motown Sound* (New York: St. Martin's Press, 1985), 183.

15. Otis Williams, *Temptations* (New York: Cooper Square Press, 2002), 136–7.

16. A lengthy Eddie Kendricks biography can be found on his website: www.ejk-online.com/ejkbio4.html. Also see Mark Ribowsky, *Ain't Too Proud to Beg: The Troubled Lives and Enduring Soul of the Temptations* (Hoboken, NJ: Wiley, 2012), 266.

17. James A. Geschwender, "The League of Revolutionary Black Workers," *Journal of Ethnic Studies* 2, no. 3 (Fall 1974): 9.

18. A. Muhammad Ahmad, "The League of Revolutionary Black Workers: A Historical Study," found at www.geocities.com/capitolhill/lobby/2379/lrbw.htm.

19. Huey's vision of a city takeover was elaborated on by Elaine Brown in *A Taste of Power: A Black Woman's Story* (New York: Anchor Books, 1993), 375.

20. Robert Allen, *Black Awakening in Capitalist America* (Trenton, NJ: Africa World Press, 1990), 89.

21. Amiri Baraka, *Raise, Race, Rays, Raze: Essays Since 1965* (New York: Random House, 1971), 43.

22. Ron Karenga, *The Quotable Karenga* (Los Angeles: US Organization, 1967), 9.

23. Ibid., 7, 8.

24. Ibid., 20.

25. The popularity of US is documented in Scot Brown, *Fighting for US: Maulana Karenga, the US Organization, and Black Cultural Nationalism* (New York: New York University Press, 2003).

26. Archie Ivy, interview by the author, April 11, 2011.

27. James Mtume, "Tripping with Black Music," *Cricket* (1969), 1.

28. Ivy, author interview, 2011.

29. Amiri Baraka, "Emory Douglas: A 'Good Brother,' a 'Bad' Artist," in *Black Panther: The Revolutionary Art of Emory Douglas*, ed. Sam Durant (New York: Rizzoli, 2006), 171.

30. Amiri Baraka, *The Autobiography of LeRoi Jones* (New York: Lawrence Hill Books, 1997), 358. Baraka's life path, as explained in his autobiography, is an

essential viewpoint for understanding the convergence of Black Nationalist consciousness with political activism.

31. Discussion of Baraka's forays into Newark politics can be found in Baraka, *Autobiography*, and Komozi Woodard, *A Nation Within a Nation: Amiri Baraka (LeRoi Jones) & Black Power Politics* (Chapel Hill, NC: University of North Carolina Press, 1999).

32. Brown, *Fighting for US*, 120–1.

33. Huey Newton, "Huey Newton Talks to the Movement About the Black Panther Party, Cultural Nationalism, SNCC, Liberals and White Revolutionaries," in Philip Foner, *The Black Panthers Speak* (Cambridge, MA: Da Capo Press, 1995), 50.

34. Brown, *Fighting for US*, 67.

35. Baraka, *Raise, Race, Rays, Raze*, 130.

36. Seale, *Sieze the Time: The Story of the Black Panther Party and Huey P. Newton* (New York: Vintage, 1973), 238.

37. Michael Torrence, interview with author, March 12, 2012.

38. Emory Douglas, interview with author, March 18, 2004.

39. Emory Douglas, "The Lumpen: Music as a Tool for Liberation," in *Black Panther*, November 7, 1970.

40. Brian Ward, *Just My Soul Responding: Rhythm and Blues, Black Consciousness and Race Relations* (Berkeley: University of California Press, Berkeley, 1998), 414.

41. Ibid.

42. Toni Vincent, interview with author, April 13, 2003.

43. A thoughtful discussion of the issue is in Bahati Kuumba, *Gender and Social Movements* (Walnut Creek, CA: Alta Mira Press, 2001).

44. Student Nonviolent Coordinating Committee Position Paper, "Women in the Movement," November 1964, found at www.wfu.edu/~zulick/341/snccwomen.html.

45. Clayborne Carson, *In Struggle: SNCC and the Black Awakening of the 1960s* (Cambridge, MA: Harvard University Press, 1981), 191–211.

46. Ruth Rosen, *The World Split Open: How the Modern Women's Movement Changed America* (New York: Viking Press, 2000), 108–110; also see the *Digital History* website, www.digitalhistory.uh.edu/database/article_display.cfm?HHID=381.

47. E. U. Essien-Udom, *Black Nationalism: A Search for Identity in America* (New York: Dell, 1964), 99.

48. Brown, *Fighting for US*, 56.

49. Amiri Baraka, *Autobiography*, 386–7.

50. *Comrade Sister: Voices of Women in the Black Panther Party*, unreleased documentary by Phyllis Jackson, 1995.

51. Jeffrey O. G. Ogbar, *Black Power: Radical Politics and African American Identity* (Baltimore: Johns Hopkins University Press, 2004), 105.

52. Ibid., 104.

53. Mzuri Pambeli, "The Black Panther Party . . . from a Sister's Point of View: An Interview of Dr. Phyllis Jackson," *Positive Action* (March–April 2007): 8.

54. V. I. Lenin, "Soviet Power and the Status of Women," November 6, 1919, found at www.marxists.org/archive/lenin/works/1919/nov/06.htm; also see V. I. Lenin, *Collected Works*, 4th english edition, volume 30 (Moscow: Progress Publishers, 1965), 120–23.

55. Frances M. Beal, "Black Women's Manifesto; Double Jeopardy: To Be Black and Female" (New York: Third World Women's Alliance, 1969), also found at www.hartford-hwp.com/archives/45a/196.html.

56. Angela Davis, *Angela Davis: An Autobiography* (New York: International Publishers, 1988), 162.

57. Angela Y. Davis, "Afro Images: Politics, Fashion and Nostalgia," in *Soul: Black Power, Politics and Pleasure*, ed. Monique Guillory and Richard C. Green (New York: New York University Press, 1998).

58. Woodard, *Nation Within a Nation*, 117.

59. Huey Newton in Foner, *Black Panthers Speak*, 52–4.

60. Marlon Brando appeared at the funeral of Lil' Bobby Hutton in April 1968. Jane Fonda appeared at Panther fundrasiers in New York. See the film *Lords of the Revolution: The Black Panthers*, written by Martin Torgoff (VH1, 2009).

61. Peniel E. Joseph, *Waiting 'Til the Midnight Hour: A Narrative History of Black Power in America* (New York: Henry Holt and Co., 2007), 254.

62. Isaac Hayes, in the film *Respect Yourself: The Stax Records Story*, directed by Robert Gordon and Morgan Neville (Concord Music Group, 2007).

63. Ward, *Just My Soul Responding*, 217.

64. Rob Bowman, *Soulsville, U.S.A.: The Story of Stax Records* (New York: Shirmer Books, 1997), 231.

65. Ibid., 238.

66. Ibid, 268. Also see the film *Wattstax*, directed by Mel Stuart (Columbia Pictures, 1973).

67. See Woodard, *A Nation Within*, 192–218; Also see "Ain't Gonna Shuffle No More" in *Eyes in the Prize*, directed by Sheila Curran Bernard and Samuel D. Pollard (PBS/Blackside, 1990).

Chapter 6: "Bobby Must Be Set Free": Panther Power and Popular Culture

1. The Lumpen, "Free Bobby Now," written by W. Calhoun, 1970, transcription from recording housed at Stanford University Huey P. Newton Foundation archives. Published by Calhoun Music Group / ASCAP.

2. Huey Newton, *To Die for the People: The Writings of Huey P. Newton* (New York: Writers and Readers Publishing, 1999), 139.

3. Safiya Bukhari, *The War Before: The True Life Story of Becoming a Black Panther, Keeping the Faith in Prison and Fighting for Those Left Behind* (New York: Feminist Press at the City University of New York, 2010), 28.

4. Nile Rogers, in *Public Enemy: Reflections of the Black Panthers*, directed by Jens Meurer (Real Fiction, 1999).

5. Afeni Shakur with Jasmine Guy, *Evolution of a Revolutionary* (New York: Atria, 2004), 61.

6. Ibid., 116.

7. Curtis J. Austin, *Up Against the Wall: Violence in the Making and Unmaking of the Black Panther Party* (Fayetteville: University of Arkansas Press, 2006), 289.

8. *Look for Me in the Whirlwind: The Collective Autobiography of the New York 21* (New York: Random House, 1971); Edward Jay Epstein, "The Black Panthers and Police: A Case of Genocide?" *New Yorker*, February 13, 1971; Paul Bass and Douglas W. Rae, *Murder in the Model City: The Black Panthers, Yale, and the Redemption of a Killer* (New York: Basic Books, 2006).

9. Donald Freed, *Agony in New Haven: The Trial of Bobby Seale, Ericka Huggins, and the Black Panther Party* (New York: Simon & Schuster, 1973), 18.

10. Ibid., 70.

11. Important narrative discussions of the demise of the BPP can be found in Austin, *Up Against the Wall*; Peniel Joseph, *Waiting 'Til the Midnight Hour: A Narrative History of Black Power in America* (New York: Henry Holt, 2007); and Ollie Johnson III, "Explaining the Demise of the Black Panther Party" in *The Black Panther Party Reconsidered*, ed. Charles E. Jones (Baltimore: Black Classic Press, 1998).

12. Hugh Pearson, *The Shadow of the Panther: Huey Newton and the Price of Black Power in America* (Reading, MA: Addison-Wesley, 1994), 138.

13. Ibid., 138–39.

14. Reginald Major, *A Panther Is a Black Cat* (New York: W. Morrow, 1971), 144.

15. Bobby Seale, *Seize the Time: The Story of the Black Panther Party and Huey P. Newton* (New York: Vintage, 1973), 133–4.

16. James Forman, *The Making of Black Revolutionaries* (Seattle: University of Washington Press, 1997), 526; Pearson, *Shadow of the Panther*, quotes the text of Forman's speech, but the words are slightly different, although the imagery is identical.

17. Panther chants heard on the "Power!" episode of *Eyes on the Prize*, directed by Louis Massiah and Terry Kay Rockefeller (PBS / Blackside, 1990) VHS.

18. David Hilliard and Lewis Cole, *This Side of Glory: The Autobiography of David Hilliard and the Story of the Black Panther Party* (Chicago: Lawrence Hill, 1993), 182.

19. Hilliard and Cole, *This Side of Glory*, provides a detailed account of the evening of April 6, 1968.

20. Major, *A Panther Is a Black Cat*, 115.

21. Clayborne Carson, *In Struggle: SNCC and the Black Awakening of the 1960s* (Cambridge, MA: Harvard University Press, 1981), 283.

22. Ibid., 300.

23. Ward Churchill, "To Discredit and Destroy" in *Liberation, Imagination and the Black Panther Party* ed. Kathleen Cleaver and George Katsiaficas (New York: Routledge, 2001), 78.

24. Ibid., 82.

25. Sundiata Acoli, "A Brief History of the Black Panther Party: Its Place in the Black Liberation Movement," available at www.hartford-hwp.com/archives/45a/004 .html.

26. David Hilliard, Keith Zimmerman, and Kent Zimmerman, *Huey: Spirit of the Panther* (New York: Thunder's Mouth Press, 2006), 121.

27. Seale, *Seize the Time*, 64.

28. Frantz Fanon, *The Wretched of the Earth* (New York: Grove Press, 1963), 129.

29. Malcolm X and Alex Haley, *The Autobiography of Malcolm X* (New York: Ballantine, 1965), 36.

30. Acoli, "A Brief History."

31. Chris Booker, "Lumpenization: A Critical Error of the Black Panther Party," in *The Black Panther Party (Reconsidered)*, ed. Charles E. Jones (Baltimore: Black Classic Press, 1998), 347.

32. Ibid., 354.

33. Kenneth O'Reilly, *"Racial Matters": The FBI's Secret File on Black America, 1960–1972* (New York: The Free Press, 1989), 297.

34. Ibid., 357.

35. Newton, *To Die for the People*, 45.

36. James Mott, interview with author, July 20, 2007.

37. Clark Bailey, interview with author, November 24, 2004.

38. Newton, *To Die for the People*, 152. Originally printed in *Black Panther*, August 15, 1970.

39. George Katsiaficas, "Organization and Movement: The Case of the Black Panther Party and the Revolutionary People's Constitutional Convention of 1970" in *Liberation, Imagination and the Black Panther Party* edited by Kathleen Cleaver and George Katsiaficas, (New York: Routledge, 2001), 142.

40. In his memoir *This Side of Glory: The Autobiography of David Hilliard and the Story of the Black Panther Party* (Chicago: Lawrence Hill, 1993), David Hilliard comments frequently on his misgivings and misjudgements at crucial turning points in black power history.

41. Peniel E. Joseph in *Waiting 'Til the Midnight Hour: A Narrative History of Black Power in America* (New York: Henry Holt, 2007) discusses the impact of Jackson and the BPP militant activity on white radicalism, 250–51.

42. Mott, author interview, 2007.

43. William Calhoun, interview with author, July 21, 2007.

44. Elaine Brown, *A Taste of Power: A Black Woman's Story* (New York: Anchor Books, 1992) provides the most emotionally complex detail about Newton and the Party's disintegration from a firsthand account.

45. Brown, *A Taste of Power*, 285.

46. Michael Torrence, interview with the author, December 8, 2008.

47. Newton, *To Die for the People*, 113–14.

48. Leigh Raiford, "Restaging Revolution: Black Power," *Vibe* magazine; "Photographic Memory" in *The Civil Rights Movement in American Memory*, ed. Renee C. Romano and Leigh Raiford (Athens: University of Georgia Press, 2006), 238.

49. Michael Campus and Harvey Bernhard make these claims in the documentary film *Mackin' Ain't Easy*, directed by Laura Nix (New Line, 2002).

50. Dialogue from *The Mack*, directed by Michael Campus (Cinerama, 1973).

Chapter 7: "Ol' Pig Nixon": The Protest Music Tradition, Soul, and Black Power

1. An insightful analysis of Motown is in Gerald Early's *One Nation Under a Groove: Motown and American Culture* (Ann Arbor: University of Michigan Press, 1995); Also see Nelson George, *Where Did Our Love Go? The Rise and Fall of the Motown Sound* (New York: St. Martin's Press, 1985).

2. The Lumpen, "Old Pig Nixon," written by W. Calhoun, 1970, transcription from recording housed at Stanford University Huey P. Newton Foundation archives.

3. "Overwhelming feast of spectacle" in *Speak of Me as I Am: The Story of Paul Robeson*, directed by Rachel Hermans (BBC Wales/New Jersey Public Television, 1999).

4. Steven Citron, *The Wordsmiths: Oscar Hammerstein 2nd and Alan Jay Lerner* (New York: Oxford University Press, 1995), 66.

5. Extensive discussion of the lyrics to "Ol' Man River" can be found in Hugh Fordin's *Getting to Know Him: A Biography of Oscar Hammerstein II* (New York: Random House, 1977), and Citron, *The Wordsmiths*.

6. Robeson quote found in the video *Scandalize My Name: Stories from the Blacklist* directed by Alexandra Isles (Unapix Entertainment, Inc., 1998).

7. Robeson singing "Ol' Man River" in his own style can be seen in *Speak of Me as I Am*.

8. Paul Robeson, *Here I Stand* (Boston: Beacon Press, 1998), 174.

9. "No pretty songs" from Robeson, *Scandalize My Name*.

10. Harold Cruse, *The Crisis of the Negro Intellectual*. (New York: Quill, 1984), 86.

11. Robeson, *Here I Stand*, 219.

12. Tombstone shown in final frames of *Speak of Me as I Am*.

13. For discussion of black-owned nightclubs during the Jazz Age, see Ted Vincent, *Keep Cool: The Black Activists That Built the Age of Jazz* (London: Pluto Press, 1995).

14. For extensive discussion on Holiday and "Strange Fruit," see David Margolick and Hilton Als, *Strange Fruit: The Biography of a Song* (New York: Harper Perennial, 2001); Also see Angela Y. Davis, *Blues Legacies and Black Feminism* (New York: Pantheon, 1998).

15. Sara Pendergast and Tom Pendergast, *St. James Encyclopedia of Popular Culture* (Farmington Hills, MI: St. James Press, 2000).

16. Davis, *Blues Legacies*, 107.

17. Walter Mosley, *RL's Dream* (New York: WW. Norton, 2002), 73.

18. William Calhoun, interview with author, July 21, 2007.

19. George, *Where Did Our Love Go?*, 17.

20. Early, *One Nation Under a Groove*, 77.

21. Ron Karenga, "On Cultural Nationalism" in *The Black Aesthetic*, ed. Addison Gayle Jr. (Garden City, NY: Anchor Doubleday, 1972), 36–7.

22. Robin D. G. Kelley, *Race Rebels: Culture, Politics, and the Black Working Class* (New York: Free Press, 1996), 17.

23. Nina Simone with Stephen Cleary, *I Put a Spell on You: The Autobiography of Nina Simone* (New York: Da Capo Press, 1991), 89–90.

24. Daniel Wolff, *You Send Me: The Life and Times of Sam Cooke* (New York: William Morrow, 1995), 289.

25. Ibid., 291.

26. Nathaniel (Magnificent) Montague with Bob Baker, *Burn, Baby! BURN! The Autobiography of Magnificent Montague* (Urbana: University of Illinois Press, 2003), 138.

27. For discussion of People's Park, see W. J. Rorabough, *Berkeley at War: The 1960s* (New York: Oxford University Press, 1989) and Axel Shelter, "The Last Public Space: People's Park in Berkeley," seminar paper, 2009.

28. Obie Benson quoted in Ben Edmonds, *Marvin Gaye: What's Going On and the Last Days of the Motown Sound* (Edinburgh: Canongate, 2003), 96.

29. Frankie Gaye with Fred E. Basten, *Marvin Gaye, My Brother* (San Francisco: Backbeat Books, 2003), 80.

30. Peter Doggett, *There's a Riot Going On* (Edinburgh: Canongate, 2007), 536.

31. George Clinton, in the documentary *Parliament Funkadelic: One Nation Under a Groove*, directed by Yvonne Smith (PBS, 2005).

32. Jimi Hendrix, *Band of Gypsys* (Capitol Records, 1970). Mysteriously, the title of the song was changed to "Message to Love" on the first printings of the album and later CD releases, obscuring the group's homage to soul music that they had prepared.

33. Bootsy Collins, interview with author, May 27, 2011.

34. Charles Shaar Murray, *Crosstown Traffic: Jimi Hendrix and the Post-War Rock 'n' Roll Revolution* (New York: St. Martin's Press, 1991), 93. Also see David Henderson, *'Scuse Me While I Kiss the Sky: The Life and Times of Jimi Hendrix* (New York: Bantam Books, 1981).

35. Hendrix had told an interviewer in 1968 that he was working on a tribute to the Black Panthers on his upcoming album, which was *Electric Ladyland*, in which the song "Voodoo Chile (Slight Return)" is featured. Presumably, Hendrix had a Panther tribute in mind long before his 1970 dedications. Passage found in David Henderson, *'Scuse Me While I Kiss the Sky*, updated edition (New York: Atria Books, 2009), 254.

36. Dennis McNally, interview with the author, January 21, 2008.

37. Found in *The U.S. vs John Lennon*, directed by David Leaf and John Scheinfeld (Lionsgate, 2006).

38. William Calhoun, interview with author, November 9, 2002.

39. Elaine Brown, *A Taste of Power: A Black Woman's Story* (New York: Anchor Books. 1992), 185.

40. Ibid., 196.

41. Elaine Brown, liner notes to *Seize the Time* (CD Water 183, 2006).

42. Lenny Williams, interview with author, December 17, 2010.

43. Robbie Robertson in "Rolling Stone Countdown: 100 Greatest Artists of All Time, #2, Bob Dylan," *Rolling Stone*, www.rollingstone.com/music/lists /100-greatest-artists-of-all-time-19691231/bob-dylan-19691231.

44. Mike Marqusee, *Redemption Song: Muhammad Ali and the Spirit of the Sixties* (London: Verso, 1999), 144.

45. Bobby Seale. *Seize the Time: The Story of the Black Panther Party and Huey P. Newton* (New York: Vintage, 1973), 183–5.

46. Lee Bernstein, *America is the Prison: Arts and Politics in Prison in the 1970s* (Chapel Hill, NC: University of North Carolina Press, 2010), 66.

47. Calhoun, author interview, 2007.

48. Calhoun, author interview, 2007; see also the *Black Panther*, May 29, 1971.

Chapter 8:"Revolution Is the Only Solution": Protest Music Today and the Legacy of the Lumpen

1. The Lumpen. "Revolution Is the Only Solution," written by W. Calhoun, 1970, transcription from recording housed at Stanford University Huey P. Newton Foundation archives.

2. Michael Torrence, interview with author, March 12, 2012.

3. James Mott, interview with author, July 20, 2007.

4. Emory Douglas, interview with author, March 18, 2004.

5. William Calhoun, interview with author, July 21, 2007.

6. Ibid.

7. Calhoun, author interview, 2007.

8. Hugh Pearson, *The Shadow of the Panther: Huey Newton and the Price of Black Power in America* (Reading, MA: Addison-Wesley Publishing Company, 1994), 241. Pearson's account of the Cal-Pak issue is one of the most thorough. Billy Jennings also recalled in an interview that rank-and-file Panthers played music and made a popular scene out of their picket lines, and it was not entirely a dismal experience.

9. Torrence, author interview, 2012.

10. Michael Torrence, inteview with the author, December 8, 2008.

11. From interviews with Lumpen members.

12. Aaron Dixon, *My People Are Rising: Memoir of a Black Panther Party Captain* (Chicago: Haymarket Books, 2012), 270.

13. Eric Porter, *What Is This Thing Called Jazz? African American Musicians as Artists, Critics and Activists* (Berkeley: University of California Press, 2002), 164.

14. Abiodun Oyewole and Umar Bin Hassan, *On a Mission* (New York: Henry Holt, 1996), 6.

15. Ibid., 13.

16. Paris, "Are You a Hip-Hop Apologist?" commentary posted on www.guerrilla funk.com, April 18, 2007.

17. See Bruce Banter, "Atlantic Records Tries to Pimp Out 14yr Old Actress," playahata.com, August 17, 2007.

18. Dr. Boyce Watkins, "BET Has Become the New KKK," newsone.com, http://newsone.com/newsone-original/boycewatkins/dr-boyce-bet-the-new-kkk.

19. Talib Kweli, "Bushanomics" on Cornel West, *Never Forget: A Journey of Revelations* (Hidden Beach Forum 44, 2007), CD.

20. Angela Davis, speaking at Pauley Ballroom, UC–Berkeley, March 2, 2012.

21. "Power!," *Eyes on the Prize*, directed by Louis Massiah and Terry Kay Rockefeller (PBS / Blackside, 1990) VHS

22. Huey P. Newton, *To Die for the People: The Writings of Huey P. Newton*, ed. Frantz Schurman (New York: Random House, 1972), 31.

23. Grace Lee Boggs, speaking at Pauley Ballroom, UC–Berkeley, March 2, 2012.

24. Angela Davis, speaking at Pauley Ballroom, UC–Berkeley, March 2, 2012.

25. Carlos Santana speaking to Brian Copland, *7Live*, 2011.

26. Che Guevara, "On Socialism and Man in Cuba," in *The Che Guevara Reader* (Australia: Ocean Press, 2005).

Index

Page references enclosed in square brackets indicate textual references to endnotes.

AAA. See Afro-American Association
AACM. See Association for the Advancement of Creative Musicians
Abdul-Jabbar, Kareem. See Alcindor, Lew
Abu-Jamal, Mumia, xvii, 5–6, 319
Acoli, Sundiata, 240, 244, 227, 319
activist artists. See artist activism
Affro-Arts Theater (Chicago), 135, 139, 145
Africa: Algeria, 253, 254; Black Nationalist return to, 180; Congo, 143; Ghana, 143; Ivory Coast, 101; James Brown influence on music, 116; Nigeria, 116–119, 148; South Africa, 73, 110, 143, 149; Yoruba culture, 117, 139, 147, 194. See also colonialism
Africa 70 band, 117
African Heritage Ensemble, 134
African roots: Abiodun Oyewole, 321; African music physicality, 118; Afro hairstyle: see Afro; Afrocentric rap videos, 323; Amiri Baraka, 187; Aretha Franklin, 155–156, 157; Assata Shakur, 147; Afeni Shakur on Ten Point Program, 226; Black

Arts movement, 142; black cultural nationalism, 181–182; black versus Negro, 149: see also black versus Negro; dashikis, 140, 147, 193, 194; Drums of Passion (Olatunji), 148, 149; funk, 96; increasingly visible in black communities, 148; Jamaican rhythms, 114; James Brown, 96, 101, 107, 281; Jesse Jackson, 136; Ma'at moral codes, 314; Malcolm X, 12, 181; "Mdamase," 73; Miriam Makeba, 149–150; Pan Afrikan Peoples Arkestra, 184; re-Africanization of black music, 120; Ron Karenga, 189; Stokely Carmichael, 2, 277; Swahili classes, 73; Yoruba culture, 139, 147, 194
Afro, 136, 146, 149–150, 205
Afro-American Association (AAA), 62, 66, 182
afrobeat: Fela Kuti music, 116
Afro-diasporic music, 150–151
Agnes Memorial Christian Academy (East Oakland), 47, 318
Agnew, Spiro, 265, 291
Akeelah and the Bee (film), 325
Alabama: Birmingham, 143, 203, 281; Montgomery, 9–10; Muscle Shoals, 152; as Republic of New Afrika, 146; Selma, 11

"Alabama" (Coltrane), 106
Alameda County (CA), 74, xiv, 251, 300
Alameda County Courthouse, xiv, 251
Al-Amin, Jamil Abdullah. See Brown, H. Rap
Alcindor, Lew, 20
Algiers, 253, 254
Ali, Muhammad, 307
All for One Executives organization (AFO), 282–283
Allan, Lewis. See Meeropol, Abel
Allen, Ernie, 66
Allen, Robert (Black Awakening in Capitalist America), 179
al-Mansour, Khalid. See Warden, Donald
"Am I Black Enough for You" (Paul): racially self-conscious song, 193
"Amen" (Impressions), 130
"America Is My Home" (James Brown), 103
Amherst College (MA), 38
Amsterdam News (newspaper), 142
"Angela" (Lennon and Ono), 205
anthems: Black Panther Party, 16–17, 294, 298; "Say It Loud" (James Brown), 108; "A Change Is Gonna Come" (Cooke), 284; "The Payback" (James Brown), 332; "The Revolution Will Not Be Televised" (Scott-Heron), 109; "Strange Fruit" (Holiday), 274; "Voodoo Chile (Slight Return)" (Hendrix), 294, 379n35
antiassimilationism, 11, 97–99, 197–198. See also Black Nationalism
anticolonial liberation movements. See colonialism
Apollo Theater (Harlem), 89, 93–94, 100, 122
Arab Spring (2011), 331, 323, 330–331
Arabic names, 182–183, 187
"Are You Really Ready for Black Power" (Byrd), 161
Art Ensemble of Chicago, 134
artist activism: Billie Holiday "Strange Fruit," 328; doing art while others risk lives, 320–321; entertainer/activist schism, 271–272, 282; Goapele, 328; Grace Lee Boggs, 334–335; Harry Belafonte, 150; James Brown "Get Up, Get Into It, Get Involved," 320; John

Lennon and Yoko Ono "Give Peace a Chance," 328; KRS-One "Self-Destruction," 328; Lumpen concert recording, xvii; Michael Franti, 327–328; Nina Simone, 282; Paul Robeson, 271–272; Sam Cooke, 282–283; Sammy Davis Jr., 272; Stevie Wonder "Happy Birthday," 328; West Coast Rap All-Stars "We're All in the Same Gang," 328
assassination: Fred Hampton, 128, 137–138, 140, 251; James Meredith attempt, 98; Malcolm X, 11, 62, 95, 181, 225, 232, 241; Martin Luther King Jr., 20, 101–103, 136, 162, 163–164, 177, 212, 236; Robert F. Kennedy, 20, 236. See also killed
"Assassination" (Elaine Brown), 298
Association for the Advancement of Creative Musicians (AACM), 134
Atkins, Thomas, 101
Atlanta (GA), 159, 163, 209
Atlantic Records, 152, 153, 154, 212, 325–326
Attica State Prison (NY), 308
Audobon Ballroom (Harlem), 143–144
authenticity, 153, 163, 320
Autobiography of Malcolm X, 97, 108, 117, 181, 243
Autumn Records, 52
Axton, Estelle, 211, 214

Baby Huey (James Ramey), 139
Baby Huey and the Babysitters, 139
Badie, Chuck, 283
Baez, Joan, 287, 302
Bailey, Clark "Santa Rita": after Lumpen, 47–48, 318–319; Black Panther newspaper distribution night, 74; BPP weapon storehouse maintenance, 318; classical music lessons, 74; left Party, 318–319; Lumpen as Panthers, 34–35; as Lumpen member, 80, 249, 312, 318; Lumpen origins, 26–27; on Lumpen principles, 47; Lumpen vocals, 168, 263; Michael Torrence recruited Bailey, 23, 74, 75; Minor Williams association, 81; at Oakland Community School, 318; as Panther, 25, 46, 74–75, 249, 318; on Party leadership attention, 29; path to Party, 74–75;

reverse racism, 41–42; "Santa Rita" origin, 74; bus driver in Sacramento, 319; Valerie Trahan and, 42

Baker, Ella, 197

Baker, General, 174

Baldwin, James, 305

"Ballad of a Thin Man" (Dylan), 70, 303–304

Ballard, Hank, 104, 193

BAM. See Black Arts movement

Bambaataa, Afrika, 122, 324

"Banana Boat Song" (Belafonte), 150

Band of Gypsys, 293

Baraka, Amina, 200

Baraka, Amiri: on Nation of Islam, 180–181; Autobiography of LeRoi Jones, 187–188, 200; in Black Arts movement, 143, 187; Black Arts Repertory Theatre/School (BARTS), 145, 186, 187; on BPP armed march on Sacramento, 71; BPP critic, 192; Committee for a Unified NewArk (CFUN) leader, 188; Congress of African People (CAP) leader, 188, 209; National Black Political Convention, 216; on James Brown, 111; Kenneth Gibson mayoral voting bloc, 186, 188; Newark Black Nationalist politics, 179, 186; and Emory Douglas, 194; and Ron Karenga, 186, 187, 188–189, 200; at San Francisco State University, 16, 71, 187; white alliance criticism, 192, 206; working among Panthers, 187. See also Jones, LeRoi

Barrett, Aston, 114

Basie, Count, 224, 272

"Battle Hymn of the Republic," 274

Bay Area, 145; black population, 57; BPP membership, 15; Cal-Pak, 315; counterculture revolution, 55–56; Four Tops performance, 286; integrated rhythm and blues groups, 41; John George, xiii; KSOL radio, 52, 314; Lumpen band musicians, 49, 82; Lumpen single, 220–221; People's Park confrontations (1969), 286–287; Sly and the Family Stone, 52, 55, 57, 85; Third World Liberation Front, 20. See also Oakland; San Francisco

Beal, Fran, 202–203

Beatles, 13, 56, 296

Beatnigs, 328

Belafonte, Harry, 150

Bell, Al, 212, 214

Bennett, Lerone, Jr., 13

Benson, Renaldo "Obie," 287

Berkeley (CA), xv, xvi, 256, 286–287

Berry, Chuck, 134

BET (TV), 324, 326

Big Al's (San Francisco), 72

Bin Hassan, Umar, 110

Birmingham (AL), 143, 203, 281

Black and Brown trading stamps, 123

Black Arts movement (BAM): cultural centers nationwide, 145–146; cultural dimension of black power, 145, 146, 210; cultural nationalist sensibilities, 182; cultural politics, 12, 27; James Brown as pinnacle, 111–112; John Coltrane and Malcolm X as black selfhood, 144–145; Lorraine Hansberry impact, 155; Lumpen concert recording, xvii; Malcolm X black liberation metaphor, 144, 225

Black Arts Repertory Theatre/School (BARTS; Harlem), 145, 186

black capitalism: Aretha Franklin, 156; Black Awakening in Capitalist America (Allen; book), 179; Black Nationalism, 207; Cal-Pak, 315; James Brown, 99–100, 102, 104, 111, 112–113, 123; National Black Political Convention (1972), 215; Richard Nixon "Black Capitalism" campaign, 123; Wattstax (film), 214. See also black economics; capitalism

black churches: Agnes Memorial Christian Academy (East Oakland), 47, 318; Aretha Franklin secular music, 153; Barack Obama speaking style, 329; civil rights as radical act, 77; gender structure, 196; gospel as movement force, 7–8, 130–131; influence in Motown music, 279; "People Get Ready" as tribute, 129; Saint Augustine's Episcopal Church (Oakland), 248; Sixteenth Street Baptist Church (Birmingham), 203, 281; Nina Simone, 281; West Coast blacks, 58; Wo'Se Community

black churches (*continued*)
  Church (Oakland), 47, 314. See also
  gospel; spirituals
black cultural nationalism: Black Nationalism, 181–182; gender equality,
  206; Huey Newton on BPP versus,
  190–191; Kawaida (philosophy of
  cultural nationalism), 183, 200;
  "Kawaida Towers" in Newark, 186,
  188–189; linked to free jazz, 184–
  185; Lumpen and, 193–196; revolutionary nationalists versus, 189; Ron
  Karenga, 191–192; SNCC, 197–198;
  US Organization, 182–185
black culture: artist-activists, 320; Black
  Arts movement: see Black Arts
  movement; blaxploitation movies,
  257–260; cultural change, 323–327;
  dual language of coded black music,
  277, 290, 304; Grace Lee Boggs,
  334–335; individualism fissures
  in community, 323; James Brown,
  91, 124; Jimi Hendrix impact, 293;
  LeRoi Jones Black Arts Repertory
  Theatre/School (BARTS), 145;
  male chauvinism, 43: see also black
  patriarchy; Motown and Black
  Nationalists leave blues behind,
  278–280; Muhammad Ali, 307;
  "Ol' Man River" spiritual passage,
  268; "Resistance Culture," 327;
  revolutionary culture part of revolution: see revolutionary culture
  part of revolution; soul aesthetic,
  158, 215, 220; "Strange Fruit" and
  social justice, 274; Wattstax (film),
  214. See also African roots; Black
  Nationalism
black economics: AACM control of
  music, 134; after 1960, 60–61; after
  World War II, 59, 60; All for One
  Executives organization, 282–283;
  and Amiri Baraka, 186, 188–189;
  and Aretha Franklin, 156; black
  entertainers, 272; Black Nationalism support, 207; Brotherhood of
  Sleeping Car Porters, 57–58; Cal-
  Pak, 315; Chicago black jazz club
  model, 135; in Detroit, 173–174;
  Dodge Revolutionary Union Movement, 175; Fair Housing Act (1968),
  163–164; "George Jackson," 306;

Huey Newton on, 242, 313, 334;
  and James Brown, 99–100, 102,
  111, 112–113, 123; LRBW, 175–176;
  Chicago political machine, 136;
  middle class, 164; music industry,
  215, 272, 320, 324–325; NATRA,
  162; Operation Breadbasket, 136;
  per H. Rap Brown, 100; revolutionary culture part of revolution, 323,
  327; Richard Nixon "Black Capitalism" campaign, 123; Sam Cooke,
  282–283; and soul aesthetic, 158,
  215, 220
Black Entertainment Television (BET),
  324, 326
black freedom movement, 141, 155, 163,
  164. See also black revolution
Black Guerilla Army, 304
Black House (San Francisco), 145
"black is beautiful," 14, 149
Black Liberation Army (BLA), 254
Black Liberation Movement (BLM),
  240–241
black middle class, 136, 164. See also
  black economics
Black Moses, 213
black music: African music influence
  after Drums of Passion (Olatunji),
  148, 149; Black Nationalism and,
  209–211; black power transformation of, 6; on black radio, 131–132;
  Blues People: Negro Music in White
  America, 141, 186, 275; Chicago
  soul, 129, 132, 133–134, 138; corporate hijacking, 322, 324; dual
  language of, 277, 290, 304; James
  Brown in mainstream, 124; James
  Brown "Say It Loud" as turning
  point, 106–107, 111; Jimi Hendrix
  impact, 293; late 1960s music
  scenes, 185; Lumpen soul music
  aesthetic, 193; lyrical innuendos
  become harsh truths, 290; Motown:
  see Motown Records; multiple
  rhythms of, 1, 118, 120; music
  industry, 215, 272, 320, 324–326;
  packaged protest music, 168, 171–
  172; resistance music, 129, 275, 276;
  Sly and the Family Stone "Dance to
  the Music" transformation of, 51
Black Nationalism, 11, 15, 41–42, 45,
  122, 128, 135, 136, 142, 175,

178–179, 180, 183, 184–185, 188, 189, 190, 192, 196–203, 207, 208, 209–211, 216, 232, 234, 235, 238, 279–280
black newspapers and publications: Amsterdam News, 142; Freedom-ways, 142; Inner City Voice (Detroit), 175, 176; the Libera-tor, 138, 141–142; Triple Jeopardy (TWWA), 203; Umbra, 142. See also Black Panther (newspaper)
Black Panther (newspaper), 15, 16, 17, 22, 24, 26, 35, 38, 43–44, 66, 69–70, 74, 75, 78, 107, 139, 190, 191, 194–195, 201, 220, 249–250, 256, 302, 315, 365n38
Black Panther Party (BPP; Party): anthems, 16–17, 294, 298; anti-assimilation, 97; armed patrols, 68–69, 338; Betty Shabazz, 232–233; Cal-Pak, 315–316, 380n8; capitalism as enemy, 207, 240; Central Committee, 43–44, 365n48; Chicago organization, 136; codes of conduct, 244; commit-ment of members, 13–14, 15, 27, 40, 75, 222; community workers, 25, 31; duties of members, 15, 27, 44, 244, 247–249, 315; East Coast chapter struggles, 224–228, 253; Elaine Brown songwriter for, 299; Eldridge Cleaver expulsion, 45–46, 252–253; first female recruit, 70; first Panther killed in action, 236; first recruit, 128, 236; Frantz Fanon as required reading, 75, 112; gen-der equality, 42–43, 65, 200–202, 248–249; guns replaced with food, 34, 45, 170, 208, 246–247, 250, 257; impact on US culture, 14–15; It's About Time Committee, xvi; J. Edgar Hoover's virulent opposi-tion, 328–329; Jimi Hendrix and, 293–296; John Forman as minister of foreign affairs, 234; John Frey altercation with Huey Newton, 232; liberation schools, 15, 76, 248; Lionel Wilson, 47, 238, 319; LRBW schism, 178; Lumpen creation, 14; Lumpen unravel, 312; lumpen-ism as demise of Party, 245–247; as Malcolm X outgrowth, 13, 28,
240–241, 243–244; Marvin Gaye views on, 288; member names: see Black Panther Party members; membership, 244–245; in movie themes and character, 257–261; New York 21, 227–228; origins, 15, 60, 61–67; Pan Afrikan Peoples Arkestra members, 184; panther as Party symbol, 67; phases of exis-tence, 15–17, 178, 224, 246–247, 250–253, 254–255, 313; Public Enemy Number One, 238–240; public image, 222–224, 229–230, 232, 233, 234, 235, 239, 244–245, 246, 248, 252, 315; race not explicit in works, 193, 222, 240; retreat meetings, 79; revolution construct, 11–12, 16; Revolutionary People's Constitutional Convention (RPCC), 40–41, 209, 250; Sacramento armed march, 70–72, 152, 223, 230, 231; Serve the People projects, 248–249; SNCC merger, 234; Soul Day at San Quentin (1971), 306–308; Stokely Carmichael as prime minister, 234; survival pending revolution, 229, 247–250; Survival Programs: see Survival Programs; SWAT raid, 24; Ten Point Program: see Ten Point Program; US Organization versus, 189–193; violence opposed and encouraged, 245; white alliances, 192, 206–209, 294
Black Panther Party members: Aaron Dixon, 294; Afeni Shakur, 226, 227; Akua Njeri, 201; Alex Rackley, 228; Ali Bey Hassan, 227; Alprentice "Bunchy" Carter, 16, 128, 189, 190, 250; Angela Davis, 204; Assata Shakur, 146, 227, 254; Bob Brown, 137; Bobby Hutton, 128, 236; Bobby Seale, 15, 333; Chaka Khan, 139; Charles Brunson, 77; Clark Bailey, 25, 74–75, 249, 318; David Brothers, 225; David Hilliard, xvi, 16, 25, 27, 37; Elaine Brown, xvi, 16, 201, 296, 299; Elbert "Big Man" Howard, 69; Eldridge Cleaver, 21, 24; Elmer "Geronimo" Pratt, 83, 254; Emory Douglas, 16, 27, 37; Ericka Huggins, 200, 229, 300; Ernie Allen, 66; Flores Forbes,

Black Panther Party members (*continued*)
318; Fred Hampton, 128, 137, 251;
George Murray, 79; Gloria Aberna-
thy, 77; H. Rap Brown, 234; Huey
P. Newton, 15; Jack Strivers, 77;
Jamal Joseph, 226, 227; James Forman, 234; James McClain, 128, 251;
James Mott, 30; John Huggins, 16,
128, 250–251; John Williams, 177–
178; Jonathan Jackson, 128; Kath-
leen Cleaver, 37; Kenny (Mamadu
Lumumba) Freeman, 66, 73; Linda
Harrison, 107; Lonnie McLucas,
229; Luke Tripp, 177–178; Lumpen
singers, xvii, 13–14, 26–27, 29,
34–35, 248; Lumumba Shakur, 225,
227; Mark Clark, 128, 251; Mark
Teemer, 77; Melvin Whitaker, 77;
Michael (Cetewayo) Tabor, 227;
Michael Torrence, 23, 25, 74, 75;
Mumia Abu-Jamal, 5; Nile Rodgers,
225–226; Phyllis Jackson, 201; Ray
"Masai" Hewitt, 298, 318; Richard
(Dhoruba) Moore, 227; Robert
Webb, 45; Sam Napier, 45; Shirley
Finney, 77; Stokely Carmichael,
234; Sundiata Acoli, 227, 244;
Tarika (Matilaba) Lewis, 70; Toni
Vincent, xiv; Walter Turner, xv;
Warren Kimbro, 229; William Calhoun, 25, 314; William Christmas,
128, 251
Black Panther Party of Northern California, 66, 73
Black Panther Political Party, 66, 204
black patriarchy, 91, 97–98, 196–200,
200–202, 204, 206, 215, 297,
298–299
black poetry: Gil Scott-Heron, 108–109;
James Brown, 108–109, 111
black power: Angela Davis Afro as icon,
205; "Are You Really Ready for
Black Power" (Byrd), 161; Black
Arts movement as cultural dimension of, 145; blaxploitation movies,
258; BPP as necessary outgrowth,
338; civil rights movement, 6, 8,
142; cultural politics, 2, 12; Drums
of Passion (Olatunji), 149; "Fight the
Power" (Isley Brothers), 164; identity politics, 14; internationalization
of, 120; James Brown celebrating,
92, 98–99, 102, 105, 121, 122; Jesse
Jackson, 136; Malcolm X assassination, 98; March Against Fear
sparking, 11, 98–99, 198; meanings,
98–99; Mexico City Olympics, 21,
105; Nathaniel Montague, 160;
revolutionary fantasy versus revolutionary work, 321; SNCC, 197–198;
spirit of change, 322; Stokely Carmichael, 11, 98–99, 198
Black Power March. See March Against
Fear (1966)
black pride: anthems after "Say It Loud,"
108; Aretha Franklin, 156; Isaac
Hayes as Black Moses, 213; James
Brown celebrating, 91–92, 96,
97–98, 104–113, 122; Marcus Garvey, 180; Muhammad Ali, 307; soul
aesthetic, 158, 215, 220
black radio: "Burn, baby, burn," 160; in
Chicago, 161; demise after King
assassination, 162; Seize the Time,
298; inspirational music with a
message, 131; James Brown radio
station, 99–100, 102, 112–113; King
cultivated, 159; KSOL and KDIA
(Bay Area), 220; NATRA, 162;
in New York City, 161; in 1965,
131–132; popularizing black power
movement, 159; Radio Free Dixie,
160; WERD (Atlanta), 159; "We're
a Winner" banned, 132; white
owned, 131
black revolution: 1960s to 1970s, 9–13;
Angela Davis, 205; Aretha Franklin,
156; artist-activists: see artist activism; "blackness" legacy, 13; Bobby
Seale revolution revolves power,
333; "A Change Is Gonna Come"
(Cooke) as anthem, 284; cultural
revolution: see revolutionary culture
part of revolution; entertainer/activ-
ist schism, 271–272, 282; "Fight the
Power" (Isley Brothers) last of great
movement songs, 164; James Brown
urged toward radical stance, 122;
James Brown's rhythm, 96–97; John
George revolutionary who could
dance, xiii–xiv; as lifetime process,
319, 322; The Mack film and black
activists, 260; Malcolm X construct,
11–12; Negro to black, 1–2: see also

black versus Negro; Newton on BPP versus US Organization, 190–191; on personal level, 146–147; "pig" added to lexicon, 246: see also "pig" symbolism; the revolution catchphrase, 13–14; revolution requires participation, 329, 333; revolutionary fantasy versus revolutionary work, 321; revolutionary versus cultural nationalists, 189; Ron Karenga US Organization plans, 191–192; SNCC-BPP merger, 234; study of revolution, 242–245; today's rebel youth rendered invisible, 323; true revolutionary guided by love, 336; waned as soul music waned, 163

Black Student Alliance formation, 21–22

Black Student Union (BSU), 22, 23, 41, 74, 75, 190, 204, 208, 296

black women, 196, 307; Akua Njeri, 201; Angela Davis: see Davis, Angela; black cultural nationalists and, 206; Black Nationalism and, 196–203; Black Women's Alliance, 202; blaxploitation movies, 258; BPP gender equality, 42–43, 65, 200–202; Elaine Brown: see Brown, Elaine; Ella Baker as SNCC organizer, 197; Erick Huggins: see Huggins, Ericka; Fannie Lou Hamer as SNCC organizer, 197; Fran Beal, 202; in Nation of Islam, 198–199; patriarchy, 97–98, 196–197, 198; Phyllis Jackson, 201; Rosa Parks, 9, 197; Septima Clark, 197; Shirley Chisolm, 215; Third World Women's Alliance, 202–203; US Organization gender roles, 183, 199–200; women of color organizations, 202–203; "Women's Liberation Movements and the Gay Liberation Movements" (Newton), 249–250. See also gender equality

Black Women's Alliance, 202

"Blackenized" (Ballard), 193

blackness: Black Arts meet Black Nationalism, 209–211; Black Arts movement celebrating, 142; black-conscious free jazz, 185; Bobby Seale dismisses reclaiming, 192; emergence of, 13; James Brown celebrating, 91–92, 104–113, 106–107, 293; Jimi Hendrix freaky black cool, 293; John Coltrane and Malcolm X as black selfhood, 144–145; Malcolm X love of, 144; Malcolm X popularizing, 225; Muhammad Ali as initiator, 307; Nguzo Saba (seven principles of blackness), 183; as piece of black liberation, 144; Republic of New Afrika space to recover, 147; SNCC black power and exclusive black participation, 197–198; soul as catchall for, 141; soul culture celebrating, 140

blaxploitation movies, 257–260

Blount, Herman Poole. See Sun Ra

Blowfly. See Reid, Clarence

Blue Gardenia (West Oakland), 38

blues: absolute honesty of, 276; Billie Holiday, 106, 273, 274; Black Nationalists abandon, 279–280; Blues People (LeRoi Jones), 141, 186, 275; Bob Dylan respect for, 302; built around melody, 96; Chess Records, 134; coded lyrics, 129, 276–277, 280, 290, 302; Huey Newton hung with blues crowd, 59; John Coltrane "Alabama," 106; John Lee Hooker, 279; not at Motown, 278–279; Oakland as hotbed, 59; as resistance music, 276; Ron Karenga invalidating, 279–280; soul music as fusion of gospel and blues, 35–36

Blues People: Negro Music in White America (LeRoi Jones), 141, 186, 275

Bob Marley and the Wailers, 114, 115

"Bobby Must Be Set Free" (Lumpen), 35, 37, 39, 217–220, 228–230. See also "Free Bobby Now" (Lumpen)

Boggs, Grace Lee, 334–335

bombings, 104, 203, 252, 281

Booker T. and the MGs, 211, 212

Bosn's Locker, 59

Boston (MA), 38, 40, 163, 334

Boston College, 334

Boston Garden (MA), 101

Bowman, Frankie, 75, 76

Boyette, Bill, 315

BPP. See Black Panther Party

Brandeis University (MA), 203

Brando, Marlon, 209, 235, 375n60

breakfast for children programs, 15, 27, 34, 38, 44, 45, 75–77, 79, 138–139, 140, 170, 208, 239, 246–249, 250, 257, 315, 338

Brooklyn (NY), 36–37, 225

Brotherhood of Sleeping Car Porters, 57–58

Brothers, David, 225

Brown, Bob, 137

Brown, Bruce, 161

Brown, Elaine, xvi, 16–17, 27, 30, 38, 46, 178, 201, 222, 252, 255, 297–299, 300, 315, 318

Brown, H. "Rap" (Jamil Abdullah Al-Amin), 100–101, 108, 223, 225, 231, 234

Brown, James: Africa visits, 101, 117–118, 120; African rhythms, 96, 107, 281; "America Is My Home," 103; artist-activist, 320; Black and Brown trading stamps, 123; black patriarchy, 97–98; black power open dialogue, 101; black pride celebration, 91–92, 96, 97–98, 108, 121, 122; born, 93; civil rights and soul music, 4, 96; "Cold Sweat," 91, 97; Donald Warden race politics discussions, 97; "Don't Be a Drop-Out," 97, 99; Famous Flames backup and lead singer, 93; freestyle rapping, 90; "Get Up, Get Into It, Get Involved," 320; as Godfather of Soul, 90, 91, 101; Godfather of Soul, 99, 104; Gospel Starlighters began singing career, 93; H. Rap Brown Defense Fund support, 100–101; Handsome "Honey" Washington (aunt), 93; as Hardest Working Man in Show Business, 89, 91; Hubert Humphrey association, 99, 103; "I Can't Stand Myself" on A side of "There Was a Time," 89; "I Don't Want Nobody to Give Me Nothin'" on integration, 92; identity politics centrality, 93, 110; "I'll Go Crazy," 93; influence on African music, 116, 119; influence on black music, 106–107, 111; influence on Jamaican music, 114–115, 119; influence on Lumpen, 32, 33, 35, 89; influence on Michael Jackson, 111; "It's a Man's Man's Man's World," 91, 97–98; James Meredith's March Against Fear, 98–99; King assassination performance, 101–103; Live at the Apollo album, 93–94; Live at the Apollo Volume 2 "There Was a Time" 15-minute performance, 89; "Lost Someone" Brown bares his soul, 93; Lumpen stage production from, 89; "Money Won't Change You," 91–92, 97, 99; most important black man in America, 111, 124; "Mother Popcorn," 91; as Mr. Dynamite, 91; Original Last Poets tribute "James Brown," 110; "Papa Don't Take No Mess," 121; "Papa's Got a Brand New Bag," 91, 94, 95; "The Payback" as Occupy Movement anthem, 332; "Please Please Please" first recording, 93; radio station, 99–100, 102, 112–113; religious references in inflections, 35; Revolution of the Mind album and black consciousness, 122–124; rhythm revolution, 91–95; Richard Nixon endorsement, 123; "Say It Loud": see "Say It Loud (I'm Black and I'm Proud)" (James Brown); "Sex Machine," 121; Sex Machine album, 87; social activism, 99–100, 104, 106; as Soul Brother Number One, 90, 91, 94, 123; "Soul Power" Brown ending show with, 220; Stokely Carmichael calling Brown dangerous, 99; "Superbad," 121; "the One": see "the One"; "There Was a Time" as flip-side hit, 89; "There Was a Time" as history of people through dance, 90; "There Was a Time" Lumpen Theme based on, 87; "There Was a Time" stretching rhythmic contrast, 97; "Try Me," 93, 115; Uncle Tom question by Earl Wilson, 104; Vietnam troop performances, 103–104; White House consultant on race, 99; "You Can Have Watergate, Just Gimme Some Bucks and I'll Be Straight," 123

Brown, Oscar, Jr., 3, 135

Brown v. Board of Education (1954), 9, 57

Brownsville riots (1970), 36–37

Brunson, Charles, 77, 79

BSU. See Black Student Union
"Burn, baby, burn," 160, 223
"Bushonomics" (Kweli), 329
Butler, Jerry, 129, 133
Byrd, Gary: "Are You Really Ready for
    Black Power," 161; "If the People
    Only Knew (the Power of the Peo-
    ple)," 161; "To You Beautiful Black
    Sister," 161; WLIB radio (NY), 161

Café Society (New York), 273
Calhoun, Jamil, xvi, 313
Calhoun, William: after Lumpen,
    47–48, 314–315, 319; Black Student
    Alliance formation, 22; as David
    Hilliard bodyguard, 46; on Elaine
    Brown, 297; family responsibilities,
    313–314; Freedom Messengers for-
    mation, 31; James Brown influence,
    89; at KSOL as "Billy King," 314;
    left Party, 46, 313–314; Lumpen
    as Party evolution, 45; Lumpen
    leader, xvi, 26, 35, 88, 125, 168,
    217, 263, 309–310; Lumpen mem-
    ber, 312; Lumpen messages, 34,
    37–38; Lumpen origins, 26–27; as
    Mdamase, 73; on Motown sound,
    278; musical career, 72–73; "Oh My
    Lawd They Done Killed the Blues,"
    278; as Panther, 25, 314; path to
    BPP, 72–73; on "People Get Ready"
    Lumpen lyrics, 127; playing "The
    Lumpen Theme," 88; Ray Charles
    influence, 72; recording of 45 rpm
    single, 35; on Soul Day at San
    Quentin, 307; Temptations dialogue
    at performance, 168; on walkout
    with San Francisco State, 22–23;
    working with teenage sex offend-
    ers, 314–315; Wo'Se Community
    Church cofounder, 47, 314
California State Package Store and Tav-
    ern Owners Association (Cal-Pak),
    315–316, 380n8
call-and-response, 88, 218, 277
Calloway, Cab, 224
Cal-Pak (California State Package Store
    and Tavern Owners Association),
    315–316, 380n8
Campbell, Clive (DJ Kool Herc),
    121–122
Caren, Mike, 325–326

Carlos, John, 20–23, 105, 364n2
Carmen Jones (film), 150
Carmichael, Stokely (Kwame Ture):
    autobiography Ready for Revolution,
    2–3; black power chant, 11, 98, 198;
    BPP prime minister, 234; coauthor
    of Black Power book, 108; intro-
    duced George Sams to BPP, 229;
    James Brown indirect sanction, 108;
    at James Mott SNCC chapter, 77;
    King association, 2, 99; King versus
    Carmichael for leadership, 230; and
    Miriam Makeba, 150, 254; music
    as weapon, 2–3, 277; Pan African
    Cultural Festival in Algiers, 254; as
    Panther, 234; Rap Brown replacing
    at SNCC, 100; saying James Brown
    dangerous, 99; SNCC leader, 2,
    100, 198, 230, 234
Carter, Alprentice "Bunchy," 16, 126,
    128, 189–190, 250, 298
Castro, Fidel, 143, 160
"Change Is Gonna Come, A" (Cooke), 3,
    283, 284
Chaplin, Ralph, 274
Charles, Ray, 36, 37, 72, 154, 264, 268,
    272
Che-Lumumba club, 204
Cherry, Don, 185
Chesimard, JoAnne. See Shakur, Assata
Chess Records, 134
Chicago (IL), 109, 129–130, 134–136,
    137, 145–146, 161, 163, 180, 201,
    236–237, 302
Chicago Eight, 237
Chicago Seven, 237
Chicago soul, 129, 132, 133–134, 138
Chi-Lites, The, 133–134, 138
Chisolm, Shirley, 215
Christmas, William, 126, 128, 251
churches. See black churches
civil rights movement: "Amen" (Impres-
    sions) as marching music, 130;
    Aretha Franklin, 151–152, 153, 154;
    black power exploded from, 6, 8,
    99; as black revolution beginnings,
    9–11; "A Change Is Gonna Come"
    (Cooke) as anthem, 284; gospel as
    movement force, 7–8, 130–131;
    Harry Belafonte outspoken support,
    150; Jesse Jackson after King assas-
    sination, 136; King, Gordy,

civil rights movement (*continued*)
and Motown on their terms, 173;
Nina Simone's first civil rights song,
281; patriarchy, 196–197, 198;
"People Get Ready" as standard,
125, 128, 129; "Say It Loud" versus
earlier music, 106; social control
as cultural control, 323; soul music
hand-in-hand, 4, 96, 141; "Wake
Up Everybody" last of great movement songs, 164; What's Going On?
(Gaye) album eulogy for movement,
288; white alliances, 207
Clark, Mark, 126, 128, 251
Clark, Septima, 197
Cleaver, Eldridge: actively condoning
political violence, 223; author of
Soul on Ice, 108, 232; BPP gender
equality, 201; drug addiction, 319;
Elaine Brown wrote "The Meeting" for, 298, 299; expulsion from
Party, 45–46, 252; Huey Newton
admiration, 233, 241; "I'm Mad
Like Eldridge Cleaver" (MC5),
295; James Brown sanction, 108; on
King assassination, 236; Malcolm X
legacy heir, 240–241; media savvy,
232; Pan African Cultural Festival
in Algiers, 254; photographing Huey
Newton, 222–223; as presidential
candidate, 233, 246; public speak-
ing skills, 251; publicizing Huey
Newton and BPP, 232, 233, 241; at
Ramparts magazine, 60, 232; Sole-
dad Prison sentence for rape, 232;
wounding of, 21, 236
Cleaver, Kathleen, 6, 37, 86, 232, 233,
241, 258
Cleveland, Al, 287
Cleveland, James, 157
Clinton, George, 184, 292, 293
Clutchette, John, 304
Cockrel, Kenneth, 174
Cohran, Philip, 134, 135
COINTELPRO, 238–240
Cole, Nat "King," 129
Cole, Natalie, 140
Coleman, Melvin, 82
Collins, William "Bootsy," 95–96, 220,
118, 293
colonialism: BPP in solidarity against,
189; Fela Kuti, 116, 117, 119–120;

Frantz Fanon "Third World Revo-
lution," 112; global community
involvement against, 330–331, 334;
liberation movements against, 143,
179–180; Malcolm X, 12; "uncolo-
nized black selfhood," 145; US
Organization decolonizing rituals,
183
Coltrane, John, 6, 7, 106, 108, 144–145,
148
Columbia Records, 148, 151, 152, 301,
328
Combahee Women's Collective, 203
Committee for a Unified NewArk
(CFUN), 188–189
Communism, 143, 204, 271
Communist Manifesto (Marx; book), 28
Community Learning Center (Oakland),
46
"Compared to What?" (McDaniels), 291
Congo, 143
Congress of African People (CAP), 188,
209, 216
Congress of Racial Equality (CORE),
100, 130, 197
Cooke, Sam, 129–130, 264, 272, 282–
283, 284, 306
Cordell, "Lucky," 161
Cornelius, Don, xiv, 134, 161
Côte d'Ivoire. See Ivory Coast
Cotton Club (New York), 224
Coup, xv, 324
Cox, Billy, 293
Cropper, Steve, 211
Cruse, Harold, 98, 143, 270
Cuba: Assata Shakur, 146; Che Guevara,
242; Fidel Castro, 143; Robert F.
Williams, 242
cultural activism. See artist activism
cultural nationalism. See black cultural
nationalism
culture. See black cultural nationalism;
black culture; revolutionary culture
part of revolution
Cunningham, Ken "Wolf," 156

Daley, Richard J., 135–136, 236–237
dance: African music physicality, 118;
black poetry through, 90; Bob Marley "Soul Almighty" dance shouts,
115; BPP troupe of women with
Freedom Messengers, 307; "Dancing

in the Street" as civic violation, 172; Huey Newton dancing skills, 297; integration on dance floor, 4; James Brown performances, 89, 90, 102; James Brown playing on the one, 96, 122; James Brown "There Was a Time" as history of, 90; John George revolutionary who could dance, xiii–xiv; Lumpen dancers, 80–81, 218, 310, 311; Lumpen message choreography, 33; rhythm and blues, 6; soul claps at Lumpen recorded concert, 310; Soul Train (TV) as black power dance party, xiv, 216; Stokely Carmichael revolutionary who could dance, 3; "Watermelon Man" and "El Watusi," 151
"Dance to the Music" (Sly and the Family Stone), 49–51
"Dancing in the Street" (Martha and the Vandellas), 172
Dandridge, Dorothy, 150
dashikis, 193, 140, 147, 194
Davis, Angela, 38, 66, 156–157, 185, 203–206, 258, 296, 322, 332–333, 335
Davis, Miles, 7, 52, 185, 290
Davis, Sammy, Jr., 268, 272
Davis, Tyrone, 133
de Passe, Suzanne, 297
Deacons for Defense and Justice (LA), 63
Dellums, C. L., 57
Dellums, Ronald V., 58, 315
Democratic National Convention (1968), 236–237
desegregation. See integration
Detroit (MI), 145–146; Aretha Franklin, 151, 156; Black Nationalism in politics, 178–179; BPP schism with LRBW, 178; Dodge Main Plant wildcat strike (1968), 175; John Lee Hooker, 279; Lennon, Ono, Wonder concert, 296; Martha Jean "the Queen" Steinberg, 159; "Message to the Grass Roots" speech (Malcolm X), 12, 173; Motown moves to Los Angeles, 176; Motown Records: see Motown Records; multiracial working class success, 172; 1943 race riots, 173; Republic of New Afrika, 146; riots in 1967 summer,

173–174, 231; Shrine of the Black Madonna Cultural Center, 145
Dibango, Manu, 118
Diggers, 65–66
Dixon, Aaron, 294–295, 318–319
DJ Kool Herc. See Campbell, Clive
Dodge Revolutionary Union Movement (DRUM), 175–177
"Don't Be a Drop-Out" (James Brown), 97, 99
"Don't Call Me Nigger, Whitey" (Sly and the Family Stone), 54–55, 108
"(Don't Worry) If There's a Hell Below We're All Going to Go" (Mayfield), 132, 138, 291
Dorsey, Thomas, 7
Douglas, Alan, 110
Douglas, Emory: ads in Black Panther for Lumpen, 38; on Amiri Baraka, 194; on Karenga, 194; Lumpen advocate, 26, 27, 29, 43–44, 80, 194–195; on Lumpen unravelling within Party, 312–313; "Lumpen—Music as a Tool for Liberation" in Black Panther, 194–195; minister of culture for Party, 16, 27, 43, 194; Pan African Cultural Festival in Algiers, 254; revolutionary artwork, 70; Seize the Time (album), 16, 17
Dowell, Denzil, 69
Dozier, Lamont, 176
Dred Scott v. Sandford (1857), 221
DRUM. See Dodge Revolutionary Union Movement
Drumgo, Fleeta, 304
Du Bois, W. E. B., 186–187, 224
Dunn, Donald "Duck," 211
Dylan, Bob, 70, 275, 291, 300–306, 56, 300, 303–304

Earth, Wind & Fire, 134
East Bay, 49, 57–60. See also Oakland (CA).
East Oakland (CA), 38, 47, 74, 318
Ebony magazine, 134, 153, 231
educational system, 63, 64, 109
Edwards, Harry, 20, 22–23
Ellington, Duke, 224, 272
Ellis, Alfred "Pee Wee," 104, 105
Emperor Jones, The (film), 269
"End of Silence, The" (Elaine Brown), 298

entertainer activism. See artist activism

Errico, Gregg, 53

Evans, Lee, 20, 22–23

Everett, Ron, 182. See also Karenga, Maulana (Ron)

Evers, Medgar, 139, 281

"everybody is a star," 53

Eyes on the Prize (film), 333

Fagan, Eleanora. See Holiday, Billie

Fair Housing Act (1968), 163–164

Fame studios, 152

Family Stone. See Sly and the Family Stone

Famous Flames, 93

Fanon, Frantz, 75, 111–112, 242, 243, 270

Fard, W. D., 180

Farrakhan, Louis, 323–324

FBI: Alfred "Pee Wee" Ellis, 104; Angela Davis, 205; BPP intimidation, 313; can't handle black hyperbole, 227, 246; COINTELPRO, 238–240; infiltration of Party, 137, 239; J. Edgar Hoover, 238–240; James Brown, 112; Lumpen harassment, 39, 40; memo to neutralize militant black nationalists, 238; treating NCCF as Panther chapters, 83

"Fight the Power" (Isley Brothers), 164

films: Akeelah and the Bee, 325; blaxploitation movies, 257–260; Carmen Jones, 150; The Emperor Jones, 269; Eyes on the Prize, 333; Foxy Brown, 258; The Godfather, 256; Jerome Kern film biography, 268; Lillies of the Field, 130; The Mack, 60, 259–260; Othello, 269; Shaft, 213, 258; Show Boat, 267–268; Superfly, 132–133, 258; Sweet Sweetback's Baadasssss Song, 257–258; Trouble Man, 289; Wattstax, 214, 256–257; Wilma, 77

Finney, Shirley, 77

firearms. See guns

Flip Wilson Show, 155

Floyd, John, 66

Flying Dutchman records, 109

"Follow the Drinking Gourd," 276–277

Fonda, Jane, 209, 235, 375n60

"For Freedom" (Lumpen), 167–170

"(For God's Sake) Give More Power to the People" (Chi-Lites), 133–134, 138

Forbes, Flores, 318–319

Forman, James, 175, 234

Foster, Kevin, 256

Four Tops, The: "Keeper of the Castle," 163; performing in San Francisco Bay Area, 286; rejected "What's Going On?" (Benson), 287

Foxx, Redd, 292

Foxy Brown (film), 258

Franklin, Aretha: African roots rediscovered, 155–156, 157; Afro-Latin soul of the city, 151; Amazing Grace, 157; and Angela Davis, 156–157; autobiography Aretha: From These Roots, 152; born, 151; "Chain of Fools," 151, 153; Detroit early years, 151; in Detroit jail, 156; Dinah Washington as mentor, 151; Hey Now Hey (The Other Side of the Sky) album, 157; "I Never Loved a Man (the Way I Love You)" tour de force soul, 151, 152; Live at the Fillmore West album, 154; Michael Torrence on Party views of, 158; "A Natural Woman," 151, 153; 1960s transformation, 6, 7; as Queen of Soul, 151, 153, 158; Ray Charles as guest on Live at the Fillmore West album, 154; recording, 151, 152; "Respect," 3, 151, 152–154, 163; "Rock Steady," 155; singing "Ol' Man River," 264; "Young, Gifted and Black," 154–155; Young, Gifted and Black album, 155, 158

Franklin, C. L., 151

Franklin, Erma, 152

Franti, Michael, 327–328, 296

Freddie and the Stone Souls, 52

"Free Angela" (Santana), 205

"Free Bobby Now" (Lumpen): first performance, 27, 220; as first side of single, 35, 36, 220; lyrics, 35, 217; lyrics in Black Panther, 220; recording of single, 35. See also "Bobby Must Be Set Free" (Lumpen)

Free Breakfast Program Benefit (1971), 38

"Free Huey" cause, 5–6, 232–235

free jazz, 184–185

Freedom from Fear March. See March Against Fear (1966)
Freedom Messengers: backing Lumpen, 19, 49; call it quits, 312; dance troupe, 307; formation of, 30–31; membership changes, 81; as multiracial, 41, 49; "reverse racism," 41
Freedom Singers, 130
Freedomways (newspaper), 142
Freeman, Bobby, 52
Freeman, Kenny (Mamadu Lumumba), 63, 66, 73
Frey, John, 232
Fugitives, xvi
funk bands, xiv, 51
funk music: affirming, 55; African rhythms and American jazz improvisation, 148; Aretha Franklin "Rock Steady," 155; funk bands, xiv, 51; James Brown, 91, 92, 96, 97, 101, 106, 161; and the Lumpen, 297; physicality of, 118; slap bass technique, 53
Funk: The Music, the People, and the Rhythm of The One (Vincent; book), xiv
Funkadelic, 292. See also Parliament/Funkadelic
Fuqua, Harvey, 285

Garry, Charles, 237
Garvey, Marcus, 180, 223, 224
Gary (IN), 215
gay liberation movement, 249–250, 313
Gaye, Anna Gordy, 287, 318
Gaye, Frankie, 286, 288
Gaye, Marvin: Anna Gordy Gaye (wife), 287; born, 285; creative independence battles with Motown, 177; "Distant Lover," 46; forced to record "What's Going On?" by wife, 287; and Frankie Gaye, 286, 288; "Hitch Hike," 285; I Want You album, 289; icon of social soul music, 288; instrumental album for Trouble Man film, 289; introduced to Berry Gordy, 285; Let's Get It On album, 289; Michael Torrence toured with, 46, 317–318; Norman Whitfield shaping sound, 177; "Pride and Joy," 285; rarely spoke to backup band, 317–318; and Tammi Terrell, 286;

What's Going On? album, 288, 290, 335–336; "What's Going On?," 3, 6, 287–288; "You're the Man," 289
gender equality: Angela Davis as activist leader, 204, 206; Aretha Franklin "Respect," 152, 153, 154; BPP policy, 42–43, 65, 200–202, 248–249, 249–250, 300; civil rights movement patriarchy, 196–197, 198; cultural nationalists, 206; Huey Newton ambivalence toward, 65, 249–250, 313; Lenin and Marxism, 202; Nation of Islam gender roles, 198–199; Sly and the Family Stone, 53, 56; SNCC patriarchy, 197, 198; Third World Women's Alliance, 202–203; US Organization gender roles, 183, 199–200; "Women's Liberation Movements and the Gay Liberation Movements" (Newton), 249–250
George, John, xiii–xiv
"George Jackson" (Dylan), 305–306
"Get Up, Get Into It, Get Involved" (James Brown), 320
Ghana, 116, 143
"Ghetto Life" (Rick James), 164
Gibson, Jack, 162
Gibson, Kenneth, 186, 188
Gibson, "Master" Henry, 132
"Give More Power to the People" (Chi-Lites), 133–134, 138
"Give Peace a Chance" (Lennon and Ono), 328
Givin' It Back (Isley Brothers), 291
Gladys Knight and the Pips, 163, 177
global community, 330–331, 334
Goapele, 328
Godfather, The (film), 256
Godfather of Soul. See Brown, James
Golden State Studios (San Francisco), 312
Gordy, Berry, Jr., 171, 173, 177, 264, 278–279, 285, 318
gospel: Aretha Franklin Amazing Grace album, 157; "A Change Is Gonna Come," 283–284; as civil rights movement force, 7–8, 130–131; James Brown Gospel Starlighters, 93; moving from churches to streets, 130; "No More" passion, 37; power of, 8; Thomas Dorsey recording, 7

Gospel Starlighters, 93
Graham, Larry, Jr., 53
Grateful Dead, 38, 56, 295–296, 365n38
Great March to Freedom rally (1963), 173
Green, Al, 185
Gregory, Dick, 3
Gregory, Robin, 146
Grier, Pam, 258
"groupies" of Lumpen, 42–43
Guerilla Warfare (Guevara; book), 242
Guess Who's Coming Home (anthology; album), 177
Guevara, Che, 175, 242, 336
Guthrie, Woody, 275, 301

H. Rap Brown Defense Fund, 100
Haley, Harold, 251
Hamer, Fannie Lou, 197
Hamilton, Charles V., 108
Hammerstein, Oscar, II, 266–267. See also "Ol' Man River" (Hammerstein and Kern)
Hammerstein, William, 267
Hammond, John, 148
Hampton, Fred, 126, 128, 137–138, 140, 251
Hancock, Herbie, 151, 185, 205
Handcox, John, 274–275
Hanrahan, Noelle, xvii
Hansberry, Lorraine, 154–155
"Happy Birthday" (Wonder), 328
Hardest Working Man in Show Business. See Brown, James
Harlem: Apollo Theater: see Apollo Theater; Audubon Ballroom Malcolm X speech, 143–144; Black Arts movement fueled, 143; Black Arts Repertory Theatre/School, 145; black capital of the world, 224; Bobby Seale speaking on Ten Point Program, 226; Gil Scott-Heron teen years, 109; Harlem Renaissance, 224; Harry Belafonte born, 150; jazz capital of the world, 224; Keorapetse "Willie" Kgositsile, 110; Last Poets East Wind space, 110; Lumumba Shakur establishes BPP chapter, 225; Malcolm X emergence, 224–225; riots in summer of 1964, 143, 172

Harold Melvin and the Blue Notes, 163, 164
Harris, Rutha Mae, 130
Harrison, Linda, 107
Hassan, Ali Bey, 227
Hathaway, Donny, 155, 164
Hayes, Isaac, 55, 210–211, 212, 213, 291
Hazel, Eddie, 292
H-D-H songwriting team, 176, 177
Heath, Albert, 185
Heath, James, Jr., 184
Henderson, Mack Ray, 31, 32, 81, 82, 87, 105
Hendrix, Jimi, 6, 7, 56, 130, 290, 291, 293–296, 308, 379n35
Henry, Milton (Gaidi Obadele), 146
Henry, Richard (Imari Obadele), 146
Hewitt, Ray "Masai,", 298, 318
highlife music, 116, 120
Highway 61 Revisited (Dylan), 70, 302, 303–304
Hilliard, David: on Black Panther newspaper, 69–70; Elaine Brown "The Meeting" BPP national anthem, 16–17, 298; Eldridge Cleaver nonviolence killed with King, 236; on Eldridge Cleaver's admiration for Huey Newton, 241; as Huey Newton childhood friend, 64; Huey Newton made chief of staff, 251; on James Brown and Richard Nixon, 123; Lumpen origins, 27–28, 29, 80; male chauvinism hard line, 43; National Committee to Combat Fascism, 83–84; Pan African Cultural Festival in Algiers, 254; as Panther, xvi, 16, 25, 27, 30, 37; public speaking ability, 251; rap album, xvi; Seize the Time authorization, 17, 30; William Calhoun as bodyguard, 46
hip-hop, 91, 121, 122, 164, 326, 328. See also rap music
Hoffman, Julius, 237
Holiday, Billie, 106, 272–273, 274, 328
Holland, Brian, 176
Holland, Eddie, 176
homosexuality, 249–250, 313
Hooker, John Lee, 279
Hoover, J. Edgar, 112, 238, 239
Horne, Lena, 272
Houphouët-Boigny, Félix, 101
House of Umoja, 73

Howard, Elbert "Big Man," 69
Howard Quinn Printing Company, 26
Howard University (DC), 38, 146, 186, 250
Howlin' Wolf, 134
Huey P. Newton Archives, xvi
Huggins, Ericka: Alex Rackley murder trial New Haven, 229–230, 296; with Angela Davis in BPP, 204; on BPP chauvinism, 201; Intercommunal Youth Institute director, 300; in jail, 39; as James Mott's wife, 46; Lenny Williams on her BPP leadership, 300; New Haven Lumpen performance, 39; as Panther, 200, 229, 300; Revolutionary Intercommunal Day of Solidarity (1971), 38, 296; "Set Sister Ericka Free," 33
Huggins, John: with Angela Davis in BPP, 204; Elaine Brown wrote "Assassination" for, 298; killed, 16, 128, 190, 250–251, 298; Lumpen "People Get Ready" dedication, 126, 128; as Panther, 16, 128, 250–251
Hughes, Langston, 177, 224
Humphrey, Hubert, 99, 103, 112
Hutton, Bobby, 21, 71, 77, 126, 128, 236, 319

"I Can't Stand Myself" (James Brown), 89
"I Don't Want Nobody to Give Me Nothin'" (James Brown), 92
"I Have a Dream" speech (King; 1963), 7, 10–11
"I Never Loved a Man (the Way I Love You)" (Franklin), 151, 152
"I Want to Take You Higher" (Sly and the Family Stone), 54, 55
identity politics: black cultural nationalism, 181–182; black power origins, 14; BPP as beyond, 107; James Brown at center of process, 93; Last Poets "James Brown" tribute, 110; W. E. B. Du Bois "double consciousness," 187
"If There's a Hell Below We're All Going to Go" (Mayfield), 132, 138, 291
"I'll Go Crazy" (James Brown), 93
"I'll Take You There" (Staple Singers), 131, 212

"I'm Black and I'm Proud." See "Say It Loud—I'm Black and I'm Proud" (James Brown)
"I'm Mad Like Eldridge Cleaver" (MC5), 295
Impressions, The, 3, 108, 129–130, 132, 133, 210
Indiana, Gary, 215
Industrial Workers of the World, 274
Inner City Voice (newspaper), 175, 176
integration: Amiri Baraka against white alliances, 192; as anachronism, 84; armed forces, 57; black nationalism contrary to, 11; Booker T. and the MGs as multiracial, 211; Brown v. Board of Education (1954), 9, 57; Café Society in New York, 273; on dance floor, 4; Detroit as multiracial success, 172, 173, 174; Freedom Messengers, 41, 49; Gil Scott-Heron school integration racism, 109; James Brown as counterpoint to, 97; James Brown "I Don't Want Nobody to Give Me Nothin'," 92; Lumpen as multiracial, 41, 49, 208; March on Washington Movement (1941), 57; Montgomery busing, 9–10; National Committee to Combat Fascism, 83–84; Operation Breadbasket striving for, 136; Operation PUSH organization, 137; racially integrated female SNCC statement, 197; Sly and the Family Stone as multiracial, 41, 51, 56, 85; SNCC "black power," 198; Stax Records multiracial, 211; Viscaynes multiracial, 52; war industries, 57
Intercommunal Committee to Combat Fascism (ICCF), 82
Intercommunal Youth Institute, 300
intercommunalism, 242, 313, 334
Irvine, Weldon, 5
Isadore, Sandra. See Smith, Sandra
Islam. See Nation of Islam
Isley, Ernie, 291
Isley Brothers, 55, 164, 291, 306
"It's a Man's Man's Man's World" (James Brown), 91, 97–98
It's About Time Committee, xvi
"It's Summer" (Temptations), 167–168, 171

"ITT (International Thief Thief)" (Kuti), 116

Ivory Coast (Côte d'Ivoire), 101, 116

Ivy, Archie, 184, 185

Jaaber, Hajj Heshaam, 187

Jackson, Al, Jr., 211

Jackson, Brian, 109

Jackson, George, 204–205, 251, 304, 305, 308

Jackson, Jesse, 136, 137, 161, 214, 215

Jackson, Jonathan: courthouse siege, 205, 251; "Jonathan" (Elaine Brown) tribute to, 252; killed, 128, 205, 251; Lumpen "People Get Ready" dedication, 126, 128; martyred, 252; as Panther, 128

Jackson, Mahalia, 7

Jackson, Maynard, Jr., 163

Jackson, Michael, 111

Jackson (MS), 8–9, 11, 98–99, 198, 231

Jackson, Phyllis, 201

Jackson, Samuel L., 258

Jackson 5, 109, 111, 278

Jamaica, 113–115, 119, 121, 122. See also Marley, Bob

Jamal, Hakim, 182

James, Etta, 134

James, Rick, 164

"James Brown" (Original Last Poets), 110

jazz: African rhythms and jazz improvisation, 148; Bobby Seale as drummer, 61; Charlie Parker, 279; cultural nationalism linked to free jazz, 184–185, 222; Harlem as world capital, 224; Malcolm X on soul of black music, 143–144; Miles Davis, 290; 1960s transformation, 6–7; Pan Afrikan Peoples Arkestra, 184; soul and soul brother, 141; Sun Ra most esoteric, 134

Jennings, Billy "X," xvi, 37

Jerry Butler and the Impressions, 129

Jet magazine, 134

Jim Crow, 5, 58, 196–197, 211, 272, 282, 283

Johnson, Bernice (Bernice Johnson Reagon), 130

Johnson, Lyndon, 103, 112

"Jonathan" (Elaine Brown), 252

Jones, Booker T., 211

Jones, Frank, 75

Jones, LeRoi, 91–92, 98, 141, 143, 145, 186, 187–188, 200, 231, 275. See also Baraka, Amiri

Jones, Quincy, 7, 157

Joseph, Jamal, 226, 227

Josephson, Barney, 273

Julien, Max, 259

"Jungle Boogie" (Kool and the Gang), 118–119

Kain, Gylan, 110

Karenga, Maulana (Ron): Amiri Baraka as disciple, 187–188; Black Panther articles, 190, 191; black revolution plans, 191–192; blues invalid, 279–280; born Ron Everett, 182; BPP versus, 189–193; at California State University Long Beach, 189; capitalism and black economic support, 207; Carter and Huggins killings, 190; gender roles, 183, 199–200; Kawaida (Mtume; album) Karenga tribute, 184–185; name meaning, 182; Newark "Kawaida Towers," 186, 188–189; premises of black cultural nationalism, 183; sentenced for kidnapping, 189; as Swahili teacher, 183; US Organization cofounder, 182; white alliance criticism, 206

Katsiaficas, George, 250

KDIA radio (Bay Area), 220–221

"Keep Your Eyes on the Prize" (Wine), 8

Kellum, Alphonso "Country," 89

Kendricks, Eddie, 176, 177

Kennedy, Robert F., 20, 236

Kent, Herb "the Cool Gent,", 161

Kern, Jerome, 266, 268. See also "Ol' Man River" (Hammerstein and Kern)

KGFJ radio (Los Angeles), 160

Kgositsile, Keorapetse "Willie," 110

Khan, Chaka, 138, 139–140

Khan, Hassan, 139

killed: Alex Rackley, 229, 319; Alprentice "Bunchy" Carter, 16, 128, 190, 250, 298; Bobby Hutton, 21, 77, 128, 236, 319; Denzil Dowell, 69; Emmet Till, 302; first Panther killed in action, 236; four little girls, 203, 281; Frank Ward, 259; Fred Hampton, 128, 137–138, 140, 251; George

Jackson, 304, 305, 308; Harold Haley, 251; James McClain, 128, 251; John Frey, 232; John Huggins, 16, 128, 190, 250–251, 298; Jonathan Jackson, 128, 205, 251; Malcolm X, 11, 62, 95, 181, 225, 232, 241; Mark Clark, 128, 251; Martin Luther King Jr., 20, 101–103, 136, 162, 163–164, 177, 212, 236; Medgar Evers, 139, 281; non-violence, 236; Robert F. Kennedy, 20, 236; Robert Webb, 45, 319; Sam Cooke, 284; Sam Napier, 45, 46, 319; William Christmas, 128, 251

"Killing" (Lumpen), 34

Kimbro, Warren, 229

King, Billy, 314

King, Martin Luther, Jr.: assassination, 20, 101–103, 136, 162, 163–164, 177, 212, 236; Barack Obama spreading racial transcendence, 329; black power movement tension, 99; black radio cultivated, 159; Chicago political machine versus, 136; Dick Gregory comment, 3; "fatal . . . to overlook the urgency," 10–11; J. Edgar Hoover as opponent, 238; James Brown as counterpoint to, 97; as mentor to Jesse Jackson, 136; recording of speech at Cobo Hall, Detroit, 173; spirituals and movement, 7, 131; Stevie Wonder making birthday a national holiday, 328; Stokely Carmichael association, 2; Stokely Carmichael versus King for leadership, 230; Vietnam War opposition, 153, 230; "Why? (The King of Love Is Dead)" (Simone/ Irvine), 5

King Records, 93, 94

KKK, 159, 203, 273, 326

Knowland, William, 60

Kool and the Gang, 118–119

KPFA radio (Berkeley), xv, xvi

KRS-One, 328

KSOL radio (Bay Area), 52, 220–221, 314

Kuti, Fela Anikulapo, 116–120

Kweli, Talib, 329

Lady Day. See Holiday, Billie

Lake Merritt, 255

Lamppost (Oakland), 59, 256, 316

"Land of 1000 Dances" (Pickett), 8–9

Laney College (CA), 316. See also Oakland City College (CA)

Last Poets, 13, 109–110. See also Original Last Poets

Lateef, Yusef, 148

Latinized music, 150–151

law enforcement. See FBI; police confrontations

League of Revolutionary Black Workers (LRBW), 175–176, 178

Lenin, V. I., 154, 175, 202, 242

Lennon, John, 13, 205, 295, 296, 328

Levinson, Cece, 82

Levinson, David, 38–39, 41, 82

Levinson, Saul, 82

Lewis, Ramsey, 134

Lewis, Tarika (Matilaba), 70

liberation movements, anticolonial: Black Arts movement fuel, 143; Black Nationalism history, 179–180; global community involvement, 330–331. See also colonialism

liberation schools, 15, 76, 248, 300

Liberator (magazine), 138, 141–142

Life magazine, 184

Lil Wayne, 326

Lillies of the Field (film), 130

Lincoln, Abbey, 3

Lincoln, Abraham, 329–330

Little, Malcolm. See Malcolm X

Live at the Apollo (James Brown; album), 93–94

Live at the Apollo Volume 2 (James Brown; album), 89

Live at the Fillmore West (Franklin; album), 154

"Long Walk to DC" (Staple Singers), 131

Look magazine, 111

Lorraine Motel (Memphis, TN), 136, 212

Los Angeles (CA): Alprentice "Bunchy" Carter killed, 128; Angela Davis in movement, 204, 206; Aretha Franklin Amazing Grace recording, 157; Black Panther Political Party, 66, 204; Elaine Brown entertainment career, 297; John Huggins killed, 128; KGFJ radio, 160; Lumpen performance, 38; Michael Torrence at-risk youth work, 318; Motown

Los Angeles (CA) (*continued*)
moved to, 176; Patrick's Payton Place, 38; Sam Cooke "A Change Is Gonna Come" recorded at RCA Studios, 283; Sam Cooke shot by motel manager, 284; Sam Cooke Soul Station #1 recording studio, 283; Soul Train moved to, 134; Stax Records office, 214; UCLA: see UCLA (CA); US Organization base, 182; violent locale for BPP activity, 297; Watts uprising: see Watts uprising (1965); Wattstax, 214

Los Angeles City College (CA), 182, 297

Los Angeles Coliseum, 214

"Lost Someone" (James Brown), 93

Louisiana, 63, 146

Lowndes County (MS) Freedom Organization, 67

LRBW. See League of Revolutionary Black Workers

Luciano, Felipe, 110

Lumpen: after break up, 47–48, 314–319; backup band, 81–82: see also Freedom Messengers; as Black Panther Party's Revolutionary Band, 19; "Bobby Must Be Set Free," 217–220: see also "Bobby Must Be Set Free" (Lumpen); community outreach, 25, 32, 33, 47, 314–315, 318, 319; concert recording: see Lumpen concert recording; creation of, 14, 26–29; as cultural apparatus of BPP, 27, 29, 32, 44, 311, 320; cultural nationalism and, 193–196; dancing message, 33; digitized single, xvi; final performance, 46, 314; "For Freedom" BPP militant ideology, 170; "For Freedom" concert recording, 167–170; 45 rpm single: see single, 45 rpm; "Free Bobby Now": see "Free Bobby Now" (Lumpen); "groupies," 42–43; James Brown influence, 32, 33, 35, 89, 297; "Killing" militant message, 34; "Lumpen Theme" concert recording, 87–88; "Lumpen Theme" James Brown influence, 32, 87; "Lumpen—Music as a Tool for Liberation" in Black Panther, 194–195; lyrics message, 32, 33, 34, 39; member Clark Bailey: see Bailey, Clark "Santa Rita"; member James Mott:

see Mott, James (Sataru Ned); member Michael Torrence: see Torrence, Michael; member William Calhoun: see Calhoun, William; militant soul music, 165, 222; Motown as superficial, 168, 177; name meaning, 27–28, 195; "Ol' Pig Nixon" based on "Ol' Man River," 263–265, 266; "Ol' Pig Nixon" concert recording, 263–265; as Panthers, xvii, 13–14, 26–27, 29, 34–35, 39–40, 42, 44, 248, 312, 319; Party civil war, 253; as Party distraction, 43–45; "People Get Ready" concert recording, 125–127; "People Get Ready" dedication to Panthers, 126, 128; performance locations, 37–39, 40–41, 46, 250, 296, 306; "pig" as enemy of people, 16, 33, 36, 50, 126, 127, 167, 169, 193; "Power to the People" chant and John Lennon song, 296; "Power to the People" concert recording, 49–50, 86; "Power to the People" Freedom Messengers cover of "Dance to the Music," 49–50; race not explicit in works, 193, 222; Ray Charles influence, 297; resistance music that updates popular songs, 275; "Revolution Is the Only Solution" concert recording, 309–310, 311; revolutionary culture part of revolution, 306, 308; as revolutionary symbol, xv; Revolutionary Tour, 38–39, 81; Seize the Time benefit, 38; Sly and the Family Stone influence, 56; Soul Day at San Quentin performance, 306–308; soul music abilities, 32–33; soul music aesthetic, 193; unpaid, 312; unravelling, 312; Walter Turner 45 rpm owner, xv–xvi

Lumpen concert recording: "Party Music," 19; "Power to the People," 49–50, 86; "The Lumpen Theme," 87–88; "People Get Ready," 125–127; "For Freedom," 167–170; "Bobby Must Be Set Free," 217–220; "Ol' Pig Nixon," 263–265; "Revolution Is the Only Solution," 309–310, 311; backing band membership, 81–82; as book structure, 17; cassette tape of concert, xvi–xvii, 312;

dedicated to fallen Panthers, 126, 128; dedicated to Huey P. Newton, 126; dialogue on Temptations, 168; elements of live and studio-recorded songs, 312; Huey P. Newton Archives tape, xvi–xvii, 312; kicker of a close, 310, 311; master tapes disappeared, 312; recording console in Merritt College venue, 312; show packed by word of mouth, 42. See also Lumpen
"Lumpen Theme, The" (Lumpen): concert recording, 87–88; James Brown influence, 32; James Brown "There Was a Time" variation, 87; lyrics, 87–88
lumpenproletariat: Bobby Seale as, 230; BPP gender equality barrier, 201; BPP identified with, 189; BPP meaning, 27–29; Huey Newton as, 230, 240; lumpenism as BPP demise, 245–247; Malcolm X as, 240; movement based on lumpen, 178, 240, 243–244, 245–247; Newton lumpen emphasis abandonment, 250; politicized lumpen no longer imaginable, 260; socially outcast due to race and economics, 242–243
Lumumba, Mamadu. See Freeman, Kenny
Lumumba, Patrice, 143
lynching, 273, 302, 328
lyrics: "Are You Really Ready for Black Power" (Byrd), 161; "Ballad of a Thin Man" (Dylan), 303–304; "Bobby Must Be Set Free" (Lumpen), 35, 217; "A Change Is Gonna Come" (Cooke), 283; "Dancing in the Street" (Martha and the Vandellas), 172; Emmett Till song by Bob Dylan, 302; "The End of Silence" (Elaine Brown), 298; "For Freedom" (Lumpen), 168–170; "Free Bobby Now" (Lumpen), 35, 217; "George Jackson" (Dylan), 305–306; "Ghetto Life" (Rick James), 164; Goapele, 328; "It's Summer" (Temptations), 167–168, 171; "The Lumpen Theme" (Lumpen), 87–88; "The Meeting" (Elaine Brown), 299; "Mississippi Goddam" (Simone),

282; "No More" (Lumpen), 36; "Ol' Man River" (Hammerstein and Kern), 267–268; "Ol' Pig Nixon" (Lumpen), 264–265; "The Panther" (Elaine Brown), 299; "People Get Ready" (Lumpen), 126–127; "People Get Ready" (Mayfield), 125; "Power of Soul" (Hendrix), 293; "Power to the People" (Lumpen), 50; "Pusherman" (Mayfield), 133; "Respect" (Franklin), 152; "Revolution Is the Only Solution" (Lumpen), 309–310; RL's Dream (Mosley) excerpt, 276; "Strange Fruit" (Holiday), 273; "To Be Young, Gifted and Black" (Simone), 155; "What's Going On?" (Gaye), 287; "Yell Fire" (Franti), 328; "You're the Man" (Gaye), 289

Ma'at, 314
Mack, The (film), 60, 259, 260
Magee, Ruchell, 38, 296
Major, Naima, 5–6
Makeba, Miriam, 149–150, 254
Malcolm X: assassination, 11, 62, 95, 181, 225, 232, 241; Autobiography of Malcolm X, 97, 108, 117; Barack Obama borrows oratorical techniques, 329; Betty Shabazz (widow), 232; birthday Kuzaliwa celebration, 183; black revolution construct, 11–12; born Malcolm Little, 243; BPP as outgrowth of, 13, 28; direct talk on race, 92; eulogized by Hajj Heshaam Jaaber, 187; Hakim Jamal personal friend, 182; Huey Newton's impression of, 66; influence on Fela Kuti, 117; love of blackness, 144; as lumpenproletariat, 240; Malcolm X Day at San Quentin, 307; Max Stanford as confidante, 62; Mecca pilgrimage, 181; "Message to the Grass Roots" speech, 12, 173; most popular black radical, 225; Muhammad Ali relationship, 307; Muslim name, 181; Nation of Islam break, 181; Nation of Islam spokesperson, 10, 11, 28, 181; recorded speeches, 181; on soul of black music, 143–144; spiritual deification of, 144–145; as Sunni Muslim, 181

Manley, Michael, 114
Mao Zedong, 75, 175, 242
March Against Fear (1966), 8–9, 11, 98–99, 198
March on Washington (1963), 7, 10, 148
March on Washington Movement (1941), 57
Marcuse, Herbert, 203, 204
Marin County (CA) courthouse siege (1970), 128, 205, 251, 252
Markham, Pigmeat, 292
Marley, Bob, 113–115, 119
Marshall, Thurgood, 9
Martha and the Vandellas, 172
Martin, Waldo E., 7–8, 130–131
Martini, Jerry, 52
Marx, Karl, 27–28, 242
Marxism, 11, 62, 154, 202, 203, 242, 304
Massachusetts, 38, 40, 100, 101, 140, 163, 203
Matilaba. See Lewis, Tarika
Mayfield, Curtis: Bob Marley affection for, 115; BPP admiration for, 128; career as socially conscious artist, 129, 133; Chicago soul, 129, 132, 133–134; Curtis album, 138; death, 133; depth of respect for black radical community, 307; "(Don't Worry) If There's a Hell Below We're All Going to Go," 138; hard rock psychedelia, 132, 291; influence on Jimi Hendrix guitar, 130; with Jerry Butler as Impressions, 129; "Keep On Pushing," 3; "Miss Black America," 132; "Move On Up," 132, 164; "People Get Ready," 3, 125, 129, 164; publishing company formation, 130; "Pusherman," 133; Soul Day at San Quentin with Lumpen, 306, 307; style innovations, 130; Superfly (film) soundtrack, 132–133; "We People Who Are Darker Than Blue," 132; "We're a Winner," 3, 132; William Calhoun on appearance at Soul Day at San Quentin, 307. See also Impressions, The
McClain, Bobby, 311
McClain, James, 126, 128, 251
McDaniels, Gene, 291
McDonald, Michael, 72
MC5 (Motor City Five), 295

McLellan, Elvie, Jr. (Basheer Muhammad), 32
McLucas, Lonnie, 229
"Mdamase" meaning, 73
media: Arab Spring (2011) using social networking, 330–331; attacked in Oakland stop the draft protests, 223; BPP constantly addressing, 223; Donald Warden media savvy, 62, 97; Eldridge Cleaver media savvy, 232; Emmett Till trial coverage, 302; James Brown radio station, 99–100, 102, 112–113; moral atrophy, 324–325; NATRA, 162; US Organization members on Life magazine cover, 184. See also black newspapers and publications; Black Panther (newspaper); black radio; films; television (TV)
Meeropol, Abel, 273
"Meeting, The" (Elaine Brown), 16–17, 298, 299
Memphis (TN), 6–7, 20, 98–99, 101, 131, 136, 151, 211, 236
Meredith, James, 8–9, 11, 98–99, 198
Merritt College (CA): Bobby Seale as a student, 58, 62, 242; Freeman, Kenny, as student, 63; Huey Newton as student, xiv, 58, 62, 64–67, 242; Lumpen concert recording, xvi–xvii, 19, 42, 49, 126, 168; Ted Vincent as teacher, xiv; young black organizers, 58
message songs: in African musical idioms, 120; Aretha Franklin "Respect," 3, 152–154, 163; Bob Dylan, 301–304; Chi-Lites, 133–134; Fela Kuti, 116, 117, 119; inspirational music with a message, 131; James Brown, 92, 97–98, 101, 104–108, 161; late 1960s music, 220; Lumpen, 32, 33, 34, 37–38, 39; Marvin Gaye, 287–289; Motown dragged into, 177; Nina Simone "Mississippi Goddam," 281–282; Paul Robeson, 269–270; Sam Cooke inspired by "Blowin' in the Wind," 301; "What's Going On?" (Benson), 286–287. See also militant messages; music with positive message; protest music; resistance music

"Message to the Grass Roots" speech (Malcolm X; 1963), 12
Mike Douglas Show (TV), 296
Miles, Buddy, 293
militant messages: Bob Marley, 115; Brown on "Say It Loud," 108; Elaine Brown "get guns and be men," 298–299; "For Freedom" (Lumpen), 170; "Free Bobby Now" (Lumpen), 221; James Brown's music capturing, 92–93; "Killing" (Lumpen), 34; Last Poets, 109–111; Lumpen militant soul music, 165, 222; Malcolm X "Message to the Grass Roots" speech, 173. See also message songs; protest music; resistance music
Mind of the Ghetto Conference (1963), 66
Miracles, The, 279
Mississippi,, 3, 5 8–9, 11, 67, 98, 99, 146, 106, 197, 198, 231, 279, 281–282, 302
"Mississippi Goddam" (Simone), 3, 5, 106, 281–282
Moffeit, Charles, 300
"Money Won't Change You" (James Brown), 91–92, 97, 99
Montague, Nathaniel "Magnificent," 160
Moore, Richard (Dhoruba), 227
Moore, Rudy Ray, 292
Morozumi, Greg, xvi
Mosely, Roger E., 259
Mosley, Walter, 276
Motown Records, 46, 80, 97, 111, 168, 171–172, 173, 174, 176–177, 264, 277–279, 285, 291, 297, 317–318
Mott, James (Sataru Ned): after Lumpen, 47–48, 318, 319; assistant pastor of Agnes Memorial Christian Academy, 318; Black Panther newspaper distribution, 78; as Lumpen member, 30, 80, 312; New Haven Lumpen performance, 39; Oakland Community School, 318; as Panther, 30, 46; path to BPP, 76–81; Sacramento BPP chapter startup, 77; Sacramento breakfast program, 248; SNCC chapter startup, 76–77; Stokely Carmichael at SNCC chapter, 77
Mtume, 184
Mtume, James, 184–185

Muddy Waters, 134
Muhammad, Basheer. See McLellan, Elvie, Jr.
Muhammad, Elijah, 180–181, 223
Mulford Act, 70
multiracial bands: Baby Huey and the Babysitters, 139; Booker T. and the MGs, 211; Freedom Messengers, 41, 49; Lumpen, 41, 208; Sly and the Family Stone, 41, 51, 56; Viscaynes, 52
multiracial movements: BPP court Hendrix for white audience, 294; BPP white alliances, 192, 206–209; Detroit riots 1967, 173–174; Malcolm X after hajj, 181; National Committee to Combat Fascism, 83–84; Occupy Movement Oakland, 332; SNCC, 197; Third World Women's Alliance, 202–203. See also integration; white alliances
murders. See killed
Murray, George, 79
music. See black music
music as weapon, 2–3, 44, 116, 117, 119, 194–195, 277

NAACP (National Association for the Advancement of Colored People), 9, 21, 73, 75, 137, 159, 197, 215, 224, 242, 246
Napier, Sam, 45, 46, 319
Nathan, Syd, 94
Nation of Islam (NOI), 10, 11, 28, 134, 180, 181, 182, 184, 198–199, 225, 322–324
National Association of Television and Radio Announcers (NATRA), 162
National Black Feminist Organization, 203
National Black Political Convention (1972), 215, 216
National Committee to Combat Fascism (NCCF), 83–84
NATRA (National Association of Television and Radio Announcers), 162
Natural Four, 38
NCCF (National Committee to Combat Fascism), 83–84
Neal, Earl, 248
Neal, Larry, 111, 112, 143
Neblett, Charles, 130

Ned, Sataru. See Mott, James
Negro versus black, 1–2, 106–107, 145, 149
Negroes With Guns (Williams; book), 160, 242
Neighborhood Service Center (North Oakland), 63
Nelson, Billy, 292
Nelson, David, 110
New Haven (CT), 30, 37, 38, 39, 200, 219, 228–230
New Jersey, 186, 268, 292
New Orleans (LA), 72–73, 146, 162
New York City (NY): Amiri Baraka base, 186; Angela Davis captured, 205; Aretha Franklin recording, 151, 152; Atlantic Records, 152; Black Arts movement, 143, 146; black power epicenter, 224; Eldridge Cleaver base, 45; Fillmore East Hendrix concert, 294; Last Poets, 109; Lumpen performances, 38–39; Malcolm X, 11–12; New York Police Intelligence Unit (BOSSI), 228; New York 21 members, 227–228; New York University, Babatunde Olatunji student, 148; Roseland Ballroom Lumpen performance, 38–39
Newark (NJ), 146, 179, 186, 188–189, 231
Newton, Fredrika, 42
Newton, Huey P.: affection for Bob Dylan, 70, 300, 302, 303–304; Afro-American Association influence, 66; autobiography Revolutionary Suicide, 68; beaten by police, 231, 232; birthday rally SNCC-BPP merger announcement, 234; Bobby Seale expulsion from Party, 255; born, 63; BPP gender equality, 201; on BPP versus cultural nationalists, 190–191; Cal-Pak, 315; classical music fan, 64, 297; cocaine use, 254–256, 313, 319; dancing skills, 297; Fredrika Newton (widow), 42; gay liberation movements, 249–250; on gender equality, 65; Grateful Dead conversation, 295; intercommunalism theories, 242, 313, 334; John Frey Oakland police officer shot, 232; Lee Edward

Newton (brother), 64; Lumpen performance dedication to, 126; lumpenization from racial caste system, 243–244; lumpenproletariat, 28, 242–243; as lumpenproletariat, 230, 240; The Mack "Goldie" resemblance, 259; on Malcolm X, 66; Malcolm X legacy heir, 240–241; Melvin Newton (brother), 64, 67; at Merritt College, xiv, 58, 62, 64–67; militant messages of Party, 34, 45, 209, 246–247, 250, 252, 313; mythic status, 234–235, 240, 251, 256; Oakland early years, xiv, 58, 61, 62–63; Oakland Party consolidation, 15–16, 178, 254–255; as Party cofounder, 15, 16, 25; penthouse apartment, 254, 255–256; photograph with spear by Eldridge Cleaver, 222–223; political violence rhetoric, 333; Port of Oakland under BPP control, 178; preferred brand of Panther, 241; public speaking skills, 209, 251; released from jail, 209, 250, 251; Revolutionary People's Constitutional Convention (RPCC) in Philadelphia, 209; Richard Pryor as cohort, 256–257; rules of engagement for armed patrols, 69; Sly Stone parallels, 85; Soul Students Advisory Council, 63; study of revolution, 242–245; Superfly character Priest resemblance, 258; Supreme Servant, 255; Sweet Sweetback's Baadasssss Song film praise, 257; Ted Vincent as teacher, xiv; as Ten Point Program coauthor, 59, 63, 67; threatened Michael Torrence, 316; Walter Newton (father), 64; Walter "Sonny Man" Newton Jr. taught Newton street life, 64; white alliances, 206–208; women's liberation movements, 249–250
Newton, Lee Edward, 64
Newton, Melvin, 64, 67
Newton, Walter, 64
Newton, Walter "Sonny Man," Jr., 64
Nigeria, 116–119, 148
Nixon, Richard, 112, 113, 123, 263–265
Njeri, Akua, 201
Nkrumah, Kwame, 143, 242

"No More" (Lumpen): digitized, xvi; first performance, 27; as flip side of single, 36; lyrics, 36; New Haven Lumpen performance, 39; Ray Charles sound, 36, 37; recording of single, 35; Walter Turner 45 rpm owner, xvi
NOI. See Nation of Islam
Nolen, Jimmy, 89, 94
North Carolina, 95, 242, 321
North Oakland (CA), xvi–xvii, 19, 42, 49, 63, 126, 168

Oak Park riots (1969), 30
Oakland (CA): black economy, 60–61; Black Nationalism in politics, 178; black organizing tradition, 57–58; blues clubs, 59; BPP impact on politics, 46–47; Elaine Brown city council run, 46, 178; Huey Newton consolidation of Party, 15–16, 178, 254–255; Lake Merritt and Newton penthouse apartment, 255; Lionel Wilson first black mayor, 47, 238; Lumpen base, xv; Lumpen concert recording, xvi–xvii, 19, 42, 49, 126, 168; The Mack movie filmed, 259; Oakland Auditorium Lumpen and Grateful Dead performances, 38, 296; Oakland City College, 58, 64, 316; Occupy tear gas incident, 332; People's Free Medical Clinic, 248; Port of Oakland Occupy march (2011), 332; Port of Oakland under BPP control, 178; Saint Augustine's Episcopal Church, 248; Seize the Time benefit (1970) for Bobby Seale, 38; stop the draft protests (1967), 231; Sun Ra lecturing at Berkeley, 134–135; Wo'Se Community Church, 47, 314. See also East Bay; East Oakland; North Oakland; West Oakland
Oakland Auditorium, 38, 296
Oakland City College (CA), 58, 67, 316. See also Laney College (CA)
Oakland Community School, 300, 318
Oakland Sportsman's Club, 38
Oakland Tribune, 60
Obadele, Gaidi. See Henry, Milton
Obadele, Imari. See Henry, Richard
Obama, Barack Hussein, 329, 330, 331, 335–336
Occupy Movement (2011), 323, 331–333

Odetta, 3, 150
"Ol' Man River" (Hammerstein and Kern), 264–273, 284. See also Robeson, Paul
"Ol' Man River" (Temptations), 264
"Ol' Pig Nixon" (Lumpen), 263–266
Olatunji, Babatunde, 148, 149
Olatunji Institute (Harlem), 148
Olympic black power fist, 21, 22–23
Olympic boycott, 20–21, 23
Olympic Project for Human Rights, 20
"the One," 90, 95, 96, 114–115, 122
O'Neal, Ron, 258
Ono, Yoko, 205, 296, 328
Operation Breadbasket, 136, 161
Operation PUSH, 137, 214
Organization of Afro-American Unity, 143–144
Organization US. See US Organization
Original Last Poets, 110. See also Last Poets
Originals, the, 287
"Ostinato (Suite for Angela)" (Hancock), 185, 205
Othello (film), 269
Oyewole, Abiodun, 321–322, 109–110, 321, 322

Palmer, Earl, 283
Palmer, Keke, 325–326
Pan African Cultural Festival in Algiers, 254
Pan Afrikan Peoples Arkestra, 184
"Panther, The" (Elaine Brown), 298, 299
panther as BPP symbol, 67
Panther Party Chapter and Community Center, 25
"Papa's Got a Brand New Bag" (James Brown), 91, 94, 95
Paris (rapper), 324–325
Parker, Charlie, 279
Parker, Maceo, 94, 102
Parker, Melvin, 94
Parks, Rosa, 9, 197
Parliament/Funkadelic, 184, 292–293
Parliaments, the, 292
Party. See Black Panther Party (BPP)
Party Music (Coup; album), xv
Pate, Johnny, 129, 133–134
patriarchy. See black patriarchy
Patrick's Payton Place (Los Angeles), 38
Paul, Billy, 193, 291

Pauley Ballroom (UC–Berkeley), 38
"Payback, The" (James Brown), 121, 332
Peace and Freedom Party (PFP), 233
Pennsylvania, 38, 109. See also
    Philadelphia
"People Get Ready" (Impressions), 3,
    125–129, 163, 164–165
"People Get Ready" (Lumpen), 125–127,
    128
"People Get Ready" (Mayfield), 125
People United to Save Humanity (Oper-
    ation PUSH), 137, 214
People's Free Benefit (1970), 38
People's Free Medical Clinic (Oakland),
    248
People's Park confrontations (1969),
    286–287
performance venues, 107–108, 224
Persuasions, 38
Pharoahs, the, 134
Philadelphia (PA), 38, 40, 62, 209, 250,
    273, 297
Pickett, Wilson, 9, 284
"pig" symbolism, 16, 33, 36, 50, 126,
    127, 167, 169, 193, 235, 245–246,
    263–265, 288
Pink Pussycat club (Los Angeles), 297
"Please Please Please" (James Brown), 93
Poitier, Sidney, 130
police confrontations: Attica State Prison
    brutality, 308; Bobby Hutton killed,
    21, 128, 236; BPP armed patrols,
    68–69; BPP Sacramento armed
    march, 70–71; BPP targeted by law
    enforcement, 39–40, 223, 227, 230,
    235, 239, 240, 246; Brownsville
    (NY) protests of, 36; can't handle
    black hyperbole, 227, 246; Detroit
    multiracial riots 1967, 173–174;
    Eldridge Cleaver wounded, 21; Fred
    Hampton killed, 128, 137–138;
    George Jackson shot at San Quen-
    tin, 304–305; John Frey altercation
    with Huey Newton, 232; Mark
    Clark killed, 128; New Haven (CT)
    Lumpen performance, 39; New
    York 21 members, 227–228; Newark
    1967 riots, 188; 1967 summer, 231;
    Oak Park riots sparked by, 30; Oak-
    land stop the draft protests, 223;
    Occupy nonviolent civil protests,
    332; People's Park confrontations,

286–287; police as pigs, 16, 235,
    245–246, 288; San Francisco police
    raid on Party headquarters, 24, 25;
    San Francisco State TWLF, 21. See
    also FBI; killed
political theater, 14, 65, 170, 192, 246,
    251, 304, 315
political violence: COINTELPRO
    harassment, 238–239; Eldridge
    Cleaver condoning, 223; "For Free-
    dom" (Lumpen) calling for, 168–
    170; H. Rap Brown condoning, 223;
    Huey Newton on necessity, 333;
    1970 rarity, 170. See also violence
Poole, Elijah, 180
Port of Oakland (CA), 178, 332
Porter, David, 210
positive message in music. See music
    with positive message
Powell, Art, 123
"Power of Soul" (Hendrix), 293, 308
"power to the people" (chant), 39, 122,
    133–134, 138, 167, 169, 170, 195,
    263, 265, 296, 304, 310
"Power to the People" (Lennon), 296
"Power to the People" (Lumpen), 49–50,
    86
Pratt, Elmer "Geronimo ji-Jaga," 83, 254,
    298, 319
progressive soul, 291
protest music: coded protest music, 129,
    276–277, 280, 290; Curtis Mayfield
    in his own context, 307; Elaine
    Brown "The Meeting," 16–17; Elaine
    Brown revolutionary ballads, 16–17;
    Lumpen, 307–308; Nina Simone, 4,
    281–282; packaged protest music,
    168, 171–172; Paul Robeson, 269;
    "People Get Ready" tribute to coded
    protest music, 129; tradition of,
    274–275. See also message songs;
    militant messages; resistance music
Pryor, Richard, 256–257
Psychedelic Shack (Temptations; album),
    167, 172
publications. See black newspapers and
    publications
punk movement, 295
Purdim, Alafia, 110
"Pusherman" (Mayfield), 133

Queen of Soul. See Franklin, Aretha

racial caste system, 243–244, 330
racial equality, 54–55, 83–84, 92, 107–108, 329–330
racial state, 14
Rackley, Alex, 228–230, 319
radio. See black radio
Radio Free Dixie (radio), 160
Rainbow Coalition, 137
RAM. See Revolutionary Action Movement
Ramey, James (Baby Huey), 139
Ramparts magazine, 60–61, 232
Randolph, Asa Philip, 57
Rap Brown. See Brown, H. "Rap" (Jamil Abdullah Al-Amin)
rap music, xv, xvi, 90, 91, 121, 226, 228, 323–324, 330
Rare Earth, 318
Rastafarianism, 113, 115
Rawls, Lou, 129–130
RCA Studios (Los Angeles), 283
Reading, John, 60
Reagan, Ronald, 71, 78, 204, 206, 286
Reagon, Bernice Johnson. See Johnson, Bernice
Reagon, Cordell, 130
Record, Eugene, 133
"red book" (BPP), 75
Redding, Noel, 294
Redding, Otis, 116, 153, 162, 212, 284
Reeves, Martha, 176. See also Martha and the Vandellas
reggae, 113–114
Reid, Clarence, 292
Republic of New Afrika (RNA), 146–147
"Resistance Culture," 327
resistance music, 129, 275, 276–277, 280, 290, 304
"Respect" (Franklin), 3, 151, 152–154, 163
Respect label, 214
revolution: Angela Davis Afro as icon of, 205; Bobby Seale revolution revolves power, 333; as lifetime process, 319, 322; Malcolm X construct, 11–12; the revolution catchphrase, 13; revolution requires participation, 329, 333; revolutionary fantasy versus revolutionary work, 321; true revolutionary guided by love, 336. See also black revolution

"Revolution Is the Only Solution" (Lumpen), 309–310, 311
Revolution of the Mind (James Brown), 122
revolution requires participation, 329
"The Revolution Will Not Be Televised" (Scott-Heron), 13, 109
Revolutionary Action Movement (RAM), 62, 238
revolutionary culture: Amilcar Cabral, 270; artist-activists, 327, 329; culture change, 323; Frantz Fanon, 270; Grace Lee Boggs, 334–335; Harold Cruse, 270; Lumpen at Soul Day at San Quentin, 306, 308; Occupy Movement (2011), 331–332; as Paul Robeson ideas, 270; "Resistance Culture," 327; Ron Karenga, 183: see also black cultural nationalism
Revolutionary Intercommunal Day of Solidarity (1971), 38, 296
Revolutionary People's Constitutional Convention (RPCC), 40–41, 209, 250
Revolutionary Suicide (Huey Newton; autobiography), 68
revolutionary theater. See political theater
Revolutionary Tour (Lumpen), 38–39, 81
rhythm and blues (R&B): black power emergence, 8; call-and-response, 88, 218; chitlin' circuit, 53; "Dance to the Music" (Sly and the Family Stone) transformation, 50–51, 53; Gil Scott-Heron and Brian Jackson recordings, 109; James Brown, 115; at 1960s dawn, 6; religious references, 35, 218; shout-singing, 50, 222
Riley, Boots, xv, 324, 329
Riley, Clayton, 138
Riperton, Minnie, 134
RL's Dream (Walter Mosley; book), 276
RNA. See Republic of New Afrika
Roach, Max, 3, 6, 144
Roach, Raheem, 82
Robertson, Robbie, 301
Robeson, Paul, 150, 267–272
Robinson, Cynthia, 50, 52
"Rock Steady" (Franklin), 155

Rodgers, Nile, 225–226
Rodham, Hillary, 230
"Roll the Union On" (Handcox), 274–275
Roostertail's Upper Deck (Detroit), 264
Roseland Ballroom (NY), 38–39
Ross, Deverol, xvi
Roundtree, Richard, 258
RPCC. See Revolutionary People's Constitutional Convention
Rubin, Jerry, 233
Rufus, 139
Rutgers University (NJ), 186, 268

Sacramento (CA): BPP armed march on state capitol, 70–72; BPP chapter startup, 72, 77–78; Clark Bailey bus driver, 319; It's About Time Committee, xvi; James Brown influence, 94; James Mott breakfast for children program, 248; James Mott growing up, 76, 94; Lumpen final performance, 46, 314; Oak Park riots, 30; William Calhoun working with teenage sex offenders, 314–315
Sacramento City Auditorium, 46
Saint Augustine's Episcopal Church (Oakland), 248
Sam and Dave, 210–211, 284–285, 292
Sams, George, 228–229
San Francisco (CA): Betty Shabazz interview at Ramparts magazine, 232–233; Black House, 145; Black Panther Party of Northern California, 66, 73; Eldridge Cleaver in Black Nationalism scene, 232; Golden State Studios Lumpen concert recording, 312; Huey Newton dares officer to draw gun, 233; People's Free Benefit, 38; police raid on BPP, 24; Sportsman's Club, 34. See also Bay Area
San Francisco State University, 16, 20, 22, 71, 187
San Jose (CA), 20, 25, 35, 72
San Jose City College, 22, 38, 73
San Jose State University: Clark Bailey student, 25, 74; Harry Edwards instructor, 20; home of US Olympic track team, 20, 23, 25; John Carlos student, 20, 23; Lee Evans student, 20, 23; Michael Torrence student,

21, 25, 74, 75; Tommie Smith student, 20, 23
San Quentin prison (CA), 304–308
Santa Rita. See Bailey, Clark "Santa Rita"
Santa Rita Jail (CA), 74
Santamaria, Mongo, 151
Santana, Carlos, 56, 205, 335–336
Satins, the, 80
Savio, Mario, 56, 366n6
"Say It Loud–I'm Black and I'm Proud" (James Brown): as black culture watershed, 106–107; black masculine aesthetic, 91; black versus Negro, 106–107; in Bob Marley "Black Progress," 115; BPP calls superficial, 107; celebrating black pride, 91, 104–113; Gary Byrd's race-conscious soul music, 161; Stokely Carmichael on music as weapon, 3; white venues shun James Brown, 107–108
SCLC. See Southern Christian Leadership Conference
Scott, Joseph "Lucky," 132–133
Scott-Heron, Gil, 13, 108–109
Seaga, Edward, 114
Seale, Artie, 67, 238
Seale, Bobby: in air force, 61; Alex Rackley murder, 228–230; on Amiri Baraka and Ron Karenga, 192; arrested, 238; autobiography Seize the Time, 303–304; "Bobby Must Be Set Free" (Lumpen): see "Bobby Must Be Set Free"; born, 61; bound and gagged by Judge Hoffman, 237; brainstorming with James Mott, 79; Chicago Democratic National Convention, 236–237; on Huey Newton and "Ballad of a Thin Man," 303–304; Huey Newton expels from Party, 255; on Huey Newton's preferred brand of Panther, 241; in jail/prison, 30, 37, 39, 219, 230, 232, 235, 237, 250; James Mott inspired to start breakfast program, 248; jazz drumming, 61; and John Lennon, 296; lumpenization from racial caste system, 243–244; on Malcolm X assassination, 62; Malcolm X legacy heir, 240–241; Melvin Van Peebles Sweet Sweetback character resemblance, 258;

at Merritt College, 58, 62; New Haven Lumpen performance, 39; Oakland early years, 58, 61–63; Oakland mayor run, 46, 178, 315; as Party cofounder, 15, 333; portrayed BPP ideals to nation, 241; public speaking ability, 226, 230, 235, 251; publicizing Huey Newton and BPP, 241; released and reunited with Huey Newton and BPP, 314; revolution revolves power, 333; Revolutionary Intercommunal Day of Solidarity (1971), 38, 296; rules of engagement for armed patrols, 69; Sacramento armed march, 70–71, 230, 235; Soul Students Advisory Council, 63; study of revolution, 242–245; Sun Ra invitation to Oakland, 134–135; Ten Point Program, 59, 63, 67, 226

Seale, John, 79

Seattle (WA), 294–295

Seeger, Pete, 275, 301, 302

segregation. See integration; Jim Crow

Sehorn, Marshall, 162

Seize the Time (Elaine Brown; album), 16–17, 27, 30, 297, 298

Seize the Time (Seale; memoir), 303–304

Seize the Time benefit (1970), 38

"Self-Destruction" (KRS-One), 328

Selico, Ronald, 90

"Set Sister Ericka Free" (Lumpen), 33

"Sex Machine" (James Brown), 121

Sexual Freedom League, 65

Shabazz, Betty, 232

Shaft (film), 213, 258

Shakur, Afeni, 226–228

Shakur, Assata, 146–147, 226–228, 254

Shakur, Lumumba, 225, 227

Shakur, Tupac, 226, 228

Sharpton, Al, 105–107, 124

Shepp, Archie, 6, 144, 254

Shields, Del 162

shout-singing, 50, 222

Show Boat (film) , 267–268

Show Boat (stage musical), 266–267

show tunes. See Lumpen concert recording; "Mississippi Goddam"; "Ol' Man River" (Hammerstein and Kern)

Shrine of the Black Madonna Cultural Center (Detroit), 145

Simone, Nina: activist on stage, 3, 4–5; on belonging to the movement, 5; courageous social commentary, 281; entertainer/activist schism, 282; "I Wish I Knew How It Would Feel to Be Free," 164; "Mississippi Goddam," 3, 5, 106, 281–282; "To Be Young, Gifted and Black," 154–155, 193; "Why? (The King of Love Is Dead)," 5

Sinatra, Frank, 264, 268, 272

Sinclair, John, 295, 296

Sister Candace, 50

Sixteenth Street Baptist Church bombing (1963), 203, 281

SJSU. See San Jose State University

slap bass technique, 53

Sly and the Family Stone: black pride music, 108; in counterculture revolution, 56, 59; "Dance to the Music," 49–50, 50–51; "Don't Call Me Nigger, Whitey," 54–55, 108; freedom as music, 53–54; gender equality, 53, 56; "I Want to Take You Higher," 54, 55; as influential band, 51–52, 56, 85; "Love City," 85; as multigender, 51, 53; as multiracial, 41, 51; positive music, 53, 54, 56; Stand! (album), 54–55; at Woodstock, 290

Sly Stone. See Stone, Sly

Small Talk at 125th and Lenox (Scott-Heron; album), 108–109

Smalls, Tommy, 162

Smith, Sandra (Sandra Isadore), 117

Smith, Tommie, 20–23, 105, 364n2

SNCC. See Student Nonviolent Coordinating Committee

Snellings, Roland (Askia Muhammad Touré), 141, 143

social media, 330–331, 332

socialism, 15, 36, 62, 189, 242

Soledad Brothers, 204, 304

Soledad Prison (CA), 232, 304

"Solidarity Forever" (Chaplin), 274

soul claps, 310

soul culture, 6–7, 140–141, 143–144, 158, 215, 220, 293, 308

Soul Day at San Quentin (1971), 306–308

"Soul Makossa" (Dibango), 118
"Soul Man" (Sam and Dave), 210–211, 292
soul music: at apocalypse with Parliament/Funkadelic, 292; and Aretha Franklin, 151, 152, 153; black power spirit centrality, 210; Bob Marley, 115; and civil rights, 4, 96, 141; emerging with black freedom movement, 141; free-form sound, 291; fusion of black culture, black pride, and black enterprise, 158; fusion of gospel and blues, 35–36; fusion of gospel and R&B, 127; fusion of sacred and secular, 35–36, 37; James Brown, 92, 96, 115, 120; and Lumpen, 32–33, 165, 193; Marvin Gaye, 288; progressive soul as rock, jazz, blues, gospel fusion, 291; psychedelic soul, 291; representing black unity, 141, 164; sincerity and passion of artists, 92, 127, 163; "Soul Explosion" at Stax Records, 213; waned as black freedom movement waned, 163; zenith, 163, 215. See also Chicago soul
"Soul Power" (James Brown), 220
Soul Station #1, 283
Soul Students Advisory Council (SSAC), 63
Soul Train (TV), xiv, 134, 161, 216
Souls of Black Folk, The (Du Bois; book), 187
South Africa, 73, 110, 143, 149
South Carolina, 93, 136, 146
South Central Los Angeles (CA), 11
Southern California BPP chapter, 128, 204
Southern California Communist Party, 204
Southern Christian Leadership Conference (SCLC), 159, 197
Soviet Union, 296, 269
Sowell, Timothy, 314
"Spanish Harlem" (Franklin), 151
Spann, Purvis, 161
spirituals, 7, 8, 268, 276–277. See also gospel
Sportsman's Club (San Francisco), 34
Sportsman's Inn (San Francisco), 38
SSAC. See Soul Students Advisory Council

Stand! (Sly and the Family Stone; album), 54–55
Stanford, Max, 62
Staple Singers, the, 131, 212, 306
"Star Spangled Banner" (Hendrix), 7, 294
Starks, Jabo, 90
Starr, Edwin, 172, 177
Stax Records 131, 211–214, 291
Stay in School program, 99
Steinberg, Martha Jean "the Queen,", 159
Stepney, Charles, 134
Stevens, Yvette Marie. See Khan, Chaka
Stewart, Freddie "Freddie Stone,", 52–53
Stewart, Jim, 211, 212, 214
Stewart, Rose, 52, 53
Stewart, Sylvester. See Stone, Sly
Stewart, Vaetta (Vet), 52
Stills, Steven, 291
Stone, Sly, 52–54, 56, 85, 86. See also Sly and the Family Stone
"Strange Fruit" (Holiday), 106, 272–273, 274, 328
Strivers, Jack, 77
Strong, Barrett, 174
Stubblefield, Clyde, 90
Student Nonviolent Coordinating Committee (SNCC): Bob Brown as organizer, 137; Bob Dylan awed by, 302–303; BPP merger, 234; Ella Baker, 197; Fannie Lou Hamer, 197; Freedom Singers, 130; Freedom Summer, 366n6; H. Rap Brown, 234; Harry Belafonte support, 150; James Forman, 175, 234; James Mott, 76–77; Los Angeles chapter from Black Panther Political Party, 204; Mississippi Summer Project, 197; patriarchy, 197, 198; Poor People's Campaign, 25; racially integrated female SNCC statement, 197; Stokely Carmichael, 2, 198, 230, 234; Waveland retreat, 197; white membership purge, 83
Students for a Democratic Society, 137
Sun Ra (Herman Poole Blount), 134, 135
"Superbad" (James Brown), 121
Superfly (film), 132–133, 258
Supremes, the, 176, 279
Survival Programs: as BPP member duty, 15, 27; as Huey Newton retreat

from lumpen orientation, 246–247; integral component of BPP, 248; local impact, 223; membership recruitment by Lumpen, 29; most labor-intensive BPP programs, 247–250; NCCF chapters, 83; white alliance militancy fetish, 209

Sutherland, Donald, 235

Swahili, 73, 182, 183, 185

Sweet Sweetback's Baadasssss Song (film), 257–258

symbols: panther as Party symbol, 67; "pig" as: see "pig" symbolism

Tabor, Michael (Cetewayo), 227

Tamla, 176–177

Tapscott, Horace, 17, 184, 298

Teemer, Mark, 77

television (TV): BET as new KKK, 326; conscious Afrocentric rap music, 323–324; Emmett Till trial televised, 302; Flip Wilson Show, 155; Mike Douglas Show, 296; National Association of Television and Radio Announcers (NATRA), 162; today's rebel youth rendered invisible, 323

Temple University (PA), 38

Temptations, the: "Ball of Confusion (That's What the World Is Today)," 171; black pride music, 108; Cloud Nine, 171; Eddie Kendricks, 176; "Get Ready," 171; influence on Lumpen, 31, 33; "It's Summer," 167–168, 171; "It's Summer" Lumpen version, 168–170, 171; "Message from a Black Man," 108, 193; "My Girl," 171; Norman Whitfield shaping sound, 171, 177; not a church group, 279; "Ol' Man River" as best and worst of Motown, 264; packaged protest music, 171–172; Psychedelic Shack, 167, 172; psychedelic soul, 291; "Run Away Child, Running Wild," 171; social commentary emerged, 55; "Take a Stroll Thru Your Mind," 171; The Temptations in a Mellow Mood, 264; Temptations Live!, 264; William Calhoun dialogue on, 168

Ten Point Program: Declaration of Independence in, 68; Huey Newton and Bobby Seale as coauthors, 59, 63, 67; manuscript preparation, 67; panther symbol, 67; points of, 67–68; to teach people to read, 78; "You're the Man" (Gaye) master plan reference, 289

Tennessee, 99–100, 109, 112. See also Memphis

Terrell, Tammi, 285, 286

terrorists. See political violence

Texas, 61, 231

"the One": funk music, 96; influence on dance, 96, 122; influence on Jamaican music, 114–115; one and three versus two and four, 95; in "Papa's Got a Brand New Bag," 95; in "There Was a Time," 90

theater. See political theater

"Theme from Shaft" (Hayes), 213

"There Was a Time" (James Brown), 87, 89, 90, 97

Thiele, Bob, 108–109

Third World Liberation Front (TWLF), 20

Third World Revolution: of Frantz Fanon, 112

Third World Women's Alliance (TWWA), 202–203

"This Land Is Your Land" (Guthrie), 275

Thomas, Carla, 38, 212

Thompson, Jan, 42

Thorne, Richard, 64–65

Thornton, Clifford, 254

Tiki Recording Studio, 35

Till, Emmet, 302

To Be Young, Gifted and Black (Hansberry; unfinished play), 154

"To Be Young, Gifted and Black" (Simone), 154–155, 193

Torrence, Michael: after Lumpen, 47–48, 316–318, 319; approached Bobby Seale about leaving, 316; on Aretha Franklin, 158; Black Student Alliance formation, 21–22; Black Student Union leader, 23, 74, 316; Bobby McClain as uncle, 311; BPP San Francisco chapter startup, 76; Elaine Brown, 318; family responsibilities, 316; Frankie Bowman as mother, 75; on Freedom Messengers, 30–31; The Godfather, 256; James Brown influence on Lumpen, 89; and Jan Thompson, 42; leaving

Torrence, Michael (*continued*)
of Party delayed, 316; left Party,
46, 316; Lumpen as Panthers, 44;
Lumpen choreography, 33, 80–81,
311; Lumpen member, 312; Lumpen
music and message, 33; Lumpen
origins, 26–27, 29–30; on Lumpen
soul music aesthetic, 193; Marvin
Gaye tour, 46, 317–318; mother
as inspiration, 75, 76; Motown
staff writer, 46, 318; musical back-
ground, 76; as Panther, 25; path to
BPP, 75–76; police raid on BPP, 24;
recruited Clark Bailey, 74, 75; on
walkout with San Francisco State,
22; working with at-risk youth in
Los Angeles, 47, 318
Touré, Askia Muhammad. See Snellings,
Roland
Trahan, Valerie, 42
"Tramp" (Carla Thomas), 212
Triple Jeopardy (newspaper), 203
Tripp, Luke, 177–178
Trouble Man (film), 289
"Try Me" (James Brown), 93, 115
Ture, Kwame. See Carmichael, Stokely
Turner, Walter, xv–xvi
TV. See television
TWLF. See Third World Liberation Front
TWWA (Third World Women's Alli-
ance), 202–203

UCLA (CA): Angela Davis professor-
ship, 204; Archie Ivy, 184; Black
Student Union, 190; BPP guns on
campus, 184, 190; John Huggins
and Alprentice "Bunchy" Carter
killed, 128, 190, 297–298; Lew
Alcindor, 20; Ron Everett, 182
Undisputed Truth, the, 177, 291
United Front Against Fascism Confer-
ence (1969), 83
United States Olympic track team, 20
Universal Negro Improvement Associa-
tion (UNIA), 180, 224
University of California–Berkeley, 38,
58, 135, 286–287
University of California–San Diego, 204
University of Madison–Wisconsin, 38
University of Massachusetts, 140
Unruh, Jesse, 78–79

Urban League, 197
US Organization: Amiri Baraka, 187–
188; black cultural nationalism,
183; BPP versus, 189–193; gender
roles, 183, 199–200; Hakim Jamal,
182; James Mtume, 184; Kawaida
(philosophy of cultural nationalism), 183, 200; Kawaida (Mtume)
album, 184–185; "Kawaida Towers,"
186, 188–189; Kuzaliwa (Malcolm
X birthday), 183; Kwanzaa celebration, 183; mainstream reach,
184; Nguzo Saba (seven principles
of blackness), 183; patriarchy,
199–200; Ron Karenga, 182, 189,
191–192; UCLA BPP and US Organization shootout, 128, 190, 297–
298; Uhuru Day (Watts uprising
commemoration), 183; Watts riots,
182; white alliances, 207

Van Peebles, Melvin, 257–258
Vault recording studio, 297, 298
VH1 (TV), 324
Vietnam, 13, 59, 83, 103, 104, 143, 153,
177, 223, 230, 231, 233, 286, 307
Vincent, Ted, xiv
Vincent, Toni, xiv
violence, 223, 245, 328, 328. See also
assassination; bombings; FBI; guns;
killed; lynchings; police confronta-
tions; political violence
Volt, 297
"Voodoo Chile (Slight Return)" (Hen-
drix), 294, 379n35
Voting Rights Act (1965), 11
Vox Studio, 104

"Wade in the Water,", 277
Wailer, Bunny, 115
Wailers. See Bob Marley and the Wailers
"Wake Up Everybody" (Harold Melvin
and the Blue Notes), 164
Walden, Phil, 162
Wallace, Thomas, 81, 82, 87
"War" (Starr), 172
Ward, Frank, 259
Warden, Donald (Khalid al-Mansour),
62, 66, 97, 123, 182
Warren, Pam "the Funkstress," xv
Washington, 294–295

Washington (DC), 7, 10, 40–41, 103, 148, 162, 212, 250, 285
Washington, Dinah, 151
Washington, Handsome "Honey," 93
Washington, Harold, 163
Watson, John, 174
Watts Summer Festival, 214
Watts uprising (1965), 11, 36–37, 60, 97, 160, 182, 183
Wattstax (film), 214, 256–257
Wayne State University (MI), 175
We Want Freedom (Abu-Jamal), 5–6
weapons. See bombings; FBI; guns; lynchings; music as weapon; police confrontations
Weathermen, 252
Webb, Robert, 45, 319
Weird World of Blowfly, The (Reid), 292
WERD radio (Atlanta), 159
"We're a Winner" (Impressions), 3, 132
"We're All in the Same Gang" (West Coast Rap All-Stars), 328
Wesley, Fred, 104–105
West Coast Rap All-Stars, 328
West Oakland (CA), 38, 60
Wexler, Jerry, 152, 162
WGYW radio (Knoxville, TN), 99–100
"What We Want, What We Believe." See Ten Point Program
What's Going On? (Gaye; album), 288, 290, 335–336
"What's Going On?" (Benson), 286–287
"What's Going On?" (Gaye), 3, 6, 286–287
"When Will We Be Paid for the Work We've Done" (Staple Singers), 131
Whispers, the, 82
Whitaker, Melvin, 77
White, Kevin, 101
White, Maurice, 134
white alliances: BPP court Hendrix, 294; BPP white alliances, 192, 206–209; Chicago Democratic National Convention, 237; Cleavers and Peace and Freedom Party, 233; "Free Huey," 235; Lumpen "reverse racism" experiences, 41, 208; most difficult black radical issue, 206, 207; National Black Political Convention stalemate, 216

White Panthers, 295
Whitfield, Norman, 171, 177
Whitney, Marva, 102
"Why? (The King of Love Is Dead)" (Simone), 5
"Why Am I Treated So Bad" (Staple Singers), 131
Wilkins, Roy, 99, 246
Williams, John, 177–178
Williams, Lenny, 32–33, 82, 300
Williams, Minor, 81, 82
Williams, Otis, 176
Williams, Robert F., 159, 160, 242
Wilson, Jackie, 6, 133
Wilson, Lionel, 47, 238, 319
Wine, Alice, 8
Winfrey, Oprah, 325
WJBE radio (Knoxville, TN), 100, 112
WLIB radio (NY), 161
Womack, Bobby, 306
"Woman's Got Soul" (Impressions), 210
women. See black women
women-of-color organizations, 202–203
"Women's Liberation Movements and the Gay Liberation Movements" (Newton), 249–250
Wonder, Stevie, 52, 163, 177, 278, 284, 291, 296, 306, 328
"(Won't Be) No More" (Lumpen). See "No More" (Lumpen)
Wooten, Chuck, 174
World War II, 57, 59, 60, 61, 141, 164, 172, 179–180, 272
Wo'Se Community Church (Oakland), 47, 314
Wretched of the Earth (Fanon; book), 112
Wright, Betty, 292
WVON radio (Chicago), 161

Ya Salaam, Kalamu, 145–146
Yale University, 229–230
"Yell Fire" (Franti), 327–328
Yoruba culture, 117, 139, 147, 194
"you become what you sing," 320
"You Can Have Watergate, Just Gimme Some Bucks and I'll Be Straight" (James Brown), 123
Young, Neil, 291
Young, Whitney, 99

"Young, Gifted and Black" (Franklin), 154–155

"Young, Gifted and Black" (Simone), 155

Young, Gifted and Black (Franklin; album), 155, 158

"You're the Man" (Gaye), 289

Zimmerman, Robert Allen. See Dylan, Bob

"Zombie" (Kuti), 119